W9-CSX-094

third edition

SUPERVISION OF POLICE PERSONNEL

N. F. IANNONE

Inspector (ret.)
Los Angeles Police Department

Chairman, Police Science Department
Fullerton College, Fullerton, California

PRENTICE-HALL, INC., ENGLEWOOD CLIFFS, NEW JERSEY 07632

Library of Congress Cataloging in Publication Data
IANNONE, N F (date)
   Supervision of police personnel.

   (Prentice-Hall series in criminal justice)
   Bibliography: p.
   Includes index.
   1. Supervision of police personnel.   I. Title.
HV7936.S812   1980   350′.102   79–15844
ISBN   0-13-876987-7

PRENTICE-HALL SERIES IN CRIMINAL JUSTICE
James D. Stinchcomb, *series editor*

Editorial production/supervision and
      interior design by Sonia Meyer
Jacket design by Saiki/Sprung Design
Manufacturing buyer: John Hall

© 1980, 1975, 1970 by Prentice-Hall, Inc.,
Englewood Cliffs, N.J. 07632

All rights reserved. No part of this book
may be reproduced in any form or
by any means without permission in writing
from the publisher.

Printed in the United States of America

10   9   8   7   6   5

Prentice-Hall International, Inc., *London*
Prentice-Hall of Australia Pty. Limited, *Sydney*
Prentice-Hall of Canada, Ltd., *Toronto*
Prentice-Hall of India Private Limited, *New Delhi*
Prentice-Hall of Japan, Inc., *Tokyo*
Prentice-Hall of Southeast Asia Pte. Ltd., *Singapore*
Whitehall Books Limited, *Wellington, New Zealand*

Contents

THE SUPERVISOR'S FUNCTION IN
ORGANIZATION, ADMINISTRATION, AND MANAGEMENT 12

EMPLOYEE DISSATISFACTION, GRIEVANCES, AND COMPLAINTS 32

4

ELEMENTS OF LEADERSHIP,
SUPERVISION, AND COMMAND PRESENCE 43

5

THE ESSENTIALS OF COMMUNICATING 75

6

SOME PSYCHOLOGICAL ASPECTS
OF SUPERVISION

7

PRINCIPLES OF INTERVIEWING

11

PERSONNEL EVALUATION SYSTEMS 216

12

PERFORMANCE RATING STANDARDS AND METHODS 234

13

DISTRIBUTION AND DEPLOYMENT OF FIELD FORCES

257

14

TACTICAL DEPLOYMENT OF FIELD FORCES

287

To My Wife

Preface

The modern supervisor of police must be more circumspect in his relationships with people than ever before. The environment in which he must function, with its rapid technological and social changes, has demanded of him an unprecedented flexibility in his dealings with others and a highly developed capacity for balancing organizational objectives with the interests of his subordinates.

At times the supervisor will find it difficult to reconcile his own personal values with theirs. It cannot be denied that many of the issues of the counterculture movement of the last decade still exist to some degree. The expectation of administrative permissiveness, defiance of traditional behavior standards, an increased demand for the right of privacy and the authority to select and follow one's own particular lifestyle irrespective of its effect upon the organization, an open distrust of official leadership, and the right of public employees to enforce their demands by use of the strike process have left their indelible imprint upon organizational operations and have severely affected traditional supervisory practices. Often, the supervisor is unable to take that action once considered appropriate because of the constraints placed upon him by society and the law; yet, the manner in which he performs his duties within these limitations vitally affects the establishment and maintenance of a professional level of police service.

It is with these thoughts in mind that this third edition of *Supervision of Police Personnel* has been prepared. The basic tenets of supervision and leadership have not changed, and have therefore been retained. Where indicated, these principles have been modified to meet the needs of the present-day supervisor. Many recommendations have been added which will be a guide to superior leadership practices—especially by first and second level supervisors in carrying out their complex and vital tasks.

The causes of employee dissatisfactions, grievances, and complaints and some suggested guidelines for resolving such problems are included in a new chapter. Considerable new material also has been added on the techniques of handling special problems which more and more confront the police supervisor today, such as those involved in hostage negotiations, human relationships, leadership, motivation of personnel, communications, and discipline.

Experience has clearly indicated that the techniques recommended here will work well if applied with sincerity and good intent. Many of these techniques are the product of personal experiences fortified by numerous thoughtful observations by many administrators and supervisors as well as numerous nonsupervisory personnel who have dedicated themselves to law enforcement. I am grateful for their valuable contributions.

Specifically, I should like to express my sincere thanks to Professor Bruce Hand, Department of the Administration of Justice, Golden West College, Huntington Beach, California; Professor James J. Jansen, Police Science Department, Milwaukee Area Technical College; Professor Peter J. Grimes, Department of Criminal Justice, Nassau Community College, Garden City, New York; and Professor James D. Stinchcomb, School of Community Services, Virginia Commonwealth University, Richmond, Virginia, for their most helpful and stimulating contributions to the text. I am also deeply indebted to my brother, Assistant Chief of Police Marvin D. Iannone, and Captain Robert M. Smitson of the Los Angeles Police Department, and Professor Henry H. Bertch, Police Science Department, Fullerton College, for their many thoughtful and constructive suggestions during the time the text was being revised. Finally, I am most grateful for the invaluable help given by Mrs. Rosemary Barnett in the preparation of the manuscript.

For simplicity in grammatical structure throughout this text, the pronouns "he" and "him" are used generically to denote "person."

1

The supervisor's role

In modern administrative terminology, management denotes the process of directing and controlling people and things so that organizational objectives can be accomplished. Supervision, as part of the management process, refers to the act of overseeing people. It is an activity which takes place at all levels in the organization except at the work level; but nowhere is it more important than at the first level where the productive capacity of the enterprise is directly controlled. The worker's performance and morale are more strongly influenced here by his immediate superior than by any other factor in his environment. This is true not only because of the close relationships between the superior and his subordinates but also because the superior exercises such a strong influence upon the subordinate's physical and social environment.[1] It is for these reasons that the first level supervisor's job is a key position in any organization.

In the law enforcement agency, first level supervisors are of special importance because of the great need for teamwork. Upon them rests

[1] Rensis Likert and Stanley E. Seashore, "Motivation and Morale in the Public Service," *Public Personnel Review*, October, 1956, p. 271.

most of the responsibility for providing the cohesive force which welds the working force into a well-functioning, smoothly operating unit.

THE SUPERVISOR'S POSITION

People are responsible for production. The supervisor is responsible for people. He accomplishes the objectives of the organization by getting things done through people. He must be an expert in handling them to be a successful leader. To this end, he must develop the art of influencing others, coordinating their efforts, and directing them to proper goals in such a way as to obtain their obedience, confidence, respect, and loyal cooperation.

People like to be led by those whom they respect and in whom they have confidence. The first step in gaining this confidence and respect is taken when the supervisor exemplifies by his personal conduct that which he demands from his subordinates. If he then provides them proper leadership, they will respond with the highest performance, with a minimum of conflict and a maximum of satisfaction.

The supervisory officer must be adept at applying the principles of wholesome human relations with common sense so that he can best integrate the needs of employees with the goals of management. He should allow them to participate in decisions that affect them; but he must avoid crippling himself as a supervisor by carrying democratic leadership so far that his subordinates will expect him to "take a vote" before making every decision.

To many a supervisor, advancement into a position of authority involves a considerable change in life style from being a follower to being a leader and requires a radical change in philosophy and thought processes, especially in the area of human relations. As he gains experience, he will come to appreciate how his actions affect the economic security, advancement, and emotions of his subordinates. He will appreciate the effects of his activities upon their general welfare and morale. He will not become tranquilized into believing that because his morale is high, the morale of his subordinates is also high; he will recognize symptoms indicating that it is low and take corrective action promptly whenever his position permits. He will realize, as Tiffin [2] declares, that "Morale cannot be legislated or induced by logical argument; neither can it be bought for a price." He can influence it, however, if he remembers that people are interested in themselves and in the things that affect them and conducts his supervisory activities accordingly. He should let

[2] Joseph Tiffin, *Industrial Psychology* (Englewood Cliffs, N.J.: Prentice-Hall, Inc., 1944), p. 313.

them know where they stand in the organization and with their superiors and give them some indication of what the future holds for them.[3] One of their basic needs is a feeling of stability and security in their work. This should be provided for them insofar as possible because people do not perform well when they are exposed to conditions which cause tension and anxiety.

Any leader must accept the fact that his subordinates are all different. They will react in different ways at different times. They will often resist his efforts to do what they know he has to do to make the organization a better place to work. They will resist changes in their duties or assignments and some will quit if they see greener pastures elsewhere. He can expect disloyalty from some and intense loyalty from others in his complex job of managing people.

The supervisor must be able to help them establish and achieve reasonable goals. He must be able to provide answers to their many job problems, and to give them wise counsel and assurance in their personal and professional lives when the need arises, recognizing that they will not all react the same when he tries to help them. At times, they will misinterpret his motives and accuse him of meddling in their affairs; yet, their affairs are his when their performance is affected.

The supervisor is selected by management. He derives his official authority from that source, but his real authority stems from the spirit of cooperation, respect, and confidence that he is able to gain from his subordinates. He is expected to represent management's interests to the workers and their interests to management. He is a buffer between them and higher authority. He absorbs heat from above without passing it along to them. To his subordinates, he is the department. His virtues personify those of the department. If he is fair in his dealings with his subordinates, if he is considerate of their welfare, and if he is stimulating, they attribute these characteristics to the organization. If he is unjust, inconsistent, and unfriendly, they are likely to think the organization is also because he reflects, to them, what it is.[4]

In the long run, the interests of management and the worker are identical. The small differences between the two can ordinarily be resolved by the effective supervisor if he avoids prejudice, if he develops a judicial attitude by basing decisions only on the facts, if he knows the rules under which he and his subordinates must work and appreciates the intent of such rules, if he studies his subordinates to gain an understanding of them, if he leads them in a joint effort instead of driv-

[3] Alfred Lateiner, *Modern Techniques of Supervision,* 13th ed. (New York: Lateiner Publishing Company, 1975), pp. 45–52.
[4] International City Managers' Association, *Municipal Personnel Administration,* 6th ed. (Chicago: International City Managers' Association, 1960), p. 237.

ing them, and if he practices loyalty to his organization and to those with whom he works.

He is responsible for keeping his superiors informed through oral and written reports. This requires that he keep himself informed through records, research, and inspection. He is obliged to keep his subordinates apprised about matters affecting them. In doing so, he must communicate clearly by learning to avoid the barriers which hinder effective communications. He conveys official policy downward and tries to sell it to subordinates even though he sometimes does not agree with it and knows it will be resisted.

The supervisor should avoid filtering intelligence to his inferiors or superiors. He must not tell them only what he thinks will make them happy nor keep from them news which he thinks will make them unhappy. He must keep his superiors informed so that their decisions may be made on unexpurgated information, not on partial data which has been taken out of context. When he is in doubt as to how much detail he should pass on to them, he should resolve the doubt in favor of conveying too much rather than too little.

The supervisor often finds it difficult to reconcile the goals of management with the goals of the employees and the sentiments of their social group. He is often torn between the loyalties he owes both, but he must realize that the best interests of the organization must prevail. He is truly "both the victim and master of doubletalk." [5]

WOMEN SUPERVISORS

The tenets of leadership discussed in this text are as applicable to women supervisors as to their male counterparts; yet, women supervisors will undoubtedly find that considerable modification might be necessary from time to time in the manner they apply such principles in supervising some of their male subordinates because some males find it difficult to accept women in authority or to submit to their direction and control. Common sense in dealing with such attitudes will usually dictate an answer.

Most men have grown up in a culture of male dominance and many expect better performance from women than from male supervisors performing similar duties. A woman supervisor is often required to prove herself over and over. She may find that she is expected to be more circumspect in her personal conduct and performance than the

[5] Fritz J. Roethlisberger, "The Foreman: Master and Victim of Doubletalk," *Harvard Business Review*, Spring, 1945, pp. 283–98.

male supervisor because an inordinate amount of attention is focused on her. This condition may be totally unjustified but does exist, and since it does, she must dispel it as soon as possible to reduce resistance to her supervisory efforts. The solution seems to be for her to prepare herself technically for her position and to avoid scrupulously the commonly recognized leadership weaknesses in any supervisor, such as indulgence of wrongdoing or misconduct, vacillation in the decision-making process, and unfairness. If any of these characteristics are observed in a woman, they may only serve to fortify the stereotyped opinions of those who contend that women are not good leaders.

TECHNICAL AND SUPERVISORY COMPETENCE

Supervisors need not become highly skilled in every technical aspect of the job they supervise to be effective. To do so would impose an impossible burden upon them; but they should have a good working knowledge of the principal aspects of the job for which they are responsible. They must have a basic understanding of the other scientific disciplines which have contributed to the science of leadership. The psychologist has contributed to an understanding of human behavior. The sociologist has attempted to explain ethnic cultures and group relationships. The anthropologist has tried to explain the developmental aspects of society. The physical scientist has given law enforcement a vast source of technical data which has contributed to the advancement of scientific criminal investigation just as have many other disciplines.

Every supervisor should keep himself abreast of the fundamental changes in practices, techniques, and procedures in order to be equipped to carry to his subordinates that information they need to perform their jobs properly. He should prepare himself for his position by gaining a good working knowledge of the principles of organization, administration, and management. He should know and understand the principles of performance evaluation. He should become an expert in directing the efforts of his subordinates into the most productive channels. He should know how to relieve himself, through the process of delegation, of many tasks which others below him are capable of performing as well as or better than he can. In delegating routine tasks to subordinates, the expert supervisor will give them sufficient authority to match the responsibility he has imposed upon them. He will then hold them accountable for the job, but he will realize that *final* responsibility for the job is his, because he cannot shed his responsibility for a task merely by delegating it to someone else. If he delegates well, he will conserve his time for carrying out his prime duty of supervising rather than performing routine operational activities.

INSTITUTIONAL KNOWLEDGE

The supervisor should prepare himself for his position by gaining a knowledge and understanding of the policies, rules, procedures, practices, functions, and objectives of his organization. He should be thoroughly versed in the functions and operations of his local subdivision of government and should have an understanding of its relationships with other units of government. He should be fully acquainted with those allied agencies which work in conjunction with his own. Their facilities for providing rescue work, ambulance services, welfare activities, or other services should be well known to him. He should be thoroughly familiar with the local political atmosphere, although he should scrupulously avoid political entanglements and alliances which might hinder the accomplishment of his official duties.

The successful supervisor will understand the legal ramifications of his office; his obligations, liabilities, and responsibilities for the acts of his subordinates under the law; and the restrictions under which he operates. He will keep himself informed of the functions, jurisdiction, and authority of persons occupying the diverse positions in his and related organizations so that he can best carry out his coordinating activities.

In order that he may provide appropriate guidance and counsel to his subordinates, he must be familiar with the personnel rules, policies, and practices governing such aspects of the job as the selection of personnel, promotional systems, assignment policies, termination procedures, sick benefits, retirement plans, disciplinary procedures, merit ratings, leaves of absence, and vacation policies.

BASIC SUPERVISORY RESPONSIBILITIES

The common elements of supervision can be grouped under those activities which relate to the direction of people and all it implies, the control of their working environment, and the means by which the employee is developed.[6] In his day-to-day relationships with people, the supervisor is expected to concern himself with the following activities.

[6] Frank P. Sherwood and Wallace H. Best, *Supervisory Methods in Municipal Management* (Chicago: International City Managers' Association, 1958), p. 14.

As a planner

He must be an expert in planning operational activities and methods. He must be capable of inspecting work systems, conducting studies, analyzing data, and developing matured recommendations for constructive changes in organization and operation when necessary. If he is to best perform his duties, he must be able to forecast future needs of his organization as part of his planning activities, anticipate problems, and make decisions ahead of time to solve them. He should familiarize himself with work simplification practices in order to bring about greater efficiency in his organization through the streamlining of procedures, reduction of paperwork, and the effective use of personnel resources.

As a personnel officer

The supervisory officer should strive to assign his subordinates as scientifically as possible to the positions for which they are best suited and to the places and at the times they are most needed. He will place "round plugs in round holes" wherever possible because a happy worker is usually a productive one.

Studies have revealed that there is a marked relationship between productivity of an individual, his job satisfaction, and the type of supervision he has received. Employee-centered supervisors obtain better results than production-centered ones.[7]

As a trainer

The best supervisors develop their abilities to train their employees to be efficient, effective producers who gain satisfaction from their work. When the supervisor neglects to develop his capacity for the role of teacher, he deprives himself of a means of upgrading the service and ensuring that the standards of perfomance in the organization are maintained through the training process.

He must carry out his training function in all types of settings. If he is to be an effective teacher, he must gain a knowledge and understanding of the learning process, the effects of individual differences upon learning, and the psychological factors involved in teaching. He

[7] Rensis Likert, "Motivation: The Core of Management," in *Human Elements of Administration,* ed. Harry R. Knudson, Jr. (New York: Holt, Rinehart and Winston, Inc., 1963), pp. 72–75.

will become proficient in the use of a variety of techniques that will make his training activities most meaningful. He will be able to do some training at the scene of a crime, or while making a routine contact with a subordinate much as he does in a formal classroom setting.

As a controller

Every supervisor worthy of the name must learn how to control his subordinates properly. He must make proper follow-ups to determine that rules and regulations have been followed and orders properly executed. When necessary, he must take disciplinary action either positively through the process of training or negatively through punitive action. He must never obstruct corrective action when it is justified merely because of personal motives but must do everything proper, honorable, and legal to protect his subordinates from unjust punishment. At the time of recruitment when facts are in conflict, doubts should be resolved in favor of the organization because questionable persons cannot justifiably be recruited into the police service; but in disciplinary matters involving employees, the organization is bound by a policy of fairness and cannot honorably punish an employee on the basis of unfounded or unproved charges, slander, gossip, and malicious innuendos.

The supervisor must expect some mistakes from even the most able of his inferiors. Errors are bound to occur, especially with inexperienced employees. When they do, they should be treated as constructively as possible. When mistakes "of the head" are made, often the training value exceeds the harm done; but if the mistake is "of the heart," negative corrective action may be indicated to prevent a recurrence. When punishment is necessary, it should be administered promptly, without hostility or anger and never in a spirit of retribution or revenge.

Perfection should not be expected of workers since demanding this degree of excellence in performance will usually result in wasted time, frayed nerves, and frustration. Seldom will they be equipped with the physical or mental resources to render the level of performance which even approximates the perfection demanded by the perfectionist. This type of person is a wearisome individual. He is seldom satisfied with the performance he receives from others and only causes them anxiety.

As a decision maker and communicator

One of the primary functions of the supervisor is that of decision making. When he makes decisions, he often helps shape policy for the organization. If a decision is indicated, he must not vacillate. A bad decision is sometimes better than none at all. When it affects others, it should be communicated to them clearly and simply to prevent misunderstandings and resistance. When change results from decisions, those affected will often resist because the change is interpreted as a threat to their security and they are forced to make new adjustments. The resistance will usually be reduced if the need for the change is explained.

Timing of a communication which affects employees and a selection of the location where it takes place is important if it is to have the greatest acceptance. Sometimes, the sowing of a seed that a change is about to take place will allow the idea to take root in the minds of employees with a resultant lessening of their resistance to the change. The manner in which the superior officer communicates with his subordinates has a vital bearing upon their interpersonal relations. Subordinates often resent a bad manner in giving an order more than a bad order.

Leadership responsibilities

A major responsibility of every supervisor is to provide leadership for the men and women under him. To become a good leader he must possess the traits of honorableness, courageousness, and vitality. He must be reasonably intelligent. He should be a person with good common sense. He must be persuasive and flexible. He is not born with these characteristics, but he can develop his leadership ability by adopting the desirable traits he has observed in good leaders or, at least, trying to adapt those traits to his own style.

Every supervisor has an inherent responsibility to motivate his subordinates by giving them positive incentives that will encourage them to achieve and maintain a high level of efficiency. He must provide them an opportunity for personal and professional growth. They need to feel that they are progressing toward an achievable goal. He can help them by providing enlightened leadership. He will strive to overcome the inertia and dogma which impede the professionalization of law enforcement. He will give his full measure of effort and careful attention to his duties whether he likes or dislikes them and whether his efforts are appreciated or not if he is firmly committed to the tenets of his profession. He must stand by his convictions in spite of adversity. He must adhere to those high moral standards of his profession regardless of a departure from them by others. He should adopt new principles only when higher or better ones become evident.

The objectives and responsibilities of the supervisor have been outlined. Let's examine the principles, practices, and techniques which can be used in achieving these objectives and fulfilling these responsibilities.

SUMMARY

The first-line supervisor occupies a key position in any organization because of his intimate influence upon the conduct and performance of those who do the work. Coordination of people and units within the organization so that it will operate effectively is a vital function of his position. If he fulfills his responsibilities improperly, coordination is likely to be poor.

Many first-line supervisory positions are now being filled by women who sometimes find it difficult to direct and control male personnel because of stereotypes that are carried over from a culture of male dominance; yet the principles of leadership and management apply to her just as to her male counterparts.

Advancement into a position of authority requires a considerable change in philosophy and life-style of the supervisor because it involves leading rather than following others. In his leadership role, the supervisor will find that his subordinates are different. He can expect different reactions from them when he tries to help them in establishing and achieving their goals.

While the long-run interests of the organization are identical to those of the workers, the supervisor's position places upon him the obligation of resolving the minor differences that sometimes arise between them. It is his responsibility to provide representation between them. He must keep both groups accurately informed in matters affecting their mutual interests if he is to perform his role effectively.

Although supervisors need not be highly skilled in all the technical aspects of the jobs they supervise, they should have a good working knowledge of the principal aspects of such jobs. They must acquire an understanding of the basic principles of leadership and the tenets of organization and management if they are to perform their complex tasks efficiently and effectively.

REVIEW

Questions

1. Define the term "management."
2. Distinguish between management and supervision.
3. Discuss the types of institutional knowledge that the supervisor must possess.

4. What are the basic supervisory responsibilities? Discuss how they affect the supervisor in obtaining the best performance from his subordinates.

Exercises

1. Discuss the basic responsibilities of the supervisor and describe two or three practical ways he can carry each of them out.
2. Give examples of how supervisors you have known have failed to carry out their responsibilities.

2

The supervisor's function in organization, administration, and management

An organization is a structure through which people work as a group. Whenever two or more persons are associated in doing something, there is some sort of organization. It presupposes an orderly arrangement between individuals and groups, but a mechanical structure alone will not assure the effective accomplishment of organizational objectives. Direction and control must be provided so that the necessary coordination of human effort can be achieved. "There must be a means of securing compliance of individual members of a group in helping to achieve organizational goals. Unless there is a directing authority, each individual will do what he wants, when he wants, and any integrated effort and attainment will be impossible." [1] Such direction is the essence of the supervisory function.

The major portion of the supervisor's job may be categorized into three broad areas. These will involve the *leading, directing,* and *controlling* of individuals and groups formally or informally arranged. Those formally structured and recognized relationships within the organization will have superimposed upon them the informal groups with

[1] Norman C. Kassoff, *Organizational Concepts* (Washington, D.C.: International Association of Chiefs of Police, 1967), p. 11.

their own indigenous leader or leaders unrecognized on the charts. Through these natural leaders, often without bars or stripes, the wise supervisor will accomplish many of his objectives.

While the supervisor's job deals primarily with the directing of his subordinates, he must concern himself also with those *internal conditions* within the organization involving concrete matters such as environmental working conditions or the provision of equipment and those more abstract factors such as morale and esprit de corps. These factors cannot be separated from his typical administrative functions.

THE SUPERVISOR'S ADMINISTRATIVE FUNCTIONS

The major duties of supervisory personnel in an establishment differ only in degree from those of the chief executive as described in Gulick's POSDCORB:

> POSDCORB is, of course, a made-up word designed to call attention to the various functional elements of the work of the chief executive because "administration" and "management" have lost all specific content. POSDCORB is made up of the initials and stands for the following activities:
>
> _Planning_, that is working out in broad outline the things that need to be done and the methods for doing them to accomplish the purpose set for the enterprise;
>
> _Organizing_, that is the establishment of the formal structure of authority through which work subdivisions are arranged, defined and coordinated for the defined objective;
>
> _Staffing_, that is the whole personnel function of bringing in and training the staff and maintaining favorable conditions of work;
>
> _Directing_, that is the continuous task of making decisions and embodying them in specific and general orders and instructions and serving as the leader of the enterprise;
>
> _Co-ordinating_, that is the all important duty of interrelating the various parts of the work;
>
> _Reporting_, that is keeping those to whom the executive is responsible informed as to what is going on, which thus includes keeping himself and his subordinates informed through records, research, and inspection;
>
> _Budgeting_, with all that goes with budgeting in the form of fiscal planning, accounting, and control. [2]

Many of these executive functions devolve upon subordinates at all levels of the hierarchy through the process of delegation.

[2] Luther Gulick, "Notes on the Theory of Organization," in *Papers on the Science of Administration*, ed. Luther Gulick and L. Urwick (New York: Institute of Public Administration, 1937), p. 13.

Each supervisory officer in his *planning* function must forecast needs and problems and prepare plans to meet them. Those which are guides to the daily performance of operating personnel at the lower level of the hierarchy must be more detailed and meticulous than those for personnel at or near the top of the organization.

Plans enable the supervisor to make decisions in advance; but they are useless if they are not effectively communicated to personnel who are expected to follow them. Whether they are communicated by manual, written orders, or verbal commands, they should be explicit and clear. It is fundamental that, if such communications can be misinterpreted, they will be. Accordingly, standing orders and those which are complicated should be written to reduce confusion and misinterpretation.[3]

Plans may be classified into several types according to the purposes they serve. *Procedural* plans relating to standard operating procedures (SOP) are useful as guides to personnel in such activities as the serving and processing of arrest warrants, recording and processing crime or incident reports, and the processing of traffic citations. Each supervisor should constantly review these day-to-day procedures and make recommendations for changes as needs arise to increase operational efficiency.

Tactical plans are those which are prepared to meet exigencies encountered by police, such as widespread civil disorders, unusual crime problems, civil defense needs, or major disasters. These plans are usually developed considerably in advance of expected incidents and are largely based on field intelligence supplied by supervisory personnel and the expertise they are able to provide in assessing future needs. The plans are designed to guide personnel in controlling unusual happenings and restoring order as quickly and as efficiently as possible. The methods of control are substantially the same as in ordinary police operations but must be expanded to meet the requirements of each occurrence. Therefore, it is necessary that such plans be basic, flexible in nature, and adaptable to modification as the need arises.[4]

Operational plans are those designed to give guidance and direction to personnel in the performance of normal police activities. These are the plans which are guides to personnel in activities, such as the deployment and distribution of personnel or the search for suspects or lost persons.

Auxiliary services plans are those which implement normal operations, such as in the recruitment of personnel, public and community relations activities, and the like.

[3] The techniques of communicating plans to personnel are described in detail in Chapter 5.

[4] Los Angeles Police Department, *Tactical Manual*, 1976, p. i.

Fiscal plans relate to such matters as budget preparation and the use and control of funds allotted for personnel, equipment, and supplies. The supervisor should adopt the practice of recording justifications for such personnel, equipment, and supplies as the need arises. Many find a perpetual budget file useful for such purpose. They record specific data throughout the year concerning budgetary needs. When the budget period arrives, a cumulative file is available to aid them in their fiscal planning.

Policies are plans consisting of a set of broad principles which guide personnel in the accomplishment of general organizational objectives. These are generally established by top management, although supervisors and unit commanders often establish policy for operation of their particular unit.

Usually, policies are not written. They evolve from the experiences of the organization; from the established, traditional customs and standards essential to its welfare; and from legal and social constraints imposed on its activities.

Policies, such as those mandating cooperation with the news media, or prescribing that personnel enforce the law fairly and justly, or requiring personnel to be prepared to take appropriate action at all times when the need arises, are stable and change slowly because they are based on broad organizational objectives that change little.

Every supervisor should be alert for confusion in the interpretation of policy by his subordinates—especially at times when policy is changed or when subordinates join his unit from another where it is interpreted differently. When such confusion is revealed through feedback, he should promptly take whatever steps may be required to clarify the conflicts and ensure uniformity in application.

Rules and regulations are plans providing specific guides to conduct and performance. They are parameters for acceptable conduct provided by management. As principles of action and conduct, they are a means by which deviations from policy may be prevented. In content, they control explicit behavior. Therefore, they are subject to more rapid change than are policies.

In order for them to be effective, they must be current, reasonable, and clear. Above all, they must not be arbitrary—reflecting only the views of management.

Rules may be made at any supervisory level of the organization to implement policy. Whether they are made by the first-line supervisor to aid him in carrying out the functions of his unit or by higher authority, he should constantly be alert to a need for modifications so that he will be able to make appropriate, timely changes or recommendations for changes that may be indicated.

As in planning, the supervisor's *organizing* function is a perpetual one. He must continuously analyze the organizational structure within his sphere of operations to ensure that it meets the needs of the total organization in providing a medium of communication between the elements of the hierarchy; that the structure provides clear-cut lines of authority and responsibility extending downward and upward lines of accountability.

Recruitment, training, and placement are proper and necessary *staffing* functions of each supervisor. The function of recruitment, while generally thought of as primarily a responsibility of top management, is a vital function of personnel at all levels. Personal contacts and persuasion that the department is a good place to work is a proven means of recruitment which should be stressed by supervisors.

The supervisor's training function as previously discussed is closely allied to his responsibility for the proper placement of his subordinates. While every employee cannot be assigned to precisely the task he likes best, every effort should be made to place him in the niche for which he is best suited. The net result to the organization is improved performance since an employee who likes to work at a particular task is likely to be more productive than one who is discontented or bored with it. Far more effective results will be realized from the placing of a subordinate in a position that will challenge him than in one that requires something less than total effort. Boredom and monotony are most destructive of initiative and industry in an employee. The wisdom of placing round pegs in round holes has been amply demonstrated, as has the philosophy that "color-blind persons are not the best strawberry pickers."

The function of providing *direction* to subordinates and control of their activities is one which consumes much of the supervisor's time. His position embodies the decision-making process in which he is constantly engaged. He must not only collect the necessary information and evaluate it before deciding issues, but he must also communicate his decisions to subordinates through orders, instructions, and all other media available to him. He must serve as a leader in the enterprise—not to drive but to lead, direct, and control personnel. He accomplishes this by securing effective action through the judicious use of his authority and by the application of common sense and practical psychology. Whenever possible, he uses positive methods by creating realistic inducements for proper performance rather than negative methods of penalizing for improper performance. The directing function involves not only putting a prepared plan into operation but also following up through observation and inspection to determine that the work ordered is actually and properly done. A supervisor who gives an order, then fails to follow up to see that it is carried out, will soon abrogate his supervisory authority.

Perhaps no function of management is less expendable than that of *coordination* of human effort to ensure unity of action of all organizational units. This activity must occur at all levels to prevent disharmony between individuals and groups. As organizations increase in size and complexity, the need for coordination becomes greater. The degree of specialization, the area covered, the distance between elements which must work together, the skill of persons doing the work, and the dissimilarity of functions involved in the enterprise determine the need for coordination. Channels of communication and lines of authority become more indistinct as the nature of the organization increases in complexity, and often its prime mission becomes clouded in the minds of individuals who comprise it. Organizational objectives may give way to personal objectives, which will soon permeate the group and destroy its esprit de corps.

The essential activity of coordination can best be accomplished through direct communication. It cannot be accomplished by mandate. Coordination of effort is difficult, even well-nigh impossible in any effective degree, if the common objectives of the organization are not accepted by those who are expected to act in unison.

The wise supervisor will take it upon himself to develop friendly rapport with supervisors of related units allied in common purposes within and outside the organization. He will accomplish this through informal meetings, formal associations, and the maintenance of friendly relations. The interchange of personnel on a training basis for short periods of time, perhaps a month or two, will increase their understanding of each other's jobs and will tend to foster coordination. The first-line patrol supervisor assigned to the investigation division for a short training period, for example, will invariably bring to his subordinates on his return to his regularly assigned patrol post an improved, or at least a broader, insight into the problems of the investigator and his job, thus contributing materially to improved relationships between two units which have traditionally experienced friction. This increased understanding of each other's responsibilities is a paramount factor in the process of bringing about better relationships between two such units where friction occurs primarily because the people in one do not appreciate the problems of the other.

By his attitude, the supervisor can establish a climate in which the spirit of cooperation will thrive among his subordinates. Hostile, suspicious, or unfriendly relations between supervisors of allied units will invariably be reflected by unnecessary misunderstandings, friction, petty jealousies, and ill will between their respective subordinates because the supervisor's attitude will often quickly permeate his whole unit. Smooth operations will be hampered by these barriers to effective cooperation.

The degree of coordination achieved in any organization will directly approximate the level of willing cooperation between individuals in the various units that must work in harmony to accomplish the mission of the enterprise. If the organizational structure clearly provides for a system of authority so that those in charge can interrelate the various elements of the establishment and create a unity of purpose in the minds of the employees, coordination will follow.

TYPES OF ORGANIZATIONAL STRUCTURES

An organizational structure is a mechanical means of depicting, by an arrangement of symbols, the relationships which exist among individuals, groups, and functions within the organization. Lines of authority and responsibility and functional relationships between groups and individuals are shown in graphic form. Even the most innovative of modern organizational structures are but modifications or conglomerates of one or more of the basic types of organizations.

The line organization

The straight line organization, often called the individual, military, or departmental type of organization, is the simplest and perhaps the oldest type; but it is seldom encountered in its true form except in any but the smallest of establishments. The channels of authority and responsibility extend in a direct line from top to bottom within the structure. Authority is definite and absolute (see Fig. 2–1).

While the line type of organization has many advantages, it also has some inherent weaknesses which, for many organizations, make its use impractical. Perhaps its greatest advantage is that it is utterly simple. It involves a division of the work into units with a person in charge who has complete control and who can be held directly accountable for results, or lack of them.

Quick decisions can be made in the line organization because of the direct lines of authority and, because of these direct lines, each member in the chain of command knows to whom he is accountable and who is accountable to him. Because responsibility is clearly fixed, discipline is easily administered in this type of organization, responsibility for making decisions is well identified, and singleness of purpose is fostered.[5] Coordination of effort is relatively easy to achieve because

[5] E. H. Anderson and G. T. Schwenning, *The Science of Production Organization* (New York: John Wiley & Sons, Inc., 1947), pp. 161–63.

FIGURE 2-1. Line or military type of organization

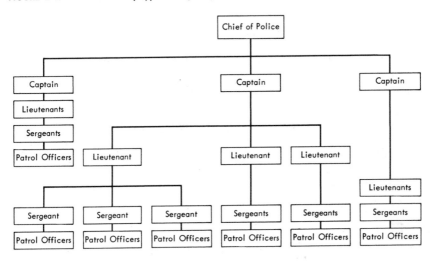

functional overlapping between units, a prime cause of friction in any organization, can be minimized.

One disadvantage inherent in the line type of organization is that supervisory personnel are too often required to perform the duties of specialists because little use is made of the latter for giving advice and counsel to line units. It is also often difficult to establish functional definition at the outset, but once it has been achieved, duplication of effort can be reduced. If jealousies exist between managers of the various units, each unit will tend to become "departmentalized," with the result that harmony of operation will be reduced and internal frictions will arise.

The functional organization

The functional organization in its pure form is rarely found in present-day organizations except at or near the top of the very largest. Unlike the line type of structure, those establishments organized on a functional basis violate the prime rule that workers perform best when they have but one supervisor. The functional organization divides responsibility and authority between several specialists, such as the person responsible for all training, the employee directing the community relations activities of all units within the department, or the officer having line authority over any employee within the department handling a case involving a juvenile. The functional responsibility of each "functional manager" is limited to the particular activity over which he has control, regardless of who performs the function (see Fig. 2–2).

Coordination of effort in this type of organization becomes difficult since the employees responsible for results may be subject to the functional direction of several persons. Discipline is difficult to administer because of this multiheaded leadership. There may be considerable conflict among the functional administrators, resulting in much confusion among line personnel. Lines of authority and responsibility are fragmented into many functional channels, making each supervisor responsible to several superiors depending upon the function he happens to be performing.

The line and staff organization

The line and staff type of organization is a combination of the line and functional types and is found in almost all but the very smallest police agencies today. It combines staff specialists or units with line organization so that the service of knowledge can be provided line personnel by specialists such as the criminalist, the training officer, the research and development specialist, the public relations officer, or the intelligence specialist. Channels of responsibility and authority are thus left intact since the specialist's responsibility is to "think and provide expertise" for the line units which are responsible for "doing." The line supervisor must remember that he obtains advice from the staff specialist, not commands (see Fig. 2–3).

In normal operations, the staff supervisor has line command only of those subordinates in his particular unit. If he and the line supervisor recognize this limitation, coordination between line and staff personnel can be achieved without undue friction. Failure to recognize these line

FIGURE 2-2. Functional type of organization

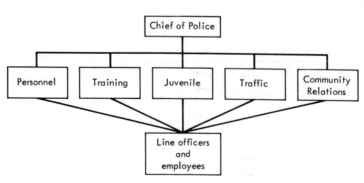

FIGURE 2-3. Line and staff organization

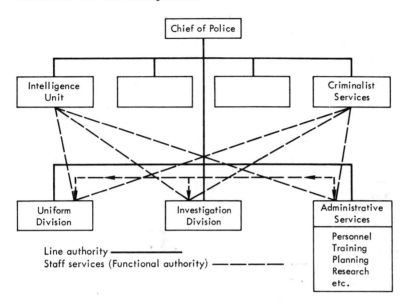

and staff relationships is the greatest and most frequent cause of friction in an organization and one of the most prominent barriers to effective coordination.

DIVISION OF WORK

Organizational structures are established to designate how work is to be divided among the various components of the establishment. Regardless of what basis is used for this division, whether work is apportioned according to *function* performed as in the laboratory, by *area* as in a system of precincts, geographical divisions, or beats, by *clientele* handled as in the case of youth activities or juvenile offenses, or by *purpose* as in public relations activities, traffic control, or the like, the division must be logical and practicable.

Usually organizations are structured according to a combination of these bases; but regardless of the way the division of work is made, if it does not result in improved operations, economies to the organization, or convenience to those served, the division should be avoided. Change in structure should never be made for the mere sake of change.

Insofar as practicable, homogeneous work should be apportioned to the same unit. Work which involves divergent functions or purposes will eventually cause friction and inefficiency if placed within one unit under the control of one supervisor.

The division of work involves not only the breaking down of a particular job into its component parts but also the recombining of these parts (synthesis) into a completed unit of work. The combining requires coordination if it is to be accomplished effectively.

The process of dividing work involves both analysis and synthesis. Anderson and Schwenning [6] stated, ". . . an incorrect synthesis might lose all the advantages gained by a correct analysis. It is conceivable that work might be divided quite minutely and then put back together . . . in some way less effective than the original."

A function of prime importance for the supervisor is that of constantly analyzing the nature of the work performed in his unit for the purpose of determining if it is effectively divided between the various units and individuals of the organization.[7] Too frequently, tasks which should be combined into one function are fragmented into several, thus breeding inefficiency. For example, considerable inefficiency might result if a patrol officer in an organization large enough to permit some degree of specialization were required to make a preliminary investigation of a crime on his beat, type the necessary reports himself, gather and preserve physical evidence and attempt to evaluate it, conduct the follow-up investigation, and then present his case in court. To perform such a variety of tasks would result in lowered productivity and quality of work.

For best results, the principle of *specialization* and the law of *productivity* as stated by Alford [8] require assigning to each worker the fewest possible kinds of tasks or operations in order to improve the quality and increase the quantity of his work, and giving him the highest class of work for which his natural abilities fit him. Only then is the greatest individual productivity possible.

UNITY OF COMMAND

In addition to providing a logical arrangement of work, organizational structure should provide clear-cut channels of authority. The principle of "unity of command" should be practiced in every organization. This principle requires that every employee should be under the direct com-

---

[6] Anderson and Schwenning, *Science of Production Organization*, p. 206.

[7] The apportioning of the patrol force by hour of the day, day of the week, and area according to relative needs for police services is discussed in detail in Chapter 13.

[8] L. P. Alford, *Laws of Management Applied to Manufacturing* (New York: The Ronald Press Company, 1928), p. 82.

mand of but one superior.[9] Thus each worker should be accountable directly to only one supervisor in normal operations. It is recognized that the principle occasionally is violated in organizations which function exceptionally well despite what is classically considered almost a fatal breach of an inviolate principle. Close analysis will probably reveal, however, that such organizations operate effectively because of exceptional leadership. Management folklore has numerous accounts of such occurrences—just as in the folklore of engineering, the bumblebee is said not to have the physical capacity to fly.

The principle of unity of command applies to those who are commanded, not to those who command. It does not relieve the supervisor from the responsibility for taking action in emergency situations that require immediate supervisory attention, decision, or disciplinary action (even against a subordinate assigned to another unit). This exception does not justify the specialist assuming command over line personnel in normal operations, although the practice is occasionally sanctioned by organizational rules. Neither does the exception make more acceptable the routine practice of some superior officers of dealing directly with operating personnel instead of through their immediate supervisors. Such practices will cause friction and tend to undermine the supervisor's authority over his own subordinates. It will invariably cause confusion, insecurity, and a lowering of the confidence of workers subjected to such habitual breaches of the principle in normal operations.

The Department of the Army stresses that, "Unity of command assures unity of effort by the coordinate action of all forces toward the common goal. . . ." It states, "Where unity of command cannot be realized [because of legal sanctions involving agencies from several levels of government, as in joint efforts to control civil disorder or provide mutual aid] at least unity of effort should be realized. The establishment of joint operations centers; the recognition of each other's capabilities and limitations; and a positive attitude will contribute to unity of effort." [10]

SPAN OF CONTROL

The principle of "span of attention," initially adopted from psychologists, refers to the number of persons one individual can supervise effectively.[11] The principle has been applied to military and administra-

9 Henri Fayol, *Industrial and General Administration*, trans. J. A. Conbrough (Geneva: International Management Association, 1930).

10 United States Department of the Army, *Field Manual 19-15, Civil Disturbances and Disasters* (Washington, D.C.: U.S. Government Printing Office, 1968), p. 2.

11 V. A. Graicunas, "Relationship in Organization," in *Papers on the Science of Administration*, ed. Luther Gulick and L. Urwick (New York: Institute of Public Administration, 1937), pp. 183–87.

tive operations as the "span of control," which relates to the number of subordinates who can be supervised effectively by one supervisor. This limit is small, from three to five at the top level of the organization, and broadens at the lower levels depending upon such factors as the capacity of the supervisor and those supervised, the types of work being performed, the complexity of the work, the area covered by it, distances between elements, the time needed to perform the tasks, the homogeneity of operations, the types of persons served, and the effectiveness of management.

The tendency in modern police operations is to exceed the bounds of effective control. Chiefs of police and other high administrative officers too frequently attempt to exert direct control over too many subordinates, and field supervisors at the operational level are expected to do likewise. The results are delay and confusion because of the "bottlenecks" which the practice causes. Rather than delegate some of his functions to subordinates, the top administrator too often attempts to retain close contact with every phase of the operation and will not relinquish his control until he comes to realize the limits of his capabilities. Until then, the total organization suffers. Superior officers should make every attempt to avoid requiring their supervisors to "spread themselves so thin" that they find it necessary to neglect their primary job of supervising because of the excessive number of details associated with the job they are given to oversee.

If good plans are made to define the tasks clearly to those who are to perform the job, if proper instructions are communicated to them, if completed staff work is practiced throughout the organization to free the supervisor and manager from unnecessary detail, if the employees receive proper training so that they require less supervision and control, and if they are given sufficient authority to perform requisite tasks, the supervisor will be able to reduce the span of detail for which he is responsible.[12]

DELEGATION OF WORK

The principle of delegation relates to the process of committing an activity to another's care. It is closely related to the principle of span of control in that even though the span of attention is excessive, the harm from it can be reduced by the delegation of much detail to subordinates. Those supervisors who refuse to allow anything to be done except under their direct control are the primary causes of the crippling bottlenecks which slow or stop effective operations.

Proper delegation frees the supervisor from many routine tasks and

[12] Kassoff, *Organizational Concepts*, pp. 26–28.

enables him to devote more of his time to broader planning activities. In addition, it provides other worthwhile benefits to employees to whom jobs are delegated. It gives them an opportunity to increase their job knowledge by performing new tasks which are not ordinarily their responsibility. It is an excellent tool for developing personnel for positions of greater responsibility and for increasing their initiative in accomplishing new tasks. Without such opportunities, workers often develop feelings of insecurity and frustration. They often begin to wonder if the boss has confidence in them or they feel that there are no avenues open to them for developing their capacity for higher positions.

While many activities can be passed down to others through the process of delegation, the supervisor cannot avoid the responsibility for such activities. Many supervisors have suffered dire consequences by assuming that a job entrusted to a subordinate relieved them of all responsibility. They should be encouraged to delegate all possible tasks to the lowest possible level in the organization where the necessary ability to perform them exists; but in so doing they do not shed their responsibility for the completion of the task and their accountability for the results.

Experience has shown that the average employee can and will accept greater responsibilities beyond his ordinary duties and will perform surprisingly well when he is delegated a task and given credit for its accomplishment, but the supervisor must exercise care that he does not delegate tasks beyond the capacity of his subordinates to perform them, that he avoids delegating only distasteful or onerous tasks, or that he does not attempt to "delegate away" his responsibility for certain basic tasks. If he fails to delegate, he has either failed to learn how, he has never really appreciated the need for avoiding routinized tasks which others can do better (and more economically), he has an overabundance of confidence in his own capacity for detail, or he does not have confidence in his subordinates.

When a task is delegated, enough authority to complete it must also be delegated, but the process must be consistent. Subordinates will be confused by a grant of total authority at one time and a total absence of it at another. Once authority has been granted, the supervisor must consistently refuse to take back what he has delegated simply because the subordinate finds the task too difficult or is reluctant to make a decision which he is perfectly capable of doing. In either case, he needs further training in how to do the task or he needs to be given assurance that he has the necessary decision-making authority.

The primary function of the manager is to preside over the process of delegation. This requires all of his judgment and much of his time.

He is constantly attempting to provide, through the means of delegation, the opportunities of growth which the people under him
demand. The strength of any organization increases with the ability
of people at all levels to accept responsibility. The assignment of
responsibility should never be static as implied by organization
charts, but should be changed with the situation and with the increasing capacity of people who are receiving proper management attention. As a responsible manager delegates responsibility to the people
below him and devotes attention to qualifying them to discharge
this responsibility well, he is developing himself as well as increasing
the satisfaction and caliber of his subordinates. [13]

Delegation may be accomplished by specific or general directive
given either in writing or orally. A simple task may be delegated in a
simple manner. A complex delegation should be supported by a comprehensive, written directive clearly identifying the problem and the
procedures to be followed if that appears necessary. It is imperative
that instructions are complete and clear lest the assignment be misconstrued, in which case the subordinate assigned the task could not be
held responsible for it. If the subordinate has been given the assignment
to provide an answer to some vague problem but does not understand
what the problem really is, his job will be unproductive and wasteful.

Once a job has been delegated, its importance explained, and
necessary instructions have been clearly given for its accomplishment,
the supervisor should discreetly follow up as needed to assure that the
employee is progressing satisfactorily. Assistance should be given to overcome obstacles the employee is not equipped to handle, but care should
be exercised that he is not given so much help that his initiative is taken
away. The process of delegation loses its value as a supervisory tool if
follow-up inspections are not made to ensure that objectives are accomplished and deadlines are met.

PERSONNEL DEVELOPMENT

The practice of delegation contributes to the development of subordinates to perform the supervisor's job in his absence or when he is unable
to act. A program of this nature is variously denominated "executive"
or "supervisory development" or simply "personnel development," which
is a more all-inclusive program of training subordinates at all levels of
the hierarchy to "take over" when necessary.

Some supervisors are reluctant to develop subordinates because of
the fear that they will become competition. However, if the supervisor's

[13] United States Army Logistics Management Center, *Principles of Management:
Special Text 38-1* (Washington, D.C.: U.S. Government Printing Office, n.d.), p. 15.

job is performed well in his absence by others who have been trained to do it, he will eventually receive credit for his efforts.

A watch commander should train each of his sergeants to take over while he is absent on vacation, days off, or sick leave. The practice of training only the senior sergeant for this duty decreases flexibility and deprives the younger supervisory officer of training which he may badly need in some emergency when the responsibility of a higher position is thrust upon him. It is better that errors be committed at a time when they can be corrected constructively under the watchful eye of an experienced supervisor than when they occur under emergency conditions, when an error might be critical. Often it is argued that the senior supervisor should never be required to operate under the direction of one of junior standing because of the adverse effect such an arrangement might have upon the morale of the senior; however, such argument is tenuous and such adverse effects, if they exist, can be avoided by adopting the executive development principle as a policy which is programmed within the agency.

The development of subordinates is essentially a problem of training wherein the subordinate's skill and efficiency are increased. This increase in his ability to render a service requiring a higher degree of responsibility enhances his confidence, gives him satisfaction, and provides him an incentive of new goals toward which he can strive. His superior gains an increased freedom from details of his operation, which enables him to devote more time to making policy, supervising, and planning.

THE EXCEPTION PRINCIPLE

Developing subordinates to take over in the boss's absence involves training just as does the exception principle, which specifies that the head of an organization should not find it necessary to act personally on each matter coming under his general jurisdiction. Rather, he should have to act only on those exceptional matters which require his personal attention.

The exception principle is inseparable from the principle of delegation. It prevails at all levels of the management hierarchy and involves the delegation of functions which, if done effectively, will free the superior from a mass of routine detail which might better be disposed of by others below him. Training is the key to the effective application of the principle. Superior officers should pass on all work possible to subordinates except that which is appropriate to the particular level that the superior occupies. He should reserve for himself only those decisions which his subordinates are not equipped to make. He should avoid becoming "bogged down" with detail so that he can be free to integrate the work being performed within his sphere of operation into that of the entire organization. As Anderson and Schwenning [14] have so succinctly stated, "It is only by consciously stripping the higher jobs of all minor tasks that artistry, ingenuity, and creative thinking are invoked or even made possible."

COMPLETED STAFF WORK

The principle of completed staff work requires that the person to whom work has been assigned through the delegation process complete it to such an extent that the only thing left to be done by the person who delegated it is to approve it. If he disapproves it, completed staff work has not been achieved since the principle requires that everything must be done which the person making the assignment would have had to do if he had the time to do the work himself.

Researching and planning projects

Usually the task assigned can be completed without an in-depth investigation and study. On occasion, however, a project requires considerable inquiry preliminary to the submission of a formal report. In such cases, the person to whom the work has been assigned must work out all details completely. All the leg work of gathering pertinent data must be performed after the approach to the problem has been carefully planned and a line of procedure decided. What data are needed? Where can it be obtained? What are the views of interested persons and those affected by the project? Consultation with specialists and a review of the related literature on the subject may furnish the answers to these questions.

Once data required for the project have been accumulated, they should be studied carefully, refined, and organized into a logical draft. Usually restudy and rewrite are required to refine the product to a point where it is suitable for presentation. The more difficult and complex the problem is, the more tempting it is to present it in piecemeal fashion.

If a plan of action is proposed, it should be well coordinated, unequivocal, and supported by factual data. Accuracy of supporting material should be unimpeachable since the superior may refer to it as supportive of his contention or request. Should he commit himself to a

[14] Anderson and Schwenning, *Science of Production Organization*, p. 106.

course of action only to find that the basis for his commitment is spurious or inaccurate, he risks embarrassment and damage to his reputation.

Ordinarily, a summary report, concise, brief, and to the point, should be included. Often, it should be placed at the beginning so that the superior can conserve time reviewing the project. Such summary should be supplemented by a more detailed section with appropriate addenda which may be referred to in the event further particulars are desired.

Finally, the person preparing the report should place himself in the position of the superior to whom it is to be submitted. Would he sign it, thereby staking his professional reputation on the contents? Would he approve it as written? If the answer to these questions is no, complete staff work has not been done. The report should be restudied and rewritten with the objective of protecting the boss from "half-baked" ideas, endless memorandums to digest, or immature proposals.

SUMMARY

Organization is a medium through which work is accomplished by individuals or groups associated with each other in doing something. Organization involves not only physical matters but psychological ones as well since it involves individual and group relationships which are welded together through the coordinating activities and leadership of managers.

The supervisor's main administrative activities are described by Gulick's POSDCORB. The planning activities of the supervisor are a constant process. Well-made plans in effect enable him to make decisions in advance to aid him in accomplishing the objectives of the organization. His organizing function is closely related. It requires that structural changes be made as the need arises to provide a more effective medium through which work can be distributed and performed. His staffing responsibilities involve the placement of subordinates into the positions for which their capabilities best fit them. Perhaps one of his most important functions as a supervisor is the training of employees so that they will produce effectively, efficiently, and safely. Much of the supervisor's time is consumed by his control activities embodied in the direction function. This is accomplished by observations and inspection.

The coordination of human effort is the function of the leaders of an enterprise which determines how effectively the elements of the organization perform in conjunction with each other. Cooperative effort is the essence of coordination. The reporting function involves the process of communicating down with subordinates, up with superiors, and across organizational channels with other units. It dovetails with the process of coordination of effort.

The supervisor is responsible for the constant and never-ending process of analyzing how work is apportioned so that the individual and group elements within the organization will be performing similar amounts of work per employee. Changing organizational responsibilities will necessitate realignment of workloads so that a logical and practical division of work may be realized. Such realignments will also require that attention be given to the number of subordinates and the amount of detail over which the supervisor exercises control. His span of control and the amount of attention he is capable of giving to his responsibilities are limited by the nature of the job and the excellence of his personnel.

The ability of the supervisor to perform his complex duties efficiently and well will depend to a large degree upon how skillfully he is able to delegate routine tasks to others and to retain for his personal attention only those exceptional matters he should handle himself. The more effective this delegation process is, the fewer bottlenecks he will create in the operations of his unit. In addition, he will be freed to engage in the broader context of planning, creative thinking, and essential external relationships. The effectiveness of this process of delegation is largely dependent upon how well subordinates have been trained both to assume responsibility for routine acts and decisions for which they are equipped and to engage in completed staff work.

REVIEW

Questions

1. List the various elements of the chief executive's activities as described by Gulick and discuss how each applies to the first-line supervisor.
2. What is meant by organization?
3. How may the supervisor best utilize the talents of the natural leaders in the organization even though they are not officially designated as such? What are these natural leaders called?
4. What are the four main bases for dividing work in the police service? Give two examples of each.
5. What is meant by the principle of specialization?
6. What is meant by the law of productivity?
7. Define unity of command and discuss the factors which affect its application.

8. What is meant by span of control? How is it affected by organizational structure? What are some of the other factors that affect span of control?

9. Discuss how the failure to delegate causes bottlenecks in an organization. Give examples.

10. Why cannot ultimate responsibility be delegated?

11. Discuss the benefits which the supervisor can derive from effective delegation.

12. What is the exception principle?

13. Define the essential nature of completed staff work.

14. How do delegation, the exception principle, and the principle of completed staff work interrelate?

Exercises

1. Prepare a simple chart of your organization or of another one. Identify the type of organization, the advantages and disadvantages of such a structure, and possible means of eliminating its disadvantages or of increasing its advantages.

2. Prepare a simple organizational chart of at least two other types of organizations. Discuss the advantages and disadvantages of each.

3. Draw a chart of an organization which you would consider "ideal" in a police organization of fifty sworn and civilian employees; one hundred; three hundred. Justify the appropriateness of each structure.

3

Employee dissatisfaction, grievances, and complaints

Every supervisor should be sensitive to the needs of employees who have real or imagined grievances or dissatisfactions. These often result from supervisory or management practices perceived by workers as a threat to their personal rights or their right to fair treatment, or an infringement on their right to privacy.

Dissatisfactions may not be expressed, but the mere fact that they are present may have the same effect in eroding ambition and initiative and causing a deterioration in morale and performance *as if they were verbalized*. Grievances, even though imaginary, should be recognized by the supervisor as being "real" in the mind of the employee who feels he has been wronged. If the supervisor is indifferent to them, resentment and hostility will occur and will quickly spread if other personnel are convinced that a fellow employee has been treated unjustly or that a wrong has not been corrected.

CAUSES OF EMPLOYEE DISSATISFACTION

Studies [1] of worker reactions in many occupations have revealed that employee complaints, grievances, and dissatisfactions arise from factors that can be broadly categorized into four areas—the working environment; harsh, abusive, tyrannical, or inept supervision; misunderstandings about policies and procedures of the organization; and management failures of various types.

These findings, although samplings, should give the supervisor many clues concerning how police officers and other employees frequently perceive organizational controls and supervisory practices that affect their personal and professional lives. He may then draw certain unmistakable conclusions about his own brand of supervision and how it may have contributed to employee discontent. Once he recognizes his shortcomings, he can set about to correct them. If he is honest about this self-evaluation, he will recognize where his performance as a supervisor might need modification.

It is not known what percentage of these reactions are valid; however, their very existence is indicative of a problem that requires some attention. Those that are invalid should not be ignored if the giving of an explanation will change an employee's attitude or correct a misconception. At least he will feel that his complaint has been considered.

There are no standard methods for handling these matters. Each must be approached with common sense and fairness.

WORKING ENVIRONMENT

Physical factors in the working environment give rise to a large portion of employee dissatisfaction. Bad lights, improper temperature, uncleanliness or inadequate restroom facilities, unsatisfactory operational equipment, and other workplace deficiencies are factors that usually require capital outlay to correct. In such cases, the supervisor is often powerless to make the necessary corrections directly but should call such deficiencies to the attention of higher management. If maintenance or service employees are subject to his direction and control, he will frequently find that more attention to their supervision will bring about

[1] Woodruff Imberman, "Letting the Employee Speak His Mind," *Personnel,* 53, No. 6 (November–December, 1976), 13–14. See also International Association of Chiefs of Police, *Managing for Effective Police Discipline* (Washington, D.C.: International Association of Chiefs of Police, 1976), pp. 200–12.

a noteworthy improvement. He must recognize that adequate physical facilities and equipment contribute to the maintenance of a high level of production and vitally affect employee morale.

INEPT SUPERVISORY PRACTICES

Poor supervisory practices account for perhaps one-third of the dissatisfaction and the negative feelings of employees. Failure to give recognition to employees when they believe they have earned it; the use of intemperate language by the supervisor; harsh, arbitrary methods in dealing with subordinates; the display of favoritism; the existence of dual standards of conduct; unfairness of supervisors in the application of rules to subordinates; excessive supervision; the existence of cliques—and all of the bad connotations usually associated with them—whether or not the supervisor is a part; and the like are commonly cited as causes of employee dissatisfaction with their leaders.

These dissatisfactions are a prime cause of complaints and grievances of various types and contribute markedly to a lowering of morale. Such employee reactions cannot be regarded merely as trivia nor can the supervisor afford to downgrade or minimize their importance. Rather, he must learn and apply the tenets of effective leadership in dealing with the problems associated with such reactions. These principles are discussed in detail in Chapter 4.

MISUNDERSTANDINGS OF POLICIES, RULES, AND PROCEDURES

Relatively few of the negative reactions of workers in many different types of occupations relate to failures of management to communicate policies and procedures effectively. Such reactions were generally confirmed by peace officers surveyed, although to a lesser degree. The results tend to indicate that managers in law enforcement agencies tend to communicate organizational policies and procedures rather well. However, since effective communications are essential to effective leadership, the supervisor must constantly work at improving his skill as a communicator so that he can minimize all problems resulting from poor communications. Suggestions for accomplishing this objective are discussed in Chapter 5.

MANAGEMENT FAILURES

Failures of management account for many of the negative reactions of workers. Toleration by supervisors of wasted time; effort, and physical resources; unjustified abuses of equipment; supervisory negligence in protecting the interests of the organization; violations of employee "due process" rights; infringement on what workers believe are their rights to privacy; arbitrary enforcement of rules and regulations; and the like are quickly recognized by employees and tend to erode organizational pride, morale, and efficiency. Employees are quick to sense the attitudes of management personnel—especially operation-level supervisors. When supervisory personnel are indifferent to the best interests of the organization, employees are prone to adopt the attitude, "If the administration wants it that way, that's the way they'll get it."

Indifference of supervisors to the squandering of organizational resources and other wasteful practices contribute to inefficient operations. Most law enforcement personnel remain in public service because they like the work. They conscientiously strive to perform their duties effectively and efficiently and resent supervisory practices that make their jobs more difficult.

Rules of conduct

Studies among peace officers have revealed some distinct dissatisfactions about organizational rules and regulations and how they are applied by supervisors.[2] Individuals who had the strongest opinions about the regulation of their personal conduct by their organization were rather explicit in their reactions. They indicated that their greatest concern was that such rules and regulations placed undue restrictions on their personal rights. They were opposed to controls governing their off-duty employment; their hairstyles, mustaches, and beards; their criticizing the organization; and their place of residence.

Personnel who had strongest feelings about departmental rules and regulations relating to the operation of vehicles, courtesy to the public, the use of physical force, the use of firearms, and other general department restrictions on conduct and performance perceived these as an interference with their ability to do good police work.

Officers who had the strongest opinions about organizational con-

[2] International Association of Chiefs of Police. *Managing for Effective Police Discipline,* pp. 200–12.

trols of their moral conduct, personal debts, the use of alcohol off duty, and the like, believed these matters to be an invasion of their right to privacy and none of the department's business.

Manner of enforcing rules of conduct

An inordinate number of officers opposed the *manner* in which organizational rules were enforced more than the rules themselves. *Inconsistency* of supervisors in enforcing all organization rules was perceived far more frequently than any other cause as a reason for this opposition.

Many officers expressed strong negative opinions about the failure of supervisors to follow the same rules which the officers were expected to follow. Many others felt that punishments were too severe for violations of rules. Only a few expressed negative opinions about supervisors failing to explain particular rules.

Undoubtedly, many of these complaints can be prevented by the supervisor if he learns how to motivate and direct his subordinates as discussed in Chapter 4.

Due process violations

Employees react strongly and often challenge management in court when they feel they have been arbitrarily deprived of some due process right.

It is obvious that their demands for greater freedom from management controls are growing. In the last decade, they have insisted on greater and greater procedural safeguards to protect them against "management infringements" on their personal rights. These demands have been reflected by due process statutes which have been enacted in some states providing for a police officers' "Bill of Rights." [3]

The recent extensions by the courts and legislators of constitutional guarantees to protect public officers' rights have further restricted organizations in exercising management controls once considered commonplace; yet, a surprising number of supervisors believe that they can still supervise as they once did.

They soon learn that some of their practices run counter to the law as court rulings become increasingly protective of employee rights. Since these decisions have varied widely from place to place, it is incumbent on every supervisor to acquaint himself thoroughly with those applicable to his jurisdiction.

[3] California Government Code, Sections 3300–3309 (1975).

He should exercise considerable care in attempting to punish his subordinates for conduct of a purely personal nature not involving their job performance, the public image of the organization, or its real interests. Such occurrences sometimes place him in a situation requiring a choice between two undesirable alternatives. Either he takes action contrary to legal rules protecting the employee and risks a court challenge that might overrule him, or he is forced to overlook conduct which he considers improper and take no action at all.

Generally, courts have ruled that an employee cannot be penalized for his acts unless it can be proved that the conduct is related to his performance of duty *and* impaired his efficiency, seriously interfered with the operational efficiency of the organization, interfered with the maintenance of good order within the organization, or that it was common knowledge that the particular conduct was prohibited.[4] This poses a rather heavy burden upon the supervisor, especially when the subordinate's behavior involves the question of whether or not the department can legally dictate non-job-related standards of conduct. Some of the most doubtful issues rise from conduct such as off-duty employment, the use of alcohol off duty, bankruptcy, failure to pay debts, immoral conduct not involving an unlawful act, and the like.

SUPERVISORY INFLUENCE ON EMPLOYEE BEHAVIOR

In dealing with behavior that is not job-related, the supervisor must be aware that his options are limited in the eyes of the law; and yet he may feel impelled to do something to correct a subordinate's demeanor which he believes to be contrary to the best interests of the organization and the individuals in it. He must consider the legal justification for his action as well as the morality of what he does if he is to set a professional "tone" within his sphere of influence.

It is in cases such as these that the supervisor's persuasive abilities are truly tested. If he is respected by his subordinates, he will be able to exert a great influence in controlling or preventing what he considers objectionable conduct that might not be legally actionable. Since people generally need a model to follow, the supervisor should find occasion to communicate his convictions to his subordinates without sermonizing. He will strive to develop and maintain in them the high standards and ideals that are characteristic of a true profession and will direct his greatest efforts toward those who have difficulty abiding by the conduct norms recognized and accepted within the organization.

4 *Bence v. Breier,* 501 F. 2d 1185 (1974); *Perea v. Fales,* 114 Cal. Rptr. 808 (1974).

The so-called "freeway therapy," "transfer treatment," or "the wheel," which may involve frequent transfer from one place, one shift, or one assignment to another, is sometimes used to remove an employee from an unwholesome environment to one of lesser exposure; but frequently, such treatment is more injurious, if not more immoral, than the conduct it is designed to cure.

Transfer may correct a problem but more often does not. All it usually does is to shift it from one place or from one supervisor to another. It may well be that transfer from one environment to another is the only solution to a problem but should not be done without consideration for other useful alternatives, such as additional training, counseling, change of assignment or partner within the unit, and the like.

RECOGNIZING EMPLOYEE DISSATISFACTION

Even though employee discontent is not verbalized, it may become more grievous to the supervisor—and the organization—than expressed grievances, and its effects may be just as devastating.

The typical symptoms that should alert a supervisor to the existence of dissatisfaction among his subordinates are similar to those symptoms of frustration described in Chapter 6. Other manifestations of dissatisfaction might be increased "blue Monday" absenteeism, a growing inattention to duty, excessive tardiness, indifference to job requirements, hostility and irritability of employees, general deterioration in performance and morale, and similar reactions.

Once the supervisor recognizes the symptoms that strong feelings of discontent are growing among his subordinates, he should try to determine what the cause might be. In doing so, he will look to the indigenous leaders among his subordinates for clues. Interviews with affected personnel, as discussed in Chapter 7, may provide additional evidence.

SUPERVISORY APPROACH TO EMPLOYEE DISSATISFACTIONS

Although many employee complaints are valid, some are not. Many of the causes for employee dissatisfaction can be prevented by the supervisor if he will consistently adhere to the basic tenets of leadership. When the working environment causes discontent which cannot be or was not prevented, the supervisor should do whatever is possible, reasonable, and just to remove the causes of dissatisfaction.

Some of these cannot be resolved directly by him because they involve established organizational policies or practices. Often, he can only inform his superiors of the effects of such factors and recommend what needs to be done.

In some cases, discontent may be caused by unfulfilled employee expectations concerning salary increases, the working environment, fringe benefits, rules and regulations and how they are enforced, and like matters. When employee demands are rejected as unreasonable, reactions often become hostile, but the adroit supervisor can do much to temper such strong feelings by his wise counsel. He must avoid commiserating with employees in such cases. Rather, he should counsel them to seek any redress they believe they are entitled to by submitting objective justification for their demands to arbitration between their representatives and management.

GRIEVANCES

When some factor in an employee's working environment causes him to complain orally or more formally, in writing, it is usually referred to as a grievance. Those grievances involving some factor not related to a contractual agreement are resolved primarily by the first-line supervisor unless he is the subject of the grievance. Then the matter is usually resolved by his superior. Those which allege that management has breached some contractual agreement with the employees are usually handled according to procedures specified in the contract. In either case, the technique is similar.

Noncontractual matters

Most grievances that do not involve a contractual matter can be resolved by the first-line supervisor without referral to higher authority. He must first obtain the true cause of the grievance by making it easy for the subordinate to discuss the cause of his complaint. Some recommended techniques for such interviews and for arriving at solutions to the problem are described in Chapter 7.

Contractual violations and grievances

When employees complain because they believe the management in an organization has breached an agreement of their contract, a more formalized procedure is usually required.

Typically, four steps are involved when dissatisfactions degenerate into formal grievances. In the first step, the supervisor or the employee representative receives the complaint. Usually, the issue can be resolved at this level. If the supervisor's inquiry reveals a true basis for the complaint, he can often take appropriate corrective action and resolve the issue there and then. Reasonableness and fairness on the parts of the supervisor, the employee, and the employee representative are essential to prompt resolution. Should attempts fail to resolve the matter at this level, the matter becomes an official grievance. This is the second step, in which the complaint is referred to a higher intermediate level of management for resolution. Third, should disagreement continue, the grievance is transmitted to the top level of management within the organization. When attempts to reach a resolution fail at this step, the matter then proceeds to the fourth step—voluntary arbitration. The typical work contract usually provides that both parties will accept as binding the decision of an impartial arbitrator.[5]

In such matters, the first step in the procedure is most critical to the employee, the supervisor, and the organization. Because of the economic cost associated with the processing of grievances through the various stages and their adverse effects upon employee morale, the supervisor must make every effort to resolve such matters at the earliest stage. Usually, an objective approach coupled with sound supervisory practices, fair play, and common sense will provide the answers to these problems.

SUMMARY

Supervisors must be alert to detect factors within the working environment that cause employee dissatisfactions. They must recognize that prompt corrective action is essential if morale and productivity are to be maintained at a high level.

Employee dissatisfactions arise from many factors, which can be categorized into four broad areas—the working environment, inept supervision, misunderstandings about policies and procedures in the organization, and management failures of various types.

Physical factors in the work environment may or may not be correctible by the supervisor (unless he has some direct supervisory responsibility over maintenance personnel) because they ordinarily involve capital outlays over which he has little control. Most of the many dis-

---

[5] Robert M. Fulmer, *Supervision: Principles of Professional Management* (Beverly Hills, Calif.: Glencoe Press, 1976), pp. 324–25.

satisfactions resulting from inept supervisory practices can be avoided if he will apply the basic tenets of leadership in his day-to-day dealings with his subordinates. In police agencies, few complaints are made by personnel about their misunderstandings of policies, rules, and procedures; however, many adverse reactions arise from the failure of management personnel to protect the resources of the organization.

Much of the discontent of employees can be associated with their opposition to rules and regulations which they construe as being an infringement on their personal rights. Of greater significance, however, are their adverse reactions to the manner in which such rules and regulations are enforced by management personnel, especially those at the working level.

These employee reactions afford many pertinent clues to the wise supervisor who will continuously engage in self-appraisal of his brand of supervision so that he may eliminate his bad practices and build on his good ones.

The supervisor who discovers among his subordinates non-job-related behavior that is not legally actionable, but is contrary to the best interest of the organization, may feel impelled to do something. In such cases, he has several options. He can take action without legal support and risk being overruled in a court if challenged, or he can overlook the conduct and do nothing. The third option will test his persuasive ability to eliminate the unacceptable demeanor by convincing his subordinates of the value of high professional standards and ideals.

REVIEW

Questions

1. What are the four categories into which employee dissatisfactions can be grouped?
2. What are some of the most prominent failures of management personnel that contribute to adverse reactions of employees?
3. What supervisory practices do employees oppose most in the enforcement of rules and regulations?
4. Describe and give an example of a due process violation.
5. What is a formal grievance?

Exercises

1. You learn that a subordinate is cohabiting with a person to whom he or she is not married. Describe how you would approach this problem if the mayor of your city mentioned it to you and suggested that you do something.

2. Describe what you would do if an employee's representative submitted a grievance to you involving a clique in your unit. What would you do if the complaint accused you of being a party to the clique?

3. Discuss the merits/demerits of "transfer treatment"; "freeway therapy."

4. Describe some of the typical symptoms of employee discontent when their dissatisfactions have not been expressed.

4

Elements of leadership, supervision, and command presence

Leadership may be defined as the art of influencing, directing, guiding, and controlling others in such a way as to obtain their willing obedience, confidence, respect, and loyal cooperation in the accomplishment of an objective. It is the human factor which binds the group together and motivates it toward goals. Leadership is truly an art. It embodies a set of basic principles the application of which facilitates human endeavor. It involves more than just a grant of authority. Parker and Kleemeier [1] make the distinction when they state,

> When men obey another because of fear, they are *yielding*. Their obedience is given grudgingly. There is little loyalty or teamwork, and no desire to give their all for a common cause. But when men *follow*, they do so willingly—because they *want to do* what a leader wishes. Herein lies the distinction between being an authority and being a leader. The leader stimulates, motivates, and inspires the group to follow willingly, even eagerly. The authority pushes and drives his men, who yield and obey because they fear the consequences of disobedience. . . .

[1] Willard E. Parker and Robert W. Kleemeier, *Human Relations in Supervision: Leadership in Management* (New York: McGraw-Hill Book Company, 1951), pp. 411–12.

There are as many levels of leadership proficiency as there are leaders. At different times and for different tasks the degree of supervisory skills called for will vary. Yet there is a close, positive correlation between organizational effectiveness and the abilities of supervisors to skillfully apply those proven principles of leadership that have evolved from the experiences of industry and the military, from the social sciences, and from other disciplines. The supervisor who has managed to learn and apply these principles will find his job easier and the productivity of his subordinates greater. Their apprehension of authority will be lessened, and their respect for their leaders will increase. The result will be better understanding and fewer conflicts of purpose between those who direct and control and those who constitute the working force of the organization.

RESISTANCE TO LEADERSHIP TRAINING

That considerable resistance to leadership training exists cannot be denied. This resistance is usually the result of the inability of some supervisors to adopt and apply realistically the principles of leadership to their own particular assignments. They perform their leadership tasks in the traditional, stereotyped fashion. They look back at the brand of supervision they have received and reflect, "If it was good enough for me, it should be good enough for my subordinates." They are apt to supervise as they have been supervised. They find this attitude difficult to change. Often, those who most need to change are those who resist change most because they believe they are already good leaders.

Some supervisors resist adopting more refined supervisory practices because many of these are intangible and require more effort than those to which they have been accustomed. They may resist because of the military connotation supervision implies in the quasi-military law enforcement organization.

The application of many proven principles of supervision may initially require more energy than do some of the hard, driving tactics to which they have become accustomed. Little do they realize that the scientific methods usually become easier than the old, unscientific approach. More often than not, they are more effective in the long run and produce better results. Becoming skillful in applying sound leadership techniques requires diligence, but every supervisor worthy of the name must recognize the need for performing his tasks in such a way as to sustain a high organizational spirit and, at the same time, achieve maximum productivity.

DEVELOPING LEADERSHIP ABILITY

Leadership ability is not inherited. There are few born leaders. Undoubtedly there are some natural endowments which affect the relative abilities of individuals to become good leaders. Some physical traits, aptitudes, intelligence, and temperament characteristics are examples.

Any reasonably intelligent person with enough forcefulness to develop his ability to inspire others to follow him can earn leadership status. He may never be recognized on the organization charts, he may never be awarded stripes or bars, but he nevertheless is a leader if others are desirous of following him. The true leader—the ideal for the organization—is the leader recognized as such formally *and* granted leadership authority not only by his organization but by his subordinates. The grant of authority by the latter is the only *real* source of authority.

The granting of formal authority does not ipso facto make a person a leader. Leadership status must be earned. The necessary qualities may be developed by training and self-discipline. When necessary, habits can be changed and emotions controlled. Mannerisms, speech, manual and mental skills, and attitudes can be altered by training calculated to develop or improve leadership ability, but this requires diligent effort. If leadership ability is learned slowly through trial and error, morale and performance are likely to suffer in the process because of the errors that are bound to creep into the supervisor's underdeveloped judgment.

The best leaders make their jobs appear easy because they have the fewest problems. They learn to recognize symptoms that problems are developing and have the fortitude to take timely preventive action before the problems become unmanageable. Those who avoid problems by sidestepping issues that should be treated forthrightly may continue to hold their positions but are bound to fail as leaders.

TYPES OF LEADERS

Many types of persons make good leaders. There is no single leader type. Most can be classified according to their individual approach to leadership under one of the following categories.

The autocrat

The autocratic leader is highly authoritative. He makes decisions without allowing subordinates to participate. They are often made to feel that they are not part of the team because they are not allowed a voice in the decision-making process. They do, however, know where they stand because he goes by the book. He directs, commands, and controls his subordinates in such a manner that no one ever forgets who is the boss. He rules through fear. He is a driver who uses his authority lavishly, demanding complete and unquestioning obedience from his inferiors. He is often thought of as the tyrant among supervisors. He is primarily leader centered, having little concern for others but considerable interest in his own supervisory status.

When conditions are unstable during periods of stress or emergency, when initiative and decisiveness are needed, when there is usually no time for permissive leadership and no time for discussion with subordinates before each decision is made, and when bold, rapid action is indicated, the autocratic leader is most likely to succeed.[2] Usually, however, he does not obtain good results over an extended period.[3]

The democratic leader

The supervisor who leads democratically, seeking ideas and suggestions from his subordinates and allowing them to participate in decision making that affects them, by and large secures the best results as a leader.[4] He uses little authority because he encourages his employees to participate with him in getting the job done. He treats them as associates in a joint venture and thereby increases their feelings of responsibility, their sense of achievement, recognition, and personal growth; but most important, he increases their commitment to the goals of the organization. This is the essence of participative management, which works well when circumstances permit employees to participate in the decision-making process.

At times, however, such as in emergent or unusual situations, purely democratic leadership will work poorly. In these cases, the most effective leaders will blend into their style more forceful measures which will produce the quick, decisive action needed. In such situations, the stronger leaders make it understood that participative management means, "I manage, you participate."

The democratic leader is keenly aware of the human factor in managing others. As an employee-oriented leader, he secures better performance from his subordinates, develops better motivation, and achieves

---

[2] Bernard M. Bass, *Leadership Psychology and Organizational Behavior* (New York: Harper & Row, Publishers, 1960), pp. 438–40.

[3] I. L. Heckmann, Jr., and S. G. Huneryager, *Human Relations in Management,* 2nd ed. (Cincinnati, Ohio: South-Western Publishing Co., 1967), p. 244.

[4] Keith Davis, *Human Relations at Work,* 2nd ed. (New York: McGraw-Hill Book Company, 1967), p. 137. See also William R. Van Dersal, *The Successful Supervisor in Government and Business* (New York: Harper & Row, Publishers, 1962), p. 21.

greater work satisfaction.[5] He ordinarily enjoys the respect of members of his group.

The free-rein leader

The leader who plays down his role as such and exercises a minimum of control seldom gives his subordinates the attention or help they need. He does not interfere with them but permits a laissez-faire operation. His failure to maintain contact is often as harmful as an excessive amount of supervision.

This type of supervision does not work well. It is an easy course for the supervisor to follow—especially when he is more concerned about being liked by his subordinates than being respected by them; but this invariably produces a climate of permissiveness. Feelings of insecurity develop among workers because they are left without the positive direction and guidance they look for and expect from their leader. As a result, morale, discipline, efficiency, and production begin to deteriorate, and the leader loses control.

SELECTING LEADERSHIP STYLE

There is no set of hard and fast rules for supervising in every work situation. Each supervisor must determine which style of leadership he thinks is best for his particular working environment. This determination must, of necessity, be based on his own personality, the personalities of his subordinates, his goals, and theirs.

All types of leadership will work with varying degrees of success if the conditions are favorable and the situation permits a particular approach. The selection of the right approach for the right situation is the key to skillful leadership.[6]

COMMAND PRESENCE AND LEADERSHIP

Command presence to some denotes a military bearing. To others, it means a distinctive type of appearance and conduct. Others believe that command presence is comprised of the same ingredients as leadership. In reality, it is a composite of all those traits. It is the natural manner of an individual indicating a complete command of his mental and

---

[5] Heckmann and Huneryager, *Human Relations in Management,* p. 244.

[6] Davis, *Human Relations at Work,* pp. 98–101.

physical faculties and emotions. It encompasses the qualities of dignity, self-assurance, and poise. It is that outward appearance which denotes that the person has the ability and qualifications to take command of any situation. When the leader has command presence, Pratt [7] observes, "Nervousness and indecision are replaced by calmness and self-control for he feels himself to be master of the situation." It is often said that command presence is best reflected by the leader who looks calmer and calmer as things get worse and worse. The leader's attitude quickly permeates a group. If he displays anxiety, they will develop it. They will not perform well in an atmosphere of anxiety and tension. Pfiffner and Fels [8] summarize this condition by stating, " . . . the supervisor absorbs heat from above instead of passing his own irritations on to his subordinates. He maintains a deportment of calmness, and evidences a high degree of emotional security, even under provocation."

ELEMENTS OF LEADERSHIP

It is impossible to draw a clear-cut line between personal qualities of leadership and the external expressions of those qualities through action. The characteristics of the leader are too closely interrelated, too interlocking, to permit complete isolation of one from another.

Indicators of good leadership

A high level of discipline in its broadest sense in an organization is perhaps the best mark of good organizational leadership. Ordinarily, if it is present, a high level of esprit de corps and morale will result together with increased efficiency.[9]

Leadership ethics

The position of true leadership places upon the leader a moral obligation to adhere strictly to the high standards of honor and integrity he expects of his subordinates and which they and his superiors have

---

[7] William V. Pratt, "Leadership" in *Selected Readings in Leadership*, 3rd ed., ed. Malcolm E. Wolfe and F. J. Mulholland (Annapolis, Md.: United States Naval Institute, 1965), p. 8.

[8] John M. Pfiffner and Marshall Fels, *The Supervision of Personnel: Human Relations in the Management of Men*, 3rd ed. (Englewood Cliffs, N.J.: Prentice-Hall, Inc., 1964), p. 169.

[9] See Chapter 9 for a discussion of the relationship between discipline, morale, and esprit de corps.

the right to expect from him. His moral code must be beyond reproach. He must not only avoid all evil, he must avoid all appearances of evil. His conduct is appraised in three frames of reference—what it actually is, what he thinks it is, and what it appears to be to others.

Psychology of leadership

The maintenance of a high level of discipline and morale requires some practical knowledge of the psychological factors which affect human behavior.[10] Few supervisors have an instinctive or intuitive knowledge of these factors. That comes only with training and experience.

To gain the willing support and cooperation of subordinates, the supervisor must learn those principles and techniques of leading them by sound logic and clear thinking rather than by driving them by arbitrary methods. He must recognize that few of them will respond consistently in the desired manner to the autocratic, dictatorial supervisory approach and that, if he uses good common sense in applying the basic principles, he will seldom be required to get things done by displaying his authority. He will find that best results will be obtained if he uses it sparingly and displays it rarely. If he demonstrates that he *is* a leader, his subordinates will recognize him as such. Since he accomplishes his objectives through the efforts of people, he must develop at least a rudimentary understanding of the things that motivate them.

MOTIVATING EMPLOYEES

All the leadership skills the supervisor manages to develop can be applied in one way or another to the motivation of his subordinates. *Motivation* involves the application of incentives which encourages a certain positive pattern of behavior and attitude and contributes to the accomplishment of organizational objectives. Unless the employee agrees with these objectives and believes they are attainable, he will not be able to commit himself to them. If he can't, he won't be motivated.

The effective supervisor will recognize the difference between giving employees a desire to produce well because of high job satisfaction and trying to force them to do so—deviously or otherwise. This is motivation versus manipulation.

Employees are stimulated to produce best when they are provided with *positive incentives* that satisfy individual needs. This satisfaction leads to pleasurable experiences. Incentives such as recognition, praise,

[10] See Chapter 6 for a further discussion of the psychology of behavior.

opportunity for development, an interesting and challenging job, and fair treatment by supervisors are strong forces in motivating people and can be directly controlled by supervisors. When incentives are properly applied, they result in satisfaction and pleasure. People tend to repeat behavior that produces these sensations and discontinue behavior that does not.

Supervisors should be constantly aware that what motivates one person may fail entirely to motivate another because of individual differences. What might be a strong motivator at one time may lose its effect after awhile.

Money and other material incentives are vastly overrated as positive motivational influences because they become weaker and weaker as physical human needs are progressively satisfied. The hungry employee is usually a good producer; but when he becomes fat, he sometimes loses his drive to produce. Motivation through the process of inspiration is unquestionably the most powerful and lasting force in forming attitudes which will induce workers to make fuller use of their potential.[11] Other positive motivators are provided when the employee derives satisfaction from his achievements, the work itself, advancement, responsibility, salary, and recognition by superiors and peers.[12]

Recognition is a strong motivating force in people. The supervisor can make good use of this force by giving employees credit for their accomplishments as a means of satisfying their drive for recognition. People obtain satisfaction from doing a job well and knowing that others—especially their superiors—have noticed their efforts. The supervisor can give this recognition if he understands the principles of objective personnel evaluations and applies them. In addition to providing recognition for deserving personnel, merit ratings will force him to appraise his subordinates periodically in relation to each other and rate them according to their value to the organization.

The supervisor should utilize every positive motivator at his disposal to stimulate his subordinates toward the highest productvity their capabilities will permit. He can assist them by establishing an atmosphere of cooperation in which each member of the organization strives on his own volition to assist others in achieving organizational objectives. He can push his subordinates or he can motivate them so that they will react favorably on their own to achieve these goals.

The supervisor can keep the productivity of his subordinates at a high level if he provides positive incentives for excellence of perfor-

11 Paul J. Meyer, "Fear—Money—Inspiration: Which Motivates Best?" *The National Sheriff*, January-February, 1968.
12 Norman R. F. Maier, *Psychology in Industry*, 3rd ed. (Boston: Houghton Mifflin Company, 1965), p. 425.

mance, as people tend to repeat behavior from which they gain satisfaction and discontinue behavior that does not produce satisfaction. His subordinates will ordinarily strive to do a good job. He can make it easier for them to do so by providing recognition for their efforts and by helping them to correct their mistakes by training or positive discipline. By avoiding inconsistent and arbitrary supervisory practices, he can gain their confidence and respect, which are vital in the process of motivation.[13]

Negative motivators such as fear, coercion, intimidation, and punishment should be avoided except when the more constructive, positive means have been tried and have failed. Negative motivators tend to cause employees to develop rather sophisticated and undesirable avoidance techniques; they soon learn how to avoid being discovered when they commit acts which may lead to unpleasant responses by their superiors.

Fear, as a negative motivator, involves threat and a degree of intimidation, but because human beings can shield themselves by developing a tolerance toward stress, fear soon loses its value as a motivating force. The employee will soon become hostile or the organization will lose him.[14] Although the use of punishment as a negative motivator has withstood the test of time, it must be used reasonably, fairly, and consistently or it will produce resentment, frustration, hostility, bitterness, and marginal performance with the low morale that accompanies these reactions.

The supervisor cannot hope to eliminate *all* practices that act as motivation barriers; but he can concentrate his efforts toward eliminating many of them. He can avoid those heavy-handed practices that impose unfair or unreasonable demands upon his subordinates. He can improve his communications with them so that they will clearly understand his directives, his goals, and the objectives of the organization. He will make that little added effort needed to increase the esprit de corps in his unit that will have such a great effect upon the morale of his subordinates. He will avoid those courses of action that cause strife, confusion, anxiety, insecurity, or mistrust within the organization. He will foster and encourage initiative among employees and reward them for their excellence of performance. He will provide training that will help them develop the competence required for their jobs. He will not just fill the position of a leader but will be one.

Studies have indicated that factors such as fringe benefits, physical working conditions, pay, security, and formal promotions do not neces-

[13] Jard DeVille, "Successful Leaders Are Successful Motivators," *Supervisory Management*, 18, No. 7 (July, 1973), 25–28.

[14] Meyer, "Fear—Money—Inspiration: Which Motivates Best?"

sarily produce improvements in performance and attitudes.[15] They only tend to prevent morale and effective performance from deteriorating. Although the supervisor at the lower levels of the hierarchy often has no direct control over such aspects of a job, he should be aware that they may affect employee efficiency adversely. When they do, he should make timely recommendations for whatever corrective action is indicated.

SITUATIONAL ANALYSIS AND SELF-APPRAISAL

The supervisor should constantly evaluate his leadership qualities in an objective manner so that he might gain some insight into his strengths and weaknesses. Does he consistently act as a leader should? How has he reacted to stressful problems? Has his behavior resulted in the most productive solution?

Honest self-appraisal is difficult because one often interprets what he does in accord with his own motives and not in accord with others' interpretations of what was done. When the supervisor recognizes his own deficiencies, he can usually correct them by systematically setting out to learn all he can about supervisory skills. The biggest problem is in honestly admitting to himself that his techniques might be wrong from time to time.

Supervisory incidents might well be reconstructed to determine if sound leadership principles were followed, if proven techniques were utilized, and if the supervisory action were objectively taken without the interference of emotion or prejudice. This does not suggest, however, that blind adherence to a mechanistic approach should be followed. Reliance on such an approach may cause supervisors to concentrate on the more superficial aspects of their relationships with employees rather than to try to gain a genuine understanding of them. Thinking, feeling people, unlike things, cannot be treated as figures in a formula. They will be quick to recognize mechanistic supervision and become resentful and dissatisfied. They may inwardly or outwardly accuse the supervisor of insincerity. A loss of confidence and respect is the likely product. Lowered morale and productivity usually follow.

LEADERSHIP CHARACTERISTICS

The traits commonly found in superior leaders would probably be found in most lists of desirable leadership characteristics. Possession of any

[15] Frederick Herzberg et al., *Job Attitudes: Review of Research and Opinion* (Pittsburgh, Pa.: Psychological Service of Pittsburgh, 1957).

particular traits certainly does not assure that a person is a good leader. He may be a gentle, kind, and friendly supervisor or a strict, decisive, and knowledgeable one. Neither may be a good leader because he lacks certain indefinable qualities that comprise good leadership.

Ideally, every leader should possess the following traits:[16]

1. Friendliness, sincerity, affection for others, and personal warmth. A long face should be seldom, if ever, the face of the leader. Neither should he have a pessimistic or negative attitude. A sincere expression of pleasure when a greeting is indicated, especially to a subordinate, has inestimable value. A person's birthday, a promotion, his wedding, or the birth of his child is one of the big events in his life. A warm, sincere handclasp or a word of congratulation takes little time and is worth every moment it takes in these and similar cases.

2. Enthusiasm for the job and all it entails. Sincerity and the ability to display it are vital traits of the leader. Zeal to do the right thing and to get the job done are extremely contagious and are quickly felt by others.

3. Ambition. Within reason, ambition is desirable; however, it must be controlled or it can become a millstone around the supervisor's neck. It should never result in the taking of credit which belongs to another. Neither should selfishness and vanity be allowed to corrode the supervisor's career.

4. Physical and nervous energy and vitality. Being a leader requires much physical and nervous stamina and a high frustration tolerance. Good leadership and hard work seem to go hand in hand. Diligence and industry are essential to effective leadership.

5. Moral and physical integrity. The real leader has moral as well as physical courage. He has a sense of direction and purpose with clear goals in mind. He has personal responsibility. He knows where he wants to go and what he wants to do. He doesn't make promises he does not intend to keep because his word is his bond. It is more important that he be trusted than liked. Subordinates expect their leaders to be honorable, to know right from wrong, justice from injustice, and to be fair with all without prejudice. A leader is expected to pursue the truth at all times. He is expected to keep his personal and professional life above reproach and, by his conduct, to be a credit to those in the organization and his profession.

6. Intelligence. It has been shown that the successful leader almost invariably has more intelligence than those he leads.[17] He has a sense of imagination and humor. He is capable of making objective observations. He has a questioning attitude which helps him in his search for the truth in all matters. He has vision and insight, for without them he

[16] See Pratt, "Leadership," pp. 2–8. See also Bass, *Leadership Psychology and Organizational Behavior*, pp. 166–67, 451; Ordway Tead, *Administration: Its Purpose and Performance* (Hamden, Conn.: Archon Books, 1968), pp. 55–70; Emory S. Bogardus, *Leaders and Leadership* (New York: Appleton-Century-Crofts, 1934), p. 105.

[17] Bass, *Leadership Psychology and Organizational Behavior*, p. 166.

will fail as a leader. He has a highly developed ability to see all sides of a question and draw commonsensical conclusions from the evidence at hand.

7. Technical skill. The most successful leader has a technical mastery of his job including the teaching skill which often takes the place of order giving.

8. Faith. The leader has faith and confidence in himself and his subordinates. Men will seldom have confidence in an individual who has no confidence in himself.

9. Verbal aptitude. A large amount of experimental work supports the conclusion that the most successful leaders are verbally capable. [18] They are persuasive and tactful. Few attributes are more important in dealing with others without generating friction.

10. Courtesy. Common courtesy demands that politeness is a civility which must be practiced at all times. The superior cannot afford to be outdone in it by his subordinates.

11. Modesty. The real leader can afford to be modest and practice humility. His accomplishments will attest to his value without his constantly reminding others of his greatness.

12. In addition, those characteristics of self-control, dependability, empathy for others short of sentimentalism, good judgment, originality, versatility, and adaptability are usually found in the most successful leaders. [19]

PERSONALITY OF THE LEADER

The personality of an individual is a composite of all his personal characteristics. As such, it plays an important part in the development of leadership ability and the ability to supervise. Every leader has the capacity to be a good supervisor. Personal traits of successful leaders should be observed and studied by the supervisor in refining his techniques of leadership. Those desirable traits should be adapted to his own natural style whenever possible. Those traits he has found undesirable in others should be avoided meticulously. For example, if he has resented inconsiderate treatment by his superiors in the past, he should avoid treating his subordinates inconsiderately.

HUMAN RELATIONS AND LEADERSHIP

The human relations aspect of supervision and leadership has developed to an inordinate degree during the last several decades. It has occupied the attention of leaders and managers to the extent that sometimes their

[18] *Ibid.,* p. 166.
[19] *Ibid.,* p. 451.

concern for the personal welfare and happiness of the individual employee has been at the expense of the organization as a whole. That consideration for these factors is important cannot be denied; yet, some supervisors are so concerned with the principle itself that they have failed to use it with common sense. They often fail to do what must be done for fear of upsetting employees. Some would no more violate what they think are the accepted concepts of human relations than criticize motherhood. With regard to the human relations movement, Megginson [20] aptly observes, "During the last quarter century, there has been an overconcern with the 'sweetness and light' doctrine and the 'happiness cult'." He asserts that when the supervisor interprets the human relations doctrine as meaning that he has no right to be critical and dissatisfied with inferior performance, he deprives his subordinates of a standard for determining the level of performance which can be reasonably expected of them. Just having happy employees is not enough. They need reasonable goals and a sense of achievement and personal development if they are to be satisfied and productive.

Pfiffner and Fels [21] said, "We need to develop a new set of social skills that will combine the new permissive and democratic approach with the continuing need to exercise authority, positive and forceful authority when called for." Supervisors who put into practice the principles of good human relations without becoming maudlin or permissive to the degree that the total organization suffers will accomplish more and will have fewer problems and conflicts than supervisors who allow themselves to become martinets, with little empathy, compassion, or understanding for others. How he handles his interpersonal relations and those indefinable, intangible social problems that arise in every organization is an indicator of the degree of his human relations ability. His problems of managing people will be lessened if he reasonably consults with them about things that affect them. This does not imply that he should take a vote before every decision is made, however.

The objective of good human relations should be the greatest production in the shortest possible time with the minimum energy and the maximum satisfaction for the producers.[22] This is the ideal of human efficiency. It is possible to achieve, but it seldom is achieved. It is a worthwhile goal toward which the supervisor should strive.

---

[20] Leon C. Megginson, *Personnel: A Behavioral Approach to Administration* (Homewood, Ill.: Richard D. Irwin, Inc., 1967), pp. 497–98.

[21] Pfiffner and Fels, *The Supervision of Personnel: Human Relations in the Management of Men*, p. 141.

[22] A. T. Poffenberger, *Principles of Applied Psychology* (New York: Appleton-Century-Crofts, 1942), p. 364.

Manner of the leader

The physical, moral, and mental attributes of the supervisor have a powerful effect upon his relations with subordinates. These traits are often reflected by his mannerisms, which afford an accurate clue to his state of mind. A look, gesture, inflection in the voice, physical bearing, or an indication of tension gives away the thoughts of an individual. As has been indicated, how an act is done is often more important than the act itself. For example, the supervisor who makes an accusation to a subordinate before learning all the facts pertinent to an issue will soon lose the confidence of his men. A worker castigated by his supervisor for tardiness when the supervisor has not taken the trouble to learn the reason for the apparent dereliction will be resentful. An employee criticized by one supervisor for doing what another superior had directed him to do has just cause for grievance when the criticism was made without the supervisor learning the reason for the act.

The supervisor will find that a calm, controlled manner will be helpful to him in maintaining the confidence and respect of his subordinates. Frequent irritation, petulance, and emotional displays—especially of temper or anger—are indicators that he lacks that self-control desirable in a leader. An outward appearance of impassiveness or calmness may be overdone, however. Sometimes a sincere showing of emotion such as pleasure or a sincere showing of appreciation for a tribute rendered by subordinates is perfectly in order. Indifference is often as out of place as emotionalism.

Language of the leader

Another outward mark by which a leader can be judged is the language he uses. What he says and the manner in which he conveys his thoughts give a clue to his mental state and the attitude behind it. They also indicate the possession or lack of good taste and breeding. His speech should be unaffected, positive, and direct, not uncertain, indecisive, and negative.

Immoderate language habitually used in the presence of others invariably produces unfavorable results. Not only order giving but all communications should be devoid of vulgar, profane, or indecent speech, or the sharp-edged tool of sarcastic language. Blunt contradictions serve no useful purpose, nor do inflammatory remarks or name calling. Language implying or expressing finality as in ultimatums should be reserved until no other recourse seems available to gain compliance, and then should be used only if the supervisor has the tools to carry out his ultimatum. Special care should be exercised to avoid talking down to others or talking over their heads for to do so will give the impression of affectation or paternalism. Either may be resented or cause subordinates to accuse him overtly or covertly of insincerity.

COMMENDING AND PRAISING OTHERS

The desire of individuals for recognition is a force the supervisor should utilize to increase substantially his effectiveness. A few words of commendation and praise, sincerely given when merited, will do much to induce continued good performance. These are much more effective tools of leadership than condemnation, criticism, or punitive action. The supervisor should follow the adage, "commend in public but criticize in private." Criticism, like commendation, should not be neglected when it is indicated. It can be constructive or destructive, depending on the manner employed in dispensing it. Supervisors are often so busy seeing that the job is done that they fail to see who does it and give credit when it is deserved.

One of the most frequent complaints of workers is that criticism comes readily but praise seldom.[23] Complimenting or giving praise when it is not merited, however, soon dilutes its value and is seldom effective. Likewise, insincere commendation soon loses its motivating effect. Dale Carnegie used the approach with great success that honest, sincere praise "wins friends and influences people" but that insincere flattery will backfire and make enemies. The most skillful supervisor will strike a reasonable balance between constructive criticism when it is needed and praise when it is earned.

REPRIMANDING AND CRITICIZING

The average supervisor all too often does not face up to his responsibilities of giving forthright criticism when it is due. He's often afraid of the repercussions from the social group if he does so. He's afraid to tell employees what they must and must not do. His subordinates must come to understand that when he says something, he really means it.[24] If they are not made to understand this, he loses his position of leadership by default.

The supervisor should never lose his temper and become angry or hostile when reprimanding subordinates, nor should he exaggerate and

[23] Thomas J. Baker, "Designing the Job to Motivate," *F.B.I. Law Enforcement Bulletin*, 45, No. 11 (November, 1976).

[24] Chris Argyris, *Executive Leadership: An Appraisal of a Manager in Action* (Hamden, Conn.: The Shoe String Press, Inc., 1967), p. 33.

overstate the reason for the criticism. He should face the issue squarely and inform the employee in private of his unacceptable behavior without equivocation, apology, or sarcasm. The employee should be given an opportunity to make a positive response concerning the issue and to save face. The response should be so structured by the supervisor that it contains some plan for improvement.[25] A "soft," intelligent approach rather than a "hard" one tends to reduce antagonism and resistance to criticism, the object of which is to bring about improvement, not to foster resentment and hostility.

KNOWLEDGE OF SUBORDINATES

Every supervisor should learn as much as he can about his subordinates, individually and collectively. He should become familiar with each individual's background, experience, education, family relationships, sick patterns, performance, and any other data that may give him insight into the subordinate's qualifications, aptitudes, potential, and motives. The process of learning about his subordinates is a continuing one. He may find that his first impressions have been fashioned on incomplete or inaccurate information and have been erroneous. As he gains more information through inspection of personnel records, observation, and personal contacts, he will develop a more accurate picture of the individual. He will learn that the personal and performance problems of subordinates may be identified with the brand of supervision they have received. He will learn that he can assist them in resolving most of these.

Once the supervisor has gained the confidence of his subordinates, he will find that they will often come to him for help. He must carefully avoid meddling into their personal lives as long as their work and the organization are not involved. He will only become involved in this case if he is asked to do so. By becoming familiar with their drives and motives, he will gain some clues to their reactions as individuals and as a group.

THE MARGINAL EMPLOYEE

The marginal employee, who will do just that amount and quality of work that will not give the organization a cause of action against him, occasionally is the cause of considerable concern to the supervisor. Such employees are invariably the source of much dissatisfaction within the

25 John R. Heron, "Thoughts on Criticism," *Supervisory Management,* 2, No. 4 (April, 1977).

peer group, which they often contaminate with their antiorganization attitude. Production and morale eventually suffer. Such persons may be or may think they are overqualified for the job they are performing and believe themselves suited for a better position which may or may not be available. They may, however, be underqualified and consequently become frustrated when they cannot achieve the goals they have set for themselves; or they may be disgruntled, frustrated, or emotionally troubled.

Supervisors often tend to ignore such problems or try to rid themselves of the employee who is, to them, a source of irritation. They can transfer him, retain him and tolerate his attitude, retain him and attempt to correct his deficiencies, or collect evidence that will support his termination.

Transfer only shifts the problem to someone else, although at times a person performing poorly in one assignment will make remarkable improvement elsewhere because he is better matched with his new job. Retention in his present position may require that he be given special attention, depending upon what is causing the marginal performance. If he is unqualified, additional training, education, and guidance supplemented at times with counseling may help. The disgruntled employee with a grievance should be given an opportunity to express the cause for his complaint. Imagined grievances are usually corrected easily by encouraging the employee to examine the real facts or by providing the facts he does not have. The disgruntled employee who has been a disciplinary problem in the past is an extremely difficult and distressing problem to the supervisor. Special counseling and recognition for his strong characteristics will sometimes motivate him to better efforts. There are times, however, despite the best efforts of the superior, when nothing short of transfer or termination will rectify the problem.

The frustrated employee and the troubled one may require special attention. Counseling or referral may help correct their problems, as described in Chapters 6 and 8.

ORDER GIVING AND COMMUNICATIONS

Ideally, order giving involves the complex process of communicating ideas in such a manner that the recipient interprets what he hears in the way the communicator intends. Each order is susceptible to three interpretations—what the person actually says, what he thinks he said, and what the recipient thinks he said.

Indistinct speech, poor selection of words, the giving of orders in a disordered or haphazard manner, the giving of too many orders at one time or too much detail in one order (assuming that the receiver understands clearly what is expected of him), and neglecting to follow up are some of the most prevalent reasons for failures in order giving.[26]

Employees are more likely to resent the way an unpopular order is given than the order itself. Persuasion is much more effective than coercion in obtaining acceptance by the workers affected. The supervisor should consider the time and place in addition to the manner in which orders are given to obtain best results. They may be direct commands, they may be framed as requests, they may be implied or suggestive, or they may consist of requests for volunteers.

The supervisor should designate one person to direct a task requiring group effort. This will provide for unity of command within the group and accountability for results. Obviously, sufficient authority must be given the person held accountable to enable him to accomplish the assignment as directed. In deciding the type of approach that should be used in a given situation, the supervisor should consider such basics as the personality of the subordinate, how much close direction he needs to do the job, his competency, and his initiative.

Direct commands

Orders may best be given by command when emergent conditions require direct, prompt action. This method of giving orders may be indicated in dealing with the lazy, careless, indifferent, or irresponsible employee or the one who refuses or neglects to obey standard operating rules or fails to respond to suggestions or implied orders. When orders are given in the form of commands, they should be simple and direct. If they are hesitatingly given, they will usually be obeyed in a like manner.

Requests

Most orders should be framed as requests. Employees will often resent the authoritarian, dictatorial method. The capable, conscientious, responsible subordinate usually requires nothing more than a request. He will construe it as an order. Older employees usually respond similarly. Orders to sensitive, nervous, or easily offended persons are usually best framed as requests. Experience clearly indicates that cooperation is

[26] See Chapter 5 for a detailed discussion of interpersonal communications.

most readily obtained through request rather than by command. Cooperation cannot be demanded. It must be won. Obviously, the supervisor should make requests to others of equal rank or status instead of making demands if he expects to gain their cooperation.

Implied or suggestive orders

Implied or suggestive directives can be employed to good effect with the reliable employee who readily assumes responsibility for a task. They are also useful in developing the initiative of subordinates since they allow considerable latitude in the method of accomplishing an assignment when immediate action is not essential.

The supervisor will express the degree of confidence he has in his subordinates by the amount of control he wishes to retain over their efforts. The amount of latitude he gives them will depend upon their reliability and capabilities and upon the nature of the assignment. The amount of confidence he has in them may be indicated by his instructions to them: for example, "Do what you think needs to be done, then let me know what you did"; or "Keep me informed about what you do"; or, "Let's talk about what you decide"; or, "Clear with me before you do anything"; or "Don't do anything without discussing it with me beforehand"; or "I'll make the decision."

Orders to inexperienced or unreliable employees should be given in a more direct manner than by suggestion or implication. The inexperienced employee will often fail to draw the intended inference or make the proper deduction from an implied order. The unreliable employee will often draw the conclusion that is most convenient or desirable for him. Implied orders are often abstract and deprive the supervisor of a follow-up tool since, if orders are subject to more than one reasonable interpretation, they are usually unenforceable.

Requests for volunteers

Occasionally, a supervisor will call for volunteers to perform a dangerous or disagreeable assignment which he cannot or should not perform himself. The call for volunteers should be used with care so that it will not become a simple expedient for escaping the responsibility of making assignments or issuing orders which are in the best interests of the organization. Neither should the supervisor call for volunteers to perform a task that he himself should perform merely because he wishes to shed his responsibility, because he considers the job beneath him, or because it involves a distasteful act.

Communicating orders

If orders are indirectly given, they will tend to strengthen ideas already present. If they are positive, they are likely to be more effective than if made in a negative vein.[27]

Verbal orders are usually satisfactory for simple tasks, especially if they have been performed before, and in emergency situations. As with many communications, a verbal order can be easily misunderstood, as can the intent of the person giving it. Details can be easily forgotten. Because of these factors, it is sometimes difficult to hold anyone accountable for failures in giving or carrying out the directive.

When other than a simple order is given, the person giving it should have it "played back" so that any misunderstandings that have resulted in the communication process can be clarified. It cannot be safely assumed that the absence of questions means that understanding has taken place.

Written orders should be used in situations where complex operations or numerous persons are affected to assure that all receive the same message. Such orders facilitate systematic follow-up and provide a basis for attaching accountability for failures.

The employee with strong qualities of independence usually knows what his job requires and how to do it. He is likely to be more responsive if he is assigned a task in broad terms and is allowed to use his ingenuity and initiative in performing the details.

The more dependent workers are more likely to prefer and depend upon more concrete and detailed assignments rather than to decide for themselves what needs to be done and how to do it.

Following up orders

The supervisor surrenders his authority little by little when he fails to follow up his orders to assure that they have been carried out. When a subordinate is directed to complete a task by a certain time, he should be required to comply as instructed. Notations regarding deadlines should be made by the supervisor on his desk calendar, pad, or notebook

[27] Poffenberger, *Principles of Applied Psychology,* pp. 93–95.

to remind him of the time he has designated for completion of an assigned task.

DECISION MAKING

One of the most frequent functions the supervisor is called upon to perform is that of decision making. It is imperative that he develop his ability to draw conclusions from facts at hand and stick to a decision unless, of course, it is manifestly improper. Even if he occasionally makes the wrong decision, the fact that he has taken positive action when action is indicated is better than if he had taken none at all. Decisiveness has a stabilizing influence upon subordinates. Indecisiveness is easily perceived. It tends to destroy confidence and lower respect. Ultimately, performance is adversely affected.

The decision-making process involves several steps. First, an awareness that a real problem exists, an appreciation of its ramifications, and a recognition of a need for a decision must be present. The proper answer to the wrong question is no solution to the real problem. To deal with the apparent problem without knowing that it is merely a symptom of the real one may result in an incorrect solution to the right problem or a solution to the wrong one. Second, facts must be obtained. Opinions of others may be needed as supportive data when subjective decisions are involved. Third, when sufficient data have been collected, they must be evaluated and analyzed. Reliability of the source of the data must be tested just as the facts themselves. Once the real problem has been identified, concentration can be directed toward the solution. Personal bias should be eliminated in the analysis. Fourth, alternative approaches leading to a logical conclusion should be decided upon and probable consequences should be weighed. Possible conflicts among those who are to implement the decision must be considered. This involves insight. The effect of each alternative upon the objective should be considered in determining the best course of action indicated by the facts at hand. Fifth, a decision must be selected from the alternative solutions. This involves value judgments in selecting the one that allows action to follow in carrying out the decision. Consideration should be given to the time and the setting in which the action is to be carried out and to the long-term results from taking one alternative over another. The pros and cons should be carefully considered and weighted. Sixth, the decision must then be communicated to those who must carry it out. Appropriate follow-up should take place so that results of the decision may be checked and evaluated. This procedure may indicate the effect of the decision in changing attitudes, altering performance, improving morale, or revealing training needs.

DRAWING CONCLUSIONS

The making of decisions or the drawing of conclusions should never be based on snap judgments. The supervisor who jumps to a conclusion before knowing pertinent facts will find his conclusions more often wrong than right. Judgment of even the most ordinary of supervisors should be right more often than wrong if he is to survive as a leader. For example, the supervisor observing an employee sitting at a desk, leaning back, and gazing out of the window may draw any one of a number of conclusions from this observation alone. The odds are against the drawing of the correct one without additional facts. The person might be just resting; he might be thinking or planning; he could be out of work or he might be lazy; he might be daydreaming or bored or he might be observing someone or something; he might simply be attempting to resolve a personal or job problem.

The wise supervisor will recognize that one cause may affect behavior in many ways.[28] The employee troubled and worried over a serious personal problem may have varied reactions. He may engage in daydreaming or fanciful imagination in attempting to escape from his problem. He may neglect his work or fail to follow safety rules. The quality of his work might decline. He may become overly sensitive to supervision. He may develop disagreeable habits or his relationships with others might deteriorate. His work might suffer by excessive tardiness or absences or he may drink to allay his worry. Any one or all of these reactions may be set in motion by one causative factor. Such problems should be approached objectively. The real reason behind the behavior may not be apparent from the reason given. The supervisor should attempt to ascertain the true explanation rather than accept the proffered one for a particular type of behavior affecting a subordinate's performance.

MODERATION IN SUPERVISION

Oversupervision is perhaps the commonest failing of inexperienced supervisors. It arises from their failure to delegate tasks, either because of a lack of confidence in their subordinates or a disinclination to re-

---

[28] See Chapter 6 for a discussion of frustration and aggression reactions.

linquish what they think are their supervisory prerogatives. When they take it upon themselves to do their subordinates' work, initiative is corroded and morale invariably suffers. They don't expect him to do their work and don't respect him for it when he does.[29]

As the supervisor's responsibilities do not permit him to be constantly on hand to help, he must train his subordinates to do what has to be done, then rely upon them to do it. If the employee is capable of performing his assigned task, he should be allowed to do so without the supervisor standing over him checking on every detail. If he cannot be trained to do the task properly, he should be assigned to another. Over-supervision, often called "snoopervision," causes loss of respect for the supervisor, creates suspicions in the minds of employees, fosters rumors, and arouses resentment. Judicious contact between the supervisor and his subordinates is welcomed by them. His presence when he is needed and the lending of a willing ear to their problems will tend to give them a feeling of security and confidence and a sense of direction.

The effective supervisor will soon learn how much attention each employee needs and direct his attention to him accordingly. Even the most efficient want some attention to give them some assurance that their good services are not going unnoticed. If a field sergeant rides with each of his patrol units on occasion, his subordinates will soon look forward to an opportunity to show their capabilities. They will not resent his presence if his supervision has been judicious, but they will feel neglected if others receive more attention than they do.

Fraternization

There is always room for forthright friendship between supervisors and their subordinates. The fact that one has been promoted to a higher position should not mean that old friendships must be severed. The extent of this friendship will vary between individuals. Friendship alone should not be allowed to become the basis of preferential treatment, however. Formal relationships should be dignified but warm, friendly, and democratic—never boorish. Overfamiliarity and the taking of unjustified liberties by subordinates, purely because of friendship, should be discouraged because they tend to corrupt respect for authority, especially when unrestrained familiarity takes place in the presence of other subordinates. When such conduct occurs between a supervisor of one sex and a subordinate of another, the results are often particularly devastat-

---

[29] William Foote Whyte, *Men at Work* (Homewood, Ill.: Richard D. Irwin, Inc., 1963), p. 387.

ing to the supervisor's position of leadership and to the morale of the organization.

Status distinctions between the first-line supervisor and his subordinates should not be allowed to become so great that he gives them the impression that he is an entirely different species. They will resent a patronizing attitude, and it will soon cause effective communications to break down between them.[30]

SETTING AN EXAMPLE

The respected leader will be imitated—consciously or unconsciously—by those he leads. He will have a valuable tool at his disposal if he sets the right example by the attitude he displays, by his conduct, and by his appearance. Rigid adherence to the requirements of good taste and convention, good breeding and behavior, without pomposity, are marks of a good leader.

He will hardly be in the best position to take remedial action against others if his own conduct is not above reproach. They will look to him to set the standard of conduct by his own demeanor. Upon it will be based much of their respect and support for him.

WOMEN EMPLOYEES

In the past, women employees tended to look upon their work as a temporary disruption to a primary obligation to their planned home lives. This trend has been drastically reduced in recent years. More than half the women in the nation between the ages of eighteen and sixty-four are in the country's working force. Almost half of these are working because of pressing economic needs.[31]

At present, law enforcement agencies are placing an increasing emphasis upon the use of women in police work. In the past, the few who were employed as officers were traditionally assigned to nonfield duties such as jail matrons, desk officers, laboratory technicians, and the like; or to field duties as juvenile investigators but only when teamed with a male officer. They are now being employed in rapidly increasing numbers to perform field duties formerly given only to men. Women also

---

[30] Whyte, *Men at Work*, p. 387.

[31] United States Department of Labor, *The Myth and the Reality* (Washington, D.C.: Employment Standards Administration, April, 1963), p. 1.

constitute a large part of the civilian force employed to perform the many service tasks that relieve sworn officers for field duties. Accordingly, many women are attaining supervisory positions. Their accountability for results is, or should be, identical to the standards required of male supervisors. Their effectiveness, like that of their male counterparts, will depend on whether they possess the characteristics leaders must have and how well they apply the principles of leadership.

Enlightened supervisors must recognize that women are legally and morally entitled to the same opportunities and considerations in the positions for which they were employed as are men. Both are accountable for their performance and behavior. The same principles of supervision must apply to both.

Women employees often have a tendency to feel they are competing with the male under great handicaps. Historically, they have not enjoyed the same privileges as have males. They have been considered inferior physically, emotionally, politically, and economically until recent years, when their status has climbed in the business, political, and financial worlds and in public service. They now fill many jobs better than do men. Their contributions to the economy are obvious.

Women tend to react to supervision much as men do. Many of the stereotyped beliefs that some male supervisors have retained are not founded on fact. Some believe that the same techniques of supervising males will fail if applied to women. Some believe that women employees are less dependable than males doing similar work and are more unstable and emotional. These concepts are usually based on isolated occurrences; they cannot be applied to all women. Stable, mature women are as capable of the same respect for their superiors, the same dependability and pride in their jobs, and the same loyalty to their organizations as are stable, mature men.

If women are made to feel they are needed and important to the enterprise, they often develop more personal interest in their jobs than do men. For this reason, some are likely to react to criticism more strongly and with greater emotion. They usually regard criticism as a personal attack upon them. To avoid criticism, they are likely to give greater attention to doing the job correctly.

When a supervisor has earned the loyalty, confidence, and respect of a competent stenographer, secretary, clerk, or other woman employee who assists him, he will find the job immeasurably easier. She will relieve him of numerous amenities he should perform but often forgets or does not have or take time to do. Her attention to detail, which he often avoids, her inclination for order and system, and her dedication usually are the direct result of her intense job interest and loyalty to one she respects.

TECHNIQUES OF SUPERVISING WOMEN EMPLOYEES

Although the same basic principles and techniques of supervision apply generally to men and women, some variations in approach are necessary in dealing with the woman employee because of her psychological and physical differences. This does not imply that she should be given special privileges merely because she is a woman.

Reactions to favoritism

Women are more sensitive than men to displays of favoritism by the male supervisor. They are prone to suspect his motives if he shows more than ordinary concern for or attention to other female employees, especially attractive ones. The supervisor should try to treat all women employees alike. His relationships with them should be as impersonal as possible.

Concern for the welfare of the woman employee

Most women are more appreciative than males of the supervisor's efforts to make the work environment more attractive or pleasant. Like men, they are susceptible to emotional and physical fatigue when their surroundings are substandard and unpleasant. Poor ventilation, improper lighting, inadequate maintenance of the equipment they use, unclean rest rooms, and the like have a tremendous effect upon them and should be corrected if the highest productivity is to be attained.

Praising the work of the woman employee

Failure to recognize and give credit for a job well done affects the woman more than it does the male employee and is one of the commonest errors of supervisors. The absence of praise or recognition is likely to be interpreted by the woman employee as an indication of her boss's disappointment. The work done, not the worker, should be given the praise. Praising the worker may be construed as flattery and favoritism by others. A sincere compliment concerning the neatness, completeness, thoroughness, or quality of a project is as much in order with women as with men.

Recognizing the individual

Women are just as capable of handling responsibility as are men. They should be given responsibility whenever possible to give them a sense of involvement with organizational goals. They often react with greater pride in their work than men do when they learn that they are responsible for a job and that they are being relied upon to accomplish it.

Courteous treatment

The common amenities expected of supervisors at all times should be particularly and strictly adhered to in their dealings with women employees. Common courtesies such as sincere expressions of appreciation for special work done or for overtime work, attentiveness to their job needs, a greeting when they arrive at work and a pleasant goodnight, polite language at all times irrespective of the kind used by them, and respectful treatment are civilities which will reap huge rewards for the supervisor in the realization of a better working spirit, greater production, and more job satisfaction among women subordinates.

SYMPTOMS OF LEADERSHIP FAILURE

There are many symptoms of leadership failures. The appearance of selfishness, suspicion, envy, failure to give credit, hypercriticism, and arbitrariness will usually denote weaknesses if not downright failure of an individual as a leader. When these characteristics manifest themselves in a person, it becomes unsafe to entrust the futures of others to him.[32]

Leadership fails more often through default than through error. Often when it is most needed, it is not present.[33] If the level of discipline in an organization is low, if its standards of conduct and performance leave much to be desired, if the organization is riddled with disloyalty, mistrust, and self-interest, its leaders have failed. The failures will inevitably result in reduced productivity, low morale, and poor organizational spirit.

SUMMARY

Organizational effectiveness is largely dependent upon the degree to which supervisors skillfully apply sound principles of leadership to everyday operations. Some supervisors fail in their primary task of directing, leading, and controlling others because they have not been able to apply these principles to their particular position. Some have been discouraged in doing so by superiors who themselves have failed to realize that the scientific techniques of leadership and supervision are, in the long run,

---

[32] Pratt, "Leadership," p. 3.

[33] Philip Selznick, *Leadership in Administration: A Sociological Interpretation* (New York: Harper & Row, Publishers, 1957), pp. 26–27.

more effective than many of the stereotyped, ineffective practices to which they have been exposed.

True leadership status can be earned by any reasonably intelligent individual if he devotes himself to the development of the traits which a leader must have. He does not gain this status from the award of stripes or bars on his uniform. The only real authority he has is that which is granted him by his subordinates. The best leaders have been the best subordinates since an individual cannot order and direct others until he has learned to receive and follow orders himself.

There is no single leader type, although most have certain common traits, among which are friendliness, moral and physical courage, personal integrity and honor, insight, a strong desire for truth, a desire to teach, and the ability to listen. No one trait can be isolated from the others since they all relate to the total character of the leader and all are interrelated.

Perhaps the single function that best marks the good leader is his ability to maintain a high level of discipline, morale, and esprit de corps. These conditions are brought about by the application of common sense and an understanding of the fundamentals of good supervisory practices. These can be most effectively related to his management activities if he has some practical knowledge of the psychological factors affecting human behavior.

Nowhere are these psychological factors more important than in the giving of orders. The supervisor should recognize that the manner of order giving is more often resented than the order itself. If it is framed as a request, it will most often be accepted and carried out without resentment. In some instances when urgent conditions exist, orders must be given as direct commands because prompt action is needed. Implied or suggestive orders may effectively be used with reliable, experienced employees. They should not ordinarily be used with the inexperienced or undependable worker. On occasion, the supervisor will call for volunteers to perform a dangerous or disagreeable task which he cannot or should not perform himself. When he uses this form of order giving, he must exercise care that it does not become a means of escaping a disagreeable job which is properly his.

Order giving involves many complex communication processes. The leader's manner, his gestures and inflections, and the time and place in which the order is given will affect the reactions of his subordinates to it. He should avoid uncertain or vacillating language because uncertainty will often be interpreted as indecision.

Immoderate, vulgar, or indecent language should be scrupulously avoided, as should sarcastic remarks in dealings with subordinates. These will only alienate them and others, who are quick to interpret such conduct as rudeness and ill breeding.

A good leader will criticize when necessary but only after he has obtained all facts upon which he has based his criticism. He will do so only in private, with rare exceptions. Whenever possible, he will praise an employee publicly where credit or recognition is earned. He will do so sincerely because insincere praise or that given grudgingly is seldom appreciated.

Good human relations practices should be followed at all times; but in so doing the supervisor must take pains to avoid becoming so concerned with the "sweetness and light" or the "kid glove" principles that he is afraid to criticize when he is dissatisfied with inferior performance or to punish when punitive action is necessary. He will strike a happy balance by being human and compassionate where he can and firm when he has to be.

The most effective supervisor will motivate his subordinates through a system of positive incentives which tend to satisfy their individual needs. He will provide appropriate recognition when it is deserved and praise when it is merited, an opportunity for personal development, challenging work, and fair treatment; but will avoid as far as possible those negative factors that induce performance through fear and intimidation.

The enlightened supervisor will avoid applying two different standards in supervising men and women. He must recognize that both are legally and morally entitled to the same opportunities and considerations in the positions for which they were employed and are accountable alike for their performance and behavior. He will use a high degree of common sense in his relationships with women employees because they are quick to sense when the male supervisor is showing too much personal interest in one of them. They will be quick to suspect him of ulterior motives or accuse him of partiality. Ordinarily, he will apply the same general principles of supervision to women employees as to males; but he will recognize that women are sometimes more sensitive to criticism, somewhat more inclined to become emotionally involved in their jobs, and generally more responsive to the physical aspects of the job environment than are men.

REVIEW

Questions

1. Why do supervisors often resist leadership training?
2. List three types of leaders and discuss the characteristics of each.
3. Define command presence and discuss how it affects leadership.

4. Discuss the principal characteristics of good leadership.

5. What are the objectives of good human relations?

6. What are the basic principles of commending and criticizing others?

7. What are the most prevalent reasons for failures in order giving?

8. List and discuss four methods of giving orders.

9. Discuss the steps involved in decision making.

10. Discuss how oversupervision occurs and the hazards that result from it.

11. Explain how the supervision of women employees differs from that of male workers.

12. List and discuss some of the basic techniques of supervising women employees.

13. What are some positive motivators? Describe how they can be used.

14. What are the major symptoms of leadership failure? Give at least one example of each.

Exercises

Checklist of 50 for leaders. The good leader will constantly review his techniques of supervision to assess his effectiveness. He will ask himself the following questions in doing so: Check your leadership ability by honestly and reasonably answering the questions *yes* or *no,* or *moderately well* if in doubt. Ask yourself what you can do to remove the questionable items. Rate yourself on the following scale: 1 point for each item marked *yes,* ½ point for each item marked *moderately well,* zero for each item marked *no:*

Totals

Score = 42 (You are probably an excellent supervisor.)

Score = 37 (You are probably a fair leader.)

Score = less than 32 (You probably need to improve.)

1. Have I made myself technically and professionally competent?

2. Do I know and appreciate the traditions of my organization?

3. Do I know thoroughly its practices and standard procedures?

4. Have I generally kept myself more fully informed about my profession than have my subordinates?

5. Have I defined my objectives clearly to my subordinates?

6. Have I tried to resolve those objectives that are in conflict?

7. Have I established clear standards of performance for my subordinates?

8. Have I let them know what these standards are?

9. Do I insist that they be met?

10. Do I actively try to reduce substandard performance?

11. Have I set performance and behavior standards for myself and followed them?

12. Do my subordinates know what they may expect from me?
13. Do I avoid self-centeredness?
14. Am I employee-centered?
15. Do I place my organization's interests before my own as I should?
16. Do I communicate well with others below, above, and horizontally?
17. Do I keep my subordinates and superiors well informed on matters affecting them?
18. Have I kept channels of communications open?
19. Do I actively lead, direct, and control subordinates?
20. Do I face my responsibilities for these functions forthrightly?
21. Do I avoid unjust criticism of my colleagues?
22. Do I avoid public criticism of others in my organization?
23. Do I give credit when it is earned?
24. Do I commend publicly?
25. Do I avoid "credit snatching"?
26. Do I respect my subordinates for what they are?
27. Do I demand respect from them by my conduct, appearance, and decorum?
28. Am I fair and impartial in meting out punishment when it is indicated?
29. Do I keep my emotions from becoming involved when I punish subordinates?
30. Do I back my subordinates to the fullest as a matter of principle when their cause is just and reasonable?
31. Do I refuse to back them when they are wrong even though such refusal may lessen my popularity with them?
32. Do I delegate as far down the line as possible?
33. Do I force my subordinates to develop their sense of personal responsibility and initiative?
34. Do I use my authority sparingly and display it seldom?
35. Do I avoid oversupervision?
36. Does my unit have pride in its accomplishments?
37. Have I actively tried to build its esprit de corps?
38. Do I practice humility?
39. Do I recognize my shortcomings?
40. Have I compensated for my shortcomings?
41. Have I retained my sense of humor in my dealings with subordinates?
42. Can I still admit that I am capable of error?
43. Do I apply the same standards of conduct and performance to both men and women subordinates?
44. Do I provide positive incentives to motivate my subordinates?
45. Do I avoid the use of negative motivators when positive incentives would possibly serve better?
46. Do I make decisions promptly, without vacillating?

47. Are my decisions the right ones in most every case?
48. Do I always obtain the essential facts before making decisions that affect my subordinates?
49. Am I a good listener in my relationship with subordinates?
50. Do I practice the Golden Rule?

5

The essentials
of
communicating

The ability to communicate clearly and concisely is the most important single skill of the supervisor because it is basic to understanding the subordinate's point of view and passing on to him the objectives of the enterprise; yet it is commonly the area of his greatest weakness and the one most neglected.[1] Too often, people are prone to take for granted that understanding takes place when they converse with each other.

The maintenance of effective communications between superiors and subordinates at all levels of the hierarchy and even between persons at the same level is considered by many to be the biggest single problem of management.[2] Without understandable communications there can be no coordination of effort. Without coordination there can be no constructive organization.

It is important for the supervisor to realize that ideas and decisions can more readily be translated into the desired action when they are communicated to others with some consideration given to the emotional

[1] Richard P. Calhoon, *Managing Personnel* (New York: Harper & Row, Publishers, 1963), pp. 268–69.
[2] F. K. Berrien and W. H. Bash, *Human Relations: Comments and Cases* (New York: Harper & Row, Publishers, 1957), p. 22 (quoting Alvin E. Dodd).

needs of the recipient and to his environment. Good communications are not only accomplished with words but with tones and deeds. Often these are more important than verbal expressions. There is much truth in the ancient adage, "actions speak louder than words." A gesture, the display of an attitude, or an inflection in the voice will often convey more meaning than will the spoken word. It is therefore well for the supervisor to review from time to time the basics of good communications practices since they all too often tend to become submerged in the day-by-day routine.

CULTURAL, ENVIRONMENTAL, AND PSYCHOLOGICAL FACTORS

Communications between persons or groups are very delicate, complex processes involving many factors—cultural, environmental, and psychological. For example, some individuals from certain ethnic groups resent the names "cop," "wop," "jughead," "pancho," "nigger," to name a few. The connotations derived from the words are offensive. Even the word "boy" is often considered insulting, depending upon the time, place, and circumstances in which it is used. The environment in which a communication takes place will often determine its effect. Accordingly, supervisors should refrain from criticizing subordinates in the presence of others, whether outsiders or peers. Likewise, a patrolman should address his superior by title in public regardless of the closeness of their acquaintance. Psychologically, the diffident, retiring individual could be dealt with more effectively perhaps with a tactful, "soft" approach rather than the direct, "hard" approach that is sometimes necessary in dealing with the aggressive extrovert.

THE PROCESSES OF COMMUNICATIONS

Word symbols are used to express thoughts. Words in themselves mean nothing. They are merely arbitrary, *symbolic* representations of something. They must be associated with some past experience or they are meaningless. For example, the word "cow" does not look like a cow and means nothing to a person who has not seen one or had one described to him. It is merely a symbol. Conversely, *signs* are the meanings that emanate from what is perceived.[3] Symbols and signs are the means the speaker uses to translate ideas to his listener. He expresses himself

[3] George T. Vardaman, "Language and Semantics," in *Proceedings of the 1962 Institute in Technical and Industrial Communications,* ed. Herman M. Weisman (Fort Collins, Colo.: Institute in Technical and Industrial Communications, 1962), pp. 8–9.

by words, gestures, facial expressions, inflections, and actions—but mostly by imprecise words—to the recipient, who hopefully absorbs what he perceives, interprets it, and reacts by words or action. The communicator then responds to the recipient's reactions. If this sequence of interaction is distorted or unbalanced, unilateral communications take place. This may result in a failure on the recipient's part to respond as expected or, worse, it may result in no action at all.

BARRIERS TO EFFECTIVE COMMUNICATIONS

The effectiveness of organizations of necessity is very dependent upon good upward, downward, and lateral communications. The latter is most important to the activity of coordinating the efforts of organizational units.

Before real communications can take place, those who desire to engage effectively in this interaction should be aware that certain barriers must be recognized, understood, and removed. When they attain this awareness and do something about it, then and only then will their communications with others become truly effective.

Failure to listen

A principal obstacle to good communications is the failure to listen to what others are saying.[4] This may result from many causes. Some of these are lack of interest in what is said, personal problems causing mental preoccupation, egocentricity, or some other psychological condition which causes inattention or inability to concentrate. Mostly, however, failure to listen results purely from a lack of effort to engage actively in this process. One cannot truly *communicate* with others by merely hearing in a passive manner what is being said. Such passiveness will more often than not stifle understanding between individuals since it will usually be interpreted as a reflection of disinterest.

Status differences

The greater the difference in status or rank, the greater will be the difficulty in achieving effective communications. Communications are easier if they travel downward from the superior than if they go upward from the subordinate. Likewise, the greater the prestige of the com-

---

[4] See Chapter 7 for further discussion of the listening process.

municator, the greater the likelihood that his communications will be effective. Gilkinson, Paulson, and Sikkink [5] found that "Speakers having prestige significantly influence listeners more than those who do not." Eisenson, Auer, and Irwin [6] also found that "Listeners tend to accept ideas from those who have prestige. . . . Listeners also tend to reject equally good ideas from those who lack prestige. . . . Speakers have prestige when listeners like them, accept them as authorities, defer to their judgment or attach importance to what they say."

Status can be helpful or it can be a hindrance. It will be helpful if the supervisor has earned the respect of his subordinates through the proper use of his authority. It can be a hindrance if he has grown apart from them to the extent that he has become unapproachable.[7]

Psychological size

Denominating all appearances of superiority, inferiority, or personal inadequacy as complexes has become a hackneyed practice; yet such psychological conditions do exist and do set up obstacles to interpersonal relations. Sometimes referred to as psychological size, these feelings often cause a bad "climate" between supervisor and subordinate and adversely affect their capacity to communicate effectively. Especially damaging to these relationships are those manifestations of superiority or impatience exhibited by supervisors in dealing with their subordinates. Often subordinates will resent having the boss talk down to them. They will resent even more the paternalistic attitude.

Should the subordinate tend toward feelings of inadequacy or inferiority, he may become especially sensitive to a "hard" approach and is likely to resent it. As a result, he will tend to withdraw even further, making two-way communications with him more difficult.

The failure of the supervisor to recognize the importance of the psychological aspects of the communication process will set up barriers difficult to overcome. An atmosphere of openness in communications is conducive to improved exchanges. An atmosphere of secrecy, evasiveness, and pressure will clog channels and impair communications.[8]

---

[5] H. Gilkinson, S. F. Paulson, and D. E. Sikkink, "Effects of Order and Authority in an Argumentative Speech," *Quarterly Journal of Speech,* 40 (1954), 183–92.

[6] Jon Eisenson, J. Jeffrey Auer, and John V. Irwin, *The Psychology of Communication* (New York: Appleton-Century-Crofts, 1963), p. 284.

[7] Dalton E. McFarland, *Management Principles and Practices,* 2nd ed. (New York: Macmillan Publishing Co., Inc., 1964), p. 567.

[8] Leon C. Megginson, *Personnel: A Behavioral Approach to Administration* (Homewood, Ill.: Richard D. Irwin, Inc., 1967), p. 531.

Noise

Noise in communications is referred to by theorists as the static that interferes with transmission of messages. This static tends to bring on *redundancy* or the repetition of the message, perhaps in a different way, to ensure that it gets across. Redundancy is inefficient in that it wastes time in repetition, but it is efficient if it helps to get the message across.[9] The extent to which noise is reduced as a distractor will largely determine how effective communications are. Psychological stress from the outside or inside, environmental distractors, and even abstractions can be considered noises which hinder communication.

Language barriers

Because of selection standards, the police supervisor will seldom encounter problems resulting from inability of his subordinates to express themselves in the language of the profession. He will, however, encounter many degrees of lucidity among his subordinates. Their capabilities of understanding will likewise vary.

When the receiver passes the state of clear understanding because he does not have the capacity for it, he starts to make mistakes, or a total breakdown in communications may follow. Ambiguities contribute to this condition. They do nothing but cause confusion. Perhaps the commonest form of everyday misunderstanding results from the assumption that what is perfectly obvious (apparently) to the sender is clear to the receiver.[10] The ability of the supervisor to express himself not only clearly, concisely, and simply but also understandably will largely determine his effectiveness.

In the interests of effective communications, words must be put together so that they mean the same thing to the listener as they do to the speaker. Distortion of meaning or the garbling of communications is usually brought about by a failure to use language that has a precise meaning to others. This failure may be overcome by projecting oneself into another's viewpoint. This is called empathy.[11]

Semantic blocks do occur at times regardless of how perfect one

[9] Harold J. Leavitt, *Managerial Psychology*, 3rd ed. (Chicago: University of Chicago Press, 1972), pp. 119, 203.

[10] John Parry, *The Psychology of Communications* (London: University of London Press Ltd., 1967), p. 84.

[11] Joseph L. Massie, *Essentials of Management* (Englewood Cliffs, N.J.: Prentice-Hall, Inc., 1964), p. 73.

thinks his communications are. Complete understanding is seldom achieved, but the chief aim of communications can be realized if meanings are conveyed to others in a way that will be understood and accepted.[12]

Van Dersal [13] states that the five hundred most used words in our language have about fourteen thousand meanings, an average of twenty-eight meanings per word. It is thus obvious that a great need exists for clarity and precision of expression if communications between individuals in the organization are to be effective.

Fear of criticism

Many individuals avoid making positive declarations because they fear being criticized. They often feel so insecure that they dislike giving others occasion to attack their observations. As a result, they too often couch their expressions in vagueness and abstraction, always leaving "an open back door" through which they can retreat if their statements are challenged. Communicating in such cases becomes difficult if not impossible. The supervisor will contribute to this condition if he editorializes upon each bit of information he receives or if he overevaluates it. The tendency to make merit evaluations on each opinion or each comment made will have a deadening effect upon communications. Soon, those who must communicate with him will avoid doing so.

Jumping to conclusions

Jumping to a conclusion on incomplete information before "hearing out" a subordinate is a tendency which supervisory personnel must suppress. Such acts will be interpreted as impatience, disinterest, and discourtesy and will contribute greatly to communication failures. The speaker trying to converse with another who refuses to listen soon will become discouraged and will discontinue his attempts because, to him, "The boss has already made up his mind. Why confuse him with facts?" Perhaps no action of the supervisor will cause more resentment than his failure to allow a subordinate to have his "day in court" before his case is judged.

---

[12] McFarland, *Management Principles and Practices*, p. 563.
[13] William R. Van Dersal, *The Successful Supervisor in Government and Business* (New York: Harper & Row, Publishers, 1968), p. 122.

Filtering

As information is passed from individual to individual, usually a distortion or dilution of content occurs. This is called *filtering*. It is a natural occurrence resulting from the tendency of individuals to repeat that part of what they have heard or otherwise learned which has had the most impact upon them.

In medieval times, it was not uncommon for the bearer of ill tidings to be subjected to harsh treatment—even death—by a king who did not wish to hear bad news. This desire to escape from unpleasant situations is not an unusual phenomenon. Some supervisors at times seem to prefer to avoid hearing the truth when it is disagreeable, thinking perhaps that they can thereby immunize themselves from responsibility or liability for what has happened by such remarks as, "Don't tell me about that," or "I don't want to hear about it"; but ignorance is rarely an excuse for inaction when action is indicated, nor does it reduce liability or accountability. This is especially true when the supervisor could keep himself reasonably informed about incidents in his unit—both good and bad—by insisting that his personnel let him know what is happening. He can thus evaluate the information himself and act accordingly. If his attitude indicates that he is unreceptive, however, he will soon shut off his sources or will hear only the pleasant information or that which his subordinates think he wants to hear. Thus, the supervisor is shielded from the unpleasant truth by those who believe that in doing so they will do him a favor by keeping him in ignorance or in good humor. Actually, they are doing him a great disservice and are exposing him to even greater liability by forcing him to make value judgments based on partial, inaccurate, or distorted information or information taken out of context through the filtering process.

The process of filtering also affects the supervisor in his downward communications. Giving employees filtered information is sometimes worse than giving them none. Besides the adverse effects filtering eventually will have on the confidence of personnel in their leaders, such distorted information will often cause rumors that are harmful to morale.

Individual sentiments and attitudes

Like it or not, management must accept the fact that people in all phases and at all levels of an establishment communicate either within their own system or in that created by the organization. Each employee interprets those communications received according to his own particular past experiences. He is apt to see what he wants to see based on his impressions of what has been said and done.[14]

The acceptance of a communication depends a good deal upon the receiver's needs, his experiences, and the environment under which the message was received. If the communication is a threat to his own goals, he may not accept it or he may accept it even though he disagrees with it, depending on how well he has been conditioned to accept discipline required in the organization. If he has a feeling of true identification with the group, he will probably accept most communications without question. In the end, the important thing is *how* he accepts them and how they cause him to react.[15]

Feelings between individuals vary extensively. Their likes and dislikes of other persons may aid or harm their communications. Attitudes, moods, and emotions likewise have a direct bearing on the type of interaction between individuals. These interactions will vary from time to time depending upon the intensity of emotions, the receptive mood of either of two persons attempting to communicate, or the attitude of one toward the other. These factors should be considered by the supervisor in selecting the time and place for communicating with his subordinates.

Intentional suppression or manipulation of communications

Intentional suppression of information which should pass from the superior to his subordinates will eventually cause a breach in upward channels. Information that should flow from the employees to management will thus be reduced. The net result will be misunderstandings. These more often than not will result in friction and the consequent lowering of production because they divert the employee's interests to himself instead of to the organization where they should be.[16] Each supervisor is obliged to keep his subordinates reasonably informed of matters that affect them. When he fails in this obligation, they will frequently respond in kind.

At times, a supervisor is approached by a subordinate who suggests directly or indirectly that a particular problem be dealt with in an irregular, improper, or illegal manner. The supervisor may rationalize to himself that the objective justifies the means used, but, fearing lia-

---

[14] Walter Wiesman, "Effecting Better Management Communication in Technical Organizations," in *Proceedings of the 1965 Institute on Technical and Industrial Communications* (Fort Collins, Colo.: Colorado State University, 1966), p. 70.

[15] Massie, *Essentials of Management*, p. 71.

[16] Walter Dill Scott, Robert C. Clothier, and William R. Spriegel, *Personnel Management: Principles, Practices, and Point of View*, 5th ed. (New York: McGraw-Hill Book Company, 1954), p. 17.

bility, gives an "official" answer for "the record" while implying by word or expression that he condones, or at least will not stand in the way of the proposal. His less-than-forthright manipulation of such information usually is easily exposed and could be exceedingly embarrassing if not actually illegal and could subject him and his organization to considerable liability.

Complexity of communications channels

The channels through which communications pass are called the *communications net*. The complexity of these channels will directly affect the speed and accuracy of messages flowing through them. The larger the number of persons involved in the interpretation of messages, the greater is the possibility that the end product will be distorted.[17] When channels are overly complex, messages will tend to be delayed at bottlenecks, which in themselves are obstacles difficult to overcome. The total effect is that senders and receivers are not brought into contact. Communications are thus stifled almost at the source.[18]

Overloading of channels

Overloading of channels causes jamming much as in the case of bottlenecks. Overloading results from lack of discrimination in separating relevant and irrelevant information. This suggests that each communicator should constantly control the quality of his messages. More messages do not mean more information.[19] If the supervisor does not establish some priorities, he will soon become bogged down in paperwork or will spend too much of his time listening to trivia rather than doing what really has to be done.

It is well for the supervisor to insist that subordinates keep him informed but too much insistence may cause resentment. The employee may feel that he is not trusted. The demands of the supervisor should be reasonable in this respect; however, his right to know what is going on to protect himself and his organization cannot be challenged. The astute supervisor will require his subordinates to keep him apprised of matters of concern to him, especially in critical operations such as vice and narcotics law enforcement. He should demand that they inform him of any occurrences when they are in doubt as to their importance. His subordinates should understand clearly that if they fail to do so, he will

---

[17] Leavitt, *Managerial Psychology*, pp. 193–95.
[18] Parry, *The Psychology of Communications*, pp. 84–104.
[19] Massie, *Essentials of Management*, pp. 71–73.

assume that they acted in bad faith and will treat them accordingly. It is true that the imposition of such requirements upon employees will tend to place a heavy burden on communications channels, but too much information is better than too little under these conditions.

Overstructuring of communications channels

Too much insistence that employees follow formal communications channels will tend to sterilize the passing of information upward, downward, and across organizational lines. Research by Bavelas [20] indicated that adherence to formal channels within the hierarchy facilitated communications, but that morale was better in systems involving informal channels.

The *direction* of communications has been found to play an important part in their effectiveness. Two-way communications are apt to be more accurate than one-way communications, and although unilateral communications are faster, they do not provide for feedback as a means of measuring understanding. Therefore, they are likely to end up in talk only. [21]

OVERCOMING COMMUNICATION BARRIERS

Rarely will a supervisor overcome all the barriers to effective communications. He can, however, overcome most of them most of the time by preparing to communicate before doing so and by employing the basic techniques of expression which have been proven successful. He must remember that communication has not really taken place until the message has reached the mind of the receiver. "Where the leader is communications-minded, grapevine, rumor-factory and so on, operate weakly. But the grapevine and other organization-harming systems flourish where the leader's communications effort lags." [22]

If the supervisor is to achieve better understanding between himself and his subordinates, he will be well advised to concentrate on removing the impediments to effective communications wherever possible. He will be materially aided in accomplishing this by adhering to the following admonishments.

[20] Alex Bavelas, "Communication Patterns in Task-Oriented Groups," *Journal of the Acoustical Society of America*, 22 (1950), 725–30.

[21] Leavitt, *Managerial Psychology*, pp. 115–17.

[22] Auren Uris, *Techniques of Leadership* (New York: McGraw-Hill Book Company, 1964), p. 146.

Determine objectives

Before communicating, he should be sure his ideas are clear in his own mind. If not, he will have scant success in conveying them to others. He should carefully analyze the matter to be communicated to determine what objectives he expects to accomplish. The more complex the communication, the more analysis it requires. He should consider the views of those to whom the communication will be directed, their attitudes, and those of other affected persons.

Before an order or directive is given, the supervisor should be certain of what he really wants others to do. Is the communication intended to obtain information, change attitudes or thinking, or alter performance? What is the most important objective?

Once these questions have been answered, the supervisor can adapt his language toward the accomplishment of his objective. He will realize that the more he structures his communication toward his primary goal, the more likely are his chances for success. He will avoid trying to accomplish too much with each communication.

The foregoing remarks suggest that there is a direct correlation between the effectiveness of communications and the total setting in which they occur. If communications are timely; if they take into consideration customs and practices and the human element, including the moods, attitudes, and emotions of the recipients; if they take place in the proper physical setting at the most propitious time; if the supervisor gives attention to their clarity and simplicity; if they are made to appeal to those affected; and if the recipient is prepared to receive, communications will accomplish most of what is intended. If they do not meet these requirements, they are likely to fail and usually do.

For example, if an order is given to officers for the first time the evening before Christmas that they must work on that holiday, unless some emergency is obvious to them, the directive is not likely to be relished, whereas if they had been previously prepared for the possibility of being required to work, the directive would have considerably more acceptance and would harm morale less. As obvious as this principle may seem, such breaches of good communication practices occur with appalling frequency.

A change in an item of equipment such as a mechanical holster (which might be especially liked by many officers) has been observed to cause a considerable amount of resentment because those affected were not prepared for the change. They construed the change as arbitrary because the basis for the decision was not understood. When the purpose of the communication or the evidence upon which it is based is conveyed to the recipients, it is far more likely to be well accepted than if no efforts have been made to prepare them for it.

Practice empathy

The supervisor should consider the views of those to whom the communication will be directed. Before issuing directives which will have widespread effect upon employees, he should confer with other persons to gain insight into the problem. He may thus gain a better understanding of the thoughts and feelings of those affected. A variety of points of view will give greater objectivity to those issuing directives. These will receive greater acceptance if others are permitted to participate in their development.

Obtain feedback

Feedback is perhaps the most important of the supervisor's tools in learning if he is communicating well. It involves simply the process of learning by observing the listener's verbal and nonverbal behavior, and by inspection and questioning whether understanding is taking place.[23] The manner in which a message is given, the tone of voice, inflections, and facial expressions have a great impact upon the acceptability of communications. The overtones accompanying these messages provide clues to the communicator as to the extent of the listener's comprehension. Such overtones are often as important in getting a message across as the basic content itself. Subtle shades of meaning brought about by choice of words will often greatly influence the listener's reception of the message. If it is possible for employees to read hidden meanings into words and overtones, the supervisor should expect them to do so and attempt to prevent this from happening.

The considerable effort that goes into the development of good communications may be wasted if the supervisor fails to follow up to determine how effective they have been. Such follow-up is essential if useful feedback is to be obtained.

Keep subordinates informed

A supervisor should keep his subordinates informed as much as possible about matters affecting them such as work plans, schedules,

[23] Leonard Sayles, "On-the-Job Communications," *Supervisory Management,* August, 1967, pp. 12–15.

policies, decisions, programs, and so on. Employees will react best to changes in plans, operations, or working conditions when they have been given some background to aid them in understanding the need for change.[24] Workers are not entitled to explanations from management as a matter of inherent right; but management will do well to explain the *why* of orders or directives whenever practicable because otherwise it risks failure to gain acceptance. Management is under no obligation to justify every decision made. To do so would clutter the decision-making process so badly that operations would be seriously impeded. On the other hand, operations can be enhanced if management "sells" its decisions to employees.

If the supervisor looks at management from the point of view of the subordinate and takes the subordinate's interests into account when formulating communications vital to his interests, greater managerial success will be achieved in the all-important function of communicating. If he makes little or no effort, the grapevine with all its potential hazards will take over.

The skilled supervisor often is able to use this medium to good advantage, but most will be well advised to use more formal and conventional methods. When the supervisor risks the use of the grapevine to communicate, he is always faced with the problem of giving more misinformation than information.[25]

Rumors can seriously impair good communications and harm morale if permitted to spread. The further they spread, the more they are likely to be embellished and the more employees tend to believe them. Therefore, the supervisor should be alert for harmful rumors so that he can promptly counter them with the truth. Once discredited, they quickly die.

Be consistent in communicating

Communications that are devised to bring about lasting results should be consistent with the long-term goals of the organization. Policies, rules, or procedures should not be changed willy-nilly. To make frequent, unnecessary changes would cause confusion and result in a general lowering of confidence of employees in management. For example, if an organization declares its intent to refrain from filing per-

[24] Federal Aviation Agency, *Management for Supervisors* (Washington, D.C.: U.S. Government Printing Office, 1961), p. 22; Laird W. Meabiea, "Employee Resistence to Change: A learned response management can prevent," *Supervisory Management*, January, 1978, pp. 16–22.
[25] Scott, Clothier, and Spriegel, *Personnel Management: Principles, Practices, and Point of View*, pp. 452–53.

sonnel complaints proved to be without merit in the concerned employee's personnel file, perhaps all such files should be reviewed and purged of such information in the interests of consistency. This would be of special importance if the personnel files were to be used for promotional purposes by oral examining boards.

Similarly, it would be eminently unfair for the supervisor to postpone communicating with his subordinate merely because both might find the interchange disagreeable. Adverse personnel evaluations or incident reports concerning unacceptable behavior or performance should be discussed with the concerned employee as promptly as are favorable ones commending him; yet many supervisors avoid making negative incident reports when they are required to discuss the matter with the concerned employee and allow him to see the report before it is filed in the personnel jacket. Neither should the application of punishment for misconduct be delayed merely because it is an unpleasant task for the supervisor. The way these activities are performed by him will have long-term effects upon morale and all its concomitants.

Make actions speak louder than words

The admonishment to "practice what you preach" has become a management principle. It is perhaps nowhere more important than in the supervisor's relationships with his subordinates. The most persuasive communications involve what is done, not what is said. This adage implies a consistent application of rules and policies to all employees. It means that the supervisor must not prescribe one course of action for his subordinates and follow another more favorable course himself.

Listen, understand, and be understood

The ability or the willingness to listen to what is being said, to understand the expressed and the true meaning of interpersonal communications, and to convey clear and understandable messages to others is dependent upon the background, experience, and motivation of the communicants. Hayakawa [26] said, "The meanings of words are *not* in the words; they are in us." Communicating is a two-way process. It involves good listening as well as good expression. One learns little by talking but a great deal by listening. Talking is an excellent secondary means of learning but only as a supplement to listening. It is the oil

---

[26] S. I. Hayakawa, *Language in Thought and Action* (New York: Harcourt Brace Jovanovich, Inc., 1972), p. 258.

that lubricates the process of listening and provides a foundation for it.[27] The supervisor must develop his listening ability if he is to achieve success in his communications consistently. He does so by developing the "big ears, little mouth" philosophy which is one of the most important and most often neglected skills in communicating.

Attentiveness to responses and concentration upon what is being said is necessary to understanding. The most effective communicator will listen not only to what the speaker says but to what he means. If this listening is half-hearted, effective communication will not occur. Rogers and Roethlisberger [28] observe most appropriately, "The biggest block to personal communications is man's inability to listen intelligently, understandingly, and skillfully to another person."

CHARACTERISTICS OF COMMUNICATIONS

Communications may be categorized into three broad groups, each with its characteristic advantages and disadvantages. Uris [29] classifies these as *autocratic, democratic,* and *free-rein.*

Autocratic

Autocratic communications can be issued with relative ease since concurrence by those affected is not sought. They have the advantage of speed and are well adapted to emergency conditions. They have the characteristic disadvantage of arbitrariness. Difficulty is often encountered in achieving general acceptance by workers because they are not afforded an opportunity to participate in decisions affecting them.

Democratic

The two-way passing of information makes democratic communication easy to understand. It permits the development of ideas and enables those affected by decisions to participate in making them. Information readily passes in both directions making it simple for the supervisor to keep informed of activities below him. Democratic communications lack the speed and directness of those which are autocratic; and, while they

---

[27] Techniques of active listening are discussed in detail in Chapter 7.

[28] Carl R. Rogers and F. J. Roethlisberger, "Barriers and Gateways to Communication," *Harvard Business Review,* July-August, 1952, p. 46.

[29] Auren Uris, *How to Be a Successful Leader* (New York: McGraw-Hill Book Company, 1953), pp. 141–44.

hold greatest promise for success in most normal operations, the supervisor will find that he must forego consultation with his subordinates when speed of operations is essential.

Free-rein

Free-rein communications provide for a minimum of contacts, thereby leaving subordinates to operate in isolation. Leadership and guidance are often absent and subordinates do not realize the benefits of two-way communications. As a consequence, misunderstandings, misapprehensions, and mistakes flourish.

The supervisor is well advised to balance his communications to the setting in which they occur. Each type has its place. None should be employed to the exclusion of the others. The type most appropriate for one set of circumstances might be totally inappropriate under other conditions.

TYPES OF COMMUNICATORS

Attempts by the supervisor to improve his ability to express himself cannot be successful until he has analyzed his shortcomings and has made a positive effort to overcome them. Is he, as Eisenson, Auer, and Irwin[30] list, a *noncommunicator*, who says no more than he thinks the situation requires? Has he failed to say something that should be said? Is he a *logical speaker*, troubled by anxieties or compulsiveness? Is he unconcerned with the impact his statements have on others? Is he the *under-talker*, who often fails to communicate when communicating is indicated? Is he the *over-talker*, who often communicates well but does not know when to stop? Is he a *tangential speaker*? Does he fail to give direct response as he is expected or does he respond to irrelevant side issues? Is he the so-called *helpless speaker*, full of self-pity and self-apology? Does he apologize for asking a subordinate to do something he is expected to do? If he does, any respect his subordinates have for him will soon be eroded.

WRITTEN COMMUNICATIONS

The supervisor is judged to a great extent throughout his career by how well he expresses himself not only orally but also in writing. His ability to study a problem; find a solution; develop proper, workable plans; and record his thoughts, ideas, conclusions, recommendations, or find-

[30] Eisenson, Auer, and Irwin, *The Psychology of Communication*, pp. 347–56.

ings in writing will be a measure of his competency in the eyes of his superiors and subordinates. Poorly written, untintelligible communications will usually result in confusion and misunderstanding and will invariably reflect unfavorably on the ability of the writer.

Any effective writing involves an organization of thoughts and ideas in a manner that will enable the reader to know exactly what the writer wants him to know. In a literal sense, anything written by a person in his official capacity involves a staff function and can be called a staff writing. Fundamentally, there is little difference between reporting and staff writing. Staff papers may consist of correspondence of all kinds, orders, directives, or briefs of formal documents. Whatever the type, the writer should follow the requisites of good staff writing and should adhere to the principles of completed staff work.

Clarity of expression

As in the case of oral communications, words and ideas must be clearly expressed. In fact, clarity is more essential in written communications since the readers are not permitted the opportunity to clarify misunderstandings as in the case of face-to-face, two-way oral communications. They can only ponder what was meant.

Excessive use of abbreviations should be avoided. As Flesch [31] asserts, they may be used with impunity whenever they are customary and will not distract the attention of the reader. If they are necessary, authorized abbreviations or those having clearly apparent meaning may be used.

Clarity of expression is all-important. If this requirement is not met, the reader will waste much time trying to decide what was meant. Confusion will result. Warnock [32] sums up the requirement of clarity of expression by saying, "A sentence must not only be capable of being understood; it must be incapable of being misunderstood."

Simplicity of style

Writers should think about the reading ability of the readers and scale their writing accordingly. Short sentences composed of simple words and careful punctuation to make the meaning clear are preferred to complex sentences and difficult words. The former are much easier to read and comprehend. Costly mistakes occasioned by misinterpretations

[31] Rudolph Flesch, *The ABC of Style: A Guide to Plain English* (New York: Harper & Row, Publishers, 1964), p. 3.
[32] Madeline Warnock, "Editing for Better Understanding," in *Proceedings of the 1962 Institute in Technical and Industrial Communications,* p. 20.

can be reduced if this practice is followed. This fact should constantly be kept in mind by the writer as he prepares his communications.

The elimination of trivia, redundant items, and nonessential detail will save the time not only of the writer but of the reader. The type and speed of action taken as the result of a report may well depend upon its clarity and the rapidity with which it is understood.

Accuracy

When a written communication is in the form of a report concerning a research project, it should be based upon the most reliable and authoritative data available. Findings must be accurate even in the most minute detail to prevent misleading those who are to rely upon the report.

Arrangement

Ideas should be arranged logically so that they may be easily followed and understood by the reader. Systematic arrangement of a paper may be accomplished with the aid of a checklist of subjects or items to be covered, an outline, and a rough draft or two. Important key points that the writer wishes to emphasize can be made more emphatic by the use of underlining, italics, boldface, script letters, or other distinctive markings to call such points to the reader's attention.

Style

The so-called newspaper style of writing ordinarily simplifies expression and facilitates understanding. The first paragraph expresses the essential elements of the paper. This is the topic paragraph. The first or topic sentence should likewise express the essence of the paragraph it introduces. Succeeding paragraphs explain and amplify the opening paragraph in such a way that each is almost self-sustaining. Thus the report proceeds from the most important ideas to the least important details, which make the main ideas more meaningful.

Summary, conclusions, recommendations, plans of action

Final paragraphs should present conclusions, recommendations, solutions, or plans of action. Summary statements are often placed at the beginning to enable the reader to capture the important aspects of the report without reading the details. Should he be interested in these, he can find them in the body of the report.

Format

The *heading* of the report should obviously indicate the title or subject. The *body* presents the main ideas or findings. The *closing* incorporates the conclusions, recommendations, and plan of action. The name of the writer should be included for purposes of accountability.

The United States Navy uses the technique of placing well-chosen cues in the left margin as guides to the material in the text. This enables those who have to do a massive volume of reading to scan the guides for material they wish to read and concentrate upon only those points of interest.[33]

MANUALS—ORDERS

Policies, procedures, orders, and rules and regulations can be easily codified into a numbered decimal system and fashioned into a manual by even the smallest agency. The manual can be used as a simple but effective means of communicating to employees uniform, detailed orders relating to the operations of the organization.

Some agencies develop separate manuals for policies, procedures, and rules and regulations. Others combine all such written guidelines into one manual appropriately numbered and arranged homogeneously into segments.

As in the case of any order, manuals must be constantly reviewed to ensure that their provisions are kept current. These reviews and recommendations for needed changes are of major importance to supervisors if they are to carry out the objectives of their organization effectively.

Modification of manuals can be accomplished as the need arises by a system of general, special, or operation orders. *General* orders are those which establish policy—the broad rules describing general objectives of the organization. *Special* orders are those issued to establish procedures or rules and regulations necessary in carrying out policy. *Operation* orders are those used to describe the procedures to be followed and the goals to be achieved in a particular event. These should

[33] Edward S. Safford, "The Velocity of Communications," in *Proceedings of the 1965 Institute in Technical and Industrial Communications,* ed. Herman W. Weisman (Fort Collins, Colo.: Colorado State University, 1966), pp. 10–16.

remain in effect only for the duration of the operation to which they relate. *Notices* are forms of orders relating to matters of general interest, such as routine notifications and scheduled events.

Most agencies make provisions to give personnel in supervisory and command positions authority to issue formal orders relating to the operation of a particular unit. As in the preparation of any written directive, great care must be exercised so that such communications will clearly state their purpose, the policy or rule established, or the procedure to be followed. Ideally, they must be written so that they are incapable of being misunderstood by even the least astute person affected.

BRIEFING

An employee will sometimes be asked to reduce a lengthy report or dissertation to give his superior a concise account of the contents. The total report should be carefully analyzed to select the important ideas or points to be covered in the brief. These should be listed. Sufficient collateral detail should then be selected from the report to provide a basis for understanding. Care must be exercised in this process to preserve the meaning of the base report and to prevent any distortion or garbling of the author's meaning. Likewise, the person preparing the brief must avoid taking the excerpts out of context. His superiors should be able to use the brief with confidence that it faithfully and accurately represents the whole writing.

EDITING

Warnock [34] admonishes writers, "After you have written your report, organizing logically, practicing proper documentation, using strong and specific words, varying your sentence lengths, following all the advice you have gleaned from countless sources, go back and read your report, preferably aloud, and listen to it. Hear what you said, not what you intended to say. . . ." If it is not right, do it over until it is.

TYPICAL DEFICIENCIES IN WRITING

There are three main reasons why written communications fail to achieve what is intended. First, the writer, because of a lack of care or an inability to discriminate between fact and nonfact, confuses his communica-

[34] Madeline Warnock, "Editing for Better Understanding," p. 23.

tions by misinterpreting the data upon which they are based. Second, the writer fails to use the most specific and concrete words to make his meaning clear. Third, the writer fails to support his conclusions by factual data.[35]

SUMMARY

The ability to communicate clearly is one of the most important and often the most neglected of supervisory skills. It is a very delicate process involving cultural, environmental, and psychological factors and can easily become thwarted by barriers between persons. The supervisor must constantly review his communicating habits to determine how effectively he is transmitting messages to others.

Communications are affected adversely by many factors. Failure to listen actively to what is being said; feelings of superiority, inferiority, or inadequacy reflected by impatience or lack of confidence; language difficulties that cause misunderstandings; and fear of being criticized or challenged, which sometimes causes the speaker to express himself vaguely or abstractly, are among the prime obstacles to effective communications. If the supervisor is prone to "jump to conclusions" before learning all the facts, he will frequently shut himself off from his subordinates because they will consider it useless to go to him with their problems. Filtering, which often causes distortion and dilution of information as it is passed from person to person, will also hamper effective communications.

Rarely can all the hindrances to good communications be removed, but they can be minimized by the supervisor if he will clarify his ideas in his own mind before they are transmitted to others—if he decides what objective the communication is to achieve and directs his efforts toward accomplishing that objective by clarity and simplicity of expression.

The wise supervisor will recognize that the manner of disseminating communications will affect their acceptance. He will realize that subtle shades of meaning will often cause his messages to be misunderstood. Misinterpretations of orders or directives will often result in costly errors. He will be able to profit from his communicating mistakes only if he will follow up to determine how they occurred and how he can avoid them in the future.

[35] Charles H. Long, "Clear Thinking and its Relationship to Clear Writing," in *Proceedings of the 1962 Institute in Technical and Industrial Communications*, p. 11.

The most persuasive communications are brought about by deeds, not words. The supervisor should not establish one course of conduct for himself and preach another for his subordinates. Neither should he expect one standard of conduct from some of his subordinates and a different one from others. Impartiality and consistency of actions must be his guides. His subordinates are justified in expecting that he will consistently apply the rules to all. He must not postpone communicating with them when they are entitled to information which affects them even though it is an unpleasant task.

Written communications require even more attention than do oral ones because readers have no opportunity to clarify meanings intended by the writer by questioning him. They can only ponder what was meant. Therefore, the supervisor must give particular attention to written orders, directives or procedures. To be most effective, these should be clearly and simply written and logically organized so that the reader will have no difficulty understanding what was intended.

REVIEW

Questions

1. Give a practical example of how cultural, environmental, and psychological factors affect communications.
2. Describe what takes place in the process of active listening.
3. How do status differences affect communications? Give examples.
4. What is meant by psychological size? Explain how this condition affects communications.
5. What is noise in communications?
6. Why does the fear of criticism often have a harmful effect upon communications?
7. What is meant by filtering, and how does it affect the process of communications?
8. Give an example of how attitudes affect communications.
9. Explain how the barriers to effective communications can be largely overcome.
10. List the three broad classifications of communications and discuss the advantages and disadvantages of each.
11. List five types of communicators and explain how their peculiarities affect their communications.
12. What is the *newspaper style* of writing?
13. What are the main parts of a written report? What should be included in each of these parts?

14. What is a brief? What are the requisites of briefing?
15. What are the main deficiencies in most written communications?

Exercises

1. Write a policy statement which your superior might wish to issue to members of your organization concerning pursuit driving. As a basis for this policy statement, assume that there have been an inordinate number of accidents resulting from pursuits and that your superior wishes to reduce these by establishing guidelines for personnel exposed to the hazards of driving under such conditions. Write a procedural order to implement this policy.
2. Write a policy statement on when to shoot. Consider legal aspects, civil liability, and the moral issues involved.
3. Write a procedural order by which the policy statement in item 2 can be implemented.

6

Some psychological aspects of supervision

The contemporary attitude toward human nature and human engineering is a relatively new concept of management. Too often people in management rise to high positions with little knowledge of the psychological factors that interfere with the productivity of their personnel. Too often persons who are highly successful in developing certain specialized skills are placed in supervisory positions with considerable power, where they prove to be bunglers in applying the fundamental skills of dealing with others. The approach of the human relations school toward supervision is a relatively new science, a science of managing human beings, which grew out of the other sciences. It was long in coming, but when it arrived it showed great promise. The new thinking was applied to a preposterous degree by some. Others refused to accept or apply it at all. The most successful managers and supervisors recognized the value of getting things done through the democratic process. They saw that people would perform better if they were made to want to perform better. As a result, they saw production and morale improve in their organizations.

Dale Carnegie made a fortune by teaching people how to get others to do what one wants. Whatever this approach is called—the charm school approach or the democratic method—it can bring excellent results when applied sincerely, with common sense, and with good intentions. If applied superficially and insincerely, it eventually will produce bad results.

The Western Electric Company spent great sums in a long study of people at work in their plant at Hawthorne, Illinois. These studies revealed that the performance of workers is more affected by factors in the psychological and social environment than by factors in the physical environment. The workers' output was affected to a greater degree by their feelings about the job, their fellow workers, supervisors, and the happenings about them than by their attitudes about the physical working conditions.[1]

The rise of worker dominance and merit systems has made it necessary for management to seek positive methods of gaining an understanding of workers and leading them into a desire to produce. Vast sums have been poured into human relations training of supervisory personnel by management in recent times. Most of this training has stressed cultural background, the psychological differences between people, and the effects these factors have upon human behavior. Undoubtedly, some good results have accrued from these efforts.

DRIVES, SATISFACTIONS, AND NEEDS

All persons have certain basic drives which motivate their behavior. They have certain satisfactions which need fulfillment and psychological needs which, in large part, govern their demeanor. It is imperative for the supervisor to understand the basic relationships of the individual's drives, satisfactions, and needs to his behavior patterns if the initial steps taken by him to prevent or relieve many of the emotional problems of his subordinates are to be most meaningful.

Drives

The commonly recognized basic human drives are the wish for *security* based on fear, apprehensiveness and avoidance; the drive for *response* derived from love, friendship, and affection; the wish for *recognition* gained from status, prestige, and social approval; and the drive

[1] Fritz J. Roethlisberger and William J. Dickson, *Management and the Worker* (Cambridge, Mass.: Harvard University Press, 1939), p. 615. See also T. N. Whitehead, *Statistical Studies in Industrial Research, Second Progress Report* (Harvard Graduate School of Business Administration, June, 1934).

for *new experiences,* including curiosity, adventure, and craving for excitement.[2] Some add the *service motive* as a fundamental drive,[3] but many disagree that this aspect of human behavior should be included as a drive.

Satisfactions

The fundamental satisfactions that the individual strives to fulfill will be found in the lists prepared by most authorities. These are (1) affection, acceptance, and security; (2) a sense of personal adequacy; (3) recognition as a personality; (4) an opportunity for accomplishment; (5) an opportunity for independence; (6) an opportunity to obtain new experiences; and (7) an opportunity to possess something or someone.

Needs

Coleman [4] lists the basic psychological needs as a feeling of *security,* a sense of *adequacy,* a sense of *self-esteem,* and a sense of *social approval.* These have a vital bearing upon the behavior of individuals.

INFERIORITY COMPLEX

Alfred Adler used the phrase "inferiority complex" to describe the psychological feeling of inadequacy. He applied this concept as a partial explanation of some of the problems of the emotional, human animal. He believed that persons have a drive for superiority and that the frustration which comes from a feeling of inferiority thwarts this basic drive. Some accept it and retain their feelings of inferiority and engage in daydreaming or fantasy to compensate. Others compensate for their inadequacies by increased effort and make themselves productive members of society.[5] The normal individual always thinks of himself in the best possible light. It is difficult for him to recognize his weaknesses, accept defeat, or admit failure. He will often resort to all kinds of subterfuges—

[2] W. I. Thomas, *The Unadjusted Girl* (Boston: Little, Brown and Company, 1931), pp. 4–40

[3] E. S. Bogardus, "The Fifth Wish," *Sociology and Social Research,* September-October, 1931, pp. 75–77.

[4] James C. Coleman, *Personality Dynamics and Effective Behavior* (Chicago: Scott, Foresman and Company, 1960), pp. 118–22.

[5] Norman L. Munn, *The Evolution and Growth of Human Behavior* (Boston: Houghton Mifflin Company, 1955), p. 470.

even to self-deception—to escape any ill thought of himself.[6] In attempting to avoid the feelings of inferiority, the individual may set unrealistic goals for himself. In his efforts to achieve these goals, he often develops a desire to gain dominance at all costs. This desire often leads him to all sorts of antisocial behavior from bullying and boasting to tyrannical action.[7]

The overcompensations or overdrives developed by such individuals in the form of intensified and exaggerated strivings to compensate for their strong feelings of inferiority become an imposing challenge to the supervisor because, in order to bring about the emotional balance of such individuals, it is crucial that their self-confidence be restored.[8]

Training might help to improve the individual's proficiency and his confidence. An assignment to a position where he can achieve added success and the satisfaction that results from it often increases the individual's self-esteem. The sincere and judicious use of praise when it is deserved often brings about similar results.

CATHARSIS

Sigmund Freud, the father of psychoanalysis, attempted to discover the causes of some psychological diseases which baffled him as a physician. He reasoned that if he could bring these problems into the open, he could learn more about their basic causes and possibly bring about a cure more readily. He discovered that if he allowed his patients to talk about their psychological ailments—to engage in catharsis—by bringing them to consciousness and giving them expression, their fears, problems, and complexes were often alleviated.

The process of catharsis is particularly helpful in reducing feelings of anxiety, guilt, fear, or hostility and failure.[9] Rogers,[10] in describing catharsis as the process of "talking or acting things out" in a permissive atmosphere, states, "We have learned that catharsis not only frees the individual from those conscious fears and guilt feelings of which he is

---

[6] Norman C. Meier, "The Psychology of Human Relations," in *Psychology for Law Enforcement Officers*, ed. George F. Dudycha (Springfield, Ill.: Charles C Thomas, Publisher, 1966), p. 133.

[7] Funk and Wagnalls, *Standard Reference Encyclopedia* (New York: Standard Reference Works Publishing Company, Inc., 1959), p. 7298.

[8] Ordway Tead, *The Art of Leadership* (New York: McGraw-Hill Book Company, 1935), pp. 224–25.

[9] Coleman, *Personality Dynamics and Effective Behavior*, pp. 342–43.

[10] C. R. Rogers, *Counseling and Psychotherapy* (Boston: Houghton Mifflin Company, 1942), p. 21.

aware, but that, continued, it can bring to light more deeply buried attitudes which also exert their influence on behavior."

Lack of knowledge or understanding is often the direct cause of debilitating anxieties, fears, and feelings of insecurity among employees. These can often be materially reduced by the supervisor if he provides those affected individuals an opportunity to talk about their feelings in an informal environment. He can then provide the necessary information that usually reduces or eliminates such apprehensions. This might be done in privacy in the coffee room, while riding with the officer on patrol, and the like.

FIXATION AND REGRESSIVE BEHAVIOR

If left unresolved, emotional ills often result in conditions of neurosis. Adults often seek infantile ways of solving their emotional problems. The adult's psychological character is generally thought to be largely a product of childhood conditions. As a screaming child he got his way, or as a result of the erratic and inconsistent behavior of his parents— sometimes succumbing to the child's tantrums and giving in to his demands as the course of least resistance, and sometimes refusing to do so— the child gains a sense of insecurity. Psychological fixation may occur at this stage of development, with the probability that the child will become a screaming, tantrum-raising man at forty or regress or develop compensations in his behavior for the shortcomings he experiences in his environment.

Symonds [11] describes regressive behavior as a "step taken by the individual in order to avoid meeting and solving some difficulty or present problem. It is an escape from reality." He describes the condition of fixation as a "defense against anxiety by stopping the process of development." It involves a concentration on some particular infantile situation which tends to block maturation. These conditions sometimes lead to serious emotional problems, as discussed later in this chapter.

THE SUPERVISOR AND THE FRUSTRATED EMPLOYEE

The supervisor is constantly dealing with people who, in one respect or another, have regressions, fixations, or overdrives caused by frustrations. When individuals are prevented from fulfilling certain conscious desires or impulses, when their basic drives, needs, and satisfactions are not

[11] P. M. Symonds, *The Dynamics of Human Adjustment* (New York: Appleton-Century-Crofts, 1946), p. 204.

realized, when they are thwarted in reaching their goals, frustrations are likely to develop. These are called goal frustrations as opposed to those due to neurotic conditions.[12] Accompanying them will be numerous problems for the supervisor to resolve.

The behavior reactions of aggression, regression, or fixation commonly found in frustrated persons [13] will demand attention. The supervisor's course will be determined in large part by the psychological impact of the frustrations on his subordinates. One thing is certain—when psychological problems interfere with performance, he must do something to resolve them. If he does not, they will invariably become more pronounced.

It would be an oversimplification to state that a single underlying cause of abnormal behavior can be easily isolated or even that such behavior can be attributed to any one causative factor. Ordinarily, many factors contribute. The supervisor must consider that a particular type of human conduct is usually the result of multiple stimuli. On occasion, however, one predominant factor can be pointed to as the primary cause of a particular course of conduct. For example, a supervisor observes a problem developing among a group of his subordinates. They have had an increasing problem of getting along with others, their performance has deteriorated, they seem preoccupied, they have missed calls and have had an inordinate number of conflicts with other coworkers and superiors. The supervisor finds that one officer has become involved in financial difficulties and the problem lately has become particularly acute. He is worried about his security. The second officer is concerned about his health. He has been ill and is troubled because of his failure to improve as rapidly as he thinks he should. The third employee is bored. He feels he has outlived his usefulness in his present job and wants to transfer. He is looking for new experiences. The fourth feels that he has not been given sufficient recognition for his work and that others are getting more than their share. All officers' problems may be but reflections of these various circumstances. The results are generally the same, although the causes may vary widely.

The supervisor must develop a clinical approach in dealing with the emotional problems of his subordinates that he encounters day by day. He must attempt to understand how these problems arise and deal with them in a practical, commonsensical way. Sometimes a workable solution cannot be found. Perhaps none could be found even by a professional who specializes in the study and treatment of emotional dis-

[12] Richard C. Calhoon, *Managing Personnel* (New York: Harper & Row, Publishers, 1963), p. 257.
[13] Norman R. F. Maier, *Frustration: The Study of Behavior Without a Goal* (Ann Arbor, Mich.: The University of Michigan Press, 1961), p. 16.

orders; but ordinarily the degree of success achieved will be directly related to the supervisor's patience and understanding and the effort he expends in helping his subordinates solve their problems.

In order to deal most effectively with the lack of emotional adjustment in others, the supervisor himself must be well adjusted. He must exhibit that he has complete emotional control of himself before he can control others. He should display a matured, philosophical attitude in his dealings with subordinates, realizing that each has a unique personality which can best be developed along certain lines. He should govern his relationships with them accordingly.

Sometimes, giving them an opportunity to talk, providing a bit of information, or giving a simple explanation are all that is required to correct an incipient problem. If the basic causes of lack of adjustment can be treated effectively rather than the symptoms only, the most valuable service will be rendered the individual as well as the organization.

THE NATURE OF FRUSTRATION

When the route to a goal is obstructed, the usual reaction is to go around the obstacle, remove it, attack it head on, accept defeat, or, if the goal is unimportant, forget it, ignore it, or deny that it ever existed. This involves problem-solving behavior since it requires some adjustment to circumstances. This is the essence of personal development.[14]

The adjusted person is capable of meeting the normal problems and solving them without undue psychological strain. Gradually, he develops the ability to meet and solve more difficult personal problems. The individual who finds it difficult to adjust to his problems develops a sense of failure. This causes frustration, irritations, emotional conflicts of all sorts, and reduced flexibility in handling other problems. If he is unable to find a satisfactory solution, his failure becomes a barrier. With it comes frustration.

The supervisor who ignores or is unaware of the employee's drive to attain a certain goal is often the very cause of frustration. He becomes the barrier. If he gives notice to the efforts of his subordinate and indicates approval of them, he assists the employee in his drive toward his goal.

BARRIERS CAUSING FRUSTRATION

A drive toward achievement of a goal may be blocked by external or internal barriers.

[14] *Psychology for Law Enforcement Officers*, ed. George F. Dudycha (Springfield, Ill.: Charles C Thomas, Publisher, 1966), p. 41.

External barriers

Those *physical* things in the environment of the individual such as a malfunctioning flashlight, a sticking door, or bad brakes on an automobile may constitute barriers to which the individual must adjust. *Human barriers* might be a nagging wife or an incompatible partner or supervisor. *Situational barriers* may consist of unpopular rules or policies, inadequate salaries, or onerous situations which affect the individual.

Internal barriers

Conflicts in motives existing within the individual may constitute internal barriers to personality adjustment. Often these obstacles are brought about by failure of the person to make adjustments to the environment in which he finds himself. The individual desiring a new and better assignment is often torn by internal conflicts which arise because he fears the added responsibility of the new position.

FRUSTRATIONS AND PERFORMANCE

As has been pointed out, frustrations may appear when job motives encounter barriers. The individual experiencing frustrations to which he is unable to adapt will usually become emotional, irritable, and inflexible. This will affect his performance. It therefore appears desirable that the supervisor examine the factors contributing to frustrations and isolate the common symptoms so that he may recognize them when they are present. He then must set about to eliminate the conditions in the job environment which lead to frustrations and work intelligently toward the relief of the consequences when frustrations occur.

If expected earnings are not realized, an employee may feel a lack of economic security. He may feel personally insecure if he is made to believe that he is inferior to coworkers. If he is frequently criticized by supervisors, if he is not kept informed regarding matters that affect him, if he does not receive adequate training for the job to which he is assigned, if he is not informed where he stands, or if he is not accepted by the group, feelings of emotional insecurity may develop. Appearances of favoritism, inconsistent application of rules and policies, and other reflections of instability in the job environment may also give rise to such feelings.

An individual may become frustrated if he does not receive recognition for his efforts or accomplishments or if he fails to gain expected promotions. He may not understand why this happened because he lacks insight into the reason for his failure or he may believe that an unfair promotional system was the cause. If he lacks an appreciation of his contributions to the entire operation, he may also experience frustration. The same results will be likely if he is not provided with an opportunity for self-expression on the job. This might be brought about by a feeling that his job is too simple for his talents or by a feeling of boredom or monotony. Failure to give the worker a sense of active participation in the total organizational objectives, a lack of encouragement to develop new skills and take on added responsibility, the exercise of excessive dominance over him by his superiors, or their failure to help him gain insight into his shortcomings may contribute to the development of frustration.

Too, employees often become frustrated when they are deprived of a feeling of personal dignity as the result of the failure of the supervisor to consider their pride and self-esteem. Excessive, inconsistent, arbitrary, or unduly strict discipline, giving rise to a feeling that they have been stripped of reasonable freedom of action, is often a cause of frustration.

Frustrations connected with the employee's off-the-job life may be reflected in his job performance. The reverse is also likely to occur. If the employee is subjected to frustrating conditions on the job, he often takes his problems home, with the result that his home life becomes a series of frustrating experiences.

Many organizations have found that family problems are materially reduced by a program in which spouses of new employees are encouraged to meet with representatives of the organization to discuss the social, economic, and psychological restraints the job often places upon the worker and his family.[15] Such programs are usually made a part of the initial training program that a new employee attends. However, even the more progressive attempts to help officers and their families cope with job pressures are not totally effective in resolving all the family problems that are bound to exist. In these cases, the supervisor must recognize his limitations. If he concludes that he is not qualified to give the necessary assistance, he should recommend that the employee seek the help of skilled, professional counselors.

Unsatisfactory home conditions or social experiences, ill health, unpleasant job conditions, or the inability to maintain a satisfactory standard of living will often have a vital bearing on the way the employee responds to his job. Stability in the home or job environment is likely to help the individual to withstand the frustrations of the other.

---

[15] John G. Stratton, "Law Enforcement Spouses Program: Review and Follow Up," *Law and Order*, 26, No. 4 (April, 1978), 56–59; see also W. C. Richard and D. D. Fell, "Health Factors in Police Job Stress," in *Job Stress and the Police Officer: Identifying Stress Reduction Techniques*, ed. W. W. Kroes and J. L. Hurrell (Washington, D.C.: Department of Health, Education, and Welfare, December, 1975).

SOME COMMON REACTIONS TO FRUSTRATIONS

Susceptibility to frustrations varies with individuals. The threshold level at which frustrations have different effects upon behavior is called the *frustration tolerance*.[16] The same situations do not cause frustrations in all individuals or may cause different degrees of frustration in different people, and, consequently, different reactions. The emotionally matured, stable person has fewer frustrations and is more capable of finding a solution to potentially frustrating conditions than is the unstable person with infantile emotional development.

Sometimes the speed with which an individual abandons his attempts to find a solution to a problem or the intensity of his frustration reaction seems to be out of proportion to the apparent cause of the reaction. A sequence of minor events may trigger abnormal behavior. The individual's frustration tolerance may seem to have disappeared. A simple explanation may or may not be available. The cause may be due to a sequence of minor frustrations. He may have had little sleep the night before, overslept, missed breakfast, had an argument with his wife, found no place to park when he arrived at work, been berated by his supervisor for being late to roll call. Although each incident singly probably would have caused little emotional disturbance, a combination of small incidents may well exceed an individual's threshold of frustration.

Intense frustration might be the result of the blocking of a great desire to attain a goal or the inability of the individual to accept a substitute goal. The nearer the goal when the individual is thwarted in reaching it, the greater the frustration and the greater will be the reaction to such frustration.[17]

Usually, if the cause of the condition is not obvious, it can be uncovered by patient counseling by the alert supervisor. Often the cause can be easily eliminated. The supervisor should realize that things cause less frustration than people because cooperation and understanding are not expected from things. Where the frustrations are caused by people, the problem can usually be removed by commonsensical action. If two partners are unable to get along, obviously the simple solution might involve determining the nature of the conflict and the reason for it and dissolving the partnership if the conflict could not be resolved. The supervisor should be constantly aware, however, of the possibility that the apparent cause of conflict may not be the real cause.

[16] David Krech and Richard S. Crutchfield, *Elements of Psychology*, 2nd ed. (New York: Alfred A. Knopf, Inc., 1969), pp. 757–58.

[17] Charles F. Haner and Patricia Ann Brown, "Clarification of the Instigation to Action Concept in the Frustration Aggression Hypothesis," *Journal of Abnormal and Social Psychology*, 51 (1955), 204–6.

Some of the more common reactions to frustrations frequently encountered by the supervisor on the job cannot be prevented because they are spontaneous. Other reactions may be tempered or the cause might be eliminated if he is alert to the symptoms of conflict.

Attack or aggression

Since human beings cannot remain static for long, they tend to meet frustration with aggression. When the aggressive behavior conflicts with social standards, suppression takes place. With suppression comes more frustration, but what has been suppressed will seek expression in some manner.[18] It must be kept in mind, however, that not all aggression is necessarily the product of frustration. Other causes may have contributed. Frustration does not inevitably lead to aggressive action. Instead, other reactions may follow.[19] These reactions will be described in following pages.

Some forms of aggression resulting from frustration are direct and undisguised. Other forms are indirect and subtle. Hostility may be present with or without physical or verbal attack or noncooperation. Attack or noncooperation reactions may not always be recognized and understood because these responses vary widely in individuals and because often the individual does not attack the barrier directly.

If anger or hostility is smoldering inside, it may result in sudden or unexpected reactions of a physical, mental, or verbal nature directed at a person or thing. Gardner and Moore [20] point out the devastating effects of hostility. They observe, "The hostile individual who seeks justification for his own inner anger and resentment in the world around him can cause havoc in an organization . . . where aggressive acts against the individual are not uncommon. In such instances, the hostile individual literally invites hostile action against him so that what started as a delusion ends in reality."

When a person is afraid to express anger or annoyance outwardly, he often engages in passive hostility symptomized by sullenness, uncommunicativeness, or grumbling. He may carry out the boss's wishes to the letter and to a ridiculous extreme. The motive is often to make the boss suffer because of his own words. The opening of communication channels might help to reduce these feelings. If the subordinate is made to

[18] A. T. Poffenberger, *Principles of Applied Psychology* (New York: Appleton-Century-Crofts, 1942), pp. 582–83.

[19] Krech and Crutchfield, *Elements of Psychology*, pp. 316–18.

[20] Burleigh B. Gardner and David G. Moore, *Human Relations in Industry: Organizational and Administrative Behavior*, 4th ed. (Homewood, Ill.: Richard D. Irwin, Inc., 1964), p. 66.

state his complaint clearly even though what he wants cannot be done, he will at least be made to realize that he has had an opportunity to express himself and that his feelings have been considered. If the supervisor overreacts, he will only reinforce the subordinate's act of complaining.[21]

Talking back, picking arguments, faultfinding, name calling, excessive criticizing, belittling, and sarcastic or bossy behavior are examples of *direct verbal attack. Indirect verbal attack* may take place in the form of rumor-spreading activities, the telling of uncomplimentary stories and jokes, and the making of disparaging remarks about the object of the attack.[22] *Noncooperation* may occur in the form of loafing, work slowdowns, wastage, excessive rest periods, absenteeism, leaving the job before the end of the day, doing only what is required, failing to help resolve common problems occurring in the work situation, or other acts indicating marginal job interest. Belligerence may be reflected in the "chip on the shoulder" attitude, sullenness, irritability, quarrelsomeness, and so forth. A physical attack on equipment or other physical facilities, or even an attack on individuals, may be the concomitant of frustration.

The tendency of the aggressor is to attack the source of the frustration. At times, he is afraid or unable to attack the person he feels is the obstacle, so he vents his anger senselessly on substitute persons or objects because they happen to be convenient. At times, a motorist, a minor offender, or an innocent bystander becomes the symbol of the frustrating barrier and is subjected to verbal or physical attack.[23] Usually, such substitutes are easy objects of aggression. They are often unable to strike back. A citizen, subordinate, or even a wife may become the victim of an aggressive act.

At other times, the frustrated individual himself becomes the object of his attack through self-criticism for failure or even self-punishment.[24] He may drink excessively, overwork, worry, engage in self-pity, or develop feelings of guilt. When the attack cannot be directed toward a specific object, the frustrated individual may remain hostile and search for other avenues of escape.

In these attack situations, the individual may become so absorbed

21 Richard M. Greene, Jr., *The Management Game—How to Win with People* (Homewood, Ill.: Dow Jones–Irwin, Inc., 1969), p. 25.

22 John Dollard, Neal E. Miller, Leonard W. Doob, O. H. Mowrer, and Robert R. Sears, in collaboration with Clellan S. Ford, Carl Iver Hovland, and Richard T. Sollenberger, *Frustration and Aggression* (New Haven, Conn.: Yale University Press, 1943), pp. 44–47.

23 Maier, *Frustration: The Study of Behavior Without a Goal*, p. 264.

24 Dollard, Miller, Doob, Mowrer, and Sears, *Frustration and Aggression*, pp. 44–47.

in his reaction that he will temporarily forget his original goal. The supervisor may then have considerable difficulty in understanding the motive of the attack. He may have even more difficulty in attempting to satisfy the motives of the individual.

Aggression has two main functions

The view generally accepted is that the first of the two functions of aggression involves the wresting of satisfaction from the outside world in the drive toward a goal which is blocked. The second involves a desire to hurt or destroy the source of the pain—those things or persons who are symbols of the barrier.[25] Both motives may require satisfaction before the attack reaction ceases. If the individual receives satisfaction of his attack motives, he may end the attack. If the initial frustration remains, however, the attack may recur. In other situations, the attack may continue for some time after the frustration stimuli have been removed. Tests with animals and humans have shown that when a need is thwarted, the frustration that occurs is likely to persist long after the original frustration-producing stimuli have ceased. When gratifying activities are interrupted and not brought to a successful conclusion, the individual is likely to continue the interrupted activity, or to have a desire to do so, long after the interruption, especially when the interruption is threatening to the individual or the desire to achieve the goal is intense.[26] This may explain the intense desire in some individuals to gamble or drink or otherwise indulge in what, to them, is a pleasant pastime. This condition may also give rise to a condition wherein the supervisor must engage in follow-up to any corrective action he may be required to take in order to prevent a recurrence of the unacceptable conduct; but he must do so in a constructive way or his acts may be interpreted as an attempt to "get him" and only worsen the problem.

If these attack motives are blocked and the person is not able to take aggressive action, he may engage in other substitutes such as noncooperation instead of criticism, or a different type of reaction such as rationalization or giving up will take place. In other cases the individual will repress his aggressive tendencies. The degree of control he exercises is directly related to the amount of punishment he is liable to sustain if he carries out his aggressive act.[27]

[25] Percival M. Symonds, *Dynamic Psychology* (New York: Appleton-Century-Crofts, 1949), pp. 72–74.

[26] George F. Dudycha, *Applied Psychology* (New York: The Ronald Press Company, 1963), p. 265.

[27] Willard E. Parker and Robert W. Kleemeier, *Human Relations in Supervision: Leadership in Management* (New York: McGraw-Hill Book Company, 1951), p. 125.

Giving up or resignation

When emotional conflicts with their resultant frustrations are frequent or continuous and attack reactions are not available to the individual, he may give up all attempts to satisfy a motive and adopt an attitude of resignation. His hope for a solution will be absent as will his esprit de corps. Discouragement will often cause bitterness or apathy. The individual will not ordinarily be responsive to praise or criticism. He must be approached patiently and given renewed hope and self-confidence. He should be helped to establish new goals and interests. Sometimes this can be accomplished by giving him added responsibility and an understanding that someone has confidence in him. If his self-esteem is not reestablished, this type of individual often becomes the marginal producer. There are frequently no readily available solutions for such a mental attitude if it involves true resignation; however, the condition may be but a temporary one reflecting a depressed state of mind and, as such, can usually be corrected along the lines just discussed. As a last resort, separation of the individual from the service may eventually be in order to preserve the morale of the organization.

Escape

An individual, finding that the efforts needed to fulfill an objective are greater than he desires to make, or facing what appears to him to be an insoluble problem, or lacking self-confidence in his ability to perform, often attempts to escape from his dilemma by physically or mentally withdrawing. If he has a problem the solution to which seems beyond his reach, he will run away from it. He will try to make himself believe that this course of action will relieve his obligation to himself or others for meeting the problem head on. He may revert to daydreaming or become ill. He may remain absent from his job, ask for a transfer, resign, or just avoid doing the task. He will often spend more effort in avoiding it than he would spend in doing it.

Escapism should not be confused with laziness or lack of motivation, wherein the employee will avoid doing what he is supposed to do because he is not inclined to put forth the necessary effort.

Psychosomatic illnesses such as headaches, stomach upset, or nervous disorders are often caused by anxieties or frustrations. They are not always actually physically caused illnesses, but are nonetheless very real to the individual. Often they are physiological manifestations intimately dependent upon the external environment.[28] Often, when the unpleasant

[28] George Saslow and Joseph D. Matarazzo, "Psychosomatic Phenomena," in *An Introduction to Clinical Psychology*, ed. Irwin A. Berg and L. A. Pennington (New York: The Ronald Press Company, 1966), pp. 270–300.

external conditions are removed or the individual is helped to face his problems realistically, the symptoms disappear.

Sometimes the individual escapes from frustrating situations by an imaginary accomplishment of his goals. This daydreaming is harmless when it stimulates him to real accomplishment, but it is more often harmful because it is not constructive. It may provide satisfaction without achievement or it may substitute for action and effort. It usually results in loss of time.

Rationalization or excuse finding

Sometimes an individual will develop certain defenses in the form of explanations or excuses to help save face or preserve his pride and excuse himself for failures to achieve his goals or fulfill his responsibilities. He will attempt to justify some action he has taken or failed to take. He may attempt to save face by blaming poor tools, improper training, or lack of it, deficient education, or some physical factor. He will do almost anything, but accept the blame himself. When he assigns it to some external object rather than to himself, he is said to have engaged in *projection*.[29] He may pass the blame on to the supervisors, saying that he should have been told of his poor work, or he may try to pass the buck to others and blame them for his failures. Blaming someone or something else may help him absorb the impact of his failure.

The person may insist that what he wanted and did not get was not important anyway. This sour grapes attitude tends to reduce in his mind the importance of the goal and makes the frustration attending the failure easier to endure.

Rationalization is a most common reaction to failure. If it causes a person to refuse to assume personal responsibility for anything, it is harmful.[30] When it impairs a person's ability to perceive things as they are and respond to reality, it becomes destructive.[31] It becomes a serious problem when the individual fools himself into believing that he has established adequate relationships with others or has done a reasonable job in carrying out his duties and responsibilities when, in fact, it is commonly known that he has done neither.[32]

Occasionally, the individual lacking confidence in himself and not

[29] Gordon S. Watkins, Paul A. Dodd, Wayne L. McNaughton, and Paul Prasow, *The Management of Personnel and Labor Relations,* 2nd ed. (New York: McGraw-Hill Book Company, 1950), p. 174.

[30] Calhoon, *Managing Personnel,* p. 260.

[31] Gardner and Moore, *Human Relations in Industry: Organizational and Administrative Behavior,* p. 65.

[32] Tead, *The Art of Leadership,* p. 225.

expecting to achieve a goal he has set for himself will find excuses in advance by magnifying all possible difficulties and then really not trying to achieve the goals. Excuse finding may protect him from the effects of frustration to a degree, but it prevents him from facing the situation and making a real effort to solve the problem confronting him. For example, he may attempt to blame a lack of recognition for his efforts upon a supervisor's favoritism rather than face the real issue of his own poor work. He is blind to the fact that he is using excuses because he regards them as sound reasoning. The excuses may not be the real reasons for failure, but to him they are good reasons. The nonperformer is likely to rationalize, "You don't get into trouble for what you don't do but for what you do." Excuses of this nature are so easily used and their face-saving protection is so satisfying that their use tends to become habitual.

Rationalization practiced by supervisors is particularly damaging to the organization when it is used to relieve the supervisor of the necessity of seriously tackling problems which are likely to be frustrating. The harm can be incalculable when he blames subordinates for his failures, or blames the boss for an unpopular order instead of selling such an order to the workers and telling them that he expects it be carried out, or if he refuses to confront a "problem employee" because "there's nothing you can do with a guy like that." All he feels he can do is to hide his head in the sand and hope the problem will go away. Other employees will soon begin to suspect his fortitude. By such failures, the supervisor will place a premium on nonconformance.

Often, these reactions will be combined with others. An individual may give up all attempts to satisfy his motives, and in addition he may mentally withdraw from the situation in an attempt to escape from reality. At other times, he may engage in excuse finding and may at the same time become aggressive with or without verbal hostility. He may even rationalize his own aggressiveness and blame it upon provocation.

Regression

At times a frustrated individual will abandon problem solving for an immature or even infantile type of regressive action. He may regress to a stage where his problem began. He may revert to earlier, less matured methods of performing his work. Some will weep or revert to infantile temper tantrums. Some will develop highly sensitive characteristics. Temperamental outbreaks become frequent with such employees because they develop extremely low frustration-tolerance levels. Often, they do not react objectively to criticism and have learned that they may gain their way more often than not by throwing a temper tantrum. Many supervisors will "back off" rather than undergo the vitriolic attacks and abusive treatment they are often subjected to by this type of individual. Their retreat may be prudent at times but generally will only tend to erode their authority. If their position in the matter is correct and justified, the attack should not deter them from doing what needs to be done.

Regression in a supervisor has particularly damaging effects. It may cause him to depart from his philosophy of firm supervision, which he feels has detracted from his popularity although it has earned respect for him in the past. He may retreat to the weaker, permissive form of supervision if he can gain ego satisfaction from it. He may stop delegating work, feeling he has lost confidence in his subordinates.

Immature reaction resulting from regression substitutes for growth and problem-solving ability. The greatest danger, however, is that it lessens a person's adequacy to perform his job.

Adler's psychology [33] assumed that individuals tend to repeat infantile acts when they have found such behavior helpful in achieving their desires. The screaming child seeking gratification of a desire will continue to use this device so long as it achieves results. The weeping employee will weep when results are achieved thereby.

The supervisor can accomplish much practical supervision if he understands Adler's concepts. Regressive reactions may be a means used to avoid unacceptable behavior. The individual avoids seeing his emotional conflicts maturely and tries to deal with them by reverting to infantile behavior. Some display childlike reliance upon their supervisor to make decisions which they themselves are perfectly capable of making. If the supervisor permits them to escape the responsibility which is theirs, he will only contribute further to the employee's regressive reactions.

Such reactions provide no constructive avenues of escape from the conflict. They often result in complete breakdown in normal employment relations.[34]

Fixation

When an individual experiences fixation, he keeps repeating a response even if it is not effective. Alternative solutions are not tried. For example, if an employee is criticized too severely for the way he performs

[33] Joel R. Butler, Felicia A. Pryor, and Henry E. Adams, "Psychoanalytically Oriented Therapy," in *An Introduction to Clinical Psychology*, ed. Irwin A. Berg and L. A. Pennington (New York: The Ronald Press Company, 1966), p. 608.

[34] Watkins, Dodd, McNaughton, and Prasow, *The Management of Personnel and Labor Relations*, p. 174.

an operation, he may become "frozen" or fixated in using the wrong method over and over. The individual often becomes inflexible in meeting new situations. His attitudes do not change. They persist despite seemingly conclusive evidence that a contrary attitude would serve better.

PREVENTING FRUSTRATION

The most obvious means of preventing frustrations arising out of the work environment is the discovery and removal of the underlying causes. This is often an extremely difficult task since the causes may not be readily apparent. Management personnel must recognize that many problems result from the human and physical factors related to the job. The work situation is a fertile source of frustrations since it restricts the worker's freedom of action and, at the same time, imposes upon him positive demands. He is responsible for meeting performance standards and is also expected to conduct himself in a manner which best serves the needs of the organization. These dual responsibilities are sometimes incompatible to the employee. The law enforcement officer might ask, "How can I do an effective traffic enforcement job and make the motoring public like it and what I stand for?" The demands of selective traffic enforcement, general public welfare, and good public relations are seemingly at odds. The officer feels the pressures from his supervisor if he does not perform his enforcement duties reasonably well; he is more often than not castigated by the errant motorist for a traffic citation and simultaneously often accused of being an "eager beaver" by his fellow officers if his performance records exceeds theirs. No wonder he often becomes frustrated.

Watkins et al.[35] observe, "Tensions arising from the interpersonal relationships on the job can be reduced mainly through improvement of the supervisory program." Knowing that frustration reactions tend to be emotional and seemingly pointless at times, the supervisor working toward reduction of frustration-producing situations must recognize the limited value of threats, coercion, arguments, or appeals to logic as a means of corrective action when aberrant behavior occurs among his employees. Instead, he will maintain a tolerant, objective, and helpful attitude without retreating to a point of permissiveness. He will keep in touch with employee attitudes and moods so that he may perceive possible causes of frustrations which can be remedied. He will remove them wherever possible. He will keep channels of communication open with his subordinates and superiors so that pertinent information may

[35] *Ibid.*, p. 179.

flow up, down, and across organizational channels. He should continuously strive to make frustrating situations more acceptable if they cannot be removed.

The supervisor should make every effort to satisfy the motives of his subordinates by helping them develop feelings of security through the process of informing them about matters affecting them and by providing them with a means of self-expression. He should keep in mind that the individual who is not well liked or the one who feels inferior or lacks social adjustment may need additional attention to help him in overcoming his sense of insecurity. Extra encouragement and attention to the training of the individual who lacks confidence in his ability may be indicated to help in relieving his feelings of inadequacy. Special effort may be needed to help such individuals achieve a level of performance which conforms at least generally with the group average. When employees are unable to reach this average, they become easily discouraged and frustrated.

Many frustrations can be prevented if the supervisor makes an effort to place his subordinates in the assignments for which they are best suited. Ordinarily, if he does this, the employee will perform best and will develop fewer frustrations arising out of his job activities.

Likewise, the supervisor will assist his subordinates greatly in reducing job-connected frustrations if he helps them to establish realistic goals. Fryer [36] stated, "When goals are adopted which are impossible or unreal, frustration is likely, resulting in uncontrolled anger, psychomotor tension, depression, remorse, embarrassment, and sometimes withdrawal from reality and a complete change of personality." The supervisor is bound to be confronted with many emotional conflicts in his subordinates. He will reduce their effects whenever possible if he cannot eliminate the conflicts themselves. He will make every effort to provide a work environment wherein each employee can best satisfy his basic drives in a manner which best comports with organizational objectives.

RELIEVING FRUSTRATION: SOME COMMONSENSICAL APPROACHES

Not always will the supervisor possess the technical ability to provide relief for a frustrating condition. Often he will not even be able to ascertain the cause; however, if he is alert, he may readily recognize symptoms of distressful emotional conflicts. He can then go about taking action to

[36] Douglas H. Fryer, "Motivation and Self-Direction," in *Handbook of Applied Psychology*, ed. Douglas H. Fryer and Edwin Henry (New York: Holt, Rinehart and Winston, Inc., 1950), p. 99.

relieve the condition by helping the troubled individual to overcome his frustrations or see them in a different light. Studies have indicated that persons are more likely to follow the suggestions of the supervisor if he has demonstrated an ability to help others solve their problems.[37]

If the frustration reaction involves aggression which the individual is unable to suppress because of his deficient control mechanisms, it would seem that relief is most adequately achieved by directing the aggression into harmless channels.[38] The individual may be directed toward constructive activity by means such as a challenge to show others what he can really do or he may be assigned added responsibilities or placed in a position that absorbs more of his energy.

The provision of an opportunity for self-expression as an important corrective technique is generally recognized.[39] Patient nondirective counseling wherein the individual is given the opportunity to engage in catharsis by talking out the situation will provide an outlet for reducing his anger, developing some objectivity, and gaining insight into his problems. It will tend to make seemingly intolerable situations tolerable. This often reveals the inconsistencies of his problems and is one of the best means of changing his interpretation of the situation. If he can be encouraged to assume an objective rather than a purely subjective view, frustration can be relieved without permitting expressions which will only worsen the matter.[40] He can usually be made to see the abusive citizen, for example, as a problem to be solved rather than as a source of frustration. If he can be given some insight into problems such as this, he might often change his interpretation of a particular problem by placing himself in the position of the other person. If aggressive behavior is involved, however, the supervisor must avoid indulging it to a point where he is only reinforcing violent behavior.

The supervisor should help relieve his troubled subordinate of frustration by providing an opportunity for the achievement of a feeling of success. If motivation results, the frustration need not be a harmful experience; but if it results in continued failure from trying to make old methods work, the effects can be devastating upon the individual. Since frustration is normally associated with goals of some sort, the

[37] Bernard M. Bass, *Conformity, Deviation, and a General Theory of Interpersonal Behavior in Conformity and Deviation* (New York: Harper & Row, Publishers, 1961), pp. 72–73.

[38] Maier, *Frustration: Behavior Without a Goal*, p. 106. See also Gail S. Fidler and Jan W. Fidler, *Occupational Therapy* (New York: Macmillan Publishing Co., Inc., 1965), pp. 41–42.

[39] Maier, *Frustration: Behavior Without a Goal*, p. 216.

[40] *Ibid.*, p. 107.

supervisor should be cautious to avoid action that will be harmful to goal achievements. When an individual gives up his desire to achieve positive, constructive goals, he is likely to give up efforts to better himself.

Since sensitivity to frustration is greater during ill health or fatigue, rest or medical attention may be considered at times. If the frustrating conditions produce severe emotional or mental disorders which persist, professional attention might be in order.

There is the tendency for some to pick up a few stray principles of psychology and psychiatry and try to apply them without a basic understanding of human behavior. A little information may be a dangerous thing. It is best, therefore, that the supervisor, in attempting to determine why certain behavior occurs, confine himself to those aspects of the personality which can be readily observed, for even the professional therapist encounters substantial difficulties in attempting to analyze human behavior. Rogers [41] said, "Psychotherapy is at the present time in a state of chaos . . . the present is a period in which the most diverse methods are used, and in which the most divergent explanations are given for a single event."

SUMMARY

A motive is a conscious or unconscious drive that prompts an individual to take action to achieve a goal. When motives are obstructed, frustration often occurs. The individual usually tries in different ways to solve his problems. If the goal is not important, he may disregard the frustration and forget the matter. If the goal is important, the usual reaction is to go around the obstacle, remove or attack it, or compensate by finding substitute goals to replace the original one. Stable, emotionally mature persons are usually capable of meeting normal problems and solving them. The unstable, infantile individual is less able to adjust to problems. He has a lower frustration tolerance. He develops a sense of failure, irritation, and emotional inflexibility. His reactions then become a real challenge to his supervisor.

The barriers blocking goals may be external or internal. Physical obstacles, human impediments, or situational factors are some of the external barriers, while internal barriers involve emotional conflicts. Either a single barrier or a combination of obstacles may give rise to frustrations.

[41] Carl R. Rogers, "Psychotherapy Today or Where Do We Go from Here?" in *Readings in Abnormal Psychology: Human Values and Abnormal Behavior*, ed. Walter D. Nunokawa (Chicago: Scott, Foresman and Company, 1965), p. 92.

The individual experiencing frustration and not being capable of adapting to it may develop aggression symptoms. He may physically attempt to attack the person or thing which obstructs the realization of his goal, he may verbally attack the barrier, or he may become noncooperative.

A common form of reaction to conflict involves hostility on the part of the individual. This reaction may be expressed by aggressive behavior against a person or thing. On other occasions, the individual may adopt an attitude of resignation, make a mental or physical withdrawal, or try to rationalize his failures and shortcomings. Each of these reactions poses a special problem for the supervisor. He should provide an opportunity for emotional security wherever and by whatever means possible. He should give his subordinates opportunity for self-expression.

Frustrations may best be prevented if the underlying causes are discovered and removed. Threats, arguments, and appeals to reason have limited corrective value in relieving frustrations. Rather, the supervisor will assist his subordinates troubled with frustrations by encouraging them to view such conflicts in their true perspective, by helping them to gain objectivity and insight into their problems. He will give each individual an opportunity to ventilate his feelings through the technique of nondirective counseling. He will assist him in developing attainable goals or subgoals if he has selected unreasonable ones. He may change the subordinate's assignment to give him an opportunity to adjust under more favorable conditions or to regain his emotional stability in a new environment. Rest or medical attention may be indicated in extreme cases. As a last resort, when other efforts have failed to find a workable solution to the individual's conflicts, psychiatric attention may be desirable.

REVIEW

Questions

1. Distinguish among drives, satisfactions, and needs.
2. Define catharsis and explain a simple method by which the supervisor might use it with a subordinate.
3. Discuss some of the reactions that might result from frustrations.
4. What are some of the overt manifestations of frustration? How may frustration reactions be covertly expressed?
5. What is the most obvious means of preventing frustrations?
6. Discuss some of the means of relieving frustration reactions once they have occurred.

Exercises

1. If you were called upon for assistance, explain how you would help an officer's spouse to adjust to his work. What factors would you stress?

2. Assume that one of your subordinates was passed over for promotion when he was at the top of a promotional list and someone below him was appointed. The subordinate becomes extremely frustrated and his work has deteriorated. Explain how you would approach this problem.

7

Principles of interviewing

An interview is an interchange of views and ideas between two or more persons. Its primary purpose is to obtain or impart information or influence attitudes or behavior. In each interview some functions common to others are involved, but each also has its own characteristics involving psychological interactions between two people with different knowledge, attitudes, feelings, and objectives. Sometimes it is difficult to reconcile these individual differences with the goals of the organization simply because an appreciation of such goals has not been adequately instilled into the minds of the members. For example, on occasion an employee will feel he has a valid grievance because his employer has not permitted him to engage in certain outside employment which involves a conflict of interest with his primary police position. The employee might find it easy to justify his rationale in such situations but difficult to accept the viewpoint of his supervisor, who demands that his subordinates consider their police employment to be of first importance.

Consulting with people is not solely the personnel officer's responsibility. It is one of the prime activities of every supervisory officer at all levels and requires a great portion of his time. If done effectively, the time spent will reap huge rewards. The skillful supervisor learns about his subordinates by hearing about them, by analyzing their work through the inspection process, and by talking with them. The last is one of his most important activities. The degree of his success in this activity is directly related to the effort expended. His technique will vary depending upon the objective to be accomplished. If he is to fulfill this objective in the most effective manner, he must develop his ability to motivate others, to change attitudes, and to obtain willing cooperation through purposeful face-to-face communications. He must also develop his working knowledge of the general principles of interviewing and counseling so that his methods can be adapted to meet the overall objective of a particular type of situation.

INTERVIEW VS. INTERROGATION

Interrogating, unlike interviewing, involves a process of questioning with the investigator usually assuming a dominant role in the relationship. True, both processes are often calculated to produce information; but the interviewer, unlike the interrogator, must often exchange his views with those of the person being interviewed. The interrogator seldom will place himself in a position of "giving" information. His job is to obtain such information without imparting any. If the latter practice is followed in the interview situation, it will often result in failure to accomplish the objectives of the meeting.

MAJOR FUNCTIONS OF THE INTERVIEW

The major functions of the interview are to obtain information (about a work or other situation, about the employee, or about a grievance); to communicate or give information (about policies or practices, or about services, behavior, or employee relationships); to motivate employees for the purpose of improving cooperation, production, or performance; to help solve personal and group problems through the consultation process; and to appraise the past, present, or future situation of the employee (with respect to his career, transfers, education, extradepartmental activities such as secondary employment, or his personal problems).

The significant characteristic about these functions is that they are involved, at least in part, in almost every interview. The differences in objectives to be accomplished will determine the amount of emphasis to be placed upon one or more of these functions. For example, the consultative approach is involved in differing degrees in many employee interviews, such as those relating to personal problems, discipline, and work progress as reflected by service ratings or job performance.

PREPARING FOR THE INTERVIEW

Good preparation for a personnel interview is just as essential to its success as it is in the case of interrogation of a suspect. Each interview requires forethought and planning. The objectives to be achieved should be carefully analyzed so that the interviewer may best direct his efforts toward those ends.

Preliminary planning

The degree of planning necessary will vary somewhat from interview to interview since each will require special consideration, depending upon the reason for conducting it. A written outline is often useful as a guide to assist the interviewer in covering salient points that he may wish to develop. This preliminary planning will be most useful if the facts available about the person to be interviewed are studied beforehand. Applications, personal history statements, files, correspondence, and other data that may give the interviewing supervisor some insight into the background of the person to be interviewed will give clues that may require further development during the interview. Preliminary planning should also involve an analysis of the point of view of the person to be interviewed—if evidence is at hand to permit this—so that potential misunderstandings may be avoided. The interviewer should analyze his own predilections and biases as well as those of the interviewee to avoid unnecessary conflicts.

The interview should be planned so that it need not be hurried. Sufficient time should be allowed to permit a relatively full development of facts and observations relevant to the situation. On occasion, there will be indicated the need for a second or third session depending on the nature of the information required. In any event, the objective should be reached without undue haste or waste of the supervisor's or interviewee's time.

Privacy

The hazards of conducting an interview in the presence of others should be recognized. The interviewing supervisor should make every effort to conduct it in privacy to help avoid possible inhibitions, which often limit frankness when persons other than those concerned are present.

Preparing questions

Questions should be prepared which may be used at first to establish the habit of answering if the question and answer technique is adopted. These should be framed so that they can be easily and willingly answered. Obviously, ambiguous, dual, or multiple-meaning questions should be avoided to prevent misunderstanding and confusion. Furthermore, they should be prepared with the objective of obtaining a true, unequivocal response. If the reply requires the interviewer to draw an inference from what is said, often such responses will be misinterpreted and further questioning will be required to obtain accurate information needed to qualify or explain the initial response. Such unnecessary use of questions might hamper free communications. Well-planned questions are sometimes necessary. They can be used to obtain maximum accuracy and completeness from responses. Inaccurate responses resulting from ill-prepared questions can be minimized if the interviewer has in mind the general and specific information he desires when he prepares certain alternative questions. These should be calculated to guide the interview into channels from which such information may be derived.

CONDUCTING THE INTERVIEW

The supervisor conducting an interview should employ a friendly, empathic attitude toward the employee interviewed. Any appearance that may be interpreted as a threat to the employee's security should be meticulously avoided, as it would likely produce results just opposite to those desired.

Opening of the interview

The interview should start on a note of obvious sincerity and reasonableness, with the interviewer stating the reason and objective simply and clearly. It should be developed in an atmosphere of friendliness, beginning on a pleasant topic, if possible, to help the interviewee to gain poise and a feeling of ease. In almost every interview, the initial conversation can relate to a matter of interest to the interviewee. Such an approach usually stimulates responses from him.

Use of questions

In using questions, an interviewer must recognize that they may guide the interview away from its true purpose. They may, however, be used to good advantage in starting the conversation or delving deeper into a specific area. Since utmost accuracy in response to the interview question is desirable, such a question should be framed in positive terms. A British psychologist, B. Muscio, found in early studies that questions framed in negative terms had a tendency to elicit inaccurate responses more frequently than did positive questions because negatives are somewhat more suggestive and cause a lessening of caution in response and decreased reliability.[1] Questions should be framed so that the trend of thought cannot be stopped by a "yes" or "no" answer. Rather they should be framed so that a continuity of thought will result and an issue can be developed as fully as need be. Likewise, questions should not lead the interviewee into a directed answer. He may try to please and, in doing so, avoid giving a true response. Questions such as, "You don't think the supervisors are stupid, do you?" or "Don't you like this graveyard shift?" may lead the interviewee into a structured answer. Rather, the question "How do you feel about working the graveyard shift?" may elicit the true feelings of the individual.

While it is true that the question-and-answer technique often plays an important part in police work, especially in the interrogation of suspects, the interview procedure wherein this technique is used is seldom entirely successful since questions seldom elicit the whole story. More frequently than not, the exclusive use of this procedure produces barriers and interferes with full communications.

ATTITUDE OF THE INTERVIEWER

Any semblance of a domineering, overly authoritative, or paternalistic attitude should be avoided since this might close avenues of communication. Ideally, mutual trust and confidence should be fostered between interviewer and person interviewed. To this end, a sincere, frank, and helpful attitude should be manifested to encourage the person interviewed to cooperate so that exaggeration and deceit may be minimized.[2]

In those interviews where the supervisor has been sought out by

[1] B. Muscio, "The Influence of the Form of the Question," *British Journal of Psychology*, 8 (1916), 351–89.
[2] W. V. Bingham and Bruce Victor Moore, *How to Interview* (New York: Harper & Row, Publishers, 1959), p. 14.

his subordinate for advice or "just talk," the supervisor should get to the problem at hand as soon as rapport is established. He should determine as clearly as possible the nature of the problem. Once the initial problem is isolated, it may require revision as the interview proceeds since the *real* problem often does not appear until it is detected from subtle indicators noted during the course of the interview. These are the clues that often lead to the true nature of what is meant. A grievance comment such as, "You know what he's like," says little but the direct question, "Just what is he like?" might force the employee to provide a more specific response.

The wise supervisor will realize that sudden and pronounced changes in his behavior in his relationships with his subordinates might be viewed with distrust by them and thus hinder personal relationships. He should, therefore, approach an interview with his usual manner, preferably friendly and calm. Any abruptness that might be inferred from the "Now, what's on your mind" approach may defeat the purpose of the interview from the beginning. Rather, an attempt must be made to develop rapport from a theme of mutual interest in good performance or continued service. These mutual interests can usually be illustrated by the problem at hand. For instance, in an interview involving a grievance, the supervisor might well at the start express his desire to remove causes for existing grievances in the interests of morale.

Rapport can be strengthened by a meticulous avoidance of argument, faultfinding, or recrimination since these acts will often force the employee to fight back to save face and, in doing so, might well destroy any accord which may have developed. The employee will seldom welcome a lecture on morality or cross-examination from the interviewer. These may be interpreted by him as an attack on his self-esteem and result in loss of cooperation. Criticism for the sake of criticism seldom accomplishes anything; but when accompanied with a sincere, objective attempt to be constructive, it can be effective without being considered a personal attack. The employee can often be led into a constructive solution to his own problem if he is encouraged to look at it objectively. The supervisor can then avoid direct criticism, which is often construed as offensive.

By displaying sincere interest in and consideration for the employee, the supervisor will start the process of building the employee's confidence. Respect, tolerance, and understanding of his viewpoints will contribute to success of the interview; and if the employee is permitted an opportunity to engage in catharsis, he may vent his true feelings and state his real opinions. The hostile employee often will not.

The arbitrary supervisor who cannot, or will not, see both sides of a problem and allows this one-sidedness to color his judgment will seldom make an interview an outstanding success. Even an officer who is lazy will resent the, "Why don't you get off the dime?" attitude of the supervisor who has made no attempt to use positive means to motivate him.

Employee-centered interview

In each interview, the person being interviewed should be the central figure at all times. This employee-centered characteristic requires that the supervisor suppress any tendency to be the dictator. He should actively engage in the "understanding listener" role. It is often said that as many superior officers climb the ladder of authority, their ears shrink and their mouths grow. Little is learned by talking—much can be learned by listening. Therefore, the wise interviewer will adopt a "big ears, little mouth" approach to the interview. He should always bear in mind that certain interviews will succeed only if the employee leaves feeling that at least he had his say. If he does not gain this impression but merely acquiesces, feeling that he "didn't have a chance," the interview must be considered a failure; and, as such, it tends to increase the barriers to good supervisor-employee relationships.

Active listening

In each interview, the successful interviewer will utilize the technique of understanding listening; and when true communication has taken place, the interviewer should adopt an attitude of active listening which will encourage the interviewee to express himself freely and stimulate continuing responses. No face-to-face communication can be effective without some listening on the part of the communicators.

The greatest learning occurs not through speaking but through the listening process, an art difficult for some supervisors. Understanding is a by-product of listening, through which one gains some insight into the speaker's desires, ideas, concepts, and attitudes. It is not a passive but an active function, which requires that the listener be actively attentive to what is said. It requires effort to listen actively and involves much more than hearing only that which one wants to hear. The listening must be a positive function so that the person speaking will be encouraged to reveal his real rather than his superficial feelings. In order that listening may be truly rewarding to the interviewer, it must be accompanied by an effort to understand what the speaker is really saying—to understand what he really means. This requires that the interviewer not only listen carefully to the declared problem but that he be observant to the hidden clues which might indicate the real problem.

Employment of the understanding-listening technique is often difficult for supervisors simply because they are not aware that the final objective of interviewing cannot be accomplished until the first objective of listening *and* understanding has taken place. This process involves considerable skill. All too often, supervisors are not good listeners because, as managers of people, they become habituated to speaking rather than listening, giving orders and directions more frequently than receiving them, and making decisions which affect others. As police officers, they often have an insistent desire "to tell" others or to get them to reveal something rather than to encourage free discussion and communications interplay between themselves and others. Often the supervisor's objective is to convince his subordinates of something or to acquire from them certain information upon which to make judgments and conclusions. Because of this, there often exists the tendency on the part of the supervisor to try from the beginning to impose his viewpoint on the interviewee rather than to attempt to understand that person's views.

In order to gain real understanding, two things must exist—a sincere desire on the part of the interviewer to gain a better understanding of others, their problem situation, and the degree of their involvement in such a situation, and a forthright approach to the interview designed to make such understanding possible. Basically, this involves a sensitivity on the part of the interviewer not only to what is being said but to the underlying feelings, attitudes, and motives which are reflected. Therefore, the interview should not be so closely structured as to discourage the person interviewed from "airing" his problem. Rather, he should be encouraged to engage in the process of mental catharsis so that his repressed feelings at the very base of the problem may be brought out. The interviewer should respond in such a limited way as to encourage such reactions. The interviewee should be helped to talk, not subjected to it. This might best be accomplished by brief natural responses to his comments; by an attentive manner, a nod of the head, a smile, an encouraging remark; or by a question framed from the interviewee's last statement. For example, should the interviewee remark, "Supervisors don't seem to take the interest in their subordinates they once did," the interviewer might repeat, "As they once did?" or "How is that?" Or if the interviewee says, "No matter how hard I work around here, I never seem to get any credit for it," the interviewer might then repeat, "You never seem to get credit?" A particular expression reflecting the attitude of the interviewee might be rephrased in the form of a question, but such a response should be framed with care to prevent adding new ideas or thoughts or directing the interview away from the real issue. For example, the person interviewed might exclaim, "I don't seem to be one of the fair-haired boys. I was passed over on the last promotional exam so I'm thinking about quitting." The response might be, "Do you feel the department has discriminated against you for some reason?" The mutual exchange that occurs produces an opportunity for the interviewer to develop rapport and for both parties to gain better acceptance of each other's viewpoints.

The process of active listening gives the person being interviewed an opportunity to understand himself better and, in so doing, to gain a different interpretation of the problem at hand. The interviewer also gains the opportunity to understand better the situation and the degree of the employee's personal involvement. In addition, the process provides a good opportunity for the interviewer to broaden the base upon which he must make judgments and take action.

The supervisor-interviewer must develop the skill of discriminating between symptoms and causes of problems in his relationships with his subordinates. In an attempt to put out the fire—the real cause of the problem—he must not get lost in the smoke screen of symptoms. This skill is one that can be gained by practice and experience.

It is not suggested that the supervisor-interviewer merely listen during the interview. This would rarely enable him to achieve his true objectives. Each situation will involve some giving and some receiving of information. The procedure does suggest, however, that the process of listening be emphasized, at least until the point is reached where understanding of the employee, his attitudes, and his views has developed sufficiently to enable the supervisor to make sound judgments and to take action as indicated. Having taken the action, he must listen to evaluate its effectiveness. On occasion, such as in the employment interview, the results will be most productive if the prospective employee is given the opportunity of free, unstructured expression; however, ordinarily the interview must be controlled to some degree to prevent excessive wandering from the subject at hand. Such necessary "structuring" can often be accomplished best by the skillful use of questions.

ELIMINATING BIAS

In his dealings with subordinates, it is fundamental that every supervisor should avoid allowing his personal prejudices and biases to color his judgment. This is especially important in the interview situation, where he must interpret overtones and draw conclusions from the oral interchanges. The effective supervisor will recognize the tendency of employees to say the things they think might impress him and thereby set up another barrier to clear understanding. He must make every effort to remove such barriers if he is to succeed in the interview. Unsound conclusions and faulty interpretations are apt to occur if he allows himself to subjectively react to the interview and permit his likes and dislikes to color his judgment. For example, merely because the supervisor has an intense dislike for drinkers, he should not shut his mind to the underlying cause of a drinking problem of a member of his unit which might be corrected and result in "saving" the employee for many productive years of service.

CONFIDENTIAL AGREEMENTS

On occasion, information will be offered the interviewer only under a confidential "agreement" arrangement. Should the interviewee proffer information under such conditions, the supervisor must carefully weigh the circumstances surrounding the offer before committing himself to accept it as a confidential communication. Once he has so committed himself, he must not breach the confidence, for to do so would grossly reflect upon his moral integrity. If such information turns out to be vital to the organization, he should endeavor to induce the employee to reveal it voluntarily. Keeping all information given to him under such conditions in strictest confidence is a basic requirement. If this cannot be done, the interviewer should avoid such "agreements." He must be prepared for unusual disclosures on occasion, however. When he is confronted with them, he should not display surprise or shock, nor should he attempt to support the employee's rationalization or give the impression of implied approval. He should avoid making any commitment or giving the impression that the information will be suppressed or withheld in confidence if misconduct is involved. Once he becomes a party to such information, he is responsible for taking whatever action is appropriate based on common sense and good judgment. He is accountable for failing to do so.

GIVING ADVICE

Often an employee with personal problems seeks out his supervisor for advice. Care should be exercised in this type of consultation to avoid providing a crutch to the employee who makes a feeble attempt—or even none—to solve what to him seems a perplexing problem. In this situation, the interviewer should avoid solving the employee's problem but should assist him in considering its ramifications and possible solutions by focusing his attention on aspects of the problem that might have been overlooked. No supervisor can afford to deprive a subordinate of the opportunity to engage in self-analysis and direction, nor can he afford to assume the responsibility for decision making, which should rightly rest on the shoulders of the employee.

Ordinarily, by encouraging him to air his problem, by giving him reassurance which he may be seeking, by suggesting alternative points for him to consider, and by enlisting his active participation in the problem at hand, the supervisor can guide the employee to his own solution by a process of reflection.[3] When the employee's problem has resulted from a lack of information, the interviewer should concentrate on furnishing the desired information rather than on giving advice.

PSYCHOLOGICAL REACTIONS

The interviewer should recognize the basic psychological aspects involved in the communication process and should avoid conditions which produce barriers or lead to faulty conclusions. He should be aware that his judgments cannot be sound if they are based on appearances alone. This factor, often called the halo effect, simply implies that, because persons look alike, one cannot accurately assume they will react alike. Thus each individual will require an independent approach in the interview. Likewise, the tendency to generalize or carry over a judgment from one particular trait or appearance to another must be avoided to prevent misconceptions and errors resulting from the belief that a person's habitual responses are transferred from one situation to another. Often the interviewer will allow an *unconscious imitation* to influence his judgment. This condition might result from the subtle moods which often permeate the interview and are transferred from it to the interviewer. Anger or hostility are emotions which are most often transferred from one person to another. It may cause an overly stern or overly cordial mood not in keeping with the dictates of the situation.

When the face value of information is questionable, it should be verified if possible; however, any hasty accusation might be best avoided until the accuracy of the information is determined, at which time an explanation from the interviewee might be indicated.

[3] Reflection is discussed in Chapter 17.

TYPES OF PERSONNEL INTERVIEWS

The most common interviews are those of an *informal* nature involving day-by-day personal contacts between the supervisor and his subordinates, those conducted for the purpose of evaluating a candidate's fitness for *employment,* those utilized to inform the employee of his *progress* on the job, those initiated by the employee who has a *grievance,* and those related to *disciplinary* actions or *separation* from the service. These will be treated in some detail in the following pages. There are numerous other types of situations, however, in which particular research projects require the interviewing of employees for specific purposes such as in job analysis and classification studies, personnel audits to fill specific personnel needs, labor relations studies, attitude surveys, polls, or salary studies. These are not treated here since they involve special research procedures not relating necessarily to the functions of the supervisor.

The informal interview

Perhaps one of the most productive sources of information which might be used by the police supervisor is the day-by-day, informal contact he has with his subordinates in office visits, inspections, at briefing sessions, in the locker room, or in the field. In each of these contacts, the adroit supervisor will employ the technique of listening and patient understanding as much as possible.

He will listen to what is meant rather than what is said because people often convey messages by subtle implication—preferring that approach to one involving direct statements.

The wise supervisor will allot some of his available field time to riding with patrol officers engaged in performing their field duties, talking informally with them, and observing their work. On occasion, the supervisor might make good use of an opportunity to join a subordinate at lunch or while making a follow-up investigation. Likewise, effective supervisors will make themselves available for after-hours interchanges with subordinates. The opportunity for coffee room conferences should not be overlooked as an exceedingly productive means of learning about personnel. The supervisor should, however, exercise great care to avoid making subtle comments or innuendoes concerning either subordinate or superior personnel which might be misquoted, misinterpreted, or misunderstood since distortions or "filtering" may start rumors or create reactions harmful to morale or barriers detrimental to good communications. In such contacts with his personnel, he should proceed on the assumption that they are likely to read hidden meaning into his comments.

A friendly approach with an expression of genuine interest in the employee, his family, problems, and interests will do much to foster true communications. Any appearance of prying should be avoided, however. The supervisor gains a splendid opportunity in such informal contacts to "establish a climate" for his subordinates—to let him know his expectations from them and to make himself approachable to them.

Employment interview

The employment interview has as its prime objective the appraisal of an applicant's qualifications for employment. The mental picture the interviewer obtains of the candidate's fitness or unfitness for the position is an excellent supplement to the more objective data obtained from the medical, psychological, intelligence, and other such examinations. This interview is a useful device for obtaining clues to other sources of information about the prospective employee such as former employment success or failure and other personal information. It provides an excellent opportunity for observing personal characteristics, behavior, and judgment under varying contrived situations, appearance, and habit patterns and may be used as a tool for obtaining subjective information such as beliefs, opinions, and attitudes not easily available from other sources. Of secondary importance is the giving of information about the position and the employing agency.

For purposes of full evaluation, the interviewer must inquire into those traits which are the best predictors of success—moral integrity, the ability to make decisions, insight into the problems of society and dealing with people, personal interests, poise, confidence, and temperament, which cannot be measured well by other tests. The supervisor must be aware, however, that the interview cannot measure with any high degree of precision slight personality differences between individuals.

The keynote of such an interview, whether it be in a group or individual setting, is that of patient listening coupled with the skillful use of suggestive questions to encourage the applicant to talk so that maximum perception can be gained into his inner nature, his mental processes, his real character, and his ability to express himself.

One of the commonest pitfalls the interviewer falls into is to assume that, if the applicant fits a given pattern in one trait, he will follow the same pattern in other similar traits. Obviously the rating of observable characteristics such as articulation ability or poise can be judged more precisely than the abstract psychological traits such as temperament or courage; but, by focusing attention on specific characteristics, the interviewer is forced to make an overall judgment in reliance on many such traits rather than on only one general impression which, if based on only one favorable attribute, may create a misleading halo effect.

Ordinarily, such interviews are too short; however, additional time should be made available whenever possible. It is suggested that a fifteen-minute interview be at least doubled. The expenditure of this added time will be well repaid if it results in the rejection of just one applicant whose unfitness for law enforcement work might not have been detected in the shorter interview.

Much information regarding the candidate's personal background can be obtained from a well-planned, personal history form completed by the applicant; however, such data often fail to reveal personality or temperament defects which might be detected by the interviewer in a face-to-face conversation.

The interview should be conducted in a cordial, informal atmosphere and in an honest, straightforward manner with the interviewer or interviewers attempting to place the applicant at ease. Any appearance of bias, discrimination, favoritism, or political patronage must be scrupulously avoided. It should be recognized that a certain amount of tension, inherent in the interview situation, will affect the applicant's responses in varying degrees. If such responses appear to be carelessly inaccurate, the suggestion that certain information can be verified may improve the respondent's accuracy. The interviewing supervisor should therefore generally avoid the "stress interview" at this stage or the "clever" approach unless there is an indication of a temperamental defect in the applicant which might be brought out by the application of a moderate amount of stress.

The interviewer should be alert for casual remarks made by the applicant upon taking his leave after the formality of the interview situation has ended. Much insight can often be gained into the inner thoughts and character of the interviewee at this time since he will often say revealing things which he might not have considered important during the interview. Likewise, comments made in an unguarded moment over a cup of coffee or lunch often provide much insight into an applicant's character.

The interviewer should bear in mind that, as a representative of management, he has an obligation to establish a favorable impression in the applicant's mind concerning the organization. The applicant should be left with a warm, friendly feeling toward the prospective employing agency, not with a feeling of bitterness which might result from an ill-prepared interview by the employer's representative who has neither the desire nor the ability to display compassion, courtesy, and understanding—even toward the most unacceptable police candidate. Bingham [4] sums up this process by stating, "The functions of the employment interview are: to get information, to give information, and to make a friend."

Information about the employing agency should be made available in an employment announcement; however, occasionally during the interview, the prospective employee will wish information which is not available from the literature provided. He should be given such data honestly and factually. It should include not only favorable information but that which involves the unfavorable aspects of the position sought. Such information should be made available promptly since it might furnish the basis for an affirmative decision by the desirable applicant who has not yet decided to accept employment.

Progress interview

The progress interview can be used effectively to inform the employee of his progress, to review his past performance, and to give constructive guidance concerning improvement required. The objective of the interview is to aid him to engage in self-appraisal. All too often, in those agencies which use periodic service rating procedures, the service rating interview is delayed until long after such reports have been prepared, if it is conducted at all. Such an interview is frequently avoided by the rating supervisor because of his reluctance to discuss any low ratings with the concerned subordinate. Progressive systems require such discussion with the employee, however, since rating reports furnish a basis for corrective training, provide opportunity for the employee to view himself as others view him, and learn from his supervisor how his past and present performance are rated and what improvement might be indicated in the future.

The wise supervisor will avail himself of all such opportunities to discuss the employee's performance as a means of aiding the substandard employee to improve his performance and commending the high producer for a job well done. Properly conducted, such interviews will have a very positive and beneficial effect upon the morale of employees.

The supervisor conducting the interview should consider the effect the discussion may have on the morale of the particular subordinate. His approach should be varied for each employee accordingly.

Facts which are pertinent to the discussion should be clearly in mind. The interviewer may find it necessary to prove a disputed point to avoid demoralizing the employee. The strengths and weaknesses about

[4] W. V. Bingham, "The Three Functions of the Interview in Employment," *Management Review,* January, 1926, p. 36.

which the conversation will revolve should be reviewed before the interview takes place. Available information should be obtained concerning the employee's background. Rating reports by other supervisors, medical history records, and other personnel data should be reviewed in preparing for the interview.

Sufficient time should be allotted for the discussion. If it is a hurried affair, the employee is likely to gain the impression that the interview is merely a formality and that the supervisor would like to get it over with as soon as possible because he is busy with more important things; yet few of his duties, in reality, are more important than this training function.

The interview should not be utilized merely as an excuse to "lower the boom." It should be conducted in a relaxed, friendly, helpful, understanding, and constructive atmosphere. The supervisor must remember that he is always in charge of the meeting and should avoid becoming apologetic or defensive about it. Neither should he make excuses for his ratings. Points should not be argued. Rather, a specific and constructive approach should be in order.

Employees seldom like vague, general comments about their performance. Therefore, the supervisor should be as specific as possible about his objectives. Good performance should be stressed at the outset with sincere, willing credit for the employee's strong points. This should then be followed by telling him in specific and constructive terms what is wrong and how he can improve. This sandwich technique allows the employee to receive objective criticism in small bits rather than in large, often harmful bites. Weaknesses should be discussed in a factual, objective manner. Personal criticism should be avoided to avert stifling the discussion. The employee should be encouraged to answer his own problems whenever possible; but the supervisor should be prepared to aid him if necessary.

The objective of the meeting should be constantly kept in mind so that collateral issues not relevant to the discussion can be avoided. It is imperative for the supervisor to convince the employee of their mutual goals, objectively and constructively, in a manner calculated to avoid bitterness and recrimination. Once this difficult problem has been overcome, a prime objective of the evaluation procedure—to improve performance—will have been accomplished. The California Highway Patrol[5] counsels its supervisors with reference to the personal development interview, "The guiding principle is that the supervisor should provide the member with a firm sense of direction for self-improvement,

[5] Department of California Highway Patrol, *Supervisor's Handbook: No. 1, Personal Development Program and Forms* (Sacramento, Calif.: Department of California Highway Patrol, 1968), p. 4.

based on those factors needed by the member to bring about his maximum development."

Excessive leniency by the supervisor seldom provides good results nor does it often produce desired reactions of changing attitudes because level of performance is largely dependent on attitudinal factors. Supervisors should not fall into the trap of being too understanding and mild. Police employees rarely respect the milquetoast supervisor; yet common courtesy and discreet forthrightness are always appreciated. The overly mild conversation may weaken the supervisor's position if he is later required to take disciplinary action against the employee for unacceptable performance. Tribunals reviewing the action may attach considerable significance to any failure on the part of the supervisor to inform his subordinates of substandard or unsatisfactory performance. Usually, they will expect that such employees will have been placed on notice that improvement is required. In the absence of such notice, disciplinary action cases are frequently dismissed or reversed.

Every attempt must be made to avoid comparing the interviewee with other individuals because this will only engender bitterness and personal animosity. The supervisor should avoid undue emphasis on the police employee's production based on raw statistics from accomplishment records. The validity of such records as a sole criterion for personnel evaluations is subject to attack and will seldom convince the employee that he has been rated fairly. Rather, the adroit supervisor will base his discussion, in the case of the substandard employee, upon careful analysis of those specific factors which reflect qualitative and quantitative performance as well as those which reflect personal relationships with other employees and the public. Fundamental to this interview is an objective and constructive manner.

The employee should be encouraged to express how he feels about his performance, and disapproval should not be shown when he does so. The art of listening should be developed and applied to each interview as was described in detail previously. The fair supervisor will be prepared to acknowledge any problem he may have caused the employee because of the supervisory methods followed without apologizing for them. This acknowledgment should be used judiciously, however, lest it provide a crutch for the employee to use for rationalizing his deficiencies. The supervisor should be aware that his relationships with his subordinates may have been interpreted differently by them from the way he had anticipated. He should look at his methods whenever possible through his subordinates' eyes to gain better insight into the effect his methods have upon them.

The interview that results in neither satisfaction nor constructive guidance for the concerned employee is wasted. It achieves nothing and should not have occurred in the first place. The interviewee should leave the interview feeling, at least, that something has been accomplished—that his efforts have been recognized; that he has gained a fresh, revitalized viewpoint; or that he has had some reassurance from the supervisor.

Each interview should be followed up to determine by casual questions, observation, or inspection if any changes have occurred in the employee's outlook, attitude, or performance. If further interviews seem indicated, they should be held as circumstances indicate. They should be made easily available to the employee should he so desire.

Grievance interview

Every supervisor should be sensitive to the needs of employees who have a real or imagined grievance. He should recognize that such grievances, even though imaginary, are always "real" in the mind of the employee who feels he has been wronged. As a result, resentment and hostility arise which quickly spread if other personnel are convinced that a fellow employee has been wronged or that a wrong has not been corrected. It is therefore incumbent on the supervisor to provide the employee an opportunity to air his grievance at the earliest moment. The cause for real grievances should, if possible, be corrected without delay. Conditions causing grievances but not easily correctable should be analyzed carefully by the supervisor. Wherever possible an opportunity should be provided for the employee to participate actively in the solution of the problem.

The employee with imagined grievances, though requiring an approach similar to that used in discussing real grievances, should be given the opportunity to see the problem in its true perspective. He will often recognize the imaginary nature of his belief that he has been wronged. Such an employee usually responds to patient reassurance, which often reestablishes his feeling of security.

The employee with an ill-founded grievance, perhaps resulting from punitive action imposed on him because of his own misconduct, often fails or refuses to recognize the need for maintenance of the particular brand of discipline to which he feels he has been subjected by the police agency. He should be allowed to talk out his problem in the process of mental catharsis. The supervisor must provide ample time for the employee to give his reasons for believing he has been wronged. Recriminations should be avoided by the supervisor since this will tend to aggravate the feeling of hostility which usually exists in this situation. Rather, the supervisor should forthrightly and patiently explain that the important consideration in the effects such punishment might have upon the officer's future career is not the severity of the punishment but the attitude with which the penalty is received.

Unless such interviews are conducted privately, with ample time, in one or more separate interviews to allow for complete ventilation by the employee, and unless they are held in an objective, constructive atmosphere, he may forever be lost to the agency as a productive, happy officer. Instead, he may become a disgruntled, marginal producer and will try to contaminate every other employee who will listen. Candor is a virtue but should be tempered on occasion by discretion and restraint on the part of the interviewer to avoid irreparable damage to the employee's pride and to prevent further recrimination and bitterness.

Problem-solving interview [6]

The supervisor frequently finds it necessary to help his subordinates to solve personal problems or otherwise adjust to a particular situation. Often called a consultation interview or the "chaplain interview," it might be likened to the function performed by the military chaplain or the police counselor.

The supervisor must approach such a meeting with a view of allowing the troubled subordinate to ventilate or air his problem. Frequently, merely by talking about the problem, the employee finds his own solution through reflection and self-analysis. Viewed in the calm atmosphere which the supervisor provides, such problems seldom appear as difficult to resolve as they do in the imagination of the employee. Often the supervisor is credited with a simple solution when in reality he provided only a patient, understanding ear, leaving the solution to the subordinate.

Disciplinary action interview

An employee against whom a disciplinary matter is pending should ordinarily be interviewed in two settings. He should be interviewed during the investigation.[7] Then he must be informed of the findings, conclusions, recommendations, and penalty, if any, stemming from the investigation when the matter has been finally resolved. It is the obligation of the supervisor to notify the subordinate of the findings in a

[6] Counseling to help employees solve many of their personal problems is discussed in Chapter 8.

[7] Interviews in connection with disciplinary investigations are discussed further in Chapter 10.

disciplinary investigation and the conclusions drawn from them as promptly as possible after conclusion of the inquiry. There are few situations that affect the officer's performance more adversely than an investigation into his conduct. While prompt interview and notification are usually indicated, the supervisor should make certain that he can perform this task objectively before attempting it. Rarely is it advisable to interview a derelict employee until the "cooling-off period" has passed to prevent anger from coloring the judgment of the interviewing supervisor.

The informative interview with the subordinate to notify him of the disposition of the investigation should be conducted promptly upon conclusion of the inquiry. This provides an opportunity for the supervisor to "clear the air" if the investigation proves that the allegations of misconduct were unfounded or if the complaint has not been sustained by the facts available. If investigation has revealed facts resulting in suspension, surrender of days off, cancellation of accumulated overtime, reprimand, or other penalty, the supervisor should accept the responsibility for informing the employee of the action to be taken. Regardless of whether the penalty is less than the accused employee expected or more, the supervisor should assume some responsibility for it since his recommendation should have played an important part in assessing the punishment. The supervisor should avoid any implication in his manner or speech that he blames a severe penalty on someone "above" or that a light penalty resulted from some defensive action he might have taken in behalf of the derelict employee. The supervisor's responsibility for maintaining discipline does not include participation in a popularity contest.

Separation interview

One of the frequent failures of the supervisors' human management functions which has a long-term, adverse effect upon the organization's image results from the neglect of someone in authority in the employing agency to discuss circumstances surrounding an employee's separation from service. An interview should be conducted regardless of the cause for separation, whether it is from voluntary or forced resignation, termination for cause, or retirement. Such an interview is especially helpful in determining useful or harmful hiring procedures. The techniques of using it should be included in supervisory training to acquaint those in supervisory positions with the need for improvement in questionable practices that might cause unnecessary and costly employment turnover.

It is most important to learn the true reason for a resignation rather than the expressed reason. Perhaps the employee has indicated that family pressures, a fearful spouse, lack of adequate pay, or adverse working conditions are the reason when the true reason involves work pressures or a capricious supervisor. Either condition is correctable. The interviewer must therefore try to isolate as specifically as possible the real reason for leaving. Whether or not he should try to persuade the employee to change his mind will depend upon the circumstances of each case.

Every effort must be taken to prevent the employee from terminating his employment with the feeling that the organization is a poor place to work. If the separation results from personal dereliction or incompetency, the interviewer seldom gains friendship for his organization if recriminations and hostility are allowed to creep into the interview. Rather, it should be conducted in as friendly a manner as possible so that the employee leaves with as little bitterness as possible. An unfriendly former employee can do inestimable harm to the organization.

Special effort should be made by supervisory personnel to take advantage of any opportunity to express gratitude to the retiring employee. Each has contributed something to the organization and should not be permitted to leave with a feeling that he was treated as if "they couldn't wait to get rid of me." It is especially important that a separation interview be conducted by the personnel officer, whatever his rank. He speaks with the formal authority of his position. All too often, he excuses his failure to "extend a friendly hand" to the retiring employee because of the press of other business; but what other activity could return so much good will, or ill will, minute for minute?

RECORDING RESULTS

When a record of the interview is desirable, upon its conclusion, the results, both general and specific, and the observations of the interviewer should be recorded promptly to prevent omissions, inaccuracies, and faulty information from filtering into the record. Often, it is desirable to prepare notes as the interview progresses (rather than to rely solely upon memory) to avoid such shortcomings in the report; however, great care must be exercised in doing so to prevent any stifling of the interviewee's responses.

EVALUATING RESULTS

The skill of interviewing can be developed just as can the skill of interrogation. Once the interviewer has learned how to listen, has made a diligent effort to learn the patience required in the process of gaining true understanding of others' viewpoints so that he may make allowances for views which may differ from his own, has diligently attempted to avoid past mistakes, has applied the general and specific principles which others have found helpful, has learned to sublimate his own biases so that he may objectively treat the problems posed by subordinates, and has made a conscious effort to focus the interview on essentials, he will have mastered the initial steps which must be taken in becoming an expert interviewer. Experience and practice are necessary in order to learn to interview well. These, however, are wasteful of time and are slow unless the interviewer profits from a systematic review of his strengths and weaknesses, modifies and improves his strengths, and avoids further error from his weaknesses. His skill can be further improved by analyzing what was said to determine the motives, feelings, views, and attitudes expressed and comparing these conclusions with those made during the interview. The interviewer must also analyze the techniques he used to ascertain if they produced free expression or stifled it. If such procedures suppressed the interviewer's responses, what might have been said or done to encourage a better response? Finally, consideration must be given to the total objective. Was such objective accomplished or, if not, how might it have been? Perhaps a change in technique would have brought about better results.

CAUSES OF FAILURE

There are indeed many limitations imposed upon the interview procedure and many combinations of factors which contribute to failures. Some interviews are unsuccessful because of a failure of the parties to communicate what is meant or to understand what is said. Others fail because of ignorance, faulty recollection, the tendency to say what one thinks he is expected to say or distortions which creep into the reporting of results when the facts are interpreted on the basis of subjective impressions rather than objective facts.

Success of the interview is dependent on factors such as the ability of the interviewer in eliciting accurate responses, the personalities of both parties, their idiosyncrasies, attitudes, and biases. The interviewer's failure to analyze the problem confronting him and to decide upon the best method of approaching it, or his failure to prepare for the interview by mastering background data, gearing it to best serve its purpose and even planning the wording of questions, might further lessen the effectiveness of the interview. When it fails for these reasons or because the interviewer cannot gain the interviewee's cooperation or understand him, techniques should be devised for preventing future failures. Most of these failures occur because the proven principles and techniques of interviewing are not adapted to the problem at hand.[8] By selecting and applying the best procedures—those found to have been most effective in many interviews—the supervisor will enjoy a continuing sense of satisfaction from the results.

SUMMARY

The effective supervisor will spend a large portion of his time talking with his subordinates, in addition to inspecting their work and observing their performance, if he is to gain the greatest understanding of them. Purposeful face-to-face interchanges with them will enable him to motivate them, change their attitude when necessary to comport with the objectives of the organization, obtain their cooperation, or help them to resolve a problem.

An interview differs from an interrogation in that the latter is primarily interviewer-centered with the dominant role played by the person asking the questions. In the interviewee-centered situation, the person responding to the prompting is most important, with the interviewer only "priming the pump" to elicit complete responses. This is the supervisor's role in his verbal interchanges with subordinates. The amount of emphasis he wishes to place on this or that technique will be dependent upon what he wishes to accomplish.

The informal interview may have as its objective the general gathering of intelligence or information to determine the level of morale or group responses to organizational objectives. The employment interview has as its objective the evaluation of those abstract traits in a prospective employee that may qualify him for employment or constitute cause for his rejection. The progress interview is primarily directed toward giving the employee some insight about his performance and progress on the job. If he has a grievance, the nature of the interview will generally dictate a different approach—one primarily of listening to learn the true rather than the ostensible reason for the grievance. Telling is reserved for clarifying misunderstandings upon which the grievance may be mistakenly based. The separation interview is utilized to determine the reason for termination so that corrective action can be taken if a voluntary resignation is based upon dissatisfaction related to the work environment. The interview may be involved with problem solving, in which case the supervisor may be asked to help the employee reach a solution to his problem. The supervisor will then lend a willing ear and indirectly encourage the employee to air his problem and arrive at

[8] Bingham and Moore, *How to Interview*, p. 7.

his own solution. The disciplinary interview is concerned with an investigation of the employee's conduct. The supervisor first interviews the subordinate complained against to determine his side of the matter. The employee is interviewed the second time to inform him of the action to be taken as the result of the investigation.

In every case, with perhaps an exception in informal interviews, the supervisor conducting an interview with a subordinate should plan ahead what he wishes to accomplish in the interview and how he will approach it. He will maintain a patient, objective attitude. He will plan his questions according to his objectives. He will refrain from giving advice. Instead, he will expertly guide the contact into constructive channels suggested by the interviewee himself.

REVIEW

Questions

1. What is the difference between an interview and an interrogation?
2. What are the major functions of an interview?
3. List the types of interviews and discuss briefly their characteristics.
4. What is meant by the principle that interviews should be employee-centered? Discuss how the employee-centered interview can be achieved.
5. Discuss the understanding-listening technique.
6. Discuss how questions might best be used in the interview process.
7. How should the interviewer generally handle an offer to give information under a confidential agreement?
8. What is meant by the term "unconscious imitation," and how might it affect an interview?
9. Discuss some of the most prevalent causes of interview failures.
10. Why should an interviewer ordinarily refrain from giving advice to the interviewee?
11. What are some of the broad steps a supervisor should take in preparing for an interview?

Exercises

Case 1: The Transfer Interview

I. The Facts

A. Personal

1. Detective (patrol officer) Leo Sparks, age 32
2. Appointed eight years ago; wife recently died; no children
3. Has received no promotions but has been assigned to investigation division for five years

4. Is the senior man in his division

5. Has been heard to say that he would quit the job if he ever had to leave the investigative assignment

B. Assumptions

1. Sparks has had several minor (almost trivial) complaints from victims of crimes he has been assigned to investigate.

2. His golf clubs have been found in his police car.

3. It is "rumored" that he is not paying attention to duty.

4. His clearance rate for cases has recently been the lowest in the division, although formerly it was the highest.

5. You have been instructed to drop one man from the division and have selected him because of the above factors, even though he is the senior man and was, until recently, one of your most productive detectives.

6. Sparks is very upset, having learned of the pending transfer before you were able to inform him.

II. The Problem

A. You are to interview this officer to tell him of the transfer since he has brought up the issue in the coffee room.

B. Your main problem is to "sell" him on the transfer and to prevent his resignation as he has threatened.

C. Employ the principles of interviewing as discussed in this chapter.

Case 2: The Grievance Interview

I. The Facts

A. Personal

1. Robert Heath, age 35

2. Appointed 12 years ago

3. Very satisfactory producer; does a very acceptable job in any assignment

4. Has a very happy home life, but is becoming unhappy with working conditions on the job

B. Assumptions

1. This officer has complained to his city councilman that he has been discriminated against by his supervisors (without naming them) in respect to assignments, days off, and vacation. He is threatening to quit his job because of it.

2. He has allegedly had a position offered him at a considerably higher salary.

3. Your department can ill afford to lose its seasoned officers since you now have several vacancies which you are having difficulty filling.

4. Your councilman, Mr. Jackson, is a strong supporter of the department and thinks someone should talk to the officer. He learned of the situation informally from the officer at a social

event. Your chief agrees that the officer is worth making an effort to save.

5. Make whatever additional assumptions required for the interview. There is no factual evidence that he has been discriminated against as alleged.

II. The Problem

A. You are to interview this officer to ascertain the nature of his grievance.

B. You are to try to change the attitude of this officer. He has become known around the station as a person with grievances but has not approached his supervisors about them.

Case 3: The Personal Problem Interview

I. The Facts

A. Personal

1. Officer Sam Peters, age 40
2. Appointed 14 years ago
3. Performance very good
4. Married (wife, Margaret, is an attractive brunette), three children, ages 9, 12, 14

B. Assumptions

1. Mrs. Peters has come to you, her husband's immediate supervisor. whom Officer Peters allegedly respects highly.
2. She states that during the last two years Officer Peters has been "chasing" another woman, a blonde, and his conduct is rapidly becoming a neighborhood "scandal."
3. No complaints have been received by the department and his conduct has apparently not affected his work.
4. Officer Peters has no record of previous disciplinary action.
5. His conduct is such that the department will undoubtedly be embarrassed soon if something is not done promptly, according to his wife.
6. Make other assumptions as required.

II. The Problem

A. You are to interview Officer Peters in an attempt to protect your department.

B. This is an initial interview.

C. Neighbors have not been interviewed, nor have the allegations of Mrs. Peters been supported by other evidence at the time you were asked by your superior to do whatever is necessary to prevent possible embarassment to the department. Other personnel have heard rumors to the effect that Peters has become involved with a woman, but none of them will admit that they have any firsthand information to support the rumor.

8

Special problems in counseling

At times, the supervisor must assume the role of counselor to his subordinates when information comes to his attention that they need his help or when they seek it either directly or indirectly. Sometimes his observations reveal that the employee's work is deteriorating. The symptoms may suggest that he is troubled with domestic difficulties, a developing physical or psychological illness, or a drinking problem.

Although the supervisor cannot be expected to administer a program of professional therapy to subordinates with serious emotional problems, he can familiarize himself with the symptoms usually characteristic of these conditions so that he may recognize them and initiate timely and appropriate action. It is in the early stages that most of these disturbances will respond best to treatment. The application of proven techniques of counseling is perhaps more essential in such cases than in most other situations involving oral interchanges between persons.

THE NATURE OF PROBLEM DRINKING

The National Commission on Marijuana and Drug Abuse has concluded from its study that alcohol dependence is without question the most serious drug problem in the country.[1] It probably involves at least five million cases, with the largest percentage concentrated among males in their most productive years, between thirty-five and fifty.[2] The problem has become one of considerable significance to law enforcement agencies, not only from an enforcement standpoint but from one involving personnel management. Consequently, many agencies are taking steps to reduce its impact by training supervisors to recognize its common symptoms so that timely corrective action may be taken.

There is insufficient evidence that alcoholism can be attributed to personality predispositions. It must therefore be assumed that any predispositions must be associated with other influences which tend to press one toward alcoholism before he will become addicted.[3]

By its very nature, police work is conducive to problem drinking. It attracts and tends to hold young men and women in the age bracket in which alcoholism most frequently occurs. The occupation is very stressful and competitive, with pressures seldom duplicated in other endeavors. If selection procedures are defective or if supervisory controls break down, the characteristics of the job sometimes contribute to the development of excessive drinking.

A person often drinks to reduce the stresses associated with his job or family, his relationships with people, or his economic responsibilities when such stresses cause confusion, anxiety, insecurity, frustration, unhappiness, or loneliness. Whatever the cause, when drinking develops into a problem, his ability to perform his job becomes impaired. He eventually becomes a major concern to his supervisor because he cannot function effectively as a police employee. In fact, aside from physical and emotional impairment and the poor image an officer portrays to the public when he smells of alcohol or demonstrates some alcohol-induced aberration in connection with his work, he often becomes a downright hazard to himself and his coworkers.

Tests involving speed and precision have revealed that the performance of the problem drinker is considerably reduced in the early stages of alcoholism. As he approaches the middle stage, a progressively greater loss of coordination becomes apparent.[4]

It might be asked, "Does not management share some of the respon-

---

[1] *U.S. News and World Report*, "Rising Toll of Alcoholism: New Steps to Combat It," 75, No. 18 (October 29, 1973), 43; Aaron T. Beck, "What to Do When You're Under Stress," *U.S. News and World Report*, 75, No. 13 (September 24, 1973), 52.

[2] Harrison M. Trice, *Alcoholism in America* (New York: McGraw-Hill Book Company, 1966), p. 39.

[3] *Ibid.*

[4] Albion Roy King, *Basic Information on Alcohol*, rev. ed. (Mount Vernon, Iowa: Cornell College Press, 1960), pp. 73–92.

sibility?" "As the problem develops not spontaneously but over a considerable period of time, why was remedial action not taken before the problem became aggravated?"

There is usually a threefold answer to these questions: The supervisor may not recognize the symptoms of deviant drinking in the early stages because he has not been trained to do so. If he does recognize them, he may not care to make an issue of the problem and thereby tacitly allows it to develop into a major one. Last, he may be forced to take disciplinary action because of misconduct by the employee brought about by drinking. However he rationalizes his failures, the supervisor still has an obligation to protect his agency from the needless and expensive loss of what otherwise might have been a highly productive employee. It therefore behooves the supervisor to familiarize himself with the characteristics of the problem and the options available to him in handling it. He must be able to recognize the difference between the chronic complainer, the hypochondriac, and the person with a psychosomatic disorder such as described in Chapter 6. He should be aware, however, that certain symptoms may appear to be associated with excessive drinking but may really signal the presence of other illnesses. He will then be in a position to make an appropriate referral to professional medical aid when necessary.

The symptoms of problem drinking and some practical methods the lay supervisor might use to cope with it through the counseling process are discussed in the following pages.

Development of the problem

As social drinking develops into problem drinking and then into an actual physiological and psychological dependence upon alcohol, the individual progresses through several distinct phases.

Jellinek and others have categorized these into three stages: an early, a middle or intermediate, and a late or acute stage. Each has its characteristic symptoms.[5] These stages may consume many months or years, with no abrupt transition from one stage to another. The progression often goes unnoticed.

A drinking problem may exist without the person being aware of it. The individual's social drinking habits begin to deviate from the usual drinking standards of his associates. He begins to solve his real or imagined emotional problems or to obtain satisfaction with the aid of

[5] E. M. Jellinek, "Phases of Alcohol Addiction," *Quarterly Journal of Studies on Alcohol,* 13, (1952), 673–84; see also Marvin A. Block, *Alcoholism—Its Facets and Phases* (New York: The John Day Company, 1965), pp. 24–30.

alcohol. These reactions place him on the broad road to addiction. He develops a variety of motives for his conduct—excitement, relaxation, increased social ability, escape, a release from pressure, a sense of euphoria, or a simple feeling of well-being.[6] His job, home life, and social life gradually become impaired. He suffers emotional and physical damage. Finally, he loses his ability to consciously control his drinking once he starts, even though he recognizes its harm.[7] It is then that he is addicted.

Symptoms of the problem

Problem drinking is exactly what the name implies. In a broad sense, when one is repeatedly affected adversely by alcohol, one is a problem drinker, regardless how slight or grave the effects are.[8] One may manifest minor symptoms such as a developing tendency toward arguments, tardiness, absenteeism, or frequent hangovers, or one may be involved in more serious breaches such as an arrest for drunken driving or a traffic accident.

An extension of problem drinking is alcoholism, in which the individual drinks compulsively—never intending to drink too much but invariably doing so. He can seldom stop of his own accord but must be given assistance, because he has lost control of his drinking.

Many of the individual's early symptoms of problem drinking go unnoticed by even his closest associates. It is believed by some that the best clue to what is developing is the recurring memory blackout.[9] He may have acted normally, he may have been fully conscious, but he cannot remember the following day what happened while he was drinking.

When these symptoms begin to appear, the supervisor should carefully watch for personality changes. Undue tensions and temperamental outbursts that did not occur before afford clues that all is not well. The development of unusual drinking habits off the job should be checked discreetly by the supervisor.

Growing domestic and financial troubles may also signal a drinking problem. The family usually is vitally affected because personal and financial irresponsibility are often associated with a drinking problem.

[6] Ibid.

[7] Trice, Alcoholism in America, p. 28.

[8] Charles R. Carroll, Alcohol—Use, Nonuse and Abuse (Dubuque, Iowa: William C. Brown Company, Publishers, 1970), p. 19.

[9] Block, Alcoholism—Its Facets and Phases, pp. 50–59; Ronald J. Cantanzaro, "Psychiatric Aspects of Alcoholism," Alcoholism, ed. David J. Pittman (New York: Harper & Row, Publishers, 1967), pp. 41–45; Carroll, Alcohol—Use, Nonuse and Abuse, p. 43.

Disharmony and anxiety within the family group are also often concomitants.

When the drinker's tolerance for alcohol increases, when he needs several drinks to obtain the effect that one gave him before, he is developing the pattern of a drinking problem. It is easily recognizable. This is a difficult condition to counter because a considerable tolerance for alcohol has become a prestige factor in our society.

The deviant drinker often manages to drink more than others by sneaking drinks now and then, by drinking faster than others or supplying them with drinks so that he can conceal the quantity of his own drinking. He may not be an uncontrolled drinker at this point but may begin to rely more and more on alcohol to bolster his tolerance for the pressures he feels. A vicious cycle often occurs. The person with stress and tension takes alcohol to relieve the tension in the early stages. Later, when the alcohol produces undesirable effects, more alcohol is taken to counter these effects.[10]

When his drinking patterns are called to the individual's attention, his resentment is symptomatic of his problem. He becomes defensive—usually denying that he has any problem at all.

It is with the approach of the intermediate stage of the disease that the employee's work habits start to deteriorate. Absenteeism increases. Usually the supervisor can recognize the clues if he is familiar with them. The employee more and more often leaves his post temporarily, offering lame or unusual excuses for his absence. The quantity and quality of his work is lower, his hangover symptoms and bleary eyes become more evident. "Sick" patterns begin to develop. These might be uncovered by close examination of a calendar prepared to show his "sick" record over a period of several years. Recurrent absences following pay days or a series of days off when other officers are usually on duty may reveal to the supervisor that he should be alert for other symptoms that might suggest a developing drinking problem.

Gradually, with the continuation of his drinking, the employee loses control over his drinking behavior. His insistence, if he talks about it at all, that he can stop drinking "any time he wants to" grows more and more obvious. In many cases, he constantly hopes secretly that some miracle will happen to help him out of his dilemma.

As his loss of control develops, he may begin to lie about his drinking, denying it when it is perfectly obvious to others. He is prone to develop three defense mechanisms: *denial*, wherein he denies using alcohol or claims that he can take it or leave it alone; *rationalization*, wherein he denies the existence of any problem; and *projection*, wherein

10 Block, *Alcoholism—Its Facets and Phases*, pp. 51–58.

he projects the blame for his problem—if he admits he has one—onto work pressures, a nagging wife, or financial difficulties.[11] He rationalizes "taking a belt" to settle him down after a particularly stressful day. He may make excuses for his recurrent hangovers. He often claims that some other chronic health problem is the cause, often misquoting his doctor.

He becomes a real supervisory headache because an inordinate amount of the supervisor's time must be devoted to him. The instances of his calling in sick without advance notice increase and require more and more last-minute changes in work schedules. He becomes a threat and an annoyance.

If his supervisors reject him because of his problem or do not understand it, he may withdraw and turn increasingly to alcohol. His tendency to brood in isolation usually grows. He may isolate himself from others even to the point of antisocial behavior.

He starts forcing the supervisor's hand. Some supervisors will give him warning after warning but will do little else in these initial episodes. However, the employee is apt to become aggressive. His conduct may become offensive with colleagues and the public, with increasing complaints against him. Other officers may refuse to work with him or may protest when assigned to do so. When they are pressed for the reason, they will often become evasive, fearing criticism for allowing him to drink on duty. Accidents and fighting off the job are clues that should not be overlooked, especially when they occur repeatedly. Such acts are common with the problem drinker.[12]

He may try to gain control over his drinking by setting a limit upon when, how much, and what types of liquor he can drink. In reality, he is making the management of his drinking a central concern of his waking hours.[13] Much of his productive work seems to be governed by his desire for a drink.

The intermediate, or middle stage of a developing drinking problem is a critical period for the concerned employee. Deceiving others, especially his supervisors and associates, about his drinking becomes common for him. If decisive action is taken when evidence that a drinking problem is developing and is impairing the employee's performance on the job, some highly desirable results can usually be attained. How-

---

[11] Cantanzaro, *Alcoholism,* p. 43.

[12] King, *Basic Information on Alcohol,* p. 77; see also Block, *Alcoholism—Its Facets and Phases,* p. 199.

[13] E. M. Jellinek, "Phases in the Drinking History of Alcoholics: Analysis of a Survey Conducted by the Official Organ of Alcoholics Anonymous," *Quarterly Journal of Studies on Alcohol,* 7 (1946), 1–88.

ever, if the supervisor delays, if his actions are characterized by vacillation and indecisiveness, if the little help offered is given grudgingly, the employee will probably continue on into the acute third stage.

Physical deterioration often sets in during the third stage. The entire spectrum of the employee's drinking behavior becomes increasingly more aggravated until he is physically and psychologically dependent upon alcohol and becomes totally unsuited for the demands of the police service. If it is at this time that severe negative corrective action is first deemed necessary, then the employee invariably becomes a total loss to the organization, either through a long-term suspension or a permanent separation from the service. If positive corrective action has been delayed until this stage, even if it is desirable to treat the person rather than punish him, the probabilities of restoring him to full productive capacity are greatly limited.

SOME OPTIONS IN TREATING THE DEVIANT DRINKER

Deviant drinking is more easily corrected in its early stages than when it becomes acute. The emotional problems associated with it are usually exceedingly difficult to reverse at this last stage. The physiological harm may be impossible to reverse.

When drinking adversely affects the employee's performance on the job or when his resultant misconduct off the job cannot be tolerated, punitive action may be indicated. Negative disciplinary action for substantive violations of rules or regulations is ordinarily followed under established procedures. However, this is not the sole recourse for the supervisor. Treatment is a much more positive course if the employee can be persuaded that he needs it. Sometimes punishment brings him to this realization. If punishment or persuasion fails to do this, his separation from the organization will become necessary. When this happens, everyone suffers—the employee, his family, his friends, his colleagues, and the organization.

Problem drinking off the job

The problem of the police employee whose deviant drinking behavior has not yet involved his job but is a matter of common knowledge may become a distressing experience for the supervisor. He is often torn between hoping the problem will correct itself or becoming involved in what many say is the employee's private matter.

Unfortunately, he will rarely be sought out for help by an employee who believes he has an incipient or actual drinking problem. Such help may be solicited by a wife, another member of the family, or a close friend, but usually only after the drinking has been going on for some time. Sometimes a colleague recognizes what is happening and calls it to the supervisor's attention. Usually, the supervisor has many subtle indicators of what is happening—even in the early stages of problem drinking—but must be alert for them and must develop the capacity to recognize them when they are present.

When counseling by the supervisor or intervention by a close friend is not practicable, the employee might be directed to secure a medical examination from the organization's physician. Professional help then becomes involved. If the physician is given full details, he is in a position to recommend further referral to a professional counsellor or an agency specializing in such cases; however, the critical objective of convincing the employee that he needs outside help is exceedingly difficult to achieve.

He will usually deny to others and to himself that he has a problem, especially during the early stages of the disease. He will seldom believe that he needs help to solve a problem he does not acknowledge. In fact, one of the most difficult phases of corrective action is that of bringing him to a realization that he has a problem and needs someone to help him resolve it; yet, this is usually as important a step as the treatment itself.

He will often resist any attempt by the organization to interfere in his private affairs. Although such resistance may be passive, he may not accept aid even if it is forced on him. The organization may then find it necessary to withhold action until the employee's drinking behavior causes his performance to deteriorate or results in an incident that requires disciplinary action.

Indirect solicitation of help

Sometimes, a trivial, seemingly unrelated question or problem will be used by an employee as an excuse for seeking help when he has a deep-seated anxiety brought about by the excessive use of alcohol. It is not necessarily true that he must hit bottom before he will realize that he needs help. Many persons reach this conclusion long before they reach the acute stage of alcoholism.[14] Under these conditions, much of the problem is solved because the employee can be helped effectively when he wants to be. What then needs to be done is to lead him to the

---

[14] King, *Basic Information on Alcohol*, pp. 124–25.

realization that drinking is the cause of his anxiety. Guiding him toward appropriate help is then a relatively simple task.

Job-involved problem drinking

When problem drinking causes the employee's job performance to deteriorate or results in misconduct that justifies negative disciplinary action, the supervisor is obligated to take action. Sometimes several other drinking-connected incidents have occurred. A written record may or may not have been made of what specific action was taken. The supervisor must recognize that the longer he waits, the less likely will be the chance of constructive behavior changes.

A decision must be made as to whether the matter will be treated as an illness and the employee retained, with or without punishment, and given an opportunity to correct the problem; or be handled solely as a dereliction calling for punitive action. If discharge is indicated, the supervisor's immediate problem is resolved.

If the course of action involves retention and treatment, the impact of what has occurred must be brought forcefully to the employee's attention. It is most important that corrective action be initiated before he becomes so deeply involved in further drinking-induced derelictions that he must be terminated. The author has experienced numerous cases in which employees terminated for unacceptable behavior brought about by a drinking problem have indicated that they would not have lost their jobs had their supervisor "knocked their ears down" when the problem first became evident.

Disciplining a subordinate for derelictions resulting from a drinking problem is not necessarily incompatible with efforts to treat the condition. Sometimes punishment applied to preserve organizational integrity brings about the crisis needed to make the employee realize that his job is at stake. In such cases, the reason for the punitive action should be made clear to him at the outset. He should be told what is expected of him. It is then up to him to live up to those expectations.[15] Telling him that he has a drinking problem and must stop drinking will do no good, nor will any attempt to convince him that he has no problem he cannot resolve himself. He does not want to be condemned for his behavior.[16] He needs to be guided towards the recognition of his problem and the realization that he needs help to overcome it. If this cannot be

[15] Al-Anon Family Group Headquarters, *The Dilemma of the Alcoholic Marriage* (New York: Al-Anon Family Headquarters, Inc., 1961), pp. 16–18.
[16] Block, *Alcohol—Its Facets and Phases*, pp. 82–86.

done because he refuses to acknowledge that a problem exists, it is unlikely that much will be accomplished by way of real treatment.

Drinking and deteriorating performance

Just as in the case of other misconduct brought about by the use of alcohol, when drinking causes an employee's work to deteriorate or drop to an unacceptable level, the supervisor is responsible for corrective action. Deteriorating performance has revealed many cases of early and intermediate stages of alcoholism before other visible or physical symptoms of the disease appear. If these conditions are ignored, they will only become worse. They will be reflected in economic loss through increased absenteeism, interpersonal problems, errors, and a reduction in the level of employee morale.[17]

Careful documentation of specific instances of unsatisfactory performance should be prepared promptly when they are observed by the supervisor. These are the basis for corrective action needed when an employee's performance becomes unacceptable. Facts indicating the cause of the deteriorating performance should be recorded. Observation for symptoms of excessive drinking in that connection is especially desirable.

COUNSELING PROBLEMS, PROCEDURES, AND TECHNIQUES

The supervisor should gain an understanding of the problems of deviant drinking and must himself accept the objectives of his role in dealing with it if he is to become effective as a lay counselor. If he doesn't accept problem drinking as a treatable condition but looks upon it only as behavior meriting punitive action for a lack of willpower and moral responsibility, his attitude will hinder any effort to resolve the matter.

Preliminary action

As with other interviewing situations, the supervisor should familiarize himself with all pertinent facts available concerning the employee, his performance records, and the details of his disciplinary history. By guiding the problem drinker toward a realization that he has a drinking problem, that he needs help in solving it, and that he cannot otherwise

[17] Frank C. Irvine, *Statement on Alcoholism* (Santa Ana, Calif.: Cannon I.T.T., 1973), pp. 7–8.

maintain an acceptable capacity for his work, the supervisor can take the first step in a course of treatment.

The counseling session

At the earliest practicable time after the supervisor has noted a deterioration in a subordinate's performance, he should discuss the matter with him. The objective should be to help the employee improve. The circumstances of each case will dictate what specific action may be needed to bring this about. The existence of symptoms of excessive drinking concurrent with the worsening performance may suggest the approach he should take.

The interview should be held in private, as is any progress interview. Sufficient time should be allotted to explore the matter preliminarily and establish a satisfactory basis for future sessions. The supervisor should anticipate that several sessions may be required to lead the subordinate to an understanding of his problem. Several short sessions may be more desirable and effective than fewer longer sessions, in giving the employee an opportunity to reflect in more detail on what took place in the short sessions. Although the supervisor may conclude quite accurately what the problem is, telling the person involved might be precisely what ought not to be done. The supervisor cannot be expected to make a medical diagnosis of the condition, nor should he try. That is a function of the professional. However, some notably successful results have been achieved by lay counselors.

Every supervisor can gain an adequate working knowledge of such problems by studying the literature and by becoming familiar with the referral agencies in the community. The important factor in a supervisor's ability to counsel well is his capacity to recognize a drinking problem and to know not only when he is not equipped to handle it but also where the person can be referred for the type of help he needs.

All the interviewing techniques at the supervisor's command should be used to make the session most constructive. The initial conversation should ordinarily be directed toward the subordinate's performance rather than toward him as an individual. Although he may be resentful of having his performance challenged, if the supervisor exhibits a sincere desire to be of help and encourages the subordinate to talk about what he thinks is interfering with his work, resentment and hostility will begin to disappear. If the supervisor talks at the right time without irritation, anger, or reproach, and without any appearance that he is sitting in judgment, he will help the person see himself as he is.

Attentiveness to what is said, looking at the problem from the employee's point of view, and establishing a comfortable relationship during the session are the three basic ingredients in effective counseling.[18] The supervisor should listen without shock or surprise while encouraging the employee to express his feelings, no matter how embarrassing they may be. He should not be expected to think through the matter at the first meeting. This should be a ventilation session in which he will begin to obtain some insight into his problem.[19]

The technique of nondirective or client-centered counseling, in which the supervisor stimulates the employee to discover his own problem and decide upon a course of action to correct it has been found to be extremely productive. It may not accomplish everything that can be done, but it can do no harm. The person is more apt to respond to a solution he works out for himself than to one the supervisor works out for him.[20]

By following this procedure, the supervisor can avoid giving advice or opinions, diagnosing the problem, and directing the subordinate in solving it. Rather, interest can be focused on how to help him gain insight into his problem.[21] In this respect, full reflection, as described in Chapter 17, should be permitted. This technique opens channels of communication and helps to keep them open if applied properly.[22] The supervisor should not attempt to interpret everything that is said, however. Rather, he should listen and ask the right questions without talking about the alcohol problem until after the subordinate "discovers" it himself.

Simply restating in question form what has been said will force the subordinate to reflect and gradually move toward a clarification of his own problems. It will tend to bring him to a point where he realizes that something is wrong.

Questions should not be over-used, as they tend to absorb too much

[18] Bruce Shertzer and Shelley C. Stone, *Fundamentals of Counseling* (Boston: Houghton Mifflin Company, 1968), pp. 357–65.

[19] King, *Basic Information on Alcohol*, pp. 124–27; Laura Esther Root, "Social Therapies in the Treatment of Alcoholics," in *Alcoholism*, ed. David J. Pittman (New York: Harper & Row, Publishers, 1967), p. 149; National Center for Prevention and Control of Alcoholism, National Institute of Mental Health, *Alcohol and Alcoholism* (Washington, D.C.: U.S. Government Printing Office, 1967), p. 33.

[20] William A. Ruch, "The Why and How of Nondirective Counseling," *Supervisory Management*, 18, No. 1 (January, 1973), 15–19; see also Philip F. Lynch, "Q and A on Alcohol," *Supervisory Management*, 18, No. 11 (November, 1973), 14–15.

[21] Robert A. Zawacki and Peter E. La Sota, "The Supervisor as Counselor," *Supervisory Management*, 18, No. 11 (November, 1973), 18–20.

[22] Daniel W. Fullmer and Harold W. Bernard, *Counseling: Content and Process* (Chicago: Science Research Associates, Inc., 1964), p. 147.

of the subject's attention. They should not be asked in a manner that will incite anger, fear, or suspicion instead of cooperation. Questions of an accusatory nature may defeat their purpose. They may appear to be innocuous enough but may imply an accusation that will be resented. For example, a question such as, "Did that [act] give you a guilt feeling?" rather than, "How did you feel afterward?" may undo much that has been done to establish rapport because it might imply some wrongdoing.

Properly phrased questions are useful for encouraging the subject to talk. They should also be used to obtain information or to lead the conversation towards matters that are more pertinent.[23]

Criticizing, censuring, belittling, moralizing, or degrading the employee or telling him how low he has sunk will do no good. These remonstrations will only cause him to lose face and contribute to his resentment. He will then resist help even more. Such conduct on the part of the supervisor will often have a fatal effect on the chances of persuading him to do something on his own accord to correct his problem.

It is important that the employee's ego be preserved, because he cannot be helped until he wants to be. He must be allowed to make his own evaluation of himself and gain insight into his problem through the process of gentle prompting. It is true that he can be forced to obtain treatment or go through the motions of it, but he cannot be forced into accepting it through fear.

Fear, unfortunately, is used too often in counseling as a prime technique, but rarely does it serve any really constructive purpose in situations involving the problem drinker. There is apprehension enough when he faces his supervisor and knows that his failures are at issue. The supervisor should reduce this fear, not by assurances which might be construed as a commitment to overlook the problem but by asking the employee what the trouble is without challenging everything he says. The greatest need is to bring out the real problem so that a solution can be reached. Fear and accusations will usually result in defensiveness, rationalization, projection, and evasiveness.

Note taking during counseling

Although a record of each contact with the employee should be kept, the taking of notes during the counseling sessions should be avoided as this procedure will only contribute to the subject's appre-

---

[23] Shertzer and Stone, *Fundamentals of Counseling*, pp. 364–65; Joseph Francis Perez, *Counseling: Theory and Practice* (Reading, Mass.: Addison-Wesley Publishing Company, Inc., 1965), pp. 13–21.

hensions and may aggravate his suspicions and increase his defensiveness. Note taking will also tend to divert the attention of the supervisor and the employee from the real issues.[24]

REFERRAL

It does not take an alcoholic to treat one any more than it takes a thief to catch one, nor is professional training a prerequisite to success in dealing with the problem drinker; however, a good deal of patience and common sense are needed if the matter is to be handled constructively—patience to weigh the issue objectively and enough common sense to recognize when the immediate resources have been exhausted. The supervisor may achieve good results in many cases despite his lack of professional training if he realizes that he does not have all the answers and recognizes when he has exhausted his own resources and those of his organization.

When the employee begins to realize that he has a drinking problem and makes a purposeful effort to help himself find the scientific reasons for it, the supervisor might suggest some appropriate literature on the subject. Then, when the employee begins to understand that he needs to find some way of facing his problems other than with alcohol, it might be suggested to him that he learn of the work of such organizations as Alcoholics Anonymous. He should then be guided into some positive effort to find an appropriate local group which may provide the needed help.[25] The supervisor should bear in mind that each case is different and that the particular organization selected by the employee should be one composed of persons with social and economic positions similar to his own.

The various chapters of Alcoholics Anonymous usually are the core to any successful referral program. The organization has built an enviable record of success with its program, which extends anonymity, confidentiality, sincerity, and help to those in need of it.

COUNSELING OBJECTIVE

The important objective of counseling is not only to get the problem drinker to give up drinking but to lead him to the realization that he can never be a moderate drinker, that he can never again use alcohol.

[24] Douglas W. Orr, *Professional Counseling on Human Behavior: Its Principles and Practices* (New York: Franklin Watts, Inc., 1965), p. 32.
[25] King, *Basic Information on Alcohol*, pp. 126–27.

Once he has come to this conclusion and makes a positive effort to do something about it, to find ways of meeting his problems other than with alcohol, the counselor has successfully accomplished his counseling mission.

EMOTIONAL PROBLEMS

Every supervisor sooner or later will observe a drastic behavior change in some subordinate whose personality has been stable and controlled in the past. The employee may exhibit a combination of many symptoms that might be early signs of a serious emotional disturbance. The supervisor is often the first and most readily available source of help. If he is familiar with these signs and what they may signify, he is in an ideal position to initiate some timely action that will help the employee.

In almost every organization, there will be a considerable number of persons who are frustrated, insecure, tense, hostile toward management, and otherwise beset with emotional problems. They may be called neurotic; but if their attitudes can be changed so that their tensions can be reduced through counseling, the entire organization will profit.[26]

As previously described, there are two occasions when the supervisor is obligated to become involved in a subordinate's personal affairs— when he asks for help, in which case his problem becomes the supervisor's also, and when the problem has affected the subordinate's performance.

Alternatives for the supervisor

Sometimes a supervisor is reluctant to add to the burdens of a subordinate who is already suffering from personal problems. The easiest alternative may be to do nothing, in which case the supervisor may find it easy to rationalize his inaction and continue to do nothing. In other cases, he may react by becoming exasperated and irritated because he must divert attention from his own affairs to the subordinate. As a consequence, he may take arbitrary punitive action of one form or another against the employee for the slightest infraction and end up causing a problem worse than the original one. At times, he may not recognize a problem because he has not bothered to familiarize himself with the signs.

The psychological conditions a supervisor often faces may be rela-

[26] Leroy N. Vernon, "Counseling in Business and Industry," in *Handbook of Counseling Techniques,* ed. Ernest Harms and Paul Schreiber (New York: Macmillan Publishing Co., Inc., 1963), pp. 262–63.

tively simple matters to deal with. Common sense, objectivity, and a large amount of patience, compassion, and understanding are called for. Sometimes, the problems are extremely complex and beyond his capacity to help. He must learn, therefore, to recognize his limitations and know when referral to professional help should be made. The following discussion relates to some conditions he frequently encounters and some common-sense solutions a supervisor as a lay counselor will find helpful.

Early symptoms of distress

Many of the symptoms that may be interpreted as clues to the onset of emotional distress are not necessarily positive indicators of such a condition; yet, any marked changes in behavior patterns in a person who previously exhibited none of them should alert the supervisor that something might be wrong, especially if a number of symptoms occur together.

Among the most prominent of these are uncontrolled emotional outbursts, excessive irritability, excessive altercations with colleagues or the public, loss of self-confidence, loss of job interest, insecurity, hopelessness, frequent short absences from the job, feelings of remorse, guilt, or self-pity, loss of ability to concentrate, pessimism, sadness, indecisiveness, sleeplessness, recurrent talks of giving up, quitting the job, or committing suicide, withdrawal from others or an inability to get along with them, feelings of persecution, and chronic fatigue or other marked changes in bodily functions. Although many of these conditions are transitory and occur in most people from time to time, if they persist, they should be cause for concern. The appearance of some of these symptoms, especially when they involve physiological changes, may dictate that medical attention should be secured.

The stress reflected by many of these conditions may indicate nothing more than low morale or poor supervisory practices. When such basic causes are corrected, it is remarkable how often the symptoms disappear.

Anxiety

Stress underlies most forms of emotional distress. Such stress may cause anxiety reactions subjectively experienced as fear, dread, or panic. The reactions that stress brings about are ways of coping with the anxiety. They may be expressed outwardly by aggressiveness or destructive acts, marital or family discord, or personality problems.

Anxiety tends to be related to external pressures. When they disappear, so does the anxiety associated with them.[27]

Destructive acts may be directed against equipment, other property, or even persons. The aggressiveness might be reflected by an increase in complaints from the public, from the person's colleagues, or from his family. The complaints usually allege excessive force, discourtesy, hostility, and the like.

If these reaction patterns are recognized as indicators that the person is trying to cope with some type of threat, something can be done to help him resolve his problem. The supervisor can be helpful by practicing empathy, by giving the employee a feeling that someone understands how he feels, is interested in him, and is reacting realistically toward the problem. A consistently warm, friendly attitude will be indicative of such interest and will give the person an opportunity to talk when he wants to.[28]

Transfer to a position where the person's strong points can be best used and where his weaknesses are not such a liability may help, although transfer is not ordinarily the best procedure to be followed to avoid disciplinary action that might be indicated. When the anxiety is deep-seated, professional help is ordinarily needed. The supervisor cannot rationalize his failure to discipline a subordinate for misconduct by reasoning that the acts are always the product of an emotional illness which can only be corrected by treatment. The supervisor and his organization assume a potential liability, if, knowing of an employee's proclivity for violence, they do nothing about it and the employee injures another person by violent acts.

When fear is the basic problem causing anxiety patterns, the employee should be given reassurance and an opportunity to talk the problem out. Once the cause of the threatening fear is brought to the surface, it will not usually appear to be so serious as was thought and the anxiety it causes will be lessened.[29]

Depression

Depressions brought about by stress may cause reactions that seriously impair performance. The symptoms may develop from a sense of loss or a threatening situation commonly associated with job pressures,

27 Orr, *Professional Counseling on Human Behavior: Its Principles and Practices,* pp. 131, 204.

28 Harry Levinson, *Emotional Health in the World of Work* (New York: Harper & Row, Publishers, 1964), pp. 50–51.

29 Orr, *Professional Counseling on Human Behavior: Its Principles and Practices,* p. 129.

a fear of failure—especially in a competitive occupation—or an over-magnification of the importance of a goal. When these conditions cause a person to become depressed, he usually loses his objectivity and sense of perspective. He tends to give up, to shun diversion that he once enjoyed. He considers himself a failure and may contemplate suicide. Physical symptoms such as heartburn, back pains, stomach trouble, and headaches are common. He may recognize these as stress symptoms or he may not, although almost everyone with whom he associates does.[30]

Everyone suffers depression of a transitory nature from time to time. They do not become depressed because they want to, and in most cases the passage of time, together with understanding, encouragement, and assurance that all will be well, will eliminate the problem. If it lingers, medical attention might be indicated. The physician can usually relieve the problem; but in severe cases where the condition does not respond to medical treatment, psychotherapy may be required.[31]

When a serious, conscientious, and sensitive employee with an intense job interest makes what he considers a serious blunder and magnifies it out of proportion, developing a depressive reaction from his guilt feelings and self-chastisement, the supervisor can help him to restore his self-esteem by making him realize that the matter was not so serious as it appeared to him. Although mistakes are not to be condoned by the supervisor, the experience gained from an honest, unintentional error often more than compensates for the harm caused. The matter may be a constructive learning experience for the employee.

Grief and loneliness brought about by the normal experiences of life may result in depression that may drastically affect the employee's performance. The depression can be lessened if the supervisor reacts with compassion and patience. The mere passage of time usually will bring about a cure. Each day that the person copes with his problem helps him to face with more equanimity the next day.

The employee mourning over the loss of a loved one can be helped if his attention can be diverted from his grief toward some physical activity, especially when his energy and interest can be focused on helping someone else. The person should not be encouraged to take a vacation "to get away from it all." This will only tend to increase his depressive reactions by focusing his attention more on his own problem than diverting it to something or someone else. Women are especially susceptible to periods of depression during late and middle age because of physiological changes that occur at that time. Medical attention—sometimes coupled with psychotherapy when severe psychological aberrations

[30] Beck, "What to Do When You're Under Stress," pp. 48–54.
[31] Nathan S. Kline, "Depression: Its Diagnosis and Treatment," *Modern Problems in Pharmacopsychiatry*, Vol. 3 (New York: S. Karger, 1969), pp. 67–74.

are present—usually does much to relieve these conditions. A good deal of patience, tact, and understanding are required in dealing with such problems.

Family discord and stress

Maslach calls excessive job stress "burnout." This condition correlates with alcoholism, all sorts of mental illnesses, suicide, and marital conflict.[32] When burnout occurs and the employee cannot resolve the stress on the job, he often transfers it to his home, where it plagues the marital relationship. The resulting discord, in turn, increases the stress and a vicious cycle results. Job stress may be only a contributing factor to marital problems or may be the direct cause; but whatever part it plays, the supervisor must recognize that family discord almost invariably will result in stress that will bring on reactions that frequently affect an individual's performance. Sometimes the reactions can be extremely severe. The affected subordinate may, for a time, give up. He may suffer severe depression, which in time may turn into resentment and anger. In this critical period the employee might react aggressively toward others, especially the source of his trouble. It is then that the need for help is the greatest. The supervisor can help temper the problem by practicing empathy and by maintaining a warm, friendly relationship that will give the subordinate an opportunity to ventilate should he so desire.

A vast array of complex causal factors are usually involved in such conflicts, and the behavior patterns that result are equally varied. In fact, all types of neuroses are associated with marital difficulties. Such conflicts often involve such delicate physical or psychological personal relationships between two people that if the supervisor becomes too deeply involved, his position in the matter will become untenable because he will eventually be accused by each—either overtly or covertly—of siding with the other.

When a marital conflict involving a subordinate has become critical and the supervisor's help is sought, he should confine his participation to listening to enough details to indicate that outside professional help is needed. He should then encourage the employee to seek such outside help.

The supervisor cannot be expected to be a marriage counselor. He can, however, at times start the subordinate on a road toward gaining some insight into his problem and making some progress toward saving his marriage by suggesting that he examine the ideas that tell him his

---

[32] Christina Maslach "Burned-out," *Human Behavior,* September, 1976.

marriage won't work and question, challenge, and rid himself of what Ard [33] calls the "irrational assumptions, ideas, values and self-defeating nonsense he is telling himself."

Often when a subordinate—especially a youthful one—comes to the supervisor with a job problem related to an incipient marital conflict, he should be encouraged to discuss the matter with his spouse rather than withdraw from the marital relationship. The supervisor should stress the value of such discussions. If they are objective, friendly, and considerate, much can be done by the parties themselves in resolving their problems. If the discussions take place in an emotion-charged setting full of anger and hostility, little will be accomplished. Many marriages that failed might have been saved had the parties made an effort to open and keep open the channels of communications between them and to talk about their problems—especially with each other. Often this has the effect of causing each to appreciate more the perspective of the other.

Should the subordinate's problem appear to have developed because he has, without realizing it perhaps, allowed his job to become more important than his family life, the supervisor should guide the subordinate to a realization that he must not attempt to derive all his satisfactions from his work at the expense of his family relationships.

This phenomenon of job satisfaction is most common in police work because of its nature. It therefore is reasonable to expect that marital disharmony might result from this fact on occasion, especially before the police wife learns to adjust to the conditions surrounding her husband's job. The supervisor should be alert to such an eventuality so that he may take preventive action should the need arise. His role is to prevent job-connected problems that might impair the performance of his subordinates without becoming involved in their marital relationships.

In some instances, transfer to a less demanding assignment might help. For example, it is commonly known among peace officers that many wives have strong objections—although they do not always express them—to assignments such as vice enforcement given their husbands. If the work begins to jeopardize the marital relationship, eventually the marital conflict jeopardizes the employee's performance. If the requirements of the employee's asignment are demanding an unreasonable amount of time, an adjustment might be in order to correct the condition.

Because of the tremendous emotional impact some marital breaches have upon the parties involved, the supervisor should practice a consider-

33 Ben N. Ard, Jr., "A Rational Approach to Clients Who Are Considering Divorce," *Los Angeles Daily Journal*, 86, No. 206 (October 17, 1973), 20–21.

able amount of forebearance and understanding of such turmoil experienced by a subordinate. The condition should never be an excuse for misconduct, however. Normally, the depressive reactions brought about by such domestic difficulties are temporary and will correct themselves if given time.

COUNSELING THE EMOTIONALLY TROUBLED SUBORDINATE

When a subordinate with an emotional problem approaches the supervisor for help, his first objective should be to examine the basic difficulties to determine if the employee has come to the right person. Any competent supervisor with a little patience and empathy can give help to an employee who has an imagined grievance which has caused some emotional stress and anxiety. This type of case involves the simple matter of encouraging him to examine the true facts so that he can recognize they are not at all what he interpreted them to be; however, when the symptoms indicate a deep-seated psychosis, professional help would be required.

As with other counseling situations, some persons unravel their problems quickly, while others will take considerable time before they come to the point. A considerable amount of patience is needed if the supervisor is to come to grips with the true problem.

In those cases where the supervisor has brought up the matter because the subordinate's performance has been adversely affected, apparently by some emotional problem, the employee might feel offended that the matter has even been brought up. He may become evasive, devious, and noncommittal. He may ask a hypothetical question—always about a friend, never about himself—calling for an answer to his own dilemma. The wise supervisor will see through this tactic and will quickly be able to arrive at the core of the matter by sifting fact from fiction.

The supervisor can reasonably expect a subordinate to do something about conditions that adversely affect his performance. If he is given an opportunity to talk, he can be helped to realize that there is something wrong that can be corrected. The process of nondirective counseling and reflective thinking, coupled with patient listening, are useful in bringing this about.

At the close of the session, the subordinate should be given an opportunity to summarize the conclusions he has reached about the problem and the course of action he has decided to take. A further session or two might be needed in helping him to resolve his problem. If some degree of improvement is not achieved by this time, however, he should be referred to professional help.

This process of referral need not be a traumatic experience to the employee. The need should be sold to him. The explanation that it is neither more unmanly nor disgraceful for a person to receive help from a professional counselor than it would be to accept help from any other professional might help make the thought easier for him to accept. The supervisor should then assist him to obtain the most appropriate help available.

SUMMARY

Alcoholism, as the most serious drug problem in the nation, involves over five million persons. Most of these are men in the age group that encompasses their most productive years. The problem has become one of considerable significance to law enforcement because the occupation attracts and holds the type of person often affected and contains the stresses that tend to press a person toward alcohol addiction.

As the social drinker develops into a problem drinker, he commonly progresses through three distinct phases—an early, a middle, and an acute stage, each with its characteristic symptoms. It is believed that the recurrent memory blackout is the most significant symptom of the start of problem drinking, although other symptoms such as the presence of frequent hangovers, absenteeism, and unusual drinking habits off the job tend to support the conclusion that the person is in the early stages of addiction. Work performance begins to deteriorate in the second stage. He begins to lie about his drinking and deny it when it is perfectly obvious to others. As his denials become stronger, he begins to rationalize his drinking, then he starts to blame his habit on others. He begins to become a real supervisory problem as he turns more and more to alcohol. In the third stage, a physical deterioration begins to set in. The employee so afflicted has become physically and psychologically dependent upon alcohol.

The employee often disqualifies himself from his job by acts of misconduct due to his addiction; his performance may begin to deteriorate. The prospect of losing his position may be the very crisis that brings him to the realization that he has a problem and needs help in solving it. The supervisor can do much to help him. He can help him to gain insight into his needs through listening and attentiveness, nondirect counseling, and reflective thinking. By following this procedure, the supervisor can avoid giving advice or opinions or diagnosing the problem for the employee.

When the employee begins to realize what course of action he must take to correct his problem, the supervisor might help him find the scientific reasons for it. He might suggest appropriate literature on the subject, then suggest that he become familiar with the work of such organizations as Alcoholics Anonymous. The employee should be guided into some positive effort to find the appropriate local group that might provide the necessary assistance.

The important objective of counseling is to help the problem drinker to realize that he must give up drinking and that he can never again use alcohol. Once this has been done, the objective of counseling has been achieved.

Counseling has other valuable uses. It can be used as a means of helping the frustrated, insecure, tense, or hostile employee who has developed anxiety or depressive reactions that are interfering with his performance. The techniques applicable to the counseling of the problem drinker are generally effective in dealing with the employee who has an emotional problem. The supervisor must apply patience, understanding, and tact in his relationship with the emotionally troubled subordinate. When the anxiety or depression is deep-seated, referral should be made to professional help.

REVIEW

Questions

1. Why is problem drinking so important to law enforcement?
2. What is primarily the cause of problem drinking?
3. What are the three stages of problem drinking?
4. What are three defense mechanisms the alcoholic will often use?
5. Why is listening so important in counseling?
6. What is nondirective counseling?
7. What is involved in the process of reflection? Give some examples.
8. Why is it necessary that the counselor avoid giving the alcoholic advice as a part of the counseling procedure?
9. What are the three main uses of questions in counseling?
10. Why is it important that the problem drinker's ego be preserved as a technique of counseling?
11. Why should notetaking not be practiced during the counseling session?
12. When should the problem drinker be referred to professional help?
13. What is the end objective in counseling the problem drinker?

14. How is anxiety often expressed subjectively?
15. How might anxiety be expressed outwardly?
16. What are some of the common causes of depression?

Exercises

1. Describe the early symptoms of problem drinking.

2. Describe what usually happens during the second stage in the development of alcoholism.

3. Explain what the supervisor might do if a subordinate's work has begun to deteriorate as the result of his drinking. Assume that the drinking is becoming a problem of habituation.

4. Conduct a simulated counseling session with a person whom it is assumed has developed a drinking habit that has caused his work to deteriorate drastically. Assume further that his work has deteriorated to a point that he could be terminated but that that course of action is to be reserved as a last resort. The person has no record of misconduct that has been induced by drinking.

5. Demonstrate how the supervisor can apply reflection in his counseling.

6. Describe how the supervisor might best handle an employee who develops a depression after he loses a son.

7. Explain why time is a great healer in some cases of depression.

8. What should the extremely sensitive person with a high job interest and a very conscientious nature be told if he developed a depressive reaction because of a serious but honest mistake he made?

9. What should the young officer be told by his supervisor when it appears that the officer has allowed his job to become more important than his family relationships? Assume that the subordinate has solicited the help of the supervisor.

10. Describe what often happens when anxiety reactions are expressed outwardly as aggressiveness.

9

Discipline: principles, policies, and practices

Discipline is often thought of in a limited sense as meaning punishment or penalty, a negative connotation. However, discipline means, more nearly, instructing, teaching, training. Its main purposes are to facilitate coordination of effort, develop self-control and character, and foster orderliness and efficiency. One of the primary measures of the level of discipline within the police force is the orderliness with which it operates. The degree of this orderliness is directly related to the conduct of the employees, which, in turn, is largely dependent upon how well the supervisor performs his duties.

The principal responsibility for maintaining an appropriate level of discipline in his unit should rest upon the immediate line supervisor.[1] He is responsible for enforcing obedience to organizational rules even though he may not personally favor them. Subordinates are bound to obey regardless of their feelings.[2] Failure to do so will disrupt smooth operations.

[1] John M. Pfiffner and Marshall Fels, *The Supervision of Personnel: Human Relations in the Management of Men,* 3rd ed. (Englewood Cliffs, N.J.: Prentice-Hall, Inc., 1964), p. 111.
[2] International City Management Association, *Municipal Police Administration,* 7th ed. (Washington, D.C.: The International City Management Association, 1971), p. 193.

If the supervisor refuses ·or neglects to consider personnel complaints against his subordinates, if he fails to investigate their delinquencies which àre called to his attention, or if he fails to take proper action when they are derelict in their duties or unprofessional in their conduct, he is not only doing himself a disservice but he is doing an injustice to his organization and other employees. Perhaps in no other activity can the supervisor distinguish himself more for his leadership ability or lack of it than by the manner in which he deals with discipline problem situations.[3]

FORMS OF DISCIPLINE

The word discipline comes from the root word "disciple," which denotes one who receives instructions from another or who follows devotedly the expressions and actions of a respected leader. It is more accurately a term used in modern administration and management to denote a form of moral or mental training, education, subjection to control and regulation, correction, and, finally, chastisement when the other, more positive means of corrective action fail.

Positive discipline

That form of training and attitudinal conditioning which is used to correct deficiencies without invoking punishment is known as positive discipline. It is constructive in nature. Its influence engenders a habitual or conditioned reaction from within the individual to the established values of the organization, its customs, and traditions. It is present when employees willingly follow the directions of their supervisors and adhere to the standards of conduct prevalent in the organization.[4]

A well-disciplined organization is one that is highly trained. It follows that an effective, efficient organization is a well-disciplined one in which the principles of positive discipline have been recognized and practiced. The members have the same individual objectives as those of the group. Such a state can only be achieved, however, when the group objectives are made known to the members and they adopt these objectives as their own.

If supervisors are thoroughly indoctrinated in their responsibilities;

---

[3] William R. Spriegel, Edward Schulz, and William B. Spriegel, *Elements of Supervision*, 3rd ed. (New York: John Wiley & Sons, Inc., 1964), p. 115.

[4] Paul Pigors and Charles A. Myers, *Personnel Administration*, 5th ed. (New York: McGraw-Hill Book Company, 1965), p. 425.

if they are expert planners, trainers, and leaders; if they assist their subordinates by demonstrating, guiding, and counseling; and if they set a good example by their conduct, positive discipline will prevail and the need for punitive discipline will be lessened. Indeed, the skill with which supervisors use this positive tool to a large extent determines the quality of their leadership and the effectiveness of the organization. Iannone [5] stated, "An organization may be considered to have been brought into the ideal state when there exists a maximum of efficiency and satisfaction [of its members] generated by techniques of positive discipline, with a minimum use of the punitive or negative discipline."

Negative discipline

That form of discipline which takes the form of punishment or chastisement is known as negative discipline. When positive methods fail to achieve conformity with accepted standards of conduct or performance, a negative type of action, punitive in nature, must follow to preserve the integrity of the organization. This form of chastisement may involve the mildest form of punishment, admonishment, or the most severe, separation from the service or criminal prosecution. Between these extremes, other penalties the supervisor may apply, short of legal prohibitions, include the oral or written reprimand, voluntary surrender of accumulated overtime, regular days off, or annual leave, mandatory deprivation of these, demotion, loss of salary, or suspension. Often, loss of regular days off, annual leave, or accumulated compensatory time is preferable to outright suspension with full loss of pay because the employee's family is not made to suffer for his derelictions. Use of these punitive forms of discipline should be reserved for the unadjusted, discontented nonconformist who has not been amenable to other, more positive methods. Punishment, then, is the first step in the process of removing him from the organization for the good of the service.

SOME ADVERSE EFFECTS OF PUNISHMENT

Although punishment may produce some undesirable effects, it must be administered at times because no alternative method of coping with a problem of misbehavior is appropriate. Some of the adverse reactions to punishment may be tempered, however, if it is administered intelligently, fairly, and consistently and if the employee can be made to

[5] Marvin D. Iannone, "A Descriptive Study of the Internal Disciplinary Program of the Los Angeles Police Department" (unpublished Master's thesis, California State University at Los Angeles, 1967), p. 13.

understand that it was necessary because of his own misbehavior, not because of someone else's.

The person punished may react with hostility and childlike behavior, especially if he considers the action arbitrary or unfair. He may become frustrated and, if he is a nonconformist with an emotional problem, he is likely to be the very one who will be most often punished.

To many employees who have been punished, such action poses a challenge to devise ways and means of avoiding discovery of their derelictions. The sleeper on the job will become harder to discover after he is once caught and punished.

Actual punishment or the prospect of it may cause a hostile, negative attitude toward the job. Marginal performance is the likely result. The employee will do just enough to avoid being punished for unsatisfactory performance and may sabotage the work efforts of others at every opportunity.

The threat of punishment and the fear it creates may be less effective in changing behavior than are the more positive methods of motivating people. This does not suggest, however, that sanctions against improper behavior are not needed.[6]

REQUISITES OF PUNISHMENT

While punishing an employee does not guarantee that his future conduct or performance will improve, it will not demoralize others in the organization if it is sensibly applied in a fair, consistent manner. Most employees will understand the need for it when a colleague's conduct tends to reflect adversely on them. In fact, most employees are highly critical when a supervisor fails to take prompt disciplinary action that they know is long overdue.

Certainty of punishment

To be most effective, punishment for even the mildest of infractions must be certain. This characteristic is perhaps the greatest deterrent to further misbehavior. Urwick[7] has attributed to Bernard Shaw the remark that "deterrence is a function of certainty, not severity."

The fear that misconduct will certainly be discovered and inevitably punished in one way or another is a powerful deterrent force

[6] I. L. Janis and S. Feshbach, "Effects of Fear-Arousing Communications," *Journal of Abnormal Psychology*, No. 48 (1953), 78–92.

[7] L. Urwick, *The Elements of Administration* (New York: Harper & Row, Publishers, 1943), pp. 87–88.

upon individuals. The fear of losing face with peers or being ostracized by one's fellow employees, especially when the act has been reproachable and is one from which all will suffer, is sometimes greater than the fear of punishment itself. Unfortunately, fear must be used as a management tool to gain conformity from some employees; yet its indiscriminate use is never justified. When its use is indicated, the supervisor should employ it with common sense.

Swiftness of punishment

Punishment must not only be certain but it must be meted out swiftly after detection and proof of the infraction if it is to be effective. Interminable delays in making necessary investigations and administering penalties while the superiors of the derelict employee mull over the matter only serves to embitter the employee involved. It will seldom have constructive effects when finally applied if it is too far removed in time from the conduct which brought about the disciplinary action.

When the supervisor is confronted with a need for disciplinary action against a subordinate, he should not hesitate to administer it. A delay might be interpreted as weakness as both the offender and other members of the group expect some action to be taken. Failure to act when action is indicated may result in the supervisor abdicating his position of leadership.[8]

In cases where criminal charges are to be made against an employee, ordinarily, disciplinary action contemplated should be held in abeyance pending resolution of those charges to avoid prejudicing him unduly in court. Too long a delay, however, may prove to be more harmful to the interests of the organization than proceeding with the administrative action.

Fairness and impartiality

When punitive action is taken against a derelict employee, it will seldom have the desired effect if it is not fairly and impartially administered. Arbitrary or capricious punishment will be resented. Likewise, if it is not applied in a constructive setting, it will have little corrective value. Nor should it be imposed as revenge for an "affront to the establishment." William H. Newman stated "it should not be given in a spirit of retribution, or for the prime purpose of humiliating the

[8] Felix A. Nigro, *Modern Public Administration* (New York: Harper & Row, Publishers, 1965), pp. 277–79.

offender. The purpose of discipline is to bring about improved conduct in the future." [9]

Often punishment is meted out by a supervisor who has allowed his anger to color his judgment. Such emotion should never be allowed to cloud fairness nor to trigger capricious or arbitrary punishment. Therefore, the supervisor discovering misconduct on the part of a subordinate should allow his emotions to cool—if they have become heated—before taking punitive action against him. Misbehavior all too frequently causes supervisors to react angrily and to show their extreme irritation. Such reactions tend to stifle constructive and more positive methods of changing behavior. Punishing a subordinate is a simple approach but not a positive one since often the supervisor can more easily punish a person for doing a poor job than show him how to do it properly.

Punishment that is intemperately or unfairly applied will be resented by employees more than when it is overly severe. It should never destroy the employee's desire to make amends for his mistakes, nor should it become a demoralizing influence upon other employees, who are quick to sympathize with and support another whom they believe has been treated unfairly even though they do not condone his conduct.

The wise supervisor knows that he himself may bear some responsibility for many of the derelictions of his subordinates because of his failure to communicate clearly with them or to train them properly. He will recognize that reprimanding or punishing a subordinate for a minor deviation often will serve no useful purpose because the well-disciplined employee will usually be the first to recognize his own mistakes and prevent a repetition of them in the future.[10]

The supervisor who finds it necessary to take corrective action against a subordinate should do so only after he has made every effort to determine if the dereliction was a mistake "of the head" or "of the heart." An inadvertent deviation from standards or an act of carelessness is one thing. Intentional misconduct is quite another. He should differentiate between the two and take action accordingly, keeping in mind that the training value gained from an error may far exceed the harm done by it.

Consistency of punishment

Punitive action for similar breaches of conduct should be somewhat uniform providing such derelictions occur under like conditions. A guiding rule which has been found useful by many supervisors is that

[9] William H. Newman, *Administrative Action*, 2nd ed. (Englewood Cliffs, N.J.: Prentice-Hall, Inc., 1963), p. 400.

[10] Felix A. Nigro and Lloyd G. Nigro, *Modern Public Administration*, 4th ed. (New York: Harper & Row, Publishers, 1977), pp. 286–90.

just that amount of punishment should be applied which will prevent further derelictions of the same nature. The penalty should fit the offense but it should also fit the individual. This is the ideal state, but it is seldom achieved. Some supervisors contend that all employees who have committed the same infraction cannot be treated just alike since some will respond more quickly to a lesser penalty than will others. If rehabilitation is accomplished without destroying the employee's morale, then what does it matter that penalties are not always equal? Other supervisors ask, "But how about the morale of other employees?" Certainly, the employee's past performance should be considered in meting out punishment. This does not suggest that one employee's breaches of conduct should be "winked at," however, and punishment administered to another for the same dereliction. To do so would violate the basic principle which requires that punishment be applied somewhat consistently.

Overly severe or excessively lenient penalties may cause a reaction from employees just opposite to that intended by the supervisor. Such penalties may make the recipient a martyr or indicate that management considers the dereliction inconsequential.[11] In neither case will the punishment accomplish what it should. Rather, it may set a dangerous precedent which may tend to "bind" management to an undesirable course of action in the future.

Training for others

Punitive action should not only serve as a deterrent to the employee against whom it is applied, but it should be a form of training for other employees to orient them to the types of acts the organization cannot and will not tolerate. Telling employees what is expected of them is a primary requisite in the establishment of an effective disciplinary program. To accomplish this training, some organizations publish in their house organ or by special notices the disciplinary actions taken against personnel. Some contend that this publication places the chastised employee in double jeopardy while others believe the benefits to the total organization more than offset the hazards of such procedures. Some maintain that if the results of disciplinary actions are published within the organization at all for training purposes, the names of those disciplined should be omitted with only the penalties and the derelictions upon which they were based briefly reported. It is argued that this accomplishes the objective of letting others know the types of actions which result in punishment. The procedure, of course, has some inherent dangers. Rumors, inaccurate guesses, and downright false con-

---

11 Newman, *Administrative Action*, p. 400.

clusions are easily nurtured, especially in the larger organizations when only brief accounts of disciplinary actions are publicized. Obviously, then, if such accounts are to be circulated throughout the organization for training purposes, they should be carefully prepared with sufficient detail to prevent speculation, guesses, and rumor. Statements of charges such as "Neglect of Duty," "Conduct Unbecoming an Officer," and the like reveal little information of training value to others. This suggests that more explanatory information be included of the nature of the act that constituted the breach of discipline. In small organizations, the facts of any particular case are usually matters of common knowledge and require little elaboration by the supervisor.

Supervisors should acquaint themselves with sufficient details of the more complex disciplinary cases so that they may explain to their subordinates when necessary the basis for punitive actions taken against employees and thus reduce morale-destroying rumors. Discussions of such matters with other employees should be conducted in an objective, matter-of-fact manner with a minimum of editorializing so that maximum training may be achieved.

Publication of names of derelict employees and concise information upon which charges against them were based can be considered one aspect of the penalty which obviously enhances its deterrent value. Except in the largest agencies, those punished for infractions are usually well identified in any event, long before penalty sheets are published. Information of this nature travels swiftly through "organizational grapevines."

While plaintiffs in civil action suits against police officers can ordinarily obtain information regarding an officer's course of conduct through discovery proceedings,[12] the organization should not jeopardize the confidentiality of its records by placing bulletins concerning disciplinary actions in locations readily accessible to the public; however, these should be easily available to members of the organization. This is especially important if the details of a disciplinary proceeding might lose its confidentiality through publication and thereby become ammunition that can be used against the officer in a civil suit arising from his actions while on duty.

DISCIPLINE BY EXAMPLE

Spriegel[13] stated, "Self-discipline precedes the discipline of others." The supervisor who has difficulty controlling himself or who follows his

---

[12] *Ogilvie v. City of New York,* 353 N.Y.S. 2d 238; *Boyd v. Gullett,* 64 F.R.D. 169 (1974); *Gaison v. Scott,* 59 F.R.D. 347 (1973); *United States v. Reynolds,* 345 U.S. 1 (1953).

[13] Spriegel, Schulz, and Spriegel, *Elements of Supervision,* p. 224.

own set of rules but expects his subordinates to follow a more rigid pattern of conduct can hardly expect them to respect him. If he cannot engage in self-discipline, he will not be able to discipline his subordinates effectively. Likewise, if he cannot follow the orders of his superiors, he can scarcely expect his orders to be followed.

UPWARD DISCIPLINE

Subordinates can exercise a form of discipline against their supervisor just as he can against them. They can do so by thwarting his attempts to exercise leadership, by forcing him to maintain constant pressure on them to gain compliance with his directions, by withholding information from him, and by doing a myriad of other things calculated to indicate their displeasure.[14]

THE RELATIONSHIP BETWEEN DISCIPLINE, MORALE, AND ESPRIT DE CORPS

Morale may be defined as a state of mind reflecting the degree to which an individual has confidence in the members of his group and in the organization, believes in its objectives, and desires to accomplish them. The exact state of morale at a particular time within an establishment is difficult to measure since it is dependent upon a multitude of factors. Among these are the quality of leadership to which the group members are exposed, the level of discipline in the organization, extraneous pressures, the existence or absence of attainable goals, remuneration received by employees, fringe benefits, and other working conditions.

Morale is a fluctuating condition. It exists within individuals and in groups. It may be high or low, moving up or down as it is influenced by a variety of stimuli. An ill-conceived act of a supervisor, an intemperate outburst, the application of an unjustified penalty, a display of partiality, an act of unfairness, or the like may adversely affect the morale of the group or the individual.

In a broad framework, morale may be measured by factors such as quality or quantity of work, the rate of turnover, the number of disciplinary cases, the number of grievances (imagined or real), the amount of absenteeism, acts of disloyalty to the organization, a sharp increase in bickering and arguments among its members, incidents involving the careless use of equipment, misuse of sick time, and the like; but the

[14] Malcolm E. Wolfe et al., *Naval Leadership* (Annapolis, Md.: United States Naval Institute, 1960), p. 33.

most obvious indicator that morale is slumping is a general deterioration in the appearance of personnel, which is usually a gauge of organizational pride. Alert supervisors will constantly attempt to assess the level of morale in the group by the extent to which these and other symptoms of employee dissatisfaction exist. If they assume that morale is always high, they will be mistaken all too frequently.

Esprit de corps, like morale, involves the existence of a sense of common endeavor and responsibility within the group. It embodies devotion to the group enterprise, cooperation among its members, and pride in its accomplishments.[15]

Discipline, morale, and esprit de corps are of equal importance, since they are interdependent. Each may flow from the others or each may adversely affect the others.[16] High morale is usually accompanied by a high level of discipline and esprit de corps. Neither a high level of morale nor esprit de corps commonly accompany a poorly administered disciplinary program. When these three occur together at a favorable level, however, efficiency will be in direct proportion. Thus the supervisor must constantly appraise the methods he employs in carrying out the disciplinary function so that he can avoid those pitfalls which cause diminution in the levels of morale and esprit de corps of his group.

REVERSALS OF ADMINISTRATIVE ACTIONS

A common belief exists among a large segment of the public that "a civil service employee cannot be fired." Such a belief is untrue as long as supervisors responsible for maintaining standards of performance and conduct properly fulfill their duties when called upon to make disciplinary investigations. Experience indicates that management is generally upheld by reviewing tribunals upon appeal by employees who have been punished for breaches of discipline in the public service.

It is true that many supervisors who initiate disciplinary action against subordinates often feel that they, not the derelict employee, are on trial when they are called upon to testify in administrative proceedings and are required to support the action taken against the defending employee. They are often subjected to a most vigorous cross-examination; however, if they have properly prepared the case, if it has been based on hard facts rather than on convincing inferences, speculation, emotion, or unsupported conclusions, and if they have meticulously

[15] United States Department of Defense, *The Armed Forces Officer* (Washington, D.C.: U.S. Government Printing Office, 1950), pp. 158–60.

[16] United States Department of the Army, *Military Leadership, FM 10-100* (Washington, D.C.: U.S. Government Printing Office, 1961), p. 38.

complied with procedural requirements established by law, their case and not the appellant's will be upheld in almost every instance.

RESULTS OF UNSUSTAINED DISCIPLINARY ACTIONS

Invariably, the poorly prepared case, carelessly investigated and lacking in documentation, not only reflects adversely upon the supervisor who investigated it but upon the organization which based punitive action upon it. As a result, the offending employee who probably should have been removed for the good of the service is returned to the job by appeal. More often than not, from that day forward, he becomes an embittered, marginal performer producing just enough to avoid further punishment and contaminating others at every opportunity. Not only does his morale suffer greatly, but the morale of all who must work with him is affected. All too often, his fellow employees who have heard only his version of the story will commiserate with him. "Far greater harm results when an undeserving employee is returned to his job because a disciplinary action cannot be sustained than if the employee had not been disciplined at all." [17]

To be sure, the prestige of management and the confidence of its employees will be lowered by each reversal of a disciplinary judgment it has made. The supervisor whose case has not been sustained frequently becomes reluctant to take further action against the same or another delinquent employee because of his former failure. As a result, his effectiveness and that of the entire unit he directs is lowered.

In those agencies where excessively liberal rules have been enacted by overzealous civil service commissions to protect employee interests, supervisors will often tolerate a substandard employee rather than remove him and contend with defending their case against him on appeal.[18]

COMPLAINT INVESTIGATION POLICY

Organizational policy will dictate the procedure to be followed in receiving and disposing of complaints against personnel. Progressive organizations will adhere to a firm policy of inquiring into each and every complaint made concerning the misconduct of personnel with perhaps

[17] Los Angeles Civil Service Commission, *Resolution on Discipline Policy,* December 9, 1966.

[18] Herbert A. Simon, Donald W. Smithburg, and Victor A. Thompson, *Public Administration* (New York: Alfred A. Knopf, Inc., 1961), pp. 329–30.

only two exceptions. Complaints against official procedures followed by the organization are not usually handled as personnel complaints, nor are those allegations too trivial to dignify as true complaints of misconduct that justify a full investigation (such as the complaint of a citizen that he saw an officer wearing his headpiece at an improper angle, and the like). The allegation should be treated as a complaint, however, if the supervisor receiving it is in doubt as to its classification. Ordinarily such incidents will cause little problem, but the organization should protect itself by a policy which requires that doubtful cases be treated as complaints. Thus the supervisor is responsible for his judgment errors and the likelihood of his being overly lax in his application of the policy will be lessened. Furthermore, the public confidence in the organization will be enhanced by a forthright policy of accepting and determining the merits of all personnel complaints through the process of investigation. In addition, the supervisors within the organization will not be unnecessarily exposed to the inherent danger attending a loose rule permitting acceptance of those complaints appearing valid on their face and rejecting (sometimes purely on an emotional basis) those which do not appear to be bona fide. Application of such a policy would be contrary to all the precepts of investigation, which hold that a conclusion should not be drawn before the facts are known. Experience has proved that some of the complaints which at first seem to be the least plausible are found to be most authentic.

OBJECTIVES OF COMPLAINT INVESTIGATION POLICY

The primary objectives in the administration of an effective personnel complaint investigation policy are to protect the integrity and reputation of the force, to protect the public interest, and to protect the accused employee from unjust accusation.

Public confidence in an organization will be fostered if it demonstrates its willingness to accept complaints against its personnel forthrightly and to give them prompt attention. Protection of the public interest is an equally important objective of a progressive complaint investigation policy. Insistent demands for police review boards and like procedures rarely originate and gain momentum in a community served by a force which has gained public confidence because it has given evidence of its desire to police itself and has recognized that it is in the best interests of the public and the agency to rid itself of unfit personnel.

It is also of great importance that the policy act as an effective protection for the employee against unjust accusations of misconduct, which often have as their objective the establishment of a basis for a civil action against him, his superiors, and the public entity for which he works.

In many jurisdictions, public entities (agencies of state, county, and local government) have been traditionally immune from civil liability resulting from wrongful acts by their employees. This immunity was based on the ancient philosophy of sovereign immunity commonly known as the divine right of kings. Public employees have always been liable for their own negligent or wrongful acts. They have been liable for compensatory as well as exemplary damages. The former were damages resulting from actual loss of wages, medical expenses, or pain and suffering. The latter damages were those awarded by the courts to punish the defendant, especially when malice, fraud, corruption, or connivance were involved in the acts which were the basis of the litigation.

It is reasonable to assume that, under prevailing legislative and judicial philosophies, the experience in many states will be similar to that of California, which now makes a public entity liable for the wrongful acts or omissions of its employees who are acting within the scope of their employment. The employee was formerly liable by himself for both compensatory and exemplary damages. He is still liable for exemplary damages but the public agency which employs him is liable along with him for compensatory damages when the acts or omissions in question were committed or omitted while he was acting within the scope of his employment.[19] The "empty pockets" doctrine of the past wherein, as a practical matter, it was useless to sue a person with empty pockets no longer applies since the treasury of a public agency may now be exposed to civil suit for the wrongful deeds of its employees. As the result of such changes in the philosophy of courts and of the legislative bodies which have enacted similar laws regarding civil liability, litigation in which the officer's conduct is at issue has increased or can be expected to increase very substantially. Thus the supervisor's responsibility in making personnel complaint investigations is increased materially. He must consider an entirely new dimension in conducting his investigations, since the financial security of his organization may be involved. Evidence which may be required for the purpose of a civil defense must be considered in addition to that involved in determining the merits of the complaint. He must be especially alert for clues which would indicate that a civil action might be filed against the officer and the department in connection with the issue under investigation.

[19] California Government Code Sections 815.2(a) and 818; see also Hast.L.J. 983.

Coroner's transcripts

Should a death result from police action and a coroner's inquest be held to determine the cause of death, the investigating supervisor should make a formal request for a transcript of the proceedings. When it is received, it should be placed in the investigation file on the incident. Provisions for interested parties to obtain such information is ordinarily provided for in the laws of the various states. These transcripts of sworn testimony have frequently been of considerable value to the officer involved and his employer in defending themselves against concocted or changed testimony in a wrongful-death action, which is sometimes filed even though the homicide has been previously ruled to be justifiable.

SUMMARY

Every supervisor should attempt to further the aims of his organization through the constructive process of positive discipline, which seeks to develop in the individual members of the force the same objectives as those of the organization. Negative discipline involving punishment should be reserved for the persons who fail to abide by the rules of the organization and cannot be corrected through the process of positive discipline. When punishment is required to correct the noncomformist, it must not only be administered swiftly and certainly, but it must be fair, impartial, and reasonably consistent. To be most effective, punishment must fit not only the offense but the individual upon whom it is imposed. If it is so severe that it engenders only bitterness and resentment in the recipient, it will not be an effective deterrent for him nor will it be training for others since it may be considered a form of revenge by the organization. Excessively lenient punishment may indicate, on the other hand, that the organization considers the deviant act inconsequential.

The supervisor can best carry out his disciplinary function if he will engage in self-discipline and set an example for his subordinates. If he follows one standard and demands that they abide by a more rigid one, they will eventually exert some form of upward discipline against him. This may take the form of work slowdowns, absences, and many other forms of subtle resistance to his leadership efforts. Soon his authority will be undermined, and he will lose much of his effectiveness.

Morale, esprit de corps, and discipline are interdependent. Each affects the others. If the level of discipline in the organization is low, morale and esprit de corps are likely to be poor, and standards of the organization will deteriorate.

The effective maintenance of these standards is dependent in large part upon a forthright policy of investigating every complaint of misconduct against employees, except those which are too trivial to dignify by formal investigation or those which are solely against the established procedures of the force.

Supervisors are often reluctant to pursue an investigation because they fear that, if an employee is separated from the service, upon appeal it is the supervisor who is on trial and not the employee. Supervisors will often tolerate the substandard employee rather than risk this eventuality.

The objectives of a complaint investigation policy should be the protection of the organization from criticism that it will not punish derelict employees, the protection of the public interest, and the protection of the employee from unjust accusation.

A new dimension has been placed upon the importance of such investigations in recent years with the enactment of legislation and the changing philosophy of the courts that have made the public agency civilly liable for the acts of its employees occurring within the scope of their employment. The supervisor must therefore not only preserve the integrity of his investigation but he must protect his organization from unjust claims. He must consider any evidence which might be used against his department in a civil action in addition to that which might reveal the truth or falsity of the accusation against the employee.

REVIEW

Questions

1. What are the two forms of discipline? Discuss the characteristics of each.
2. What are the requisites of punishment? Which of these is the greater deterrent to future misbehavior of a like nature? Discuss your reasons.
3. Distinguish between the mistake "of the head" and the mistake "of the heart." How should these mistakes affect corrective action?
4. How can subordinates exert upward discipline against a superior?
5. What are some of the means you can use as a supervisor to utilize negative disciplinary actions as training for others?
6. What is meant by morale?
7. What is esprit de corps?
8. Discuss how discipline, morale, and esprit de corps are interrelated.

9. What are some of the indicators of the level of morale in an organization?

10. Discuss some of the adverse effects that often result when an employee is reinstated to his job after he appeals his dismissal.

11. Should the supervisor make an inquiry into every complaint of personnel misconduct of subordinates? Justify your answer.

12. What are the three major objectives that a personnel investigation policy should cover?

13. Explain the doctrine of sovereign immunity.

14. What other name is this doctrine known by?

15. What is the "empty pockets" principle?

16. What liability does a city have for the acts of its employees?

Exercises

1. Your superior has assigned you to look into the operations of a unit under his command to determine what the reason might be for an excessive number of complaints against personnel of the unit. Prepare a plan of procedure you would follow in your inquiry. Justify your method of procedure.

2. Your superior believes the morale in this unit is extremely poor. He asks you to verify or disprove his suspicion. How would you proceed to do so?

3. Write a policy statement covering personnel complaint investigations.

4. Prepare a procedural order for the handling and disposition of personnel complaints and investigations.

10

Personnel complaint investigation procedures and techniques

The procedures and techniques involved in conducting a personnel complaint investigation and preparing a disciplinary action will vary somewhat depending upon the origin and nature of the complaint. The supervisor will be limited in his procedural approach by rules and regulations of his organization. His techniques of investigation will ordinarily be limited only by his imagination and ability.

CASE PREPARATION: GENERAL PROCEDURES

The general procedures for handling minor infractions observed by the supervisor in the course of his activities will involve a discussion of the incident with the concerned employee, an on-the-spot warning or admonishment given when indicated, a record made of the incident for future reference, and follow-up to determine the effect of the warning. The procedure which will be followed by the supervisor in initiating appropriate action in response to a more serious complaint from within or from outside the department will follow a general pattern. First, the exact nature of the alleged misconduct must be ascertained from the complainant. Broad generalizations such as, "I am being harassed by the police," do not state a cause for investigation unless the complainant can specify the exact nature of the harassment. Second, an inquiry must be initiated for the purpose of determining the merit of the complaint (and the degree of culpability of the accused officer if investigation supports the allegation). Third, conclusions must be drawn from the facts collected and recommendations made concerning the disposition of the case. Corrective action may be indicated or the case may be closed if the evidence does not reasonably support the allegation. Fourth, if corrective action is decided upon, it must be administered. Fifth, the supervisor should follow up to ascertain the effect of any disciplinary action, especially if it is negative.

SOURCES OF COMPLAINTS

The following discussion will consider first those investigations initiated as the result of complaints by supervisors who have observed infractions or complaints based on information received from inside the organization that an employee has committed a breach of conduct and, second, complaints of others from outside the organization. The first type may be called the *internal complaint*. The latter is designated the *external complaint*.

Internal complaints

Internal complaints are those emanating from within the organization such as those made by report auditors who report upon deficiencies or irregularities found in reports, jailors who report upon improper conduct of employees in the treatment of arrestees or prisoners, supervisors who observe misconduct and initiate disciplinary action, and so forth.

External complaints

External complaints are those which come from persons outside the organization. These may be classified as *primary complaints*—those received directly from alleged victims of police action or debtors—and *secondary complaints*, or second-party complaints—those from persons who are not themselves victims but complain on behalf of others. Such complaints may be made by attorneys, elected officials, or representatives of organized groups, parents, or others whose attention has been directed to possible deviant behavior through observation or who act as the spokesman for others in complaining of such behavior.

OBSERVED INFRACTIONS

The extent of the action taken in a given case will be determined by the nature of the infraction. Many minor deviations involving the employee whose work is somewhat substandard, who has drifted into bad habits, who has committed a minor breach of regulations, or who has otherwise engaged in conduct which is not acceptable can be disposed of at the time they are observed by the supervisor by a warning or admonishment from him. Such reproof should obviously be given only when the act of the employee does not require immediate and more severe disciplinary action.

Discuss in private

In every such instance of an observed breach of discipline, the supervisor should call the matter to the attention of the employee *promptly and in private.* Rarely indeed can a castigation in the presence of fellow employees or of the public be justified. On occasion, however, it may become necessary to stop a continuing breach of order.

Sometimes the supervisor will learn that a misunderstanding of rules and regulations has been the cause of a minor breach of conduct. If so, he should clarify the matter to prevent a recurrence. The supervisor should assure himself that the subordinate understands specifically the nature of his dereliction and what is expected of him in the future. This can be accomplished by having him "play back" what *he* understands is expected of him. This procedure will ensure that the subordinate cannot later validly claim as a defense that he misunderstood instructions should the incident recur.

Record results

Except in very minor cases, a record of the circumstances of the incident and the action taken should be made in every instance where a breach of discipline requires punitive action by the supervisor. Such records may vary from a brief notation in the sergeant's activity log or on the control card maintained for each officer if the infraction is a minor one, to an incident report [1] for an infraction requiring only an on-the-spot warning or admonition, or to a full, detailed report for a more serious dereliction requiring review by higher authority and possible punitive action. Such records will provide documentation in the event of a recurrence of such unacceptable conduct.

The recording of the incident without calling the act to the offending employee's attention or otherwise confronting him with it is indefensible since, in essence, such procedure involves a charge being made against him without giving him an opportunity to be heard. He will be resentful when he ultimately learns that a written record of his act has been placed in his file without his having been apprised of the matter. A secondary, but nonetheless important, side effect which should be avoided is a general weakening of supervision when such covert practices are permitted.

Some supervisors tend to avoid making a negative incident report when they are required to discuss it with the involved subordinate or allow him to see it before it is filed. Conversely, such supervisors are often prone to overdo these reports when they involve commendatory incidents. Although such conduct is an evasion of responsibility, it is nevertheless a natural psychological reaction for most persons to do those things which produce a pleasant experience and to avoid those activities which are unpleasant. This psychological truism explains such occurrences but does not excuse them. Supervisors should be expected to face the problems they encounter forthrightly and take whatever corrective action may be indicated.

Follow-up

In order to determine if the initial discussion was successful, the supervisor should discreetly make a follow-up inquiry, which may consist of a casual conversation with the offending subordinate, observations to determine if improvement has taken place, or whatever additional investigation may be necessary. A follow-up discussion with the subordinate may be necessary if no improvement has occurred. Such an interview should involve discussion, clarification of misunderstandings which may have contributed to the incident, understanding of what is expected, suggestions for improvement, playback, warning when indi-

---

[1] An incident report may be used as a formal record of a minor censurable act (or a meritorious act deserving formal recognition) when a full, detailed report is not indicated, such as in cases of minor mishandling of equipment, tardiness, improper uniform, and the like. These report forms should be simple and easy to make, or they will not be used to full effect.

cated, recording of results, and perhaps referral to higher authority with a recommendation for punitive action when circumstances indicate.

Every supervisor should be aware that the selection and training of a police officer to a point where he has become a productive employee is a costly venture and draws heavily upon the resources of the force. Therefore, every effort must be made to prevent the eventual loss of an officer when he could be saved if his minor deficiencies are intelligently, purposefully, and positively dealt with by his supervisor before they are beyond correction. For example, the police supervisor serves neither his own best interests nor those of his organization or of his subordinates if he tolerates or "blinks at" an incident, however minor, involving drinking on duty (excepting, of course, in those few assignments requiring such activity on occasion). It has been an unfortunate experience in many forces that such conduct all too often becomes eventually so aggravated as to require the termination of an employee who represents a considerable investment to the force and who might otherwise have been of considerable value to it rather than an embarrassment that could have been avoided by proper treatment of the problem when it was small.

It is not suggested that the supervisor become a martinet in his adherence to rules and regulations; however, he should not overlook conduct which requires corrective action merely to foster his own popularity.

PRIMARY AND SECONDARY COMPLAINTS

Taking primary complaints

Supervisors taking personnel complaints from aggrieved citizens should listen courteously and attentively and should avoid any facial expressions or statements indicating disbelief. When the complaint is patently false, a different approach may be indicated.

Occasionally the complaint, while made in good faith, is based on misinformation or misunderstanding. The supervisor should then make the necessary explanations or provide the information needed to clarify the issue. Often this is all that is necessary to satisfy the complainant. When it is not, the matter should be processed in accordance with departmental practices.

Supervisors should avoid acting as arbiters when complaints involving the validity of police action are received with no allegation of misconduct. Adjudication of such matters as traffic citations and arrests is within the province of the court or jury hearing the facts, and "curbstone justice" in such instances can lead only to eventual accusations of "ticket fixing" or "quashing a case if you know the right people." Such complaints should be referred as gracefully as possible to the courts for adjudication. Where police action has been patently unjust or improper, however, the supervisor should follow established procedures to correct such injustices; if misconduct exists on the part of his subordinate, appropriate corrective action should be initiated.

Second party complaints

Complaints received from second parties on behalf of an alleged victim of police action should not be rejected merely because they are not made directly by the person claiming he has been aggrieved. Bona fide complaints from whatever source should set the wheels of investigation in motion to determine all the facts in the matter.

Anonymous complaints

Complaints coming from unidentified sources should be treated with the greatest caution and discretion because of the great impact they may have upon the morale of employees involved. Each such complaint should be considered upon its own merit. Unfortunately, no rule of thumb can dictate whether an investigation should or should not be initiated in such cases; however, no agency can afford the risks of rejecting a complaint for lack of merit solely because it comes from an anonymous source. Experienced supervisors will recall that some of the most serious and bizarre police personnel incidents have been brought to light by anonymous information.

INTERVIEW OF COMPLAINANT

Persons making complaints while intoxicated should always be reinterviewed when they are sober. It has been found that, at this time, they will often temper their original complaint, change it, or withdraw it completely when sober reflection indicates to them the injustice of the complaint. For example, sobriety often enables them to recollect what happened to property they thought was taken by arresting officers. (Complaints from intoxicated persons will be discussed in considerable detail below.)

When accusations have been brought to the attention of the department by second parties such as ministers, attorneys, parents, and so on, the investigating supervisor should insist upon interviewing the complainant personally to obtain his firsthand version of the incident.

During this interview, the investigator should neither commit his organization to a particular course of action regarding the investigation, the disposition of the complaint, or penalties, nor should he indicate directly or by implication his impression regarding the merits of the accusation, the culpability of the accused officer, the history of past complaints against him, or his proclivities to commit the type of act complained of. Facts uncovered during the investigation may cause the supervisor to regret his editorializing and may cause his superiors and himself considerable embarrassment if their judgment, based on mature consideration of the facts, does not coincide with his own premature commitments.

The supervisor should be alert for expressions of the complainant indicating his possible motives for complaining. These may provide valuable clues which will often assist in the investigation. For example, it is not unusual for a person who has been arrested to complain that the arresting officer relieved him of his money. He may find this accusation, however unjust, a more convenient explanation of the loss of his paycheck than the true fact that he lost his money in a bar, gambling game, or some other activity equally difficult to justify to his spouse.

A check of records should be made and the interview report should indicate if the complainant has had previous encounters with the police, the nature of the charges against him, and whether similar complaints of misconduct were made by him against the arresting officer in other police contacts. This information may help in assessing his credibility, or lack of it, and in determining the merit of his allegations.

COMPLAINTS FROM INTOXICATED PERSONS

Frequently, complaints against police personnel are made by intoxicated persons who have been arrested by the police. Less frequent are those complaints from intoxicated victims of crime. Such complaints will tax the judgment of the supervisor since many prove to be totally without merit and are made by the arrestee in an attempt to evade further criminal action; however, the complaint should not be discredited merely because it is made by an intoxicated person who is the subject of police action. The supervisor must exercise the greatest caution and discretion in treating complaints made under these circumstances. When complaints of loss of personal property are made under conditions giving the supervisor reasonable cause to believe the complaint has some merit, immediate steps must be taken to determine how such loss occurred— to protect not only the interests of the complainant but also the integrity of the police agency and, above all, that of the accused officer if he has been subjected to an unjust accusation or hint of wrongdoing.

Under such circumstances, the supervisor should promptly examine the police premises in which the arrestee was detained and the police vehicle in which he was transported. It has been the experience of many supervisors that property is frequently concealed in police premises or vehicles by arrestees who later complain that their property has been stolen by the arresting officer. The motives behind such complaints are obvious. Supervisors, jailors, searching officers, and booking officers are therefore sometimes prone to discredit such allegations—sometimes at considerable risk because of the occasional meritorious complaint. When a series of complaints are received, supervisors should be especially alert for the pattern of conduct which may be indicated.

RECORDING COMPLAINTS

Oral complaints should be reduced to writing as soon as practicable after they are received, when the facts are usually most readily available. Occasionally, a verbatim record of the accusation may be indicated because of its nature. Usually, however, a carefully made record of the substance of the complaint will serve as a basis for the investigation. The policy of the organization will dictate whether a crime report must be made when a complaint alleges a criminal act.

In recording complaints against police personnel, the supervisor should avoid including as part of the report his subjective observations. He should, however, record objective evidence which comes to his attention such as the existence of conflicts in the complaint, intoxication of the complainant, the existence of particular motives in the making of the accusation, and other evidence which might be useful in the investigation and subsequent proceedings.[2]

COMPLAINT INVESTIGATION

The techniques of investigating personnel complaints will not vary substantially from those employed in other investigations. A few cautionary admonitions should be recited at this point, however, since ordinarily no criminal act is involved. Most complaints against personnel involve

[2] Prior to May 29, 1961, in California, complainants who were proved to have knowingly and falsely accused police officers of misconduct were subject to criminal prosecution. However, in *People v. Marco Delmus Johnson*, CRA 4520 (May 29, 1961), the majority of the Appellate Department of the Superior Court stated that to apply such a law (i.e., making a false police report in which a police officer is knowingly and falsely accused of misconduct) to a "Personnel Complaint" as opposed to a crime report constitutes an abridgment of a citizen's right to petition his government for redress of a grievance under the First Amendment of the U.S. Constitution. The

noncriminal misconduct only. Furthermore, experience reveals that over half the complaints received from all sources, both from inside and outside the department, cannot be supported by investigation or are conclusively found to be without merit. Finally, an unusual amount of discretion must be exercised by the supervisor conducting a personnel investigation because his approach will have a vital effect upon the morale of the force.

The protections given an employee by "due process" provisions in the law and in collective bargaining agreements must be meticulously observed by the investigating supervisor—not only for morale purposes— but to comply with such legal restraints imposed on him.

Avoid premature conclusions

The investigating supervisor should avoid drawing a conclusion regarding the merits of the complaint until all the evidence has been collected. He should exercise the greatest of care to avoid unnecessary discussion of the merits of the complaint with subordinates before the case is concluded since his statements are apt to be misconstrued. If he appears defensive toward the accused subordinate prematurely, he subjects himself to the criticism of superiors, and rightly so. If he hastens to a conclusion concerning the employee's guilt before learning all the facts, he risks seriously impairing employee morale by his attitude.

Although the supervisor may tend to be influenced in his investigation by his personal feelings, he should approach the inquiry as objectively as possible. If he is reluctant to collect facts adverse to his subordinate's interest, his organization suffers since effective corrective action will become impossible. If he fails to make a complete and proper investigation, or makes none at all, the incident may never be resolved because evidence which might have cleared the accused officer was not uncovered. The officer may live under a cloud of suspicion, doubt, and uncertainty thereafter because the supervisor did not do his job.

Prevent aggravation

In some instances involving allegations of serious misconduct supported by evidence which points to the incontrovertible conclusion of guilt of the accused employee, the supervisor must take steps to prevent

---

same reasoning must be applied to municipal ordinances covering the same subject since this area of law has been preempted by state law.

It appears likely that such a ruling will spread in light of present trends in the appellate courts' interpretations of a citizen's rights under the First Amendment.

the matter from becoming more aggravated. Protective custody of the employee involved or his actual confinement may be indicated in instances of felonious conduct. In less serious cases in which the errant employee cannot be continued on duty, the supervisor may find it desirable to send him home with instructions to report back at a later specified time. Should the breach of conduct involve intoxication of the type that does not indicate more severe action at that time than relieving the employee from duty, he should be taken home by a supervisory officer rather than by a colleague. Often, a secure place is available at the station where an intoxicated employee can be isolated until he becomes sober, should that course of action be practicable.

An alternative procedure available to the supervisor in preventing further aggravation in some cases permitted by departmental rules is that of continuing the employee on duty but assigning him to remain at home subject to call until such time as the matter is resolved. In effect, this places him under "house arrest." Since the employee is considered to be on duty in this case, necessary control can be maintained over him without exposing him to further hazards which might only subject the organization and the employee to more embarrassment during the period in which the matter is being resolved. In other cases, he might be relieved from duty until completion of the investigation which will permit a disposition of the case.

Arrest and booking of employee

Physical arrest and formal booking of an accused officer should be made only after the chief officer of the organization has been made fully aware of the circumstances of the matter. It is he who must answer inquiries of other city officials or the press. Therefore, he must be kept informed of such important happenings in his department.

Serious misconduct of a peace officer involving felonious crimes such as bribery, morals offenses, theft, and so on will invariably result in considerable adverse publicity for the entire force; yet the bad effects will be minimized in the eyes of the public if the organization will demonstrate its willingness to police itself by uncovering such employee breaches and dealing vigorously with them. Less serious offenses, though technically low-grade misdemeanors, such as traffic infractions, intoxication, and the like ordinarily can be disposed of administratively within the organization. Such infractions should rarely be handled by "on-the-spot arrest." Should later developments indicate that criminal action must be taken against the employee, a complaint can be secured from the local prosecutor at any time. Such a course of action is not inimical to the public interest since administrative punishment within the law enforcement organization has traditionally been far more severe than criminal penalties.

In cases where a police employee of another agency is involved, his own department should be promptly informed of the circumstances. At times, it is desirable to turn the investigation over to them, especially when the conduct involves a serious breach of a department rule but is not a crime.

Promptness of investigation

Delays in beginning a complaint investigation and failures to pursue it diligently to a conclusion can only hamper the inquiry. Witnesses often forget details with the passing of time, stories may be concocted, and evidence sometimes disappears with the result that the findings become less and less reliable. It should be stressed again that investigations of cases which are not clearly resolved usually serve no useful purpose either to the accused employee or to the organization. To the contrary, the case often creates a doubt whether the employee was not culpable of the act alleged.

Collecting negative information

Investigating supervisors sometimes fail to record information from bystanders who were in a position to observe what happened in the incident under investigation but say that they saw or heard nothing. Such negative evidence usually has little probative value but may be exceedingly important in refuting the testimony of such persons who may later appear as witnesses in a civil trial and testify that they witnessed the entire occurrence.

Personnel record check

Personnel records of the accused employee should be carefully scrutinized for evidence that he has previously been the subject of similar complaints. Their existence may point up the need for a closer examination of his conduct. Valuable clues to the employee's pattern of behavior may be revealed by a series of similar complaints.

When the allegations involve failures in performance, personnel evaluation reports should be analyzed for evidence that the officer has been previously warned or admonished concerning his performance.

Considerable difficulty would be encountered in bringing a successful action against an employee for general unfitness or substandard performance if his supervisors had rated his performance satisfactory in their periodic service ratings.

Time sheets, attendance records, and daily performance logs may reveal evidence of false statements regarding duty activities. Accomplishment reports may reveal substandard performance in relation to established norms but should be viewed with caution since quantitative records are seldom, in themselves, true indicators of the employee's worth.

Interviewing the accused employee

At some time during the investigation, the investigating supervisor must decide when the accused employee is to be interviewed. There are no hard and fast rules governing this decision. Each case must be decided on its own merits. At times, the interview should be conducted at the very beginning of the inquiry. This procedure might be indicated where the accusation is minor or where the accused person has certain information that is needed before the inquiry can be continued. For example, if an allegation is made that an officer misappropriated certain property he had taken from a suspect, the accused employee might easily be able to explain what happened to the property. An interview with the employee in connection with a serious dereliction under investigation should generally not be conducted until the full accusation has been recorded and as many facts as practicable concerning it have been collected and reviewed by the investigating supervisor. Departmental policy and the nature of the complaint will usually dictate whether a written, stenographic, or taped statement should be taken of the interview and whether the investigatory procedures to be followed are explained to the concerned employee.

The supervisor should scrupulously avoid the tendency to draw a conclusion before the investigation is completed as previously discussed. He should be especially careful to avoid discussing the merits of the case with other subordinate officers not concerned in the inquiry. The investigator's function is to obtain facts, not to give out information. At this stage of the inquiry, every effort must be made to avoid disparaging the employee with his family and fellow workers either by the method of interviewing him, making necessary searches, or otherwise conducting inquiries in their presence.

The investigating supervisor should approach this contact with the accused employee as an interview, but he may find it necessary to complete it as an interrogation, depending upon the nature of the accusation.

It is imperative that the interview with the accused employee be approached in a matter-of-fact manner, giving him a full opportunity to explain his side. No apology need be given for the action taken since disciplinary investigations are an important and necessary part of the supervisor's responsibility to his organization. His manner, however, should reflect an objective, unbiased attitude with no indication that a preconceived conclusion had been reached.

Should a dereliction under investigation indicate that separation from the service is desirable, the supervisor should avoid coercing the employee to resign in lieu of disciplinary action, since such action might result in reversal by the courts and a reinstatement of the employee. Allowing an employee to resign in lieu of disciplinary action is largely a matter of organizational policy. Voluntary resignations are generally more final than forced separations from the service, as the latter must often withstand court action to bring about reinstatement along with the risk that the employer will be required to pay the back salary due the employee.

Should the employee be permitted to resign in lieu of administrative punishment, the supervisor should refrain from promising or implying that the resignation will bring immunity from any further action, civil or criminal. The supervisor is rarely in a position to offer such immunity.

Likewise, statements made as ultimatums should be avoided. The supervisor may not be in a position to take the action indicated by his ultimatum because of legal limitations prohibiting coercion, duress, or undue influence, or because of a disinclination by his superior to take a particular course of action merely because it was thought by the supervisor to be appropriate.

Legal counsel

The investigating supervisor should be guided by the law in his jurisdiction and past practices in his organization whether to grant an accused employee's request for legal counsel before or during the fact-finding interview. The right to consultation *prior* to questioning delays the proceedings and implies a right to counsel *during* the questioning. Counsel should not generally be permitted during this stage of the inquiry. If counsel is permitted, a later claim may be made that such procedure is a general practice and that the denial of counsel at the particular inquiry in question was arbitrary and unfair. Recent cases [3]

[3] *Boulware v. Battaglia*, 478 F. 2d 139 (1973); *Mobil Oil Corporation v. National Labor Relations Board*, 482 F. 2d 842 (1973); *National Labor Relations Board v. Quality Manufacturing Co.*, 481 F. 2d 1018 (1973); *Texaco Inc. Houston Producing Div. v. National Labor Relations Board*, 408 F. 2d 142, 168 (1969).

in federal courts have held that employees have no right to legal representation during such interviews; however, if the investigation becomes accusatory, that is, the focus is on the employee as a suspect in a criminal case, then he is protected the same as any other person.

Written statements

The nature of the investigation will dictate whether formal, verbatim statements should be taken from the accused employee concerning his version of the incident, whether a memorandum report from him will suffice, or if a summary report by the interviewer is indicated. Supervisors are prone to require the accused to make an employee's report too frequently. Such reports seldom give a complete account of what happened. Rarely do they satisfy the requirements of the investigation, especially when the accused is expected to make admissions against his own interests. Invariably, inaccuracies or omissions require reinterviewing the employee. It is often said that "you can tell the truth without convicting yourself." This philosophy implies that the truth can be rigidly adhered to by telling only part of the story and conveniently omitting the incriminating part. It is the supervisor's responsibility to arrive at the truth of the matter. He must do so by whatever proper means present themselves. Generally, he can accomplish most by asking directly the questions he expects answered.

Requiring the accused to make a written report of the incident presents a further danger. The accused is often unwittingly made the subject of rumor which can, and usually does, start with the typing and distribution of the report. Such an event should be avoided whenever possible because of the adverse effect rumors and gossip concerning matters of this nature have upon morale. Handwritten reports without routine distribution will, of course, eliminate some of these problems. In those cases where they are obtained, they should contain a specific, unequivocal answer to each and every allegation by the complainant. Unless such a response is made to every issue in the accusation, the investigation cannot be complete.

Avoid face-to-face encounters

Despite the dramatic success of fictional investigators in face-to-face confrontations, experienced supervisors have found that only upon the rarest of occasions would a situation arise in which it would be advisable to bring the complainant and the accused employee together in a face-to-face encounter. Seldom will anything beneficial to the investigation be accomplished by this procedure, but it could well make a bad situation worse. Claims and counterclaims, if not downright violence, can easily be precipitated in such volatile situations involving the accused and his accuser. If the case is serious enough to require a "show-up" for identification purposes, the supervisor can easily make the necessary arrangements without risking the possible complications which might result from a confrontation of the parties.

Pictures of employees might suffice for the purpose of identification if such is necessary. The guidelines set forth by the courts [4] should be followed in this process to ensure fairness and impartiality to all parties involved. Several photographs should be selected showing individuals with dress, features, pose, and complexion similar to those of the accused. The person making the identification should not be influenced or open to suggestion in his attempt to select the right photograph. Nor should he be given reason to conclude or guess that the photographs shown him include the picture of the person to be identified. The ultimate purpose of this procedure must be kept in mind—to arrive at the truth.

If an apology is demanded by the complainant for an act allegedly involving misconduct of an officer, the supervisor should not allow the apology to settle the matter even if an apology is forthcoming. To do so would establish a dangerous precedent. Other personnel would soon come to believe that all they need to do to escape punishment for their misdeeds is to apologize.

Searches

One of the most distasteful of the supervisor's investigative responsibilities but, on occasion, a most necessary one is the making of a search which might involve an officer's person, his private vehicle, his locker and effects, or his home. The need for a search might be indicated in conjunction with an investigation of a complaint such as one alleging that an employee misappropriated property. The task becomes especially onerous for the investigator and equally distressing for the employee when the allegation is made by an intoxicated arrestee; however, when

---

[4] See *Simmons v. United States*, 36 LW 4227 (1968), for additional guidelines in making identifications by photographs. While the procedures suggested by the United States Supreme Court are "ideal" in criminal cases, they are not required in all cases. Such procedures might even be impractical at times. Generally, however, they may be applied with good effect in administrative proceedings. The main objective would be to lessen the risk of misidentification. Neither the manner used in displaying photographs nor the pictures themselves may be "unfairly suggestive"; see also *Biehunik v. Filicetta*, 441 F. 2d 228 (2d Cir. 1971), cert. denied 403 U.S. 932 (1971).

the decision has been made by the supervisor to follow this course of action, he should proceed with the search with the utmost tact and discretion. Whenever possible, the search should be made with the employee's consent. Searches of his personal property without his consent are limited by the many rules of law that have evolved under the Fourth Amendment. These rules are applicable to administrative disciplinary proceedings as well as criminal trials [5] and should be adhered to meticulously by the supervisor.

Some courts have held that searches of departmental property such as lockers, police vehicles, and desks, generally may be conducted without a warrant;[6] but rulings in some states may depart from the general rule because past practices in an organization have led the employee to believe that he may expect privacy in the use of such equipment or facility. Under such circumstances, the employee may be protected from a warrantless search of this type of department property. Therefore, the supervisor should be fully aware of the search and seizure rules in his particular jurisdiction so that he may avoid the exclusion of evidence which has been seized in violation of the employee's reasonable expectation of privacy or other Fourth Amendment rights.

Whenever practicable, searches should be made in private. The matter can be disposed of with a minimum of resentment if the subordinate is convinced of the need for such steps to protect him from future aspersions which might result from a failure on the part of the investigating supervisor to follow what might appear to be a necessary investigative procedure. A forthright approach by the supervisor will tend to reduce the adverse effects to morale often accompanying such incidents.

A search of the vehicle or effects of the accused should be made in his presence. Should a search of his residence become necessary because of the nature of the complaint and the evidence, steps should be taken to make it in the absence of other members of the employee's family to avert the implications and the irreparable harm to family relations which might result from the mere fact that the search had been found necessary. Regardless of what evidence is revealed, such searches often will result in a total loss of an employee as a productive member of the organization. If incriminating evidence is revealed, the employee may be lost to the service through termination, or if he is severely punished, he will in all probability lose much of his organizational zeal. If the search is nonproductive, it will often cause irreparable harm to his morale. This is often in direct proportion to the selling job done by the super-

[5] *McPherson v. New York City Housing Authority*, 365 N.Y. S. 2d 862 (1975).

[6] *Peo. v. Tidwell*, 266 N.E. 2d 787 (1971); see also *United States v. Katz*, 389 U.S. 347 (1968).

visor. In any case, it is incumbent upon the supervisor to take whatever investigative steps are indicated within the framework of the law.

Lineups

An employee may be ordered to participate in a lineup to have him identified by a complainant and may be disciplined for refusing; but the lineup must not be unfairly suggestive.[7] The order to submit to this investigative procedure should be made in writing if he refuses, as discussed later in this chapter.

Investigative aids

The investigating supervisor should not overlook the many aids at his disposal in making a complete inquiry into the circumstances of a personnel complaint.

A polygraph examination might be of value to the inquiry, but its limitations should not be forgotten. It is not infallible. It is not yet considered an absolute indicator of guilt or innocence regardless of the qualifications of the operator. Use of this device on an officer should be reserved for the most serious of complaints and should be carefully controlled by the policy of the organization. Approval of its use should be reserved to the highest officer of the department or his delegate because of the adverse impact upon morale which might result from the indiscriminate use of the instrument in personnel investigations. The supervisor should remember that this device is merely an aid to his investigation, not a crutch for him to rely upon. It does not take the place of a thorough investigation but may be a useful supplement to it. On occasion, it is an effective means of determining the veracity of the complainant's accusations, and if doubt exists as to their truth or falsity, it might be resolved by this means.

Courts have given qualified approval of the use of the polygraph in personnel investigations:

> While lie detector tests do not as yet have enough reliability to justify the admission of expert testimony based on their results, . . . it does not follow that such tests are completely without value. It is well recognized that polygraph tests are commonly used by law enforcement agencies in the investigation and detection of crime. . . . Such tests can serve to guide police investigators in their hypothesis. [8]

[7] *Biehunik v. Felicetta*, 441 F. 2d 228 (1971); *Stoval v. Denno*, 385 U.S. 293 (1967).

[8] *Frazee v. Civil Service Board of the City of Oakland et al.*, 170 C.A. 2d 333 (1959); see also *Roux v. New Orleans*, 233 So. 2d 905 (1969); and *Chambliss v. Board of Fire and Police Commissioners*, 312 N.E. 2d 842 (1974).

An unwilling officer accused of misconduct can properly be ordered to submit to such an examination by the chief administrative officer of the organization:

> It is . . . a violation . . . for any police officer to refuse to disclose pertinent facts within his knowledge even though such disclosure may show, or tend to show, that he himself has engaged in criminal activities. [9]

In still another decision by a District Court of Appeals, it was held that:

> We do not suggest that appellant's refusal to obey the order is any evidence of guilt or knowledge of the identity of the guilty party. We do hold that, in the light of his sworn duty to aid in the investigation of crime, the order that he complete the [polygraph] test . . . was reasonable. Appellant's refusal to obey the order impeded the investigation of a criminal offense and amounted to insubordination and unofficer-like conduct, thus warranting his discharge.[10]

It is thus apparent that, in many jurisdictions, the courts will support the right of a public organization to protect itself from unscrupulous employees. While the provisions of the Fifth Amendment to the United States Constitution will protect the employee from being required to answer questions that may tend to incriminate him for a criminal offense, the amendment does not give him a constitutional right to his employment but does protect him from being forced to answer questions not related "narrowly and directly" to his duties or the investigation being conducted.[11] Obviously, when the employee's statements are to be used against him in a criminal prosecution, he should be given his Miranda rights.[12] If he is not, his statements will be excluded at the trial with few exceptions. If an employee answers a question in response to a direct order, his statements will be admissible against him in an administrative hearing; but if he is threatened with the loss of his job

[9] Christal v. Police Commission, 33 Cal. App. 2d 564 (1939). See also Uniformed Sanitary Men v. Commissioner, 283 Federal 2nd., 364, wherein the court held that if employees availed themselves of the Fifth Amendment privilege and refused to answer questions, their employer could properly dismiss them. See also Nelson v. Los Angeles, 362 U.S. 1 (1960), in which the court upheld a dismissal of employees for refusing to answer questions as to their conduct on the job.

[10] McCain v. Sheridan, 160 Cal. App. 2d 174 (1958). See also Gardner v. Broderick, 392 U.S. 273 (1968).

[11] Gardner v. Broderick, 393 U.S. 273 (1968); Furutani v. Ewigleben, 297 F. Supp. 1163 (1969); Spevak v. Klein, 385 U.S. 511 (1967).

[12] Miranda v. Arizona, 384 U.S. 436 (1966).

if he does not waive his privilege against self-incrimination and answer the question, the coercion makes any of his incriminating answers involuntary and inadmissible in a criminal proceeding.[13]

An employee's refusal to submit to a scientific test that would aid the organization in the investigation of a criminal offense would make him subject to discharge. Such an order should be given in writing whenever possible if an employee refuses to comply with an oral directive. It has long been the law that any reasonable order to an employee is enforceable administratively, and the courts have been reluctant to interfere if arbitrariness or capriciousness is not shown or if there has been no breach of procedural requirements such as might be contained in a police officer's "Bill of Rights" in a contractual agreement. Refusal of such an order by an employee would properly be considered unbecoming conduct for which he could be punished.

Physical tests

Blood, urine, or breath tests are often helpful to prove or disprove intoxication when this condition is in issue. Objective symptoms of intoxication are not always sufficient to provide conclusive proof of this physical state. When an accused employee is requested to submit to such test or tests, they should be administered in private, by a supervisor if possible, to avoid embarrassing him unnecessarily or causing rumors unjustifiably.

Other scientific devices, tests, and equipment should be utilized when investigative procedures indicate their need. The law governing the seizing and use of nontestimonial evidence in connection with a personnel investigation is generally the same as that relating to criminal investigations.[14]

Investigative techniques common to other police investigations should be employed to enable the supervisor conducting the inquiry to arrive at the truth of the matter; however, when these techniques are used, he must abide carefully by the employee's constitutional safeguards and by local rules or contractual provisions that may be more restrictive than the law in protecting employee rights. The supervisor should exercise the utmost tact and diplomacy in this sensitive area of complaint investigations since these ordinarily involve noncriminal misconduct.

[13] *Garrity v. New Jersey,* 385 U.S. 493 (1967); *Varela v. Commissioners,* 383, P. 2d 62 (1962).
[14] *Schmerber v. California,* 384 U.S. 757 (1966); *Krolick v. Lawrey,* 308 N.Y.S. 2d 879 (1970).

REPORTING PROCEDURES

Basic to all police reports but of special importance to complaint investigation reports are the requisites of accuracy and completeness. All allegations of misconduct made by the complainant must be answered. Each report should contain a brief account of the complaint, the details of the investigation of each and every accusation, and the findings.

Investigative report

The report of the investigation should ideally contain a heading, a statement of the complaint, a summary of the investigation, the details of the investigation, conclusions and recommendations (when requested by higher authority or required by rules and regulations), and addenda.

The *heading* of the report will follow the format established by the organization and will ordinarily contain the details which identify the reporting supervisor, the person to whom the report is directed, the date and time of the report, and other details which may be required.

The *complaint* (sometimes referred to as the subject) should contain a brief statement of the accusation, the name of the accuser, and that of the accused. The *who, what, where, when, how* (and sometimes *why*) should be recapitulated in this section of the report to provide those who review it a brief description of the subject matter. A typical complaint section of a report would contain the following information:

> *Complaint.* Winthrop J. Spinning alleges in a letter to the department that he suffered a twisted shoulder as the result of unnecessary force used upon him when he was arrested for being intoxicated by officer James S. Jones, #23, on (date) at (place).

The *summary of investigation* section should contain a concise account of the material findings of the inquiry. This section gives the reviewer a complete but brief résumé of all the evidence obtained which is germane to the complaint. Extreme care should be exercised in preparing such summary statements to avoid misleading those who wish to familiarize themselves with the circumstances surrounding the incident without studying the details of the investigation. Busy administrators often find it necessary to rely upon summary statements of occurrences to keep abreast of current happenings so that they may keep their superiors informed and deal intelligently with news-gathering services, complainants, and other interested parties. In effect, the summary is an overview of all evidence obtained, whether tending to prove or to disprove every allegation of the complaint.

Unless requested by his superior to give his opinions, the investigating supervisor should refrain from editorializing in his report since to do so would usurp the function of higher reviewing authority, which ordinarily reserves the right to draw ultimate conclusions from the facts presented. This does not suggest, however, that the investigator should avoid pointing out conflicts which he has discovered in the evidence. These are of value to the reviewer, especially in complex investigations. The data assembled should be reported in a factual manner so that an intelligent, informed, and just conclusion can be drawn.

The *investigation* section of the report should contain a detailed account of the inquiry to which the reviewer might refer for particulars beyond those contained in the summary of investigation section. This section should report the substance of verbatim transcripts of witnesses' statments or those of the accused or the complainant. These substantive statements must be carefully prepared to preserve the integrity of the total report.

In the *conclusions* section of the report, the investigating supervisor should report the conclusions he has drawn from the inquiry but only after he has been requested to do so by a superior or if required to do so by departmental rules. The responsibility for drawing conclusions at times places an extremely difficult burden upon the supervisor. Little difficulty will be encountered in those cases wherein the evidence unequivocally points to the innocence or guilt of the accused employee; however, where the evidence conflicts and the complaint can neither be sustained nor disproved, the supervisor is often hard put to arrive at an objective conclusion because of his personal involvement in the investigation.

Ordinarily, he will not be required to draw a formal conclusion from the investigation for his superiors, since the "jury function" is their prerogative.

Recommendations, when required by departmental procedures or requested by superiors, should be placed in a section similarly titled. The investigator's familiarity with the case and the accused employee may enable him to render valuable aid in appraising the merits of the case for his superiors; however, this section is normally omitted from the report since ultimate disposition of the case is usually reserved for superiors.

Some public agencies [15] recommend a schedule of suggested cor-

[15] See California Personnel Board, *Supervisor's Handbook—3: A Guide to Employee Discipline* (Sacramento, Calif.: California State Personnel Board, 1965), pp. 25–36. See also "A Resolution on Discipline Policy" adopted by the Los Angeles Civil Service Commission on December 9, 1965. The suggested penalties are considered only as guides to supervisory personnel in assessing penalties.

rective actions for typical derelictions. These schedules, when available within an agency, may be used as guides by supervisors in recommending corrective action for personnel who have committed a breach of conduct. The supervisor should be mindful, however, that the penalty to be imposed should not only fit the dereliction but should fit the individual. For similar infractions, a penalty that might demoralize one employee may be insufficient and ineffectual for another.

In recommending punishment, the supervisor must consider the totality of circumstances surrounding the commission of the act. The motive and intent with which it was committed will necessarily influence his judgment. Deliberate violations of established standards of conduct or offenses involving moral turpitude will usually require a far more severe punishment than offenses resulting from ignorance or carelessness. The latter can usually be resolved by application of positive disciplinary measures.[16]

In the *addenda* section of the report are included such supporting data as verbatim transcripts of statements, arrest reports, crime, evidence, or property report, booking information, exemplars, descriptions of physical evidence, and so forth.

Pagination and cross-references

For ease in referring to the component parts of the investigation report, each page should be numbered. After summary statements, cross-references to the page or pages from which the summary was taken should be included in parentheses. Such references are invaluable in conserving the time of busy administrators who must review such reports.

Avoid offensive terminology

Terms such as "suspect" used in referring to the accused employee or the complainant who happens to be the subject of a criminal matter should be avoided in personnel investigation reports. Neither should the complainant be referred to as "the arrestee" if such references can be avoided. These appellations will often be offensive to the complainant, the public, or a jury and may result in criticism that the investigation has been unjustifiably "slanted" in favor of the officer should they appear in press accounts. Proper names are more descriptive and should be used in lieu of terms that might be considered derogatory.

[16] O. W. Wilson, and Roy Clinton McLaren, *Police Administration*, 4th ed. (New York: McGraw-Hill Book Company, 1977), p. 145.

CLASSIFICATION OF COMPLAINT INVESTIGATIONS

A simple but effective classification such as that adopted by the Los Angeles Police Department [17] has been found highly useful in classifying cases after investigation has been completed so that they will reflect the findings in the matter when filed in personnel files.

When the facts obtained support the complaint, the case is classified as *sustained*. When the evidence indicates that the act complained of did in fact occur but was legal, proper, and necessary, the case is classified as *exonerated*. For example, in an incident wherein the complainant alleges that excessive force was used upon him by an officer in making an arrest but investigation reveals that the force was made necessary by the complainant's resistance and was not excessive under the circumstances, the classification "exonerated" is placed on the case to indicate that there was no evidence of improper conduct on the accused officer's part.

The *unfounded* classification is used to indicate that the act complained of did not in fact occur and that the complaint was false. Those cases which cannot be resolved by investigation, either because sufficient evidence is not available or because of material conflicts in the evidence, are resolved in favor of the accused employee and are classed as *not sustained*. Should investigation reveal that the employee was guilty of misconduct not part of the original complaint, the case might be classified *Misconduct Not Based on the Complaint*.

CHARGES AND SPECIFICATIONS

When investigation supports the complaint, the due process provisions of the law ordinarily require the employee be given written specifications of the charges upon which a penalty or hearing is to be based. A preferred procedure in drafting charges against the employee for misconduct is to prepare them in terms of *specific violations* described in rules and regulations as unbecoming conduct. Ordinarily, the courts will not uphold a broad, vague charge only of unbecoming conduct.[18]

DISCIPLINE AND THE PRESS

The supervisor conducting a personnel investigation is often confronted by members of the news media pursuing a "lead" related to the matter under inquiry. Obviously, a premature release of details of the investiga-

[17] Los Angeles Police Department, *The Department Manual*, 3/820.20.
[18] *Bence v. Breier*, 419 U.S. 1121 (1975); *Perea v. Falis*, 114 Cal. Rptr. 808 (1974).

tion before it has been completed would be improper and might jeopardize the entire inquiry. However, deceit will be resented and may result in the publication of a news story based upon inaccurate information gleaned from unreliable sources and adverse to the interests of the department. Usually, reporters will appreciate a frank explanation of why a release cannot be made at the time and an assurance that it will be made when the case has been completed. This procedure presupposes that there exists within the department a policy of full cooperation with the news media and that news releases, when made, will emanate from an authorized source.

NOTIFICATION TO COMPLAINANT

In the interests of good public relations, the complainant should be notified of the disposition made in the matter when the investigation has been completed and the case resolved. Even though the complaint has been sustained by the investigation, the communication should state only in general terms that appropriate action has been taken to prevent a recurrence of the act without indicating the specific penalty imposed upon the employee. When the specific penalty is communicated to the complainant, he will often be dissatisfied with the action taken since he is not aware of all the findings in the case and is uninformed of the past record of the officer, either good or bad. He will sometimes declare the penalty too severe. More often, he will believe it to be too lenient; his judgment may be clouded by his personal involvement, because he usually will feel that he has been the victim of police action.

When the investigation reveals that the complaint was unfounded in fact or that the officer should be exonerated because the act upon which the complaint was based was legal and proper and made necessary by the failure of the complainant to cooperate, he should be forthrightly appraised of such conclusion and the general reasons therefor.

NOTIFICATION TO THE ACCUSED EMPLOYEE

In addition to the notice given the complainant that final disposition has been made in the incident, the accused should be promptly informed of the conclusions drawn from the investigation and the action to be taken, if any. Some agencies communicate this information on a simple form established for the purpose. In addition, a copy of the communication to the complainant can be sent the employee with good effect when the case is classed as unfounded or when he is exonerated of the charges. This procedure will do much to relieve his anxiety.

Rarely will the employee be exposed to a more harrowing and emotionally upsetting experience than when he is the subject of an investigation of a personnel complaint alleging a serious dereliction. Therefore, it is of utmost importance to his morale that he be informed at the earliest possible time when the matter has been finally resolved.

ADMINISTERING PENALTY

When a penalty is to be imposed, it should be administered promptly to have greatest effect. It should not be used as a threatening device but as a constructive tool of supervision. It will usually be accepted by employees if they have confidence in its reasonableness and necessity; but if it is used as a club, it will often result in resentment and downright resistance to supervision.

To delay administering a penalty when one has been imposed, merely because it is a disagreeable supervisory task, is inexcusable. This does not mean, however, that the execution of a nominal penalty such as a voluntary surrender of days off or compensatory time accumulated cannot be delayed somewhat, at times, upon the mutual agreement of the employee and the department. For example, a short suspension or loss of days off might best be executed when the deployment demands of the shift requires the least personnel or when a delay in executing a supension will avert the imposition of an unreasonable hardship on the employee.

DISCIPLINARY FAILURES

A certain portion of all disciplinary actions fail because supervisors do not know how to make personnel investigations. The answer to this problem is training. Other disciplinary actions fail to accomplish their objectives, not because of the insufficiency of the evidence, but as a direct result of the failures of the investigating supervisor to fulfill his responsibilities. He avoids doing what has to be done in fulfilling his obligation to maintain departmental disciplinary standards either because of his overprotectiveness or defensive attitude toward his subordinates or his disinclination to do anything that might hurt one of them, even one whose actions have brought discredit on other members of the law enforcement profession. His failures are often the result of his fear of disapproval from those with whom he works. On occasion, he will fail to investigate complaints completely, if at all, or his delays in making prompt inquiry into personnel breaches often result in the destruction or disappearance of evidence which might otherwise have been collected, cooling of witnesses, or downright concoction of stories which will prevent any possible resolution of the matter. Fortunately, such failures are not common, but when they do occur, the supervisor responsible does a grave disservice to his organization by contributing to a general lowering of its prestige and public confidence in it, not to speak of the disservice he does to his hardworking, dedicated subordinates who subscribe fully to the organizational standards of conduct and are proud of their professional stature. Furthermore, his well-intended protectiveness might harm rather than help the accused employee who is innocent of any wrongdoing but is merely in need of someone to collect the evidence to prove his innocence unequivocally so that the matter will not be the subject of further doubt.

SUMMARY

Once the exact nature of a personnel complaint is ascertained, the supervisor must initiate an inquiry to determine the facts surrounding the case. Conclusions must then be drawn from all the evidence secured and corrective action taken when indicated or the case closed without punitive action when the facts absolve the accused person.

The supervisor investigating a complaint against his subordinate must pursue every channel of investigation available to him in seeking the truth. He must remain objective in his approach and avoid drawing a conclusion of innocence or guilt before the facts are known. Traditional investigative procedures generally should be followed; however, since ordinarily the complaint involves an allegation of noncriminal conduct, it is imperative that the employee and the complainant be treated with equanimity to prevent, insofar as possible, shattering the morale of the employee or destroying the confidence of the complainant in the integrity of the force.

Promptness of investigation is essential to prevent loss, destruction, or contamination of evidence and to minimize the adverse effects of long, drawn-out inquiries of this nature upon employee morale. When the case has been resolved, both the complainant and the accused employee should be promptly notified of the conclusion reached. If punishment is to be imposed upon the employee, the amount or degree should not be specified in the communication to the complainant notifying him of the disposition of the case. Likewise, if investigation reveals that the accusation is without merit, this fact should be brought forthrightly to his attention.

The taking of disciplinary action against subordinates imposes upon supervisors the obligation to use discipline forthrightly and impersonally as a constructive tool of supervision rather than as a threatening device to secure compliance with departmental standards of conduct.

REVIEW

Questions

1. What are internal complaints? Give examples.
2. Where do primary and secondary complaints originate? Give examples of each.
3. Discuss anonymous complaints and how you would handle them.
4. How would you handle a complaint from an intoxicated person?
5. If a complaint has been made against one of your employees, why should his personnel record be checked as part of the investigation?
6. Why should face-to-face encounters be prevented between the accused employee and his accusor?
7. What are the general procedures a supervisor should follow when he discovers a minor infraction on the part of a subordinate? A serious complaint?
8. If you received a complaint concerning a serious incident involving one of your subordinates but the complainant was not able to identify him, what means of identifying him would you use? What precautions would you take if the incident involved a criminal offense?
9. If a search of a subordinate's person, locker, private vehicle, or residence is indicated, how would you accomplish it in each case? Discuss the general procedures you would follow.
10. Generally, what are the sections of a typical personnel investigation report and what information should each contain?
11. What are some of the common failures of supervisors in making personnel complaint investigations?

Exercises

Assume that you are a field supervisor. You observe or your attention is called to the following incidents involving personnel under your direct supervision. Explain how you would handle each in a manner that would not be in conflict with legal and administrative rules.

1. Over a period of time, you have noted one particular officer has been slow in responding to calls between 2 A.M. and 5 A.M. His explanations have not satisfied you but you do not have evidence to dispute them. You suspect that he is sleeping.

2. While you are conducting roll call, an officer arrives late. Upon entering, he creates a disturbance, then interferes with the proceedings by whispering to other officers.

3. Your vice officers have received several complaints that a gambling game is taking place in the back room of a bar. They investigate and arrest several persons for illegal gambling. One of them is your subordinate officer. He is off duty. The vice officers call you to the scene and ask your advice. What would you advise? Would you handle the incident differently if the officer was on duty at the time? Explain. Would you handle the incident differently if the officer involved were assigned to another unit of your department? What would you do if he were a member of a neighboring force?

4. While checking your officers at the end of watch, you observe one of them take a box of groceries from the police vehicle and transfer it to his own.

5. For some time, you have been hearing rumors that some of your subordinates have been frequenting a bar and drinking illegally after closing hours. You check the bar one-half hour after closing time and find two of your officers drinking there. One is intoxicated. They are both off duty, but are in uniform.

6. You follow up on a call and find one of your subordinates involved in a minor traffic accident. He is not in uniform. You observe that he has been drinking but do not conclude that he is under the influence of alcohol. The other party to the accident maintains that the officer is intoxicated. How would you proceed? How would you handle the matter if the officer were intoxicated? Explain.

7. You receive a call from a collection agency that one of your subordinates has failed to pay a bill for medical services after repeated requests from the physician. The officer assures you that the matter will be taken care of promptly. Two weeks later, the collection agency notifies you that the officer has not contacted them to make arrangements to pay the debt. Would your disposition in this case be different if, upon the first interview with the officer, he claimed the charge was excessive and therefore in dispute? Explain.

8. You follow up on a call in which one of your subordinate officers has arrested an intoxicated person. The arrestee, a pedestrian, is well dressed, intelligent, and appears to be a responsible citizen when sober. He tells you that not more than five minutes before your arrival, the officer stopped him and asked for identification, which he produced from his wallet. He alleges that the officer took his wallet, examined it, and when it was returned to him, a twenty-dollar bill was missing. He says that when he complained, he was placed under arrest.

9. One of your subordinates, whom you consider a very promising young officer, tells you that he is planning to quit because of pressure he is receiving from his wife and family. He believes he can be more

successful in some other endeavor, although he likes police work. He indicates that his wife is opposed to the job because of the bad working conditions, irregular hours, low pay and prestige, and the hazards of police work.

10. You receive information from a person who declines to identify himself that one of your subordinates arrives home nearly every morning at about the time the informant arises. According to the informant, the officer frequently unloads cartons or packages from his car and carries them into the house. This observation usually takes place about 8:00 A.M. The officer identified is assigned to the 11:30 P.M. to 7:30 A.M. watch. The informant thinks that the property may be stolen because he has seen it carried into the house and garage so regularly.

11

Personnel evaluation systems

Organizations are judged by their records of achievement. The military establishment is judged by its ability to win battles, the industrial enterprise by its capacity for making profit for stockholders, the law enforcement agency by its ability to suppress unlawful activity. In each of these activities, the factor that determines whether there is to be victory or defeat, profit or loss, order or disorder is the personnel who constitute the organization. In order for those responsible for planning programs and directing the many projects of the enterprise to accomplish their mission most efficiently, they must be able to utilize effectively the skills and abilities of their most costly and important resource—manpower. To do this, the capabilities of employees must be known and a means must be provided to assess their level of performance in comparison with what is desired.

OBJECTIVES OF THE RATING SYSTEM

Service ratings, personnel evaluations, employee appraisals, merit ratings, or whatever the system is called will provide one tool for measuring employee capabilities and giving management an inventory of them, and they will provide a means for supervisors to record systematically at specified intervals their opinions regarding the performance of subordinates. Such systems will also establish a basis for rewarding or penalizing personnel and for explaining to them why they are or are not progressing satisfactorily. Evaluations based on sound, objective data are unparalleled as a foundation upon which the supervisor can help a substandard employee develop a program to improve his performance. Properly administered, the system will also be a valuable tool in placement and promotion of personnel, in the administration of merit pay increases, disciplinary proceedings, and similar matters.

In addition, supervisors will be given a means for measuring those abstract traits of their subordinates which cannot be easily measured otherwise. Absences, tardiness, production, or accomplishment measured quantitatively can easily be measured directly. Not so with such traits as loyalty, the ability to get along with others, and temperamental stability, to name a few.

Every supervisor rates formally or informally

Every supervisor worthy of the name engages constantly in the process of comparatively rating subordinates, whether there is a formal or informal rating system or none at all. In small agencies an informal rating system may serve management well because everyone knows everyone else, but in larger organizations, it is found that, in the interests of efficient management, a more formalized system is necessary so that an individual employee's progress may become a matter of record. This will give management a tool for comparing his performance with that of other employees in similar assignments in other parts of the organization.

No system of measuring the qualities of a human being is perfect because personal bias and subjectivity cannot be entirely eliminated from the appraisals. Any system that yields reasonable results when used skillfully is better than none at all provided the appraisal measures what it is intended to measure.[1]

In those agencies where no evaluation system has been adopted, each supervisor is left to his own devices to evaluate his personnel comparatively. More often than not, such ratings become highly subjective and are of little value in providing management an accurate source of information concerning employee skills. Furthermore, management is deprived of a ready means of determining what has been done, what is being done, and what needs to be done.

---

[1] Leonard R. Sayles and George Strauss, *Managing Human Resources* (Englewood Cliffs, N.J.: Prentice-Hall, Inc., 1977), p. 308.

A CASE FOR EVALUATION SYSTEMS

"It might be expected that service rating plans would be generally accepted and approved. This is far from the case. No aspect of personnel administration has had a stormier history than that of service ratings. No rating plan has yet received acceptance, and most have suffered violent criticism and frequent modification." [2]

Evaluation systems have been established in some organizations because of legal requirements. In other establishments, enlightened administrators have adopted a system as a means of improving employee morale by giving employees recognition in proportion to the excellence of their performance. Since the desire for recognition is one of the basic human drives, it is often found that the effectiveness of the working force is dependent, at least in part, upon the recognition it receives from management for its efforts. The personnel evaluation system should serve as a means of providing at least a degree of the recognition employees desire.

Rating reports carefully made and judiciously used serve as a valuable aid to the organization in the maintenance of reasonable performance standards and in the administration of a progressive training, placement, promotion, executive development, or salary program based on merit. If they are made and filed without further reference, they serve no useful purpose other than that they have focused the supervisor's attention upon the specific characteristics of the employee. There can be no denial of the cost of administering these programs. It is considerable; but management must weigh the costs in terms of the results achieved or achievable from them.

Impartial administration of an evaluation system should make it obvious to personnel that at least an effort is being made by management to eliminate snap judgments and favoritism in the personnel relations program and that an attempt is being made in good faith to reward the most faithful producers by objectively giving credit where it is due. The extent to which this is done will determine, in large part, the degree of employee confidence in the whole process.

As an administrative tool, the data obtainable from personnel evaluations are useful in a progressive personnel management program. Personnel evaluations are valuable devices for determining if employees should be granted tenure or if they are entitled to earn or retain longevity or merit pay. The converse is also true. They are instruments which can be useful as one basis for determining if employees should

---

[2] International City Managers' Association, *Municipal Personnel Administration,* 6th ed. (Chicago: International City Managers' Association, 1960), p. 142.

lose merit pay. Industrial concerns often utilize evaluation reports to determine the order of laying off personnel or reemploying them.

As clinical instruments, rating reports not only are valuable in giving employees credit for superior performance but they also afford a basis for calling attention to inadequate performance. They cannot be equaled when used as a basis for constructive employee counseling. They provide an excellent means of establishing production and accomplishment standards within the organizational unit. When properly prepared, such reports may be effectively used to support disciplinary actions and reveal training needs.

Properly administered personnel evaluation systems can be useful to administrators in research activities such as the refinement and validation of personnel relations techniques. These systems are helpful in evaluating the selection process since they provide some clues to the correlation between job success and the testing program. To date "police profiles" based upon psychological testing have not been developed to any high degree of effectiveness in selecting police candidates.

Evaluation reports are useful in assessing with some accuracy the effectiveness of a training program at the operating level. They often provide data upon the degree of police efficiency as it is influenced by the presence or absence of a good field training program.

When rating reports are utilized as one basis for promotion, ratings over a period of years by many supervisors will tend to be a highly accurate appraisal of the employee's worth—far more accurate generally than an appraisal by an oral examining board which observes the candidate for a relatively short interview. These reports should thus afford a fertile source of information concerning a candidate's suitability for promotion based on his past performance and many individual supervisory appraisals. Thus the importance of evaluating employees for promotability in addition to evaluating them on their productivity and institutional value is obvious.

CAUSES FOR RATING SYSTEM FAILURES

There are many causes for rating system failures. Some of the most prominent of these causes are described in the following pages.

Indifference

Regardless of how sophisticated the rating procedures or how important the program, it will be successful only if the raters or those rated really want it to succeed. Either the system is destroyed through the indifference of supervisors to the need for accuracy in rating or the administrators of the organization fail to support the program actively and their passivity discourages those raters below and causes them to lose interest in it. When the system fails because of the disinclination of management to make it work, morale inevitably suffers.

Employee pressures

Even the persons rated may thwart the evaluation system by sheer pressure, especially when the level of their performance as reflected by ratings forms a basis for their pay. Employee groups sometimes are solicited to bring formal, organized pressure to bear upon management when merit pay is withdrawn—unjustifiably, in the eyes of the employee—on the basis of performance rating reports. If it appears that the employee's welfare must be protected, often the employee group will vigorously press management to justify its action.

Even individual employees bring a kind of pressure to bear upon the entire system. When they view their rating reports and see their defects being made a matter of formal record, they often become hostile and resentful. The marginal employee is usually the most vociferous and may attempt to embarrass his superiors by accusing them of prejudice.

Those supervisors who really believe in the program and honestly want it to work soon become discouraged when the brunt of employee pressures disproportionately falls upon their shoulders. Unfortunately, some of them soon lose their zeal for honest evaluation with the result that their ratings become riddled with inaccuracies and consequently are useless as management tools. Experience has shown that some supervisors will go so far as to change their rating reports on an employee if his complaints are loud enough.

Failure to train raters

Systems devised to provide a means of assessing employees will ordinarily not survive, or if they do will be relatively noneffectual, unless training is provided for those who are to do the rating. They must be given an understanding of the objectives which a properly administered evaluation program should meet and be made aware of the means of avoiding the common errors that cause inaccuracies in ratings and reduce their value.

The common errors which too often creep into personnel evaluations are the most noticeable and troublesome deficiencies in any rating program. They can be reduced considerably by training the raters to become more objective and more sophisticated in their rating methods.[3] Training the raters is the key to the successful administration of the rating system and is its most usual source of weakness.

When standards of measurement of employees are not consistently applied from unit to unit or when difficulties are encountered in attempting to compare ratings from several divisions of the organization, the deficiencies can usually be traced to the lack of training or failure on the part of management to clearly define rating traits.[4]

Another cause of failures in rating programs results from the neglect of management to give raters an opportunity to learn rating procedures under supervision. Rating failures can be reduced through regular conferences among supervisors wherein rating problems and solutions are discussed, proposals for modifications in procedures or methods are presented and considered, and common agreements are reached concerning rating standards which should prevail in the organization. Without this training, it is highly probable that the system will collapse because of its inefficiency and uselessness.

Rating abuses

A rating system is bound to fall into disrepute if personnel rated come to lose confidence in it because it has been abused by management. Ratings should be utilized only as they were intended. Once the purposes for which they were adopted have been announced, their use should be confined to those purposes. They are most commonly used in promotional examinations, as a basis for assignment, or for merit pay raises. A broadening of this use may be necessary from time to time, but such changes should be mutually agreeable to management and employees. A breach of faith with them may cause the whole system to be subtly sabotaged.

Slipshod procedures

Rating reports often affect a person's entire career; therefore, those made carelessly may have serious consequences. Slipshod, inaccurate methods affect every person in the organization because each is a ratee or a rater. In some cases he may be both. Even nonsupervisory personnel have to rate other personnel on occasion. For example, the patrolman

---

[3] Paul Pigors and Charles A. Myers, *Personnel Administration: A Point of View and a Method,* 8th ed. (New York: McGraw-Hill Book Company, 1977), pp. 298–99.

[4] See Dale Yoder, *Personnel Principles and Policies: Modern Manpower Management,* 2nd ed. (Englewood Cliffs, N.J.: Prentice-Hall, Inc., 1959), pp. 339–41.

acting as a training officer to orient the new recruit in field procedures invariably must rate the new employee. Peer rating is also often practiced in training situations. Ratings made perfunctorily by raters who have evaded their responsibility lose most of their value and become administrative trivia. In either event, they are probably not worth the time invested in preparing them, and sooner or later the entire system will fail.

Rating shortcuts

A personnel evaluation system worthy of the cost should not be compromised by shortcut methods. Experience has shown that abbreviated versions of rating scales devised to economize on time at the expense of accuracy have been responsible for a high percentage of failures.

GATHERING AND RECORDING PERFORMANCE DATA

The competence of the rater, the effort he expends in observing and recording evidence of the behavior of his subordinates, his judgment in weighing and evaluating this evidence, and his fairness in applying it to the service rating procedure directly reflect the type of training he has received, the degree of his attitudinal conditioning, and the "climate" established for the system by management.

The first-line supervisor, usually a sergeant in the police service, is the key figure in any rating system since his job involves the productivity of the officers under his command. If he accomplishes his objectives as a leader and discharges his responsibility to his organization, he must continuously collect and record evidence reflecting the quality of service being rendered by his subordinates so that he may periodically evaluate them. If he is required to rate them, he will be forced to learn more about them and about the job they are performing. He must know at least generally how the work should be done and how it is being done by every person in the particular unit over which he exercises supervisory control. This knowledge is gained by keeping abreast of technical developments in the field of law enforcement and allied professions, by inspecting results of operations, and by follow-up observations.

The method of accumulating evidence about his subordinates' performance may be established as a matter of practice and policy. The techniques used by supervisors may vary according to their individual needs. Some agencies have adopted an incident report form to be used to record commendable or censurable performance of a minor, routine nature. These reports should be retained during the rating period, as they form a substantial basis for performance evaluations. They should then be placed in the employee's personnel folder or destroyed. Some supervisors prefer to record observations in a separate file for future reference. Still others record incidents in the supervisor's log and later transfer these notations to a file or a control card kept for each officer. Whatever system is used to record such incidents, the evidence is helpful in making periodic rating reports more objective.

The memory of the supervisor alone will not store the multitude of observations he makes each day on his subordinates. If he relies on recollections alone, his ratings are likely to be based on broad impressions rather than on specific, objective data. The larger the span of control of the supervisor and the more frequent the changes in the supervisory staff, the greater are the needs for written documentation of a subordinate's performance.

Critical incident technique

The critical incident technique involves the collection of objective data about an employee's performance which can be used as a basis for more effective performance ratings. Critical incidents indicating superior or unsatisfactory performance are reported as they are observed and can be used as an objective standard for ratings about which raters can agree. Vague, abstract trait ratings which often reflect personal bias can thus be minimized. Such data dealing with specifics rather than abstractions are also valuable as a basis for counseling employees about their performance.[5]

RATING TRAITS

Rating forms will usually list from four to twelve traits or characteristics which must be considered by the raters. Investigation has revealed that not over twelve traits should ordinarily be used for best results.[6] Figures 11-1 and 11-2 indicate a typical form of a rating report used by the Los Angeles Police Department.

Evaluation reports for probationary officers of all ranks should be made at least once per month during the probationary period to give the broadest picture of the employee. These should be carefully considered as one of the criteria for giving probationary officers tenure.

[5] J. C. Flanagan, "The Critical Incidents Technique," *Psychology Bulletin*, No. 51 (1954), 357–58.

[6] Michael J. Jucius, *Personnel Management* (Homewood, Ill.: Richard D. Irwin, Inc., 1959), p. 279.

FIGURE 11-1. Personnel Rating Report (courtesy of Los Angeles Police Department)

LOS ANGELES POLICE DEPARTMENT

01.78.0 (2-75)

PERSONNEL RATING REPORT

☐ SEMI-ANNUAL ☐ TRANSFER ☐ SPECIAL ☐ PROBATIONARY-PROMOTIONAL ☐ PROBATIONARY POLICE OFFICER ☐ PROBATIONARY CIVILIAN

FOR COMPLETION INSTRUCTIONS REFER TO MANUAL SECTIONS 3/760 AND 5/1.78.

NAME (LAST, FIRST, MIDDLE)		SERIAL NO.	CLASSIFICATION	GRADE	DIVISION OR BUREAU
DUTY ASSIGNMENTS (E.G., SENIOR DESK)	JOB CODE	PERIOD COVERED MONTHS	FROM		TO

CHECK-BOX RATING SECTION (Items I thru 4). The below categories of employee performance consist of various sub-factors (e.g., Common Sense). The sub-factors should be rated as follows:

Strong (+), Average (leave space blank), Weak (−). If not observed sufficiently to rate, draw a line through the word descriptor. Make an over-all rating for each category by placing an "X" in the righthand column.

Columns: UNSATISFACTORY | SATISFACTORY | EXCELLENT | OUTSTANDING

I. PERSONAL CHARACTERISTICS
☐ APPEARANCE ☐ PRESENCE OF MIND ☐ EXPRESSIVENESS
☐ LOYALTY ☐ DIPLOMACY ☐ PHYSICAL FITNESS ☐ COMMON SENSE ☐ ADAPTABILITY
☐ ☐ ☐ ☐

2. INTERPERSONAL RELATIONSHIPS
☐ WITH PEERS ☐ WITH PUBLIC ☐ WITH SUBORDINATES ☐ WITH SUPERIORS
☐ ☐ ☐ ☐

3. DUTY PERFORMANCE
☐ INITIATIVE ☐ PERSEVERANCE ☐ COMPLIANCE WITH RULES
☐ RESPONSIVENESS TO INSTRUCTIONS ☐ PUNCTUALITY ☐ QUALITY OF WORK ☐ THOROUGHNESS
☐ CARE & USE OF DEPARTMENT EQUIPMENT ☐ RELIABILITY ☐ QUANTITY OF WORK
☐ ☐ ☐ ☐

4. MANAGEMENT CAPABILITIES (How well does employee:)
☐ LEAD? ☐ INSPIRE HIGH MORALE? ☐ ORGANIZE?
☐ DELEGATE? ☐ DIRECT? ☐ PLAN? ☐ DEVELOP PEOPLE? ☐ ACCEPT RESPONSIBILITY?
☐ ☐ ☐ ☐

5. Did this employee receive an unsatisfactory rating on the report prior to this report? If "yes", has improvement been shown? Indicate previous unfavorably rated item(s):
☐ YES ☐ NO ☐ YES ☐ NO

6. Indicate the number of each of the following items involving this employee during the rating period:
___ Favorable incident reports ___ Preventable Traffic Accidents
___ Commendations (Explain briefly) ___ Disciplinary action - other than T/A (Explain briefly)

7. POTENTIAL FOR INCREASED RESPONSIBILITY? (Place an "X" by the most appropriate statement)
☐ HAS ADEQUATE TRAINING AND EXPERIENCE, AND HAS DEMONSTRATED POTENTIAL FOR INCREASE RESPONSIBILITY.
☐ HAS ADEQUATE TRAINING AND EXPERIENCE, BUT HAS NOT DEMONSTRATED POTENTIAL FOR INCREASED RESPONSIBILITY.
☐ LACKS ADEQUATE TRAINING AND/OR EXPERIENCE, BUT HAS DEMONSTRATED POTENTIAL FOR INCREASED RESPONSIBILITY.
☐ LACKS ADEQUATE TRAINING AND/OR EXPERIENCE, AND HAS NOT DEMONSTRATED POTENTIAL FOR INCREASED RESPONSIBILITY.
☐ PRESENT ASSIGNMENT DOES NOT AFFORD OPPORTUNITY FOR OBSERVATION OF POTENTIAL FOR INCREASED RESPONSIBILITY.

8. Considering the requirements of the Department, my attitude toward having this employee under my command is:
☐ I WOULD BE PLEASED TO HAVE THIS EMPLOYEE.
☐ I WOULD BE WILLING TO HAVE THIS EMPLOYEE.
☐ I WOULD PREFER NOT TO HAVE THIS EMPLOYEE. (EXPLAIN)

FIGURE 11-2. Supporting data to Personnel Rating Report (courtesy of Los Angeles Police Department)

9. NARRATIVE EVALUATION OF THIS EMPLOYEE. Support overall rating. No. 10. Also, consider the following as applicable: NEEDS---in the areas of training, education, and experience; GOALS---have they been established and met; PHYSICAL FITNESS---results of must recent test and/or employee's own programs; MERIT PAY---if not recommended, explain reasons fully.

10. OVERALL VALUE TO THE DEPARTMENT. Rating must reflect this employee's eligibility to receive the appropriate merit pay.

☐ UNSATISFACTORY   ☐ SATISFACTORY   ☐ EXCELLENT   ☐ OUTSTANDING

Recommendation for non-certification to withhold or remove merit pay.

11. PROBATIONARY EMPLOYEES ONLY. List and explain consecutive days off in excess of 7 for S/L, IOD, M/L, SUSP., AWOL, or ABSENT during this rating period (include dates):

RECOMMENDATION: ☐ FURTHER OBSERVATION   ☐ PERMANENT STATUS   ☐ TERMINATION

12. RATING SUPERVISOR: (Immediate Supervisor)

SIGNATURE _____ RANK & TITLE _____ DATE _____

13. CO-RATING SUPERVISORS:

SIGNATURE _____ RANK & TITLE _____ DATE _____

SIGNATURE _____ RANK & TITLE _____ DATE _____

SIGNATURE _____ RANK & TITLE _____ DATE _____

SIGNATURE _____ RANK & TITLE _____ DATE _____

14. EMPLOYEE'S COMMENTS: (Optional)

15. EMPLOYEE'S SIGNATURE: This signature does not necessarily indicate agreement with this report. I have received a copy of this report.

SIGNATURE _____ RANK & TITLE _____ DATE _____

16. REVIEWING SUPERVISOR:

SIGNATURE _____ RANK & TITLE _____ DATE _____

17. If eligible, is this employee, on the basis of this rating report qualified to receive or continue to receive merit pay?

☐ YES   ☐ NO (Explain and complete a Form 15.2.0 requesting non-certification to withhold/remove merit pay).

18. APPROVING COMMANDING OFFICER:

SIGNATURE _____ RANK & TITLE _____ DATE _____

The supervisory officers' rating form should be constructed to focus the rater's attention on the many traits and characteristics required for a supervisory position. Space should be provided for evidence justifying extremely high or low ratings and for specific comments by the rater relative to characteristics of the person rated not covered elsewhere on the report.

TRAIT RATING FOR PROMOTIONAL EXAMINATIONS

The Personal Qualifications Appraisal developed by the San Diego City Civil Service Department to guide members of oral examining boards in rating police candidates for promotion is illustrated in Figure 11–3.

CATEGORIZING TRAITS

Rating traits and abilities can be grouped into broad categories such as *personal characteristics* (needed for the job), *ability* (to perform the duties of the position), *performance* (quality and quantity of work), *overall value to the organization* or *suitability for promotion*. Additional or fewer categories may be used depending upon the purpose to be served by the rating report.

The traits selected for rating purposes should be examined critically to assure that they are as specific as possible, that the trait which is to be measured can be relatively easily observed and uniformly evaluated by all raters, that it will describe an actual characteristic required by the job, that it will be common to the largest possible number of employees, and that it will be selected so as not to overlap into others, which would tend to defeat the purpose of the rating.[7]

The following are some subcategories of rating factors:

Personal Characteristics	*Ability*
honesty	stability
character	initiative
attitude	job knowledge
appearance	judgment
persistence	common sense
imagination	
loyalty	

[7] *Ibid.*, p. 280.

Form R-9a (Rev.)

SAN DIEGO CITY CIVIL SERVICE

Index Code: 10.2911

PERSONAL QUALIFICATIONS APPRAISAL

NAME _____ POSITION TITLE _____ DATE _____

INSTRUCTIONS: Ask yourself how this candidate compares with those who are doing work of this kind and how he compares, trait by trait, with other candidates for the position. Show by a check (✓) that point on each scale where, in your judgment, the candidate stands. At the close of the interview, assign a final percentage score, make appropriate comments and sign the appraisal form --- ALL IN INK.

1. APPEARANCE: What do you think of the applicant's personal appearance and dress?	Unfavorable	Unimpressive	Acceptable	Above Average	Excellent
2. ALERTNESS: Does the applicant appear alert and intelligent?	Often Misunderstands	Slow to Grasp Subtleties	Average Keenness	Bright and Quick	Unusually Alert
3. EMOTIONAL STABILITY: Is the applicant at ease and well poised?	Easily Disconcerted	Self-Conscious	Good Self Control	Superior Self Command	Exceptional Poise
4. PRESENTATION OF IDEAS: How does the applicant present his ideas?	Confused & Illogical	Some Difficulty	Moderate Clarity	Clear & Effective	Unusually Clear and Convincing
5. ABILITY TO GET ALONG WITH OTHERS: Does the applicant inspire confidence and command loyalty?	Unpleasant or Abrupt	Somewhat Tactless or Antagonistic	Likeable & Friendly	Arouses Cooperation	Extremely Inspiring
6. DECISIONS AND JUDGMENT: What do you think of the applicant's judgment?	Notably Lacking	Poorly Considered	Acceptable Judiciousness	Firm, Well Considered Answers	Exceptional Soundness
7. GENERAL FITNESS FOR THE POSITION: Consider your overall evaluation of the candidate, based on a composite of the above traits plus any additional traits or qualifications which are important in the position, as indicated below in your comments.	Unsuited for this work	Not quite up to Standard	Would make an Average Employee	Definitely Above Average	Outstanding

COMMENTS: _____

Appraisal Score _____ %
(NOTE: 70% is the minimum passing score.)

EXAMINER _____

Performance	*Suitability for Promotion*
quality of work	leadership ability
quantity of work	administrative ability
accuracy	job knowledge
attention to duty	acceptance of responsibility
perseverance	ability to organize
efficiency	decision-making ability
supervision required	

SETTING STANDARDS OF PERFORMANCE

The first-line supervisor plays a prime part in setting standards of performance for his subordinates. If he exacts anything less than full and honest performance from them, he is negligent in his own duty. They must be thoroughly indoctrinated in what he expects from them. In turn, they have the right to know what they may expect from him. They must recognize that he is responsible for the manner in which the police function is performed by them in the area in which they operate. They should also be made to understand what he expects from them by virtue of their particular assignment. Subordinate personnel too often do not know, other than in very abstract terms, what their supervisors expect simply because they have not been told. Often the scope of their responsibilities has not been delineated.

Every supervisor in the patrol service, for example, must make it clear by every means at his disposal that officers are theoretically accountable for crime in their assigned area or beat, for enforcement of the law selectively to reduce the incidence of traffic accidents resulting from accident-producing violations, for providing an acceptable level of service for those in need of it, and for other police activities calculated to reduce crime when patterns begin to appear. The supervisor must let his subordinates know that, in addition to the rating bases noted above, they will be rated also on the manner in which they observe and report police incidents and conditions requiring correction, such as inadequate street lighting which might be corrected to reduce crime, engineering changes which might be needed to reduce traffic accidents, or exposed hazards which might be better controlled to reduce the incidence of juvenile delinquency.

In letting his subordinates know what he expects of them, the supervisor will be performing a training function and will give them a basis for understanding what standards will be used to measure and evaluate their effectiveness. They will then recognize what should be done, how they are expected to do it, and what degree of competency is expected of them. Regardless of their assignment, they are entitled to know this. When they do, certain standards will emerge based on their relative productivity, both qualitative and quantitative. These then can be used as goals toward which the employee can strive when he is told where he stands in comparison with other employees and with established norms.

RATING CRITERIA

Some of the many criteria which have been found useful by supervisors as a basis for rating the performance of personnel are listed below. Obviously, evidence must be collected which demonstrates the employee's value to the organization. Some of this evidence will be accumulated for specific periods, usually monthly, in accomplishment reports. This must be interpreted with great care, however, since such data usually measure quantitative production only and do not equate it with the quality of the work done. Because of this shortcoming and because such data do not lend themselves to the measurement of the more abstract traits which are important in the police officer's job, accomplishment reports are perhaps one of the least useful devices in the evaluation of personnel.

Some of the following criteria may not be applicable in all personnel appraisals because of the particular assignment of the employee, but all of them are easily adaptable for most field assignments and can be easily evaluated through the process of inspections. Effective supervisors often gain much valuable information regarding their subordinates by riding with them on patrol, where their capabilities can be measured through firsthand observations.

Patrol and traffic personnel

1. Are officers keeping themselves informed of what is happening on their beat or in their area? Are they making use of pin maps or police incident summaries to gain an awareness of crime, or traffic accident patterns as they develop, or exposed hazard areas?
2. Are officers familiar with crime, delinquency, and traffic trends in their area of responsibility?
3. Are officers familiar with patrol techniques and are they performing their patrol functions effectively?
4. How many errors are observed in their reports? Are reports complete and accurate?

5. What is the quality of traffic enforcement citations issued? Are traffic citations reasonably related to accident-producing violations on a selective basis? Do citation books, turned in for inspection and filing when completed, reveal quality enforcement effort, or do they disclose an inordinate number of "apple orchard" citations? Do errors or erasures appear on file copies?

6. Are preliminary investigations made carefully? How do officers preserve evidence?

7. Do activity logs reflect a high proportion of quality arrests based on observation? Do the officers' repressive patrol activities appear to be adequate? Do these activities involve adequate random inspections of business and residential premises and places exposed to criminal attacks, vehicle checks, and so forth?

8. What is the quality of field interviews with pedestrians and motorists, juveniles and adults, as reflected by field contact reports?

9. What type of "police image" do the officers make in their personal and public lives?

10. How do the officers handle assigned calls? Do the follow-up inquiries and observations by the supervisor reveal that they lack enthusiasm, self-assurance, confidence, ability, or interest in handling called-for services?

11. Does their court performance reflect poise, fairness, and preparation?

12. How do the subordinates care for their personal equipment and that of the organization?

13. Do the employees' medical records reflect a favorable attitude toward the job, or does their medical history reveal an inordinate use of sick time? Do sick "patterns" reflect evidence of "malingering"?

14. How do the employees relate to other members of the organization, fellow workers and superiors, and the public?

15. Do the employees observe the usual safety precautions in their work?

16. Does the organization receive an unusual number of complaints about the officers' performance or conduct?

17. Do officers strongly support their superiors and the organization, or are they passive or antagonistic?

18. What is the "growth" potential or promotability of officers?

19. Is the overall quantity of their work acceptable?

20. What is their overall worth to the organization in comparison with others doing similar work?

Investigative personnel

Some criteria which may apply, in addition to those listed for patrol and traffic officers, are these:

1. Are follow-up calls made promptly in the interests of good investigative procedures and public relations?

2. Is the officer thorough and systematic in his investigative activities?

3. What percentage of his assigned cases are cleared by investigations? What percent are cleared by arrest resulting from investigations? Are clearance rates bona fide; that is, are they cleared by arrest or directly by investigative activity or are there an excessive number cleared improperly by weak and inadequate "modus operandi" factors?

4. Does he have an unusual backlog of cases which have not had preliminary follow-up calls made?

5. Do progress reports reflect satisfactory progress on his assigned cases, or does it appear that the investigator is directing his efforts primarily toward the investigation of those cases which are newsworthy or which may earn him some special recognition?

6. Does the officer enjoy a high conviction rate on cases he has investigated? Do records reveal that an unusual number of his cases which have been submitted to the prosecutor for complaint are rejected because of improper or inadequate case investigation or preparation?

7. How effectively does he deal with juveniles who have been involved in police incidents?

8. Does he keep complete and accurate records of his investigative activities?

9. Does the investigator work well with a minimum of supervision?

10. Does the investigator's court performance indicate thorough investigation and case preparation?

Staff or auxiliary personnel

Additional criteria which are useful as a basis for rating personnel assigned to staff or auxiliary activities are these:

1. Does the employee complete his assigned projects promptly, thoroughly, and objectively?

2. Does he practice the principles of completed staff work or does he require an inordinate amount of direction?

3. Do his reports meet accepted standards for staff writings?

4. Do his relations with operating personnel reflect a clear understanding of his organizational function as an "advisor" rather than a director?

SUMMARY

Personnel evaluation systems are a valuable tool for giving employees recognition for their efforts, for revealing operational deficiencies which might be corrected by training, for uncovering weaknesses in selection procedures, for placing and promoting personnel, for establishing a basis for merit pay, and for providing an inventory of the capabilities of the manpower of the organization.

The basic objectives for which the system was adopted in the first place must continuously be kept in mind by those who are responsible for its success if they are to make it a useful and effective management tool. The system must be used as it was intended. Abuses will be considered a breach of faith by the employees and may become a cause for them to bring pressures to bear which will thwart the objectives of the program.

Of perhaps the greatest importance to an evaluation system is the training of the persons who are to do the rating. The rater's competence in carrying out the objectives of the program reflects the type of training and attitudinal conditioning he has received. The training should be directed toward giving him a fuller appreciation of the need for judging subordinates in objective terms from a viewpoint of the service they are rendering rather than from a personal standpoint of likes and dislikes. The rater should be made aware of the means at his disposal to collect evidence that can be used as a factual basis for evaluations. A rating philosophy should be impressed upon him so that he will see the purpose and value of ratings. Such indoctrination will give him an understanding of the program which may lessen the tendency for him to consider this periodic task as a routine drudgery. The positive aspects should be stressed rather than the negative ones, which emphasize why the system is bad and cannot be made much better.

Once traits have been selected and the rater has been made aware of the shades of meaning of the rating terminology, he can apply rating criteria to performance standards. He will thus be able to assess the employees according to their relative value to the organization.

REVIEW

Questions

1. Discuss the uses that can be made of the data obtainable from an effective service rating system.
2. List and discuss the causes for service rating system failures.
3. Discuss some of the methods for gathering and recording employee performance data which can be used as a basis for personnel evaluations.
4. What are the main categories into which traits and abilities of employees should be grouped for rating purposes?

5. Give several of the most important subcategories under each of the main groupings in the preceding question.

6. Discuss the rating criteria that the supervisor may utilize in appraising traffic and patrol personnel; investigative personnel; staff and auxiliary personnel.

Exercises

1. Develop a rating form for the evaluation of probationary officers.

2. Prepare a rating form for the evaluation of all personnel other than supervisors.

3. Prepare a rating form for supervisory personnel. Include instructions for its use.

12

Performance rating
standards
and methods

Rating systems are inherently subjective since they involve a personal audit by one person of another's conduct or performance. Many of the personal traits supervisors are called upon to evaluate cannot be measured by precise tests. One of the inherently difficult problems in the police service is that of fairly comparing persons assigned to widely different tasks. Extreme difficulties are encountered in trying to compare the performance of the detective with that of the jailor, or the performance of the patrol officer with that of the staff officer.

RATING STANDARDS

It is recognized by most supervisors that many of the observations they make of their subordinates cannot be completely objective; yet if these observations are systematically made and recorded for the prime purpose of eliminating bias, which is likely to occur if ratings are based on inadequate evidence, they will provide an excellent basis for trait evaluation involved in personnel rating systems. The biggest problem seems to be the selection of a rating method which will yield the most reliable results. Some of these methods will be discussed in the following paragraphs.

Ranking employees

Many of the earlier systems such as those of the military used the technique of ranking all employees in a particular group according to their relative overall value to the organization. This method of "ranking" or "scaling" ratings is still widely used. It ranks employees from highest to lowest in the unit or on the basis of most valuable to least valuable. If a unit contained twenty persons performing similar functions, each would be rated on his relative position within the group. The most valuable employee would be ranked number 1 of 20. The least valuable would be ranked number 20 of 20 in terms of overall value to the organization.

This method is simple and easy to administer, but it has the disadvantage of lacking common standards of measurement, especially when employees from widely different assignments must be compared. Furthermore, the employee ranked highest in a large, nonselected group might be of less value to the organization than the employee ranked lowest in a unit where employees are carefully selected. When this method of ranking employees is used, the supervisor is forced to make meticulous appraisals of his subordinates or risk the danger of hurting morale and being accused of arbitrariness or favoritism. Rarely will his judgments be in accord with the individual opinions of many of those evaluated who are often prone to overrate themselves in comparison with others.

Selected employee standard

Accuracy may be improved when the rater compares each employee with others who have been selected as having the greatest value to the organization, who are in the middle group with average value, and who are considered as having the least value. The rater is thus able to rank those employees rated by him by comparing them with other representative employees whom he has selected through personal knowledge as being of greatest, average, or least value to the organization. Standards are thus established which can be used effectively as criteria for ratings in smaller organizations where the varying capabilities of employees are generally known and usually agreed upon by raters. In the large organizations, raters are limited in the selection of representative employees by their own past experiences. Therefore, a larger number of selected employees will be used as the standard of comparison with the consequent lessening of the uniformity initially intended.

Additional standards may be selected which will tend to increase rating flexibility and accuracy. For example, accuracy can be increased if additional employees are selected who are representative of not only the outstanding, average, and unsatisfactory group of employees but of intermediate groups as well. These may include above-average (but not outstanding), below-average (but not unsatisfactory), and so on.

Ideal employee standard

Instead of using selected employees who are representative of certain groups of personnel with varying values to the organization, ideal employee descriptions may be developed to avoid the necessity for changing criteria when the selected employees leave the unit or the organization or their performance becomes such that they can no longer be used as a pattern for ratings. The rater is instructed to decide in his own mind the attributes, professional qualities, and performance of the *ideal* employee performing a similar function to that of the employee to be rated and make the rating in comparison with this standard.

Whatever criteria are used, however, it is of utmost importance that they be applied uniformly by all raters or the system will not yield reliable results. Precise guidelines developed by the organization for raters will contribute materially to the achievement of this uniformity.

Numerical standards

When quantity of production is most important to an organization, descriptive standards may be used to advantage in measuring accomplishments. These are often expressed numerically; however, such measurements are difficult to apply to the many abstract traits which are important in police work.

In a purely arithmetic method, the rater gives a numerical grade to each trait on the rating form according to the degree to which the employee possesses it.[1] Predetermined weights are established by the organization for the various traits. The numerical grade given each trait

---

[1] The grade may be expressed in percentages, on a 1 to 5 or 1 to 10 point scale, or on some other scale selected by the organization as a guideline representing various degrees of the employee's proficiency or the extent to which he possesses a trait.

by the rater multiplied by the weight assigned that trait equals its value points. By totalling value points, the organization is able to rank each employee arithmetically according to his overall value.[2]

This weighting adds the element of subjectivity to the rating, since weights assigned to traits are estimates of the value of each in comparison with others.

Table 12–1 depicts a typical trait scale and the simple method of deriving value points for the various traits being assessed which are used in arriving at total value points for the employee.

The arithmetic rating scale for use as a guide in determining total value points assigns numerical values to each trait or performance factor and gives each a weight as illustrated in Table 12–1 and Figure 12–1. This increases the flexibility of the report. These guides may be provided on a separate form or may be preprinted on the rating instrument. Figure 12–2 is an example of a numerical rating system in which each performance factor is given a numerical value of 1 to 5 points according to the degree of proficiency of the rated employee in that factor. Figure 12–3 provides an example of that part of a rating report in which excellent or deficient performance may be described to support the numerical rating. (See pages 240 and 241.)

TABLE 12-1. Trait rating by arithmetic standard method

	Personnel Rating Report				
Trait	Numerical Rating	X	Trait Weight	=	Value Points
Initiative	5		2		10
Dependability	4		3		12
Judgment	4		4		16
. . . .					
Total Value Points					38

Numerical Rating Scale

1	2	3	4	5
Unsatisfactory (or needs improvement, etc.)	Fair (satisfactory but below average, etc.)	Average	Very good (above average, etc.)	Outstanding (or excellent, superior, etc.)

[2] Michael J. Jucius, *Personnel Management* (Homewood, Ill.: Richard D. Irwin, Inc., 1959), pp. 274–77.

Orange County Sheriff's Department
PERFORMANCE EVALUATION REPORT

NON-SUPERVISORY

NAME		CLASS TITLE	DIVISION

PERIOD COVERED BY EVALUATION REPORT
FROM: TO: ASSIGNMENT

RATING INSTRUCTIONS:

1. Check each item box.
   + STRONG   √ STANDARD
   − WEAK   N NOT OBSERVED
2. Rate each factor by circling the appropriate number.
3. Multiply the circled number by the weight for each factor and write the results in the "score" column.
4. Add the "score" column and record the sum.

Use spaces below for comments. Ratings other than competent should be substantiated in writing. Use reverse side for additional space.

1. Examples of work well done; Superior performance:

PERFORMANCE FACTORS	RATINGS (1=UNSATISFACTORY, 2=IMPROVEMENT NEEDED, 3=COMPETENT, 4=HIGH COMPETENT, 5=OUTSTANDING)	WEIGHT	SCORE (RATING X WEIGHT)
QUANTITY			
☐ AMOUNT OF WORK PERFORMED ☐ COMPLETION OF WORK ON SCHEDULE	1 2 3 4 5	25	
QUALITY			
☐ ACCURACY ☐ NEATNESS ☐ THOROUGHNESS ☐ ORAL EXPRESSION ☐ WRITTEN EXPRESSION	1 2 3 4 5	25	
WORK HABITS			
☐ PUNCTUALITY ☐ ATTENDANCE ☐ COMPLIANCE WITH ORDERS ☐ INTEREST ☐ INITIATIVE ☐ RESOURCEFULNESS ☐ AGGRESSIVENESS	1 2 3 4 5	15	
PERSONAL TRAITS			
☐ EMOTIONAL STABILITY ☐ MATURITY ☐ ATTITUDE ☐ COMPATABILITY WITH OTHERS ☐ PERSONAL APPEARANCE ☐ COMMAND PRESENCE ☐ LOYALTY	1 2 3 4 5	15	
ADAPTABILITY			
☐ PERFORMANCE IN NEW SITUATIONS ☐ PERFORMANCE UNDER STRESS ☐ PERFORMANCE WITH MINIMUM INSTRUCTIONS ☐ ABILITY TO LEARN	1 2 3 4 5	10	
JOB KNOWLEDGE			
☐ TECHNIQUES ☐ PROCEDURES ☐ SKILLS	1 2 3 4 5	10	
		100	
		SUM	SUM

2. Performance deficiencies; Suggestions for improvement or continuing development:

3. General comments (e.g., over-all performance, progress since last report, plans, goals; any other remarks):

This report represents my best judgement of the employee's performance based on my observations and knowledge.

RATING SUPERVISOR _____ DATE _____

I have read and approved this report.

DIVISION COMMANDER _____ DATE _____

This report has been discussed with me.

EMPLOYEE'S SIGNATURE _____ DATE _____

F 2021-54

Forced choice standard

Once traits are selected which are considered to be the most important indicators of quality of performance, several options can be provided from which the rater must select the one that most closely describes the performance of the person being rated. The options can be given a numerical value to indicate the subject's overall rating or the options may be classified in broad terms such as poor, fair, good, very good, excellent, or other descriptors indicative of the rater's assessment of each trait.

In this standard of rating, the rater must select only one choice for each trait evaluated. Only one trait should be considered at a time to avoid an unconscious bias that often creeps into trait ratings when several traits are considered together. Similarly, the rater should disregard any general impression he has of the person being rated to avoid undue influences on the independent ratings of traits. The rating should be a true report of how the person rated performs his work— not a personal analysis of that person.

Highest or lowest ratings for the various traits should not be based on only one favorable or unfavorable talent or event; however, such extreme ratings should be supported by objective evidence which is more than just one person's subjective opinion. The making of these extreme ratings should not be avoided because of this requirement, for to do so would result in commission of the error of central tendency discussed in later pages and would tend to discredit the entire rating. Rather, when justified, such ratings will provide the rater with an opportunity for giving credit when it is due for meritorious service or to take action necessary to improve the performance of an employee rated in the lowest column.

Figure 12–4 shows some selected examples of options that can be easily developed for the various traits to be rated. (See page 242.)

RATER CHARACTERISTICS

Evidence indicates that the best supervisors are usually the best raters. They are more faithful to their rating responsibilities than are the poorer supervisors and are less likely to commit the error of leniency by overrating the poor performers. The better supervisors are found to be more discriminating and generally more objective than their less effective colleagues.[3]

[3] W. E. Kirchner and D. J. Reisberg, "Differences Between Better and Less Effective Supervisors in Appraisals of Subordinates," *Personnel Psychology*, 15 (Autumn, 1962), 295–302.

FIGURE 12-2. Performance Appraisal Report (courtesy of Orange, California, Police Department)

CITY OF ORANGE
POLICE DEPARTMENT

EMPLOYEE: _____

RATING PERIOD: _____ TO _____

DIVISION: _____

ASSIGNMENT: _____

PERFORMANCE APPRAISAL REPORT (PEACE OFFICER)

TYPE: _____

STATUS: _____

PROB. REC.: _____

RATER INSTRUCTIONS: Enter number in appropriate scale column box on each item. Marks **above** or **below** COMPETENT are discussed under appropriate heading on attached page. Refer Department Memoranda #6 for complete instructions.

"TYPE": Refers to whether this appraisal is annual, bi-annual, or quarterly. If "Special," enter "exceeds standards" or "sub-standard."

"STATUS:" Refers to the employee's present employment status; probationary, hire, promotion, permanent.

"PROBATION RECOMMENDATION:" If the employee is on probation, enter recommendation for continued probation; extended probation; termination; or permanent appointment.

"5"...OUTSTANDING — Clearly exceeds normal expectations of proficiency.

"4"...EXCEPTIONAL — Exceeds normal expectations of proficiency.

"3"...COMPETENT — Is reasonable and consistent with normal expectations of proficiency.

"2"...IMPROVEMENT NEEDED — Is not quite reasonable and consistent with normal expectations of proficiency.

"1"...UNSATISFACTORY — Is clearly not reasonable and consistent with normal expectations of proficiency.

"0"...NOT OBSERVED

PERFORMANCE FACTORS (ELEMENTS)	SCALE
1. JUDGMENT - PROBLEM SOLVING	
a. Ability to set priorities on work.	
b. Ability to handle a number of tasks at one time.	
c. Ability to make on-the-spot decisions.	
d. Ability to organize required work.	
2. ORAL COMMUNICATIONS	
a. Ability to impart information.	
b. Ability to interpret and apply oral instructions.	
c. Ability to express oneself orally.	
d. Ability to maintain confidential police information.	
3. MEMORIES	
a. Ability to observe, recognize and interpret.	
b. Ability to learn and apply procedures.	
c. Memory for instructions and directions.	
4. BEHAVIOR ELEMENTS	
a. Satisfactory personal conduct and integrity.	
b. Tact and diplomacy.	
c. Emotional stability.	
d. Ability to maintain an ethical attitude.	
5. PERSONAL CHARACTERISTICS	
a. Punctuality.	
b. Reliability and dependability.	
c. Cooperative with others.	
d. Demonstrates initiative in the performance of duties.	
6. WRITTEN COMMUNICATIONS	
a. Correct use of grammar, punctuation, spelling.	
b. Clarity of reports.	
c. Ability to proofread and direct appropriate correction.	
d. Effectively report all required elements.	

PERFORMANCE FACTORS (ELEMENTS)	SCALE
7. PHYSICAL AGILITY - CONDITION	
a. Ability to perform the physical tasks and duties as required by the classification.	
8. KNOWLEDGE OF MODERN POLICE ORGANIZATION AND PROCEDURES	
a. Knowledge of City and Department policy and procedures.	
b. Knowledge of Department Rules and Regulations.	
9. KNOWLEDGE OF APPLICABLE CRIMINAL LAWS-CODES	
a. Knowledge of search and seizure guidelines.	
b. Knowledge of laws of arrest.	
c. Knowledge of applicable codes used regularly in this assignment.	
10. STRESS	
a. Ability to work under pressure.	
b. Ability to work rapidly.	
c. Ability to shift tasks as priorities change.	
SUPERVISORS ONLY	
11. KNOWLEDGE OF MGMT/SUPERVISION/HUMAN RELATIONS	
a. Knowledge of current principles of Management and supervision.	
b. Knowledge of principles of human relations.	
12. KNOWLEDGE OF TRAINING AND INVESTIGATION PROCEDURES	
a. Knowledge of conducting applicable investigations.	
b. Knowledge of current training principles and procedures.	
13. SKILL IN HUMAN RELATIONS	
a. Sets and maintains effective levels of performance for personnel.	
b. Gaining compliance while maintaining morale.	
c. Establishes and maintains effective working relationships.	
d. Observes a need and initiates appropriate action.	

OPD P-42 (6-76)

DISTRIBUTION: WHITE: Department Personnel File   YELLOW: Ratee's Unit/Division File   PINK: Ratee

FIGURE 12-3. Performance Appraisal Report—review and narrative (courtesy of Orange, California, Police Department)

ORANGE POLICE DEPARTMENT
PERFORMANCE APPRAISAL REPORT

SECTION 1 PERFORMANCE EXCELLENCE | Describe examples of work, performance and/or assignments that have been done well.

_____
_____
_____
_____
_____

SECTION 2 PERFORMANCE DEFICIENCIES | Describe specific examples of performance deficiencies. Describe suggestions for improvement, continuing development or re-training:

_____
_____
_____
_____
_____
_____
_____

SECTION 3 GENERAL COMMENTS | Describe progress since last report; agreed-upon goals set for next rating period, overall performance factors:

_____
_____
_____
_____
_____
_____
_____
_____

RATER	REVIEWER(S)	RATEE
• I have read and understood the "Guide to Performance Appraisals."	• I have read and understood the "Guide to Performance Appraisals."	• I have read and understood the "Guide to Performance Appraisals."
• I have regularly and directly observed the performance of employee on the elements which I evaluated.	• I have read this appraisal and received a copy	• I have read this appraisal.
	REVIEWED BY:_____ DATE:____	• I have discussed this appraisal with the rater.
SIGNATURE_____ DATE____	REVIEWED BY:_____ DATE:____	• I have received a copy of this appraisal.
TITLE_____	REVIEWED BY:_____ DATE:____	SIGNATURE_____ DATE____

OPD P-42 (6-76)   DISTRIBUTION: WHITE: Department Personnel File YELLOW: Ratee's Unit/Division File PINK: Ratee

241

Consider the quality and accuracy of reports made.
(Personnel matters, field investigations, complaints, etc.)

| Extremely tardy and careless. Reports quite often inaccurate. | Inclined to be careless. Reports sometimes unacceptable. Needs reminding to get work in. | Acceptable reports. May be too fast and inaccurate, or slow and accurate. | Reports done with few errors and with greater dispatch than usual. | Unusually good complete reports. Work accurate and reliable. Always on time. |

Consider the judgment of this employee. Is it sound and unbiased?
Do his decisions conform to the policies and practices of
the Department and of his own unit?

| Handles situations clumsily; ignores departmental policy, rules, and lines of authority. Makes decisions too hastily and illogically. Prejudice indicated. | Judgments often illogical. Tends to overlook departmental policy and rules. Prejudice sometimes indicated. | Acts judiciously under most circumstances. Usually adheres to departmental policy and rules. | Judgments impartial and logical, in keeping with established policies and procedures, with rare exceptions. | Thinks soundly and logically. Advice respected and sought by associates. Considers all factors without confusion. |

Consider attention and concentration on work and routine matters.
His attitude toward departmental rules, policies and procedures.

| Kills time. Welcomes interruptions of duties. No particular interest in work. Continually violates rules. Fails to enforce rules. | Works intermittently; dawdles and gossips; sometimes violates rules. Regards service as "just a job." Little progress shown. | Works fairly steadily; displays a moderate interest and enthusiasm for the job. Seldom breaks rules. Steady progress. | Interested and enthusiastic about all phases of work. Seldom distracted by other matters. Always on the job. Always observes regulations. | Outstanding enthusiasm. Treats job as a career. Is an incentive to associates in work attitude and observance of rules. Shows unusual progress and application. |

Consider ability to handle assignments without detailed instructions
or supervision. Is some initiative shown in daily work?
Has he some original suggestions for improvements?

| Has to be told every step to take. No imagination. Has no suggestions for an improved service or conditions. | Needs some instruction and supervision. Routine worker; has few ideas outside of usual line of duties. | Requires little supervision. Has an occasional good suggestion for bettering the service. Shows some imagination. | Works well without supervision. Often presents useful ideas and methods. Takes hold of work with will and initiative. | Absolutely reliable in following through on assignments. Always alert for improvements and effective shortcuts. |

FIGURE 12-4. (cont.)

Consider how subject utilized experience and information.
How he increases his information and skill in handling assigned work.

Inadequate knowledge of job. Makes no effort to learn. Has to ask same questions repeatedly.	Has a fair background of information but does not use it to advantage. Shows little interest in learning more about job.	Knows his job reasonably well; picks up information readily. Seldom asks second time about the same information.	Knows his job well and uses previous experience to advantage. Seldom has to ask questions.	Thoroughly familiar with work to be done. Learns rapidly. Can "take over."

Lenient supervisors who rate all their subordinates alike are covertly disrespected. The outstanding employee is penalized while the marginal one is rewarded, simply because the rating officer did not have the personal interest, or perhaps the ability, to prepare a thorough, accurate service rating report based on the objective evidence he has bothered to gather. The preparation of these reports is directly dependent upon his ability to observe and record evidence of the type of performance of his subordinates, his judgment, patience, and understanding in dealing with them; and his ability to lead, to maintain discipline and morale, and otherwise to control them. These same abilities are involved in all his supervisory activities. Indeed, they are in direct proportion to his proficiency as a supervisory officer. If his rating attitude is one of leniency, morale problems will inevitably result. The industrious, dedicated officer will ask why he should continue to extend himself when he gets little or no more credit for his efforts than the lazy officer who rarely works diligently. In addition, employees tend to believe that most supervisors are influenced by personal relationships—either good or bad—more than they are by performance. Lenient raters tend to support this belief. Strict but fair raters are usually approved by almost all subordinates. At least, if they are honest with themselves, they will realize that this type of rater is doing the best job he knows how to do with the tools or evidence at hand. The unfair rater will rarely, if ever, receive the approbation of his subordinates.

Every supervisor should realize that he is evaluated informally by his subordinates on the basis of how his personnel evaluation duties and responsibilities are performed. No wonder so much importance is attached to employee ratings. The economic life of the employee is directly affected by the evaluations he receives from his superiors. Promotions and related salary increments, longevity pay, tenure, seniority rights, and other job benefits are often directly involved. If the ratings are used as management tools and are improperly or carelessly made, irreparable harm is often done the employee's career. If he demands nothing else, he will insist on fair and impartial treatment from his superiors. In turn, if the supervisor gives his subordinates little else, he owes them this.

Certain broad characteristics are usually found in supervisors who excel in rating their subordinates. Some of the most common of these qualities are these:

> They are able to distinguish facts from feelings or impressions.
> They are able to weigh the performance of their subordinates against a consistent standard. They accomplish this by establishing "norms" of conduct and performance as a point of departure for rating personnel.
> They are able to base their ratings on objective data whenever possible without allowing subjective emotions, individual likes and dislikes, or biases to influence them.
> They are careful to avoid committing the error of rating on the basis of vague, general impressions. They make every effort to rate on the basis of individual, personal traits.
> They are systematic and thorough in recording accurate data relating to their observations of employees throughout the rating period.

Unfortunately, some raters allow strong personal idiosyncrasies to influence them in their appraisal of subordinates. Strong, often unreasonable, likes and dislikes sometimes cause clouded vision and result in seeing only good in some officers and bad in others. Adequate records of observations may dissipate this prejudice and favoritism. The more confidence subordinates have in the objectivity of the rating system, the less likely they will be to complain, to offset poor ratings by "playing politics," or to develop a defensive attitude. The most effective raters are those whose temperament and personality are well balanced. It is not necessary that they be intellectually superior to be effective.

COMMON RATING ERRORS

Invariably, when ratings fail to accomplish their true purpose, it is found that the fault lies not in the form used but in the rater. Either he has prepared the report merely to fulfill a policy or legal requirement, or because the activity adds just another burden to his already overworked position, he has become indifferent to or unconcerned with the probable results of carelessly prepared reports and completes them in the easiest way possible. Even the simplest of forms can achieve a very beneficial effect if care is given to their preparation. A thoughtful, simple narration of the rater's appraisal of a subordinate sometimes is more meaningful than complicated formulas which attempt to equate the various personal traits by a series of checkmarks in boxes. The quality of personnel evaluations, then, is largely a matter of attitude—the attitude of the rater. It is therefore a truism that the training of the raters is the most important requisite in the administration of a successful evaluation system. Yet even with training, some errors do creep into the rating process. The following are some of the most common.

Error of leniency

The error of leniency is by far the most common of all errors in the rating of personnel.[4] It occurs when the rater marks an inordinately large number of the rating reports in the highest one or two categories such as Very Good and Excellent, or perhaps Excellent and Outstanding, depending upon the particular terminology used in the report form. Occasionally, such forms include a percentage figure denoting the percentile within which the ratee is marked in comparison with other persons rated. The lenient rater will mark an excessive number of his subordinates in the upper 20 per cent or upper 10 per cent and fewer in the lower ranges.

This tendency to "overrate" has many obvious dangers, foremost of which is the damaging effect it has on the morale of the truly outstanding workers. They will soon begin to wonder if it really pays to work diligently when the less proficient employee receives the same rating anyway.

This marked tendency to rate high results in what is called a skewed curve with an excessive number of personnel rated in the upper range. Such a tendency is a perfectly human one but should be avoided to preserve the integrity of the rating system. Often the rater who commits this error will start overrating his subordinates because of his intense desire to be popular and to be liked by them. He will lower ratings only when he is offended by an overt act committed by the ratee.

The error of leniency is contagious. It has a tendency to spread rapidly from one supervisor to another who feels compelled to overrate his subordinates so that they may compete favorably with others who have been rated too high by an overly lenient supervisor. "The effects are to force ratings so drastically high that they are useless as management tools and to create unrealistic employee confidence when improvement in performance is really needed and quite possible."[5]

A supervisor is likely to "overrate" his subordinates if they are to

[4] International City Managers' Association, *Municipal Personnel Administration*, 6th ed. (Chicago: International City Managers' Association, 1960), p. 147.

[5] International City Managers' Association, *Municipal Personnel Administration*, p. 147.

see their ratings or if the supervisor is defensive and feels that he is protecting a deficient employee.[6]

Research by Kirchner and Reisberg [7] shows that the error of leniency seems to occur more frequently in ratings by the less effective supervisor, who also tends to attach a higher degree of emphasis to the more static employees who "don't rock the boat," while the better supervisors are more discriminating in their ratings and attach more significance to an attitude of progressiveness in their subordinates.

Error of personal bias

Raters often tend to rate higher than is justified those persons they know well and like, and those who "subscribe to the same platform" as the supervisor. Those who are not liked or who are not compatible with the supervisor's own particular philosophies are likely to be rated lower than is justified.

This tendency toward bias in ratings should be guarded against as it destroys the validity of ratings. Such bias can be reduced if the rater tests his rating by asking himself if it was influenced by the fact that the employee is like (or unlike) himself. If it was, then the rater must reappraise the facts upon which he based the rating.

Supervisors must likewise consciously guard against overrating subordinates merely because they have been selected by him or are working in his particular unit. True, ratings of individuals selected for a specialized unit because of their special abilities may be generally somewhat higher than ratings of a large, randomly selected group where the distribution of ratings follows a normal, bell-shaped curve; but when 80 or 90 percent of the personnel in a certain group are rated in the top category or very near the top, the effect is that there is no normal curve of distribution of ratings showing differences in performance. Thus, all ratings are open to question and are often considered unreliable.

The conclusion of a superior that all his employees are good "because they work for me," or "if he works for me, he must be good," is absurd. Such philosophy applied to a rating program usually results in other supervisors becoming reluctant to penalize their own subordinates by attempting to make honest, objective ratings when they know others are not using objective standards. This attitude also tends to penalize the best employees because it reduces the spread in the ratings and places

---

[6] Richard S. Barrett, *Performance Rating* (Chicago: Science Research Associates, Inc., 1966), pp. 23–26.

[7] Kirchner and Reisberg, "Differences Between Better and Less Effective Supervisors in Appraisal of Subordinates," *Personnel Psychology*, pp. 295–96.

all personnel of the unit in about the same rating category. Some supervisors feel that this may ingratiate them with their subordinates, but the best employees, as previously indicated, will resent having to "carry" the worst, and they will resent the failure of their superior to give honest credit where it is due.

Error of central tendency

All too often, raters will group their ratings near the center of the rating scale with few ratings at the bottom or top. This tendency to avoid the extremes on the rating scales usually results from a policy requiring justification for extreme ratings. Again, outstanding employees are penalized by being unjustifiably rated lower than they should be, while those personnel who should be rated at the lowest part of the scale are rewarded by the lazy supervisor who is either indifferent to the effects of his neglect or is disinclined to take the trouble to collect sufficient data to justify high or low ratings. In either case, the organization suffers as well as the better employees. This error of central tendency is especially common when no system has been devised by the individual rater or the organization to gather adequate, specific, and objective information which could be used to defend or justify a high or low rating.

Halo effect

The tendency of raters to rate in terms of a very general impression rather than on the basis of specific traits is commonly referred to as the halo tendency.[8] It occurs when the rater thinks in terms of the "good" or the "poor" officer and groups all the ratings for that individual at the high or low end of the scale. This often occurs when the rater has been unduly influenced by the error of related traits or the error of overweighting of incidents, which are discussed in the following paragraphs.

Error of related traits

Sometimes referred to as *logical error* or *association error,* the error of related traits is committed when the rater gives similar ratings to traits which seem to be similar. For example, this rating error is made

[8] E. L. Thorndyke, "A Constant Error in Psychological Ratings," *Journal of Applied Psychology,* 4 (1920), 25–29.

in reports when the rater assumes that if a person has good judgment he must also have good presence of mind, if he is attentive to duty he must have a high degree of initiative, if his physical health is good his mental health must also be good, if he is dependable he must also be cooperative, or if he makes errors he must be fatigued.

Each trait must be considered by the rater by itself. If he associates several traits, he is apt subconsciously to allow one to influence another similar one and thus reduce the accuracy of his ratings.

Error of overweighting

The tendency of raters to be unduly influenced by an occurrence, either good or bad, involving the ratee near the end of the rating period is known as overweighting. This rating error often occurs when one or more outstanding occurrences near the end of the rating period are out of proportion to the average performance during the entire period. When ratings are influenced by such events, they cannot be supported. They may be inordinately high or low depending upon the nature of the occurrence and its effect upon the rater. Such ratings are often influenced by factors much like those resulting from the halo effect especially if the rater has not diligently kept himself informed about the standard performance of his subordinates.

Error of subjectivity

The error of personal bias is often confused with the error of subjectivity; but close examination of the two will reveal subtle differences. The error of subjectivity occurs when the rater is unduly influenced by one or two characteristics which have special appeal to him. The cooperative or pleasant officer, for example, is sometimes rated much higher because of these traits than his overall performance justifies.

The rater must constantly be alert to the possibility that he may harm morale if he fails to utilize the objective data available to him and bases his ratings on subjective influences and idiosyncrasies which will have the tendency to distort his appraisals.

It must be recognized, however, that human traits cannot be measured with mathematical precision. The rater must consider the ratee's progress, his accomplishments—both qualitative and quantitative—and the probabilities of his future patterns of performance being generally similar to what they have been in the past. Any projection of such performance patterns must be founded on what has been learned of the individual's previous behavior. For example, the rate at which a person produces is only one factor to consider in rating him. If the rater is appraising a person and attempting to predict his suitability for promotion to a position wherein the activities and responsibilities are quite dissimilar to those of the present rank, all those traits which contribute to competency in the new position such as attitude, initiative, leadership ability, and the like must be considered. At best, a series of educated guesses would be involved in such projections; but these are perfectly acceptable if carefully made because workers who are good performers and who possess those basic characteristics desirable in a leader can be trained to be good supervisors.

EVALUATION PERIOD

Evaluations should be prepared from evidence collected during a particular rating period. Ratings for an established period should not be contaminated by observations carried over from some other period.

VALIDITY AND RELIABILITY OF RATINGS

Raters must be given a deep appreciation of the great need to make evaluation reports valid and reliable indicators of performance if they are to have maximum value as tools of supervision. If they do not reflect with reasonable accuracy the relative competency of personnel, their capabilities, and their value to the organization, the effort and expense involved in making them is largely wasted.

Validity

A valid report is one which is an accurate measurement of the ability it purports to measure. Valid reports actually reflect the officer's value to the organization in terms of specific traits which are related to his work such as get-along-ability, industry, attention to duty, cooperativeness, and so forth. If the report is truly valid, it will not measure something it is not supposed to measure. If the form requires that certain traits or characteristics be measured which have little bearing upon the traits and abilities required for the particular job, then the validity of the rating form as a measure of the individual's competency is lowered. Likewise, if trivia are emphasized, then the form's value is further reduced.

Obviously, in modern police agencies which are involved in highly complex activities of varied types, it would be impractical, if not almost impossible, to gear a separate rating form to each job assigned. Therefore, it is necessary that at least the core traits and abilities necessary for the police job be included in the rating form if it is used for all nonsupervisory personnel. In some organizations, a rating report is especially constructed for evaluating supervisory or management personnel because skills and traits necessary for these positions differ somewhat from those required for personnel performing nonsupervisory tasks.

The rater must exercise care to avoid weighting all traits and abilities equally since the job being performed by the person rated may not require the same abilities—at least the same amount of a particular ability— that another job may require. For example, a police laboratory assignment may not require the same administrative ability as might a supervisory assignment. Unbalanced emphasis upon a particular trait being assessed will reduce the validity of the rating. Leonard [9] observed, "It is generally conceded that a rating system is just as valid as its design and the degree of intelligence, judgment, honesty and understanding of the rating instrument, exercised by the rater."

Reliability of ratings

A rating report is said to be reliable if it measures consistently and reasonably accurately—even if not perfectly—each time it is used. If several persons, using the same information, rate an individual substantially the same, then their ratings would be a reliable measure of the employee's abilities; however, raters rarely have the same abilities to observe, collect, and report evidence regarding the performance of subordinates with the same degree of accuracy and objectivity. Therefore, training must focus the raters' attention on means of bettering the collection and use of data. The ideal rating, of course, is one in which the results are not unduly influenced by subjectivity or chance but are based on sound, objective evidence.

RATING METHODS

The method selected for rating personnel depends in part upon the individual needs of the organization and the preference of the raters. Each method has its merits and shortcomings.

[9] V. A. Leonard, *Police Organization and Management*, 2nd ed. (Brooklyn, N.Y.: The Foundation Press, Inc., 1964), p. 109.

There is general agreement that, whatever method is selected, when ratings are made under supervision so that instructions are understood and some controls are exercised over them, their quality improves.[10] Bittner [11] found in the army that the quality of ratings was higher when they were reviewed by a superior familiar with the performance of those rated than when no such review was made.

Composite ratings

Some supervisors prefer to rate their subordinates individually with the superior officer of the unit making a composite rating from the several individual appraisals, usually by a process of averaging the ratings. Occasionally, the ratings of the various supervisors will be identified on one composite report by the use of numbers or symbols keyed to the names of the raters which are listed on the form. The shortcomings of this method are readily apparent. Extreme ratings will tend to be in agreement while midrange ratings will often be in conflict. In addition, all individual raters often do not have access to the same evidence. Some who have had limited opportunity to make observations upon a particular subordinate will, of necessity, base their ratings on general impressions rather than on specific, factual, observed evidence. Before the more abstract personal traits of individuals can be accurately measured, many observations must be made.

Group ratings

In the police service, a common practice followed is to make group ratings of individual employees in a conference of supervisory officers. For example, all first-line supervisors who have supervised the officer rated over the rating period rate him by conferring. By pooling observations, discussing factual evidence, and preparing a group rating with which the raters agree, the tendency to overweight the evaluation is reduced, individual biases are tempered, and a rating norm can be established by the group for more accurate ratings. The disadvantage of this method is that a biased (but articulate) supervisor may unduly prejudice the other raters in favor of or against the person being rated.

Group conference ratings should always include the names of the

10 Barrett, *Performance Rating*, p. 122.

11 R. Bittner, "Developing an Industrial Merit Rating Procedure," *Personnel Psychology*, 1 (1948), 410–18. See also Lee Stockford and H. W. Bissell, "Factors in Establishing a Merit Rating Scale," *Personnel*, September, 1949, p. 110.

participants on the report form. Theoretically, raters who are properly trained in the procedure of personnel appraisals will always make reasonably accurate ratings; however, this rarely occurs, and, as the result, superiors and examining boards reviewing such reports are often inclined to "rate the rater" before they attempt to assess the rating itself.

Individual trait rating

It is recommended by many who are experienced in the merit rating process that raters should be encouraged to rate each employee on one characteristic at a time rather than to rate each employee completely before rating another. It is argued that the halo effect is increased when only one employee is considered at a time until his rating is completed because of the good or bad influence one trait has upon another; whereas, if only one trait is considered at a time for all employees being rated, a more desirable norm can be achieved. The logic of this contention is sound. The supervisor may, however, find it difficult at times to rate separate items separately. Some may have to be considered together because of the effect each has upon the other. For example, in the police service, quantitative production reflected by the number of traffic citations issued or the number of arrests made will be definitely affected by the quality of the traffic citations or arrests. The officer issuing numerous "apple orchard" citations should not receive greater quantitative credit than that given the officer who writes considerably fewer violations but of a much higher selective enforcement quality. The same applies to quantitative and qualitative arrests.

DISCUSSION OF RATING WITH EMPLOYEE

Perhaps one of the greatest uses to which personnel evaluations can be put is their discussion with the person rated.[12] The supervisor is provided an opportunity to commend or thank his subordinates formally for their high level of performance during the rating period or, in the case of marginal or substandard employees, to help them when improvement is indicated. If carefully made, the rating report provides a medium for showing the employee how he is measuring up to standards or how he may be falling short of them in his performance.

Some supervisors believe that discussion of ratings with personnel

---

[12] See Chapter 7 for further discussion of the progress interview.

accomplishes little and only leads to controversy; however, the training value of such discussions is readily apparent and undoubtedly the benefits outweigh the liabilities if they are conducted in a constructive manner. Unfortunately, it must be stipulated that some interviews do not accomplish what is intended because, if they are conducted for the purpose of informing the substandard employee of his weaknesses, they are inherently threatening, not only to the supervisor who is expected to be constructively critical of his subordinate but to the subordinate who is on the receiving end of the criticism. This threat is an obstacle to effective communications between the two and, over a period of time, causes a lessening of such face-to-face contacts with a weakening of the whole system resulting.

The interview

The interview with the employee calls for a degree of tact and forthrightness if it is to have maximum effect. Rating officers invariably have little difficulty in interviewing the high producer. Difficulty is usually encountered in approaching the marginal or substandard employee. Often supervisors find this an onerous and unpleasant task, easier to avoid than face; but if the interview is approached objectively, they will be able to make it a constructive training device.

At the conclusion of the interview, a substandard employee should be asked to recap his understanding of what was agreed upon and what is expected of him in the future. Such playback will eliminate any real or feigned misunderstandings which may be claimed later.

Follow-up to rating interview

Arrangements should be made in the supervisor's schedule for follow-up observations which will provide clues to the effectiveness of the interview. These observations will often assist him in determining the usefulness of the plan the employee has been helped to make and if the specific objectives set for him have been realized. It should be made clear to him that help will be readily forthcoming if needed. He should also be informed that future discussions regarding his performance will be held. If present weaknesses are to be corrected, a specific date might well be set for follow-up discussions. The interview and the follow-up contacts should be conducted on a friendly, helpful, and positive basis.

WRITTEN NOTIFICATION OF RATING

Some superior officers utilize the written notice procedure to inform the employee of his overall rating. This technique is effective as a method of commendation but has serious limitations if utilized to replace the face-to-face interview with the employee whose work needs improvement. This procedure does not afford a suitable medium for full discussion and goal setting, which are desirable and which can be accomplished in the progress interview.

SUMMARY

One of the biggest problems in performance evaluations is the selection of a rating method which will yield reliable results. Employees may be ranked, they may be rated on the basis of a comparison with selected employees, or in comparison with the ideal employee, or they may be rated on a numerical basis. Whatever standards the supervisor is expected to use as guides in interpreting the performance norms of his subordinates should be clearly defined. He should be made conscious of the difference between ability and performance. Procedures should be standardized so that all raters may perform their tasks uniformly.

The performance standards which emerge from an effective rating system will give employees the clues to what is expected from them. These standards will serve as goals toward which they can strive when they know where they stand in comparison with other employees.

The supervisor responsible for rating his subordinates must be fully aware of the common errors which creep into ratings so that he may avoid inaccuracies that penalize the better performers. The error of leniency will cause his appraisals to be inordinately generous while personal bias will tend to destroy their usefulness as accurate measures of the level of an employee's performance. When almost all ratings are grouped near the center of the scale because of the reluctance of the rater to defend extremely high or low ratings, this error of central tendency penalizes the best and rewards the poorest employees. The halo effect will likewise reduce rating accuracy as will the error of related traits wherein the rater unconsciously allows one trait to influence another merely because both seem to be similar. Subjectivity of ratings and the undue influence of one incident near the end of the rating period upon the evaluation of an employee for the entire period will adversely affect the report's value as a management tool.

Whether the composite, group, or individual trait rating method is followed, the rating process should be supervised so that the raters will apply a common standard in their ratings. Such supervision will improve their quality. Their value will also be enhanced if the reports are accurate indicators of the ability they purport to measure and if they measure consistently and reasonably accurately each time they are used for they will then be statistically valid and reliable instruments.

Upon completion of periodic ratings, they should be used as a basis for discussing with each employee his performance—commendable, acceptable, or unsatisfactory. Substandard performance can often be corrected by planning a course of action for him, stimulating him to improve his performance, and following up to ensure that he is making acceptable progress.

REVIEW

Questions

1. Discuss the rating standards and methods commonly used in rating systems to compare employees.
2. What broad characteristics are usually found in supervisors who excel in rating subordinates?
3. List the seven common rating errors and discuss how each error is committed.
4. Distinguish between reliability and validity in rating reports.
5. What are the most common rating methods? Discuss the advantages and disadvantages of each.

Exercises

Assume that you have rated your subordinates on a 1 to 10 basis for the following traits, abilities, performance, and value to the organization. A rating of 10 represents the outstanding employee, while a rating of less than 5 represents the deficient one who needs to improve. You are to interview the concerned employee, whom you have rated as indicated below, for the purpose of informing him of his deficiencies and assisting him to establish a program for self-improvement. Make any assumptions reasonably required for the interview.

Quality of work	4
Quantity of work	6
Knowledge of job	7

Initiative   3
Loyalty   5
Cooperation with fellow employees   5
Diplomacy and tact in dealing with public   4
Personal habits   4
Emotional stability   5
Overall value to department   4

13

Distribution and deployment of field forces

Every police administrator is faced with the problem of providing a certain level of service to his community with a specified number of personnel. The total number of officers available to him will vary from community to community depending upon many factors among which are budget limitations, the availability of qualified applicants, the extent and kind of crime, or the level of police service demanded by the public. Many police functions do not lend themselves to precise time and motion studies, which might enable the police administrator to determine precisely his total police personnel needs. Therefore, rules of thumb and experience will usually dictate the amount of public monies allotted for policing the community. Despite almost universal police manpower shortages in American cities, the police administrator can make maximum use of the resources he has by distributing his personnel in accordance with some basic scientific logic—that of assigning them to the *places they are needed at the times they are needed in proportion to the relative need for their services.*

The apportionment of field officers available in accordance with the demand for services as revealed by statistical data, is a scientific approach defensible against pressure groups in a particular area de-

257

manding added police protection at the expense of another area. Invariably, there is only a certain amount of service available, and it should be apportioned on a more logical basis than emotion, political considerations, or mere guesswork.

FIXED POST POSITIONS

The assignments of personnel to fixed post positions such as jailor, desk officer, vice officer, or supervisor of shift or watch is a relatively simple task. These positions must be manned regardless of the number of officers on patrol duty. The number of officer personnel required for these posts must be provided *in addition* to those made available for field patrol. Likewise, the determination of the number of officers needed for some field duties such as traffic direction or accident investigation can be accomplished with ease as the need for such services can be determined by simple observation or time measurements. In larger departments having traffic law enforcement and accident investigation units, these can be apportioned according to the criteria of time measurements and the requirements to investigate fatal accidents and those involving personal injury. Not so with the patrol force.

PATROL ALLOTMENTS

Many functions of the patrol officer, such as repressive patrol and crime prevention activities, are intangible, and the need for these activities is not susceptible to accurate measurement. Therefore, the total number of officers assigned to the patrol force will usually be based on estimates, which in turn rely heavily on records of past experience and operations.

ASSIGNMENTS BASED ON PROPORTIONATE NEED

When the determination of the percentage of the total force to be allotted to patrol activities has been made, the problem of distributing assigned officers according to the proportionate need for their services must be met. The most effective service will not be afforded a community if patrol personnel are assigned in *equal* numbers to shifts, to the days of the week, or to beats of equal geographic size on a "flat" basis. Rather, if most police incidents occur during the night, then obviously most of the patrol force should be assigned to nighttime duty to meet the need for police service during that time if the scientific principle of proportionate need is to be followed. Likewise, the assignment of patrol personnel to days of the week according to the proportionate need for their services would be indicated, as would their assignment to areas according to this principle. Other collateral benefits, more specific in nature, which would result from such distribution of personnel would be a degree of equalization of work loads of officers throughout the hours of the day, the days of the week, and the areas of the city. Thus each officer could justifiably be held accountable for the police problems within his area of responsibility. He would, ideally, have the same amount of work assigned and therefore the same time available for preventive patrol as would other officers.

Obviously, in very small organizations, where it takes all personnel available to provide minimal patrol services twenty-four hours per day, scientific distribution may not be possible. In departments that have found it necessary to use unpaid volunteers or reserve officers to fill shortages, these should be distributed on the same basis as are the regular personnel.

Selection of factors to determine proportionate need

The determination of proportionate need for the distribution of the patrol force depends upon selection and use of factors which indicate the extent of the police problem in a given city. Herein lies the element of subjectivity since the selection of factors which reflect the nature of the police problem is, in large part, a matter of opinion. Each administrator should select those factors which he believes most accurately reflect the police problem in his community. He must equate each factor chosen with others. These will not necessarily remain static because the nature of the problem will change from time to time. It is recognized that certain occurrences are more valid as measuring devices than others. Experience has shown that some criminal offenses are more subject to control by police patrol than are others. Crimes such as robbery, burglary, auto theft and thefts from autos, thefts from persons, and aggravated assaults are either indicators of the need for police services or are more responsive to patrol activities than are many other offenses such as crimes against persons.

There are numerous factors that indicate to some extent the nature of the police problem. Attempts to use all of them would probably yield few benefits and no greater accuracy than would the use of a limited number of carefully selected items.[1] Some of these factors are:

[1] N. F. Iannone, "Factors in Patrol Distribution" (unpublished manuscript, Los Angeles Police Department, 1950), p. 20. Comprehensive studies revealed slight, almost insignificant, differences in apportionment of personnel based on a twenty-six factor formula from apportionment based upon a formula of seven selected factors with

Part I offenses (except crimes against persons)
Part II offenses
Selected major offenses (which respond most readily to police patrol)
Misdemeanor arrests by patrol officers
Felony arrests by patrol officers
Juvenile offenses known to the police
Street mileage
Number of calls for service
Time spent handling calls for service
Population (in residence)
Population density (including transient and work population)
Property loss from crime
Autos stolen
Autos recovered
Number of attractive police hazards
Number of public gathering places
Number of traffic accidents (fatal and injury) investigated by patrol units
Traffic accidents (total including property damage)
Number of ex-felons in residence
Citations issued by patrol officers

Weighting of factors

Factors should be carefully analyzed to determine their usefulness as criteria representing proportionate need for the expenditure of available patrol time. Obviously, some factors do not place the same demands on patrol time as do others. A preliminary investigation of a robbery involves more time than does the issuance of a traffic citation, therefore, a system must be devised to equate these police statistics so that they will be given appropriate emphasis in computing proportionate police needs. This may be accomplished by a system of *weighting* of selected factors. Such weightings are admittedly subjective, but they provide a fairly accurate measure for determining relative police needs. For example, selected crimes and attempts may be given a weight of three because of their general responsiveness to police patrol. Radio calls handled by patrol units may be double weighted because they represent a clear-cut, tangible need for police service. Adult and juvenile felony

---

carefully chosen items weighted. A study by Marvin D. Iannone, "A Study and Analysis of the Methods Employed by the Patrol Bureau and Geographical Patrol Divisions of the Los Angeles Police Department in the Distribution of Personnel" (unpublished manuscript, California State University at Los Angeles, 1965), p. 19, revealed that minor variations in choice of factors do not result in any great change in distribution patterns.

arrests by patrol personnel may be double weighted since the making of felony arrests involves more of the patrol officer's time than do most arrests for lesser offenses. Misdemeanor arrests, property loss, fatal and injury traffic accidents, vehicles recovered (by place of recovery), population (residence), and population density (including transients) are often not weighted.

The use of certain factors, as indicated above, and their relative weights should be reassessed periodically for the purpose of determining the current nature of the police problem which must be met. The amount of property loss factor may cause distortions in statistical data in small cities with few property losses. In larger cities, this condition will not ordinarily make the data unreliable, especially if the few extremely large losses of property are eliminated from computations. Places of recovery of vehicles is included because these vehicles are often used in the commission of other crimes and recovering the vehicles requires patrol time to handle. Street miles is a far more reliable indicator of the need for patrol time than square miles because patrol time is involved in going from place to place in performing the many kinds of police activities. Response time involved in answering calls may be used instead of street miles, but data are far more difficult to obtain. Furthermore, response time is often distorted by other factors, such as road conditions, police zeal, and the like. Population figures represent problems of patrol work load not reflected in other factors. Population density factors reflect the relative number of activities initiated by the police, such as those occasioned by an increase in juvenile activities during seasonal surges, increased problems brought on by industrial or residential development, and so on.

The formula can be used to compute the *overall average percent of the police problem* (which represents the proportionate need for police service with certain statistical adjustments to increase accuracy) by hour of the day, day of the week, and by area of the community. The use of different weights and factors might be indicated because of such conditions as extreme area to be covered, extreme density of population with small area to be patrolled, or severe seasonal fluctuations in population. Such decisions are individual and may vary widely from city to city.

Collecting data

After the factors to be used to distribute available patrol personnel are selected, steps must be taken to collect the necessary statistical data. Some of these are collected by each organization in connection with routine records keeping. These data should reflect the need for police service by hour of the day, day of the week, and area of the city.[2] In large agencies, the data which have been accumulated and punched on cards from information reported by officers may be collected from data-processing machine records. The information can be easily tabulated by reporting district and time. For distribution purposes, the data may be collected, tabulated, and assembled on a sample basis, for example, the first month in each quarter, to gain adequate, representative data.

The use of sophisticated electronic equipment for information retrieval in an elaborate deployment system is extremely costly and will often not produce more satisfactory results than the deployment of patrol personnel selectively by use of a simple, basic formula.

In small departments, this information can be relatively easily tabulated by hand from radio call and disposition reports, officers' daily logs adapted for tabulating, crime, or similar reports. Annual studies of work load ordinarily will suffice; however, if new territory is annexed, or territory is lost, or if a sudden population shift occurs because of development or redevelopment, an immediate study should be made to provide a current basis for distribution and deployment.

Additional data are obtainable from planning groups and from the federal government, which periodically gathers social and economic data in its census studies. These data may be useful in analyzing and forecasting the incidence of crime. Since the federal government collects these data and assembles them according to specifically defined areas known as Federal Census Tracts, the police administrator desiring to make use of this valuable material will establish crime reporting districts and beats which coincide with the federal census tract boundaries. The data from both sources may then be correlated. This may not always be practicable because geographical barriers may require some alterations in beat layout, as discussed later, while having no effect upon the area covered by the census tracts. Such tracts are relatively stable while beat boundaries are subject to change as the geography is altered by freeways, storm drains, parks, and other physical changes or as the need for police services changes because of the growth of new industrial or business centers or residential tracts.

---

[2] Some police reports do not reflect the time or area of occurrence accurately. The exact place where a robbery was perpetrated after the victim was kidnapped and moved from one place to another or the exact time a burglary occurred when all that is known is that it took place between one date and another would not be possible to report. Such occurrences should be distributed, for statistical purposes, to days of the week and hours of the day (unless the day is known) in the same relative proportions as in those cases where the time of occurrence is known.

OVERALL AVERAGE PERCENTAGE OF POLICE NEEDS

The method of utilizing the basic distribution formula in computing the average percentage of police need by hour of the day, day of the week, or area is identical except that raw data are tabulated according to time or area as needed. For example, if five factors were being used by a particular department with some of the factors weighted as illustrated in Table 13-1, the average percentage of police need by shift and day of the week would be computed as indicated.

Determination of shift hours

In order to determine the chronological distribution of personnel, the average percentage of police need must be determined by hour of the day and by day of the week. The first group of data is used in establishing shifts, while the second group of data is utilized to determine how patrol personnel should be distributed throughout the week to best meet policing needs. Thus the supervisor has some guides in making assignments for days off, vacations, or training, and also in planning ahead to allow for the sick time he should anticipate.

Ordinarily, the first or second level supervisors will not be called upon to compute the number of patrol personnel to be assigned to each shift. The patrol division commander will make such determinations; however, the shift commander and the field supervisors must apply identical techniques in distributing personnel throughout the week and to beats. They should understand the methods utilized by their commanding officer in order to appreciate the many facets involved in the

TABLE 13-1. Average need by day of week—day shift

	Selected Crimes (X 3)	Radio Calls (X 2)	Felony Arrests (X 2)	Property Loss	Misdemeanor Arrests	Overall Average
Sunday	27.0%	16.0%	18.0%	22.8%	13.4%	10.8%
Monday	33.3	17.1	21.6	16.0	16.4	11.6
Tuesday	42.0	18.0	19.3	15.0	14.6	12.1
Wednesday	51.6	26.0	23.4	6.0	14.5	13.5
Thursday	37.1	35.5	26.0	12.0	22.6	14.8
Friday	54.0	42.0	41.0	10.3	12.0	17.7
Saturday	55.0	45.4	50.7	17.9	6.5	19.5
Totals	300.0%	200.0%	200.0%	100.0%	100.0%	100.0%

distribution of field patrol officers. The supervisors are responsible for conveying information and intelligence to their superiors relative to unusual policing requirements which may alter the total number of personnel made available for field patrol and, consequently, the number to each shift. The police administrator will ordinarily review statistical data at predetermined intervals to determine if the distribution of field forces needs to be revised to meet current problems. The supervisor will also constantly observe operations to determine whether changes are indicated in the distribution of his subordinates on a chronological or geographical basis.

The formula for distributing patrol personnel scientifically will apply only to the total number of patrol officers available for *motorized field patrol,* as previously indicated. This number can easily be determined by subtracting from the total number of officers assigned to the patrol division those personnel required to accommodate all fixed posts.

A determination of the hours when shifts would begin and end is presented graphically in Figure 13–1. By plotting the police needs by hour of the day on a graph, the supervisor can readily determine by observation the most practicable hours into which shifts should be established. Inspection will indicate that, if eight-hour shifts are to be used,

FIGURE 13-1. Shift hours (percentage of police need by hour of the day; data taken from Tables 13-2 and 13-3. Deviations from average hourly needs are graphically shown.)

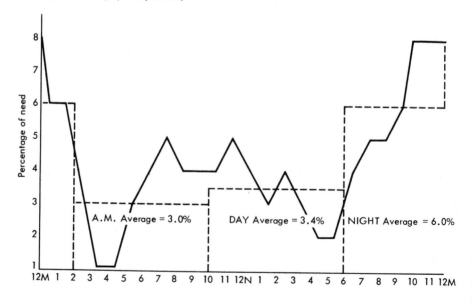

they would probably be arranged in this particular instance to start at 2:00 A.M., 10:00 A.M., and 6:00 P.M., and end at 10:00 A.M., 6:00 P.M., and 2:00 A.M. respectively.

Ordinarily, shifts should not be changed during periods of high police activity since field patrol units available to respond to calls for services are reduced somewhat while shifts are being relieved. Ideally, changes of shifts should be arranged so that they may be made during periods of relatively low police activity. Obviously, morale of the patrol forces and the effects of unusual hours of duty upon the health of officers must be considered to some extent in determining shift hours. For example, shifts starting at 4:00 A.M., 12:00 noon, and 8:00 P.M. would often work a hardship upon personnel and should ordinarily be avoided by the police administrator, although an overlapping shift starting at 8:00 P.M. and ending at 4:00 A.M. (often referred to as a midwatch), to provide for added police patrol in periods of peak activity during the nighttime, might be in order.

So-called "split shifts" in which officers work a few hours, are relieved for a period, then return to complete their tours of duty should also be avoided because of the adverse effects they have upon morale. There are times, however, when such arrangements are desirable for officers wishing to further their education or attend to other personal needs during the middle of their shift. "Split shifts" are sought after by such personnel.

Ordinarily, however, each shift should be planned for a continuous eight-hour period. Three shifts are usually preferred to four or five. When a fourth or fifth shift is superimposed upon the basic three, area responsibility usually becomes indistinct, car plans must be changed during a shift, and communications are often unnecessarily complicated. The result is lessened efficiency.[3]

In establishing shift hours, *actual* hourly need for service should not deviate widely from the *average* hourly need. The 4:00 P.M. to 12:00 midnight shift in Table 13–2 shows the *actual hourly need*,[4] deviating considerably from the *average* hourly need. Unless extraneous factors such as unusual situations brought about by a highly transient popula-

---

[3] Car or beat plans are established for the purpose of assigning available field units to specific areas or beats depending upon the number of units available on a particular shift. Planning of the number of beats to be patrolled on a given shift enables the supervisor to establish area responsibility and facilitates radio communications with assigned units.

[4] The percentage of hourly need (proportionate need for police services during that hour) is derived from the computations of total need for police services utilizing all selected factors (in the formula) representing the total police problem.

TABLE 13-2. Method of shift selection based on deviations of actual hourly needs from average hourly needs

	4 P.M. to 12 M. Shift		6 P.M. to 2 A.M. Shift	
	Hourly Need*	Deviation From Average Hourly Need (±)	Hourly Need	Deviation From Average Hourly Need (±)
4 P.M. – 5 P.M.	2%	3%	–	–
5 – 6	2	3	–	–
6 – 7	4	1	4%	2%
7 – 8	5	0	5	1
8 – 9	5	0	5	1
9 – 10	6	1	6	0
10 – 11	8	3	8	2
11 – 12 M.	8	3	8	2
12 M. – 1 A.M.	–	–	6	0
1 A.M. – 2	–	–	6	0
Total percentage need per shift	40%	–	48%	–
Average percentage of hourly need	5% (= 40 ÷ 8)	–	6% (= 48 ÷ 8)	–
Total percentage deviation from average hourly need	–	14%	–	8%
Adjusted total shift deviation	–	5.6% (= .14 × 40)	–	3.8% (= .08 × 48)

*Percentage of hourly work loads for the hours 2 A.M. to 4 P.M. have been omitted for simplicity. Data for all 24 hours would be recorded when three or four shifts are to be selected.

tion and the like are involved which would justify a distribution of personnel on a basis other than a purely statistical one, the shift from 6:00 P.M. to 2:00 A.M. would be more desirable since the actual hourly need in that shift deviates less from the average hourly need than does the 4:00 P.M. to 12 midnight shift (8 per cent versus 14 per cent).

To compute the proportionate need for police service for each shift, it is only necessary to tabulate the *overall average* percentages of the police problem for each hour of the day (as computed by the formula) and add the percentages for the consecutive eight-hour periods selected for each shift. Determination of the overall average percentages for a shift is illustrated in Table 13–1, where computations have been made to indicate the need in the day shift for each day of the week.

Inspection of Tables 13–2 and 13–3 reveals that the 4:00 P.M. to midnight shift ends at a period of peak work load. This is graphically illustrated in Figure 13–1. Such an arrangement of shift hours would result in either considerable overtime on that shift because of late calls or an increase in criminal activity in exposed places during a period of reduced police patrol occasioned by a change of shift. In selecting shift hours, however, it must be remembered that all three shifts must be considered. Benefits derived from the selection of certain hours for one shift may be offset by disadvantages arising from the hours that must therefore be selected for the other shifts.

TABLE 13-3. Hourly need for police services

		Hourly Need*	Total Need for 8 Hours Ending With This One	Average Hourly Need
12 M. — 1 A.M.		6%	... 44%	5.5%
1 A.M. — 2		6	...... 48%	6.0
2 — 3		3		
3 — 4		1		
4 — 5		1		
5 — 6		3	36%	4.5
6 — 7		4	... 32%	4.0
7 — 8		5	...... 29%	3.6
8 — 9		4	.... 27%	3.4
9 — 10		4	.... 25%	3.0
10 — 11		4		
11 — 12 N.		5		
12 N. — 1 P.M.		4		
1 P.M. — 2		3	33%	4.1
2 — 3		4	... 33%	4.1
3 — 4		3	...... 31%	3.9
4 — 5		2	.... 29%	3.6
5 — 6		2	.... 27%	3.4
6 — 7		4		
7 — 8		5		
8 — 9		5		
9 — 10		6	31%	3.9
10 — 11		8	... 35%	4.4
11 — 12 M.		8	...... 40%	5.0
Total		100%		

*Fractional percentages omitted.

Adjusted total shift deviations

In order to adhere to the requirements that shifts be selected for greatest efficiency so that the *actual* hourly need will have the least deviation from the *average* hourly need (as illustrated in Table 13–2), the total percentage of deviation from average hourly need for each shift can be adjusted to provide an additional guide in the selection of the hours for each shift. Adjusted shift deviations will indicate which of the alternative shift arrangements contain the least deviation and therefore, in the absence of extraneous factors apart from statistical considerations, will most efficiently and equitably distribute the manpower available.

The total shift deviation is adjusted for statistical purposes to dis-

TABLE 13-4. Total deviation from average hourly need and percent of adjusted total shift deviation*

Shift Hours	Total Need for Police Services	Average Need for Police Services	Total Deviation from Average Hourly Need	Adjusted Total Shift Deviation
6 A.M. – 2 P.M.	33%	4.1%	3.4%	1.1%
2 P.M. – 10 P.M.	31	3.9	9.2	2.9
10 P.M. – 6 A.M.	36	4.5	20.0	7.2
Total	100			11.2
7 A.M. – 3 P.M.	33	4.1	3.4	1.1
3 P.M. – 11 P.M.	35	4.4	13.0	4.6
11 P.M. – 7 A.M.	32	4.0	16.0	5.1
Total	100			10.8
8 A.M. – 4 P.M.	31	3.9	3.4	1.1
4 P.M. – 12 M.	40	5.0	14.0	5.6
12 M. – 8 A.M.	29	3.6	13.0	3.8
Total	100			10.5
9 A.M. – 5 P.M.	29	3.6	5.8	1.7
5 P.M. – 1 A.M.	44	5.5	12.0	5.3
1 A.M. – 9 A.M.	27	3.4	11.0	3.0
Total	100			10.0
10 A.M. – 6 P.M.	27	3.4	7.0	1.9
6 P.M. – 2 A.M.	48	6.0	8.0	3.8
2 A.M. – 10 A.M.	25	3.0	9.0	2.3
Total	100			8.0

*Adapted from: *Assigning Patrol Personnel 1 - Distribution* (Anaheim, California: Litton Instructional Materials, Inc., Litton Industries, 1966), p. 44.

tribute the deviations in hourly work load more accurately throughout the entire shift. Deviations from the average hourly needs may be plus or minus; however, whether these are overages or underages is disregarded since the important consideration is how much of a deviation there is from the average hourly need.

The *adjusted total shift deviation* is the product of the total percentage deviation from the average hourly need multiplied by the total percentage of need per shift (see Table 13–2).

Table 13–3 illustrates a tabulation of *actual hourly needs* for police service and the total need for several different eight-hour periods from which the *ideal* shift selection will be made.

Table 13–4 data have been computed from the raw data shown in Table 13–3 and illustrates the *total percentage of need* for police service per shift, which data are utilized in the mathematical process of distributing available field personnel. In addition, the *adjusted total shift deviation* is utilized, as illustrated in Table 13–2 in the selection of the most desirable shift arrangements on a purely statistical basis. These data (illustrated in Table 13–4) indicate that the 10 A.M.–6 P.M., 6 P.M.–2 A.M., 2 A.M.–10 A.M. shifts would be the preferred arrangement because they have the least adjusted total deviation.

OVERLAPPING OF SHIFTS

On occasion, because of inordinately high workloads at certain hours of peak police activity, it will be desirable to institute overlapping shifts to meet the need for police services. This should be avoided, however, unless the problem of deviation from the average is serious at the end of one shift and at the beginning of another. Such overlapping shifts, often called midwatches, should be eight consecutive hours long to avoid the necessity of requiring officers to work split shifts. The four–ten (four-day workweek with ten-hour shifts) plan, discussed later, has built in excesses in overlapping of shifts.

The same techniques of determining proportionate need for the overlapping shifts and the most desirable shift hours should be used as in the case of three eight-hour shifts illustrated in Table 13–4 except that, instead of computing the necessary percentages showing the need for three eight-hour shifts, data would be tabulated to show various combinations of hours for shifts so that adjusted total deviations for each period could be determined. The twenty-four hour period with the least adjusted total deviation would be the most desirable arrangement and, statistically, the most efficient. *Data should be tabulated so as to avoid using the same statistics twice.* Thus, if a 6 P.M. to 2 A.M. overlapping shift were to be utilized, the various arrangements of hours for which the percentage of adjusted total deviation would be computed might be:

6 A.M.–2 P.M.	or	7 A.M.–3 P.M.	or	8 A.M.–4 P.M.	*etc.*
2 P.M.–6 P.M.	or	3 P.M.–6 P.M.	or	4 P.M.–6 P.M.
6 P.M.–2 A.M.	or	6 P.M.–2 A.M.	or	6 P.M.–2 A.M.
2 A.M.–6 A.M.	or	2 A.M.–7 A.M.	or	2 A.M.–8 A.M.

Problems of overlapping of shifts

When additional units are deployed on an overlapping shift basis to meet peak activity, the supervisor must consider some of the adverse effects to efficiency and morale which might arise if he does not make assignments with care. Generally, as previously outlined, to maintain beat responsibility, to avoid the problems which arise from dividing this responsibility between two or more units, and to prevent morale problems which invariably occur when one of the two or more units assigned to a beat is permitted to "jump" the most interesting calls (the "cruiser car effect"), it is desirable to use a larger car plan, that is, to reduce the size of beats and utilize more units to cover the larger number of smaller beats. This, in effect, gives each unit a smaller area to cover and yet provides an equalization of work load between all patrol units. When additional units in overlapping shifts are assigned to beats already assigned to other units or given "area-wide" assignments as "cruiser cars," the supervisor is unable to establish clear-cut area responsibility, the problems of follow-up are increased, and control of such units generally becomes more difficult. It is recognized that the change of car plans during a shift often complicates communications and beat coverage, but such problems can be easily overcome if units are fully informed of the required changes in beat coverage when car plans change. Confusion will consequently be minimized and changes will become simple routines. Maps showing beat boundaries and reporting districts in the various car or beat plans should be standard equipment for each patrol unit kit. These will provide a ready reference for officers affected by changes in their beat area brought about by a change in car plan during a tour of duty. The communication center and each field and station supervisor should be similarly equipped.

Such maps can be easily made by simply tracing from the control map onto plain white paper of standard loose-leaf size the beat boundaries of each of the various car plans. Boundary sheets should be clearly identified, and each map should be appropriately titled. Reporting districts should be identified to facilitate reporting of police incidents from which the necessary data can be secured for distribution and deployment purposes.

DISTRIBUTING AVAILABLE FIELD PATROL PERSONNEL

When the most desirable shift arrangements have been made, the matter of distributing the available field patrol personnel to shifts involves the simple matter of multiplying the number of officers available for *field patrol* by the total percent of need for each shift. This, then, is shift distribution on the basis of proportionate need.

Providing for relief

Since the area covered by patrol beats must be policed every hour of the day and every day of the week throughout the year, provision must be made for the relief of officers who are on days off, vacation, sick leave, training assignments, or military leave of absence, or are off duty for some other reason. This relief factor will vary from agency to agency, depending upon local policies and practices. It may be simply determined by computing the actual number of days the *average* officer assigned to the patrol force is available for duty. Fixed post positions must be covered just as must field patrol assignments. By dividing the number of days per year that the average officer is available for his field duties *into* the number of days the area in each beat must be covered per year (365) the number of officers needed to cover a beat for one full shift for one year can be readily determined. Thus, if the average officer is entitled to two days off per week (104 days per year), twenty-one vacation days, ten days for sick leave (on the average) and training assignments, for a total of 135 days, he would be available for his patrol duties only 230 days per year. The relief factor thus would be nearly 0.6 since 0.6 of one man's time would be spent in relieving another officer who is absent because of regularly assigned days off, sick or training leave, or vacation. Expressed in another way, 1.6 officers would be required to cover one field position every day of the year on the average.

Unusual shortages of personnel on one shift because of unforeseen happenings such as excessive injuries or long-time sickness usually can be solved by borrowing from other shifts so that the unusual absences can be spread over all shifts rather than absorbed by any one.

ASSIGNMENTS BY DAY OF WEEK

The determination of the proportionate need for police service for each day of the week is ordinarily a shift commander's responsibility. He ordinarily delegates it to a field sergeant.

The first step is to arrange statistical data by the day of the week rather than by the hour of the day as was done in selecting shift hours. Identical factors are used in computing percentage of need. Separate tabulations are made for each shift to determine the nature of the problems occurring at the various times of the day. Obviously, the need for police services is not equal for each day of the week any more than it is for all hours of the day.[5] Therefore, personnel must be distributed by the shift supervisors according to the proportionate need on the various days of the week if the most efficient use is to be made of the available personnel and the most effective service is to be provided the community. Obviously, such factors as the need for some two-officer units should be considered in making personnel adjustments for shifts having such requirements. A different number of personnel would be required for each day of the week on each shift if they are to be distributed scientifically. When two-officer patrol units are used, the number of beats which can be covered by a given number of personnel must be reduced by one for each two-officer unit. This factor must be kept in mind when car plans are established.

If sixteen officers were assigned to a shift for field patrol and if the relief factor were 0.6, the supervisor would have ten officers to distribute, on the average, each day of the week; but, since each day of the week would require a different amount of patrol, the supervisor would distribute the seventy officer-days of work which would be available on a proportionate need basis throughout the week. Table 13–5 illustrates the percentage of need for each day of the week, the number of personnel assigned to work on each day, and the number which can be absent.

This simple method of distribution will allow the supervisor to assign days off in accordance with plans made a month or more ahead of time. With a little additional effort, he can give his subordinates many of the days off they desire and still retain sufficient personnel on duty to provide the proportionate amount of police service indicated for each day of the week. Other factors than purely statistical ones must

[5] Frank E. Walton, "Selective Distribution of the Police Patrol Force," *The Journal of Criminal Law, Criminology and Police Science,* November-December, 1958, p. 387.

TABLE 13-5. Distribution of night-shift personnel by day of week

	Percentage of Need for Police Service*	Number Working	Number Off Duty
Sunday	10.8	8	8
Monday	11.6	8	8
Tuesday	12.1	9	7
Wednesday	13.5	9	7
Thursday	14.8	10	6
Friday	17.7	12	4
Saturday	19.5	14	2
Totals	100.0	70	42

*The computations are made on the basis of sixteen men available on this shift for field patrol assignments and a relief factor of 0.6. Fractions have been rounded.

be kept in mind when work schedules are prepared, however. The astute supervisor will recognize that statistics may provide the "ideal" distribution patterns, but special needs of his subordinates may dictate some modifications. The basic objectives of scientific deployment and distribution can still be reasonably met without destroying morale by becoming overly arbitrary in assigning days off.

Projections for some weeks in advance showing the number of personnel available for each day of the week, the number of days off allowable, and the relative work load needs will give the shift commander a suitable guide in preparing his assignment sheets. Barring extraordinary losses of officer-days through some unforeseen event, he can rely upon such projections as reasonably accurate guides in distributing his personnel.

Statistical data may indicate the need for services changes from time to time, or unusual police problems may arise suddenly. Changes in distribution may be required without an opportunity for long-term planning. These exigencies can be met with little difficulty by rescheduling of days off, canceling compensatory time off or vacations, or drawing personnel from other shifts to meet the needs of the moment. Some departments use reserve teams or squads which can be easily deployed for any special enforcement problems that arise. If, however, a mechanical, "flat" system of distribution is employed wherein personnel are distributed equally throughout the week, those working Saturday might have twice the work load as those working Sunday. Inflexibility and inefficiency are the by-product of such distribution practices.

CAR PLANS

Once field personnel have been distributed to the various shifts, usually by the commanding officer of the patrol division, the shift commander and field supervisors must deploy them to beats or patrol car districts. Statistical data obtained by using the same formula as in the case of the selection of shifts are tabulated to show the percentage of need by areas. Data can then be grouped into Federal Census Tracts or reporting districts (which usually should be coextensive). This will make possible a comparison of crime statistics with socioeconomic data collected in the federal census and will indicate the relative police problem in each district.

Data are accumulated for each reporting district on a chronological basis to show the relative need for police services by hour and day. Unless geographical considerations make it essential, census tracts should not be split into more than one reporting district. To do so would unnecessarily complicate beat layout. In some cases, isolated areas may be so located as to justify splitting a census tract and maintaining separate statistical data for each portion to determine how it should best be covered in each of the various car plans.

Establishing car plans

Data collected *for each shift* from reporting districts may be utilized by the supervisor to establish a variety of car plans so that a given area may be covered according to its proportionate need on any day of the week or at any time of the day. Separate car plans must be established for each shift to equalize workloads for all field officers assigned to the shift. The boundaries for the beats in a six-car plan on the day shift might well be different from the boundaries of the beats in a six-car plan on the graveyard shift because of the shifting police problem at various times of the day. A congested industrial area might present quite a different police problem on the day shift when plants are open than on the night shift when they are closed.

The car plan in use usually will be dictated by the number of officers on duty available for field patrol. If two-officer units are utilized, adjustments will be necessary accordingly. For example, Table 13–5 would indicate that an eight-car plan to cover the eight beats into which the area has been divided should be utilized for the night shift on Monday when one-officer units are used. A ten-car plan would be indicated for Thursday since ten officers would be required on that day to meet the dictates of proportionate need.

Although a perfect arrangement is seldom possible, contiguous reporting districts should ideally be grouped like building blocks into beats so that each will contain as nearly as practicable an equal percentage of the total police problem. The variously grouped beats thus become car plans.[6] Each beat in a ten-car plan would theoretically contain 10 per cent of the police problem. Each beat in a five-car plan should contain as nearly as possible 20 per cent of the total problem. Experience will play a prime part in car plan arrangement. By experimentally arranging beats according to *ideal percentage of work load and most desirable boundaries,* the supervisor will soon approach a variety of reasonably effective car plans from which he can select those most workable. Beats will not be equal in area since area, *as represented by street miles,* is only one factor used in determining relative need for patrol. The problems might well be condensed in certain areas and widely distributed in others. Figures 13–2, 13–3 and 13–4 illustrate typical four-, eight-, and nine-car plans for patrol units. Figure 13–5 depicts a totally different, three-car arrangement for accident investigation units, illustrating how policing patterns vary.

Data on proportionate need, arranged by reporting district (census tract) as shown in Table 13–6 and recorded on a map of the area, will

TABLE 13-6. Night-shift work load by reporting district

Reporting District	Night Shift Work Load	Reporting District	Night Shift Work Load	Reporting District	Night Shift Work Load
1401	3.345	1425	2.610	1455	.735
1402	3.240	1427	1.755	1456	2.750
1403	4.385	1428	1.380	1457	2.002
1404	1.795	1429	1.285	1459	2.580
1405	2.861	1431	2.013	1466	1.861
1406	1.705	1432	1.868	1467	2.583
1407	2.945	1433	1.251	1469	2.933
1408	1.295	1434	1.705	1481	1.411
1409	1.525	1435	1.295	1483	2.861
1411	1.752	1437	.845	1485	1.604
1412	1.030	1438	1.295	1486	1.432
1413	.920	1439	1.293	1487	2.613
1414	1.625	1446	1.295	1489	2.511
1416	1.210	1447	1.380	1491	1.021
1417	.895	1448	.461	1492	2.212
1419	1.860	1449	.589	1493	1.406
1422	1.280	1453	1.210	1497	3.065
1423	1.432	1454	.860	1499	3.020
1424	1.910				

[6] Marvin D. Iannone, "A Study and Analysis of the Methods Employed by the . . . Los Angeles Police Department in the Distribution of Personnel," pp. 24–25.

FOUR-CAR PLAN
P.M. WATCH

FIGURE 13-2. Four-Car Plan—P.M. Watch (courtesy of Los Angeles Police Department)

EIGHT-CAR PLAN
P.M. WATCH

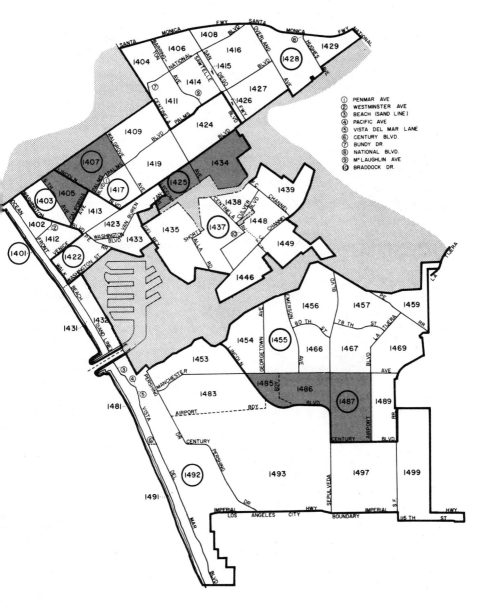

① PENMAR AVE
② WESTMINSTER AVE
③ BEACH (SAND LINE)
④ PACIFIC AVE
⑤ VISTA DEL MAR LANE
⑥ CENTURY BLVD.
⑦ BUNDY DR
⑧ NATIONAL BLVD.
⑨ McLAUGHLIN AVE
⑩ BRADDOCK DR.

FIGURE 13-3. Eight-Car Plan—P.M. Watch (courtesy of Los Angeles Police Department)

NINE-CAR PLAN
P.M. WATCH

FIGURE 13-4. Nine-Car Plan—P.M. Watch (courtesy of Los Angeles Police Department)

THREE-CAR PLAN
P.M. WATCH

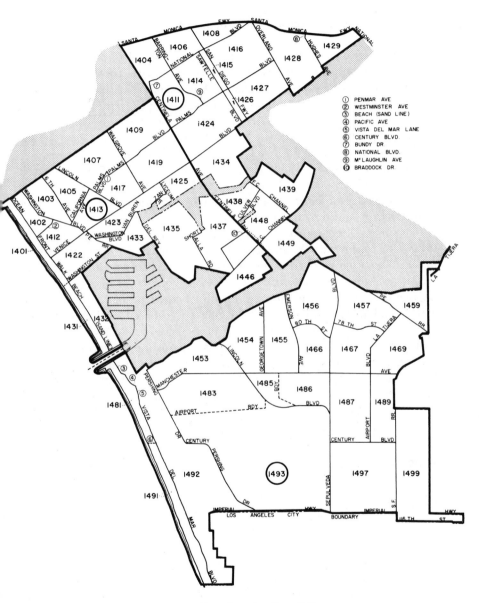

① PENMAR AVE
② WESTMINSTER AVE
③ BEACH (SAND LINE)
④ PACIFIC AVE
⑤ VISTA DEL MAR LANE
⑥ CENTURY BLVD.
⑦ BUNDY DR.
⑧ NATIONAL BLVD.
⑨ McLAUGHLIN AVE
⑩ BRADDOCK DR.

FIGURE 13-5. Accident Investigation Division. Three-Car Plan—P.M. Watch (courtesy of Los Angeles Police Department)

best portray the most desirable combinations which may be arranged into the various car plans as illustrated in Figure 13–6.

Physical factors affecting beat arrangement

Usually, some experimentation will be required to achieve best results in developing car plans since some subjective considerations are involved in selecting beat boundaries. For example, as previously mentioned, beat boundaries should not ordinarily split reporting districts, for to do so would unnecessarily complicate the reporting of police incidents requiring patrol time. However, on occasion this may be imperative to avoid geographically isolating a portion of the area. To assure that patrol units have easy access to all areas of their respective beats, natural or man-made barriers such as mountains, rivers, storm drains without ample crossovers, freeways, and other obstacles must be considered in addition to purely statistical information.

Primary streets such as major thoroughfares which form reporting district or census tract boundaries should ordinarily be given preference for beat boundaries over secondary streets, which often do not provide area-wide access. Extreme distances between boundaries of a beat should be avoided. Dead-end or short streets obstruct access to the total area of a beat and usually do not present sufficient exposed police hazards to justify using them as boundaries where considerable overlapping of patrol takes place from contiguous beats. Again, the supervisor will rely heavily upon experience to give him the insight into the nature of the police problems which, combined with objective statistical data, will enable him to equalize the work load among his subordinates according to time and area.

FOUR–TEN PLANS

The administrative decision whether an organization will adopt a revised work week plan involving four ten-hour days is one which will invariably be made by top management. The methods for determining the relative need for police services by time and place will be the same as for traditional selective enforcement deployment systems. Such computations will ordinarily fall within the scope of a supervisor's duties.

Many organizations in the private sector have adopted various types of revised workweek schedules such as the four-ten plan with considerable success; however, in law enforcement agencies that provide public services twenty-four hours per day, usually by way of three or

REPORTING DISTRICT MAP

Workload for
Night Shift:

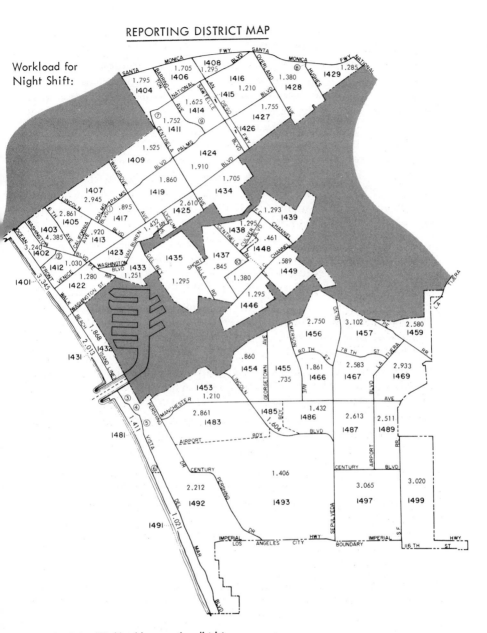

FIGURE 13-6. Workload by reporting district

four shifts, any substantial extension in the length of the traditional workday will necessarily produce a certain amount of shift overlap unless other tasks are found for personnel during these overlapping periods. Whether this will result in inflexibility and inefficient use of manpower or produce other uneconomic results on low-intensity workdays will depend on the care with which the plan is supervised. Ordinarily, under a traditional system of deployment, on days when the demand for police services is highest, a fourth shift—overlapping two other shifts—can be used to accommodate the problem; however, when shift overlap becomes a mechanical process *every* day of the week because of the length of the workday for each employee under a four–ten plan, inefficient use of manpower is likely to result and may more than offset benefits derived from the plan.

Four–ten plans have been studied extensively by many law enforcement agencies. It has been found that workers generally favor the shorter workweek because of the added time it provides for leisure, education, moonlighting, and the like. From an overall management point of view, however, most law enforcement organizations have concluded that the potential benefits were not sufficient to justify adoption of such a plan. These conclusions were based upon problems associated with the fatigue factor, the control of the increased moonlighting made possible for employees, the need for additional equipment to accommodate extra personnel during overlapping periods of duty, the potential need for greater salary budgets to pay employees at overtime rates for work exceeding eight hours per day, and a host of related reasons. A few organizations which have used it in the past have modified it extensively and have found that it has produced acceptable results. Others have abandoned it completely. Despite its shortcomings, some have been forced to retain the plan because of employment contracts.[7]

---

[7] The California Commission on Peace Officer Standards and Training, *The "Ten Plan" in California Law Enforcement Agencies* (Sacramento, Calif.: Commission on Peace Officer Standards and Training, 1973). See also Riva Poor, ed., *4 Days, 40 Hours: Reporting A Revolution in Work and Leisure* (Cambridge, Mass.: Bursk and Poor Publishing, 1970); Paul Brown, "'Cycle Scheduling' for Eight and Ten Hour Days," *Police Chief*, XLI, No. 4 (April, 1974); Thomas J. McEwen, *4–10 Plan: Police Explore Potential of 4-Day Workweek* (Washington, D.C.: National Criminal Justice Reference Service, No. 1, April, 1972); Earle W. Robitaille, "Ten Hour Shift Study–'Ten Plan,'" *Journal of California Law Enforcement*, 5 (July, 1970); William A. Allen, "Four Day Work Week: Another Approach," *The Police Chief*, January, 1973; Redondo Beach Police Department, *Project Ten: Final Evaluation Report* (Redondo Beach, California, Police Department, March, 1975); Downey Police Department, *Project Overlap* (Downey, California, Police Department, 1974); Niel A. Martin, "Some Reservations About the 4-Day Week," *Supervisory Management*, November, 1971.

SUMMARY

The police administrator can make maximum use of personnel available to him by distributing them scientifically to the places they are needed at the times they are needed and in accordance with the proportionate needs for their services. The most effective and efficient service will not be provided if personnel are assigned in equal numbers to shifts, to the days of the week, or to beats of equal geographical size since to do so would make impossible an equalization of the work load among officers and the establishment of area responsibility.

Proportionate need can be established with some accuracy by the development of a formula which has been found useful by many enforcement agencies in distributing and deploying personnel chronologically and geographically. The factors which could be used in such formula are numerous; however, the police administrator should select those which he believes most accurately measure the particular problem in his community. As some factors such as selected major crimes place a greater demand upon patrol time than do other factors, a system of weighting them must be devised so as to place appropriate emphasis upon them when comparative police needs are computed.

Statistical data are collected from routine record keeping of crime data and from the federal government, which periodically gathers socioeconomic information in its census and tabulates it by Federal Census Tracts. Thus, the administrator and supervisor can utilize not only local crime and police problem data but can correlate it with federal census tract information; but to do so, reporting districts which coincide with these census tracts must be established.

The first consideration in the distribution of available field patrol personnel must be given to their assignment by shifts. Data tabulated by hours of the day, weighted in accordance with factor weighting, and computed according to the formula will reveal the most desirable shift hours. Shifts should be selected which contain the least deviation of actual hourly needs from the average hourly needs so that policing requirements will remain as nearly consistent as possible throughout the shift. Graphs showing the need by hour of the day will often make the selection of shift hours obvious; however, a computation of adjusted total shift deviations is a more precise method of establishing shifts. The matter of distributing field personnel available for patrol duty to shifts then becomes a matter of simple arithmetic computation.

Once personnel are allocated to shifts, the supervisor must determine how they would be assigned to meet the varying needs for police services by day of the week. The same factors are used for computing the need for service by the day of the week and by each shift as were used in determining proportionate need by shift. The difference is in the arrangement of the data by day and shift instead of by the hour.

The number of officers needed for relief of those who are not available for duty must be considered so that days off, vacations, and other leaves may be allotted on an equitable basis with enough personnel left to meet the daily proportionate need for police services. The relief factor is ascertained by determining how many officers are necessary to cover one beat at all times on one shift for a full year. By dividing the number of days the position must be covered during the year by the number of days the average officer is available for duty, the number of officers needed to cover it can easily be computed.

Geographical beats should be established so that they each represent an equal share of the work load. These may be developed by plotting geographically the extent of the police problem from the same formula used in determining shift hours and daily need for services. Recording of the data by area and by shift on a reporting district map will be useful in determining beats and car plans.

Consideration must be given to geographical factors in addition to purely statistical data in the establishment of beat boundaries. Major thoroughfares, secondary streets, storm drains, freeways, mountains, and so forth will influence the setting of these boundaries so that isolation of certain areas can be avoided and work can be properly apportioned on a logical basis. The establishment of beats will enable the supervisor to develop car plans which can be utilized depending upon the number of officers available for field duty on the various days and shifts. Car plans are developed like building blocks through the process of combining contiguous reporting districts into beats with work loads as equal as possible. If five officers are assigned for one-officer patrol units, a five-car plan would be used. Ten one-officer units would require a ten-car plan.

When overlapping shifts are utilized, larger car plans should be used to increase the number of beats covered and decrease the area each unit covers to avoid the adverse effects to morale which often result when two or more units are given joint responsibility for a particular area.

REVIEW

Questions

1. What is meant by proportionate distribution of the patrol force?
2. Name at least five fixed post positions.
3. List twenty factors that might be considered in developing a dis-

tribution formula and describe which of these would be most valid as measures of police need.

4. Why should certain of these factors be weighted when they are used in the formula?

5. How is the overall average percentage of the police problem determined from the formula?

6. If a burglary report indicated only that the offense was committed within a two-day period, how would you establish a time element for the crime for statistical purposes?

7. What is the adjusted total shift deviation? Why is this adjustment made?

8. How is the average hourly need for a shift determined?

9. Discuss the pros and cons of overlapping shifts.

10. How is the relief factor computed?

11. What are car plans? How are they established?

12. Should car plans be the same on all watches? Explain how they might differ.

13. Why should reporting districts generally be coextensive with Federal Census Tracts?

14. Enumerate and discuss some of the physical factors affecting beat arrangements.

Exercises

1. Assume that you have thirty-six officers assigned to your shift. Four of these are assigned to fixed post positions. Using the data contained in Table 13–1 (Average need by day of week—day shift), prepare a duty assignment roster showing the number of officers to be deployed on each day of the week and the number off duty. Assume further that the relief factor is 0.5 for your department.

2. Using the work load data recorded on the reporting district map (Figure 13–6), prepare a three-car plan and a seven-car plan. If you utilize physical factors (other than statistical data) in your car plan arrangements, justify such use.

3. From the information contained in Table 13–3 (Hourly need for police services), compute the *percentage of adjusted total shift deviation* for the following shifts:

   5:00 A.M.–1:00 P.M.
   1:00 P.M.–9:00 P.M.
   9:00 P.M.–5:00 A.M.

4. Compute the percentage of adjusted total shift deviation for the following shift arrangement (which incorporates an overlapping shift) by using the data contained in Table 13–3.

   6:00 A.M.–2:00 P.M.
   2:00 P.M.–6:00 P.M.

6:00 P.M.–2:00 A.M.

2:00 A.M.–6:00 A.M.

5. In the graph in Figure 13–7, indicate the best arrangement for three regular shifts and one overlapping shift. Work load data are plotted to the nearest one-half per cent. Discuss the reasons for the shift arrangements you have selected.

6. If you had 142 officers assigned to *field* patrol duty, approximately how many of these would be assigned to each shift that you selected in Exercise 5?

FIGURE 13-7. Percentage of workload by hour of the day

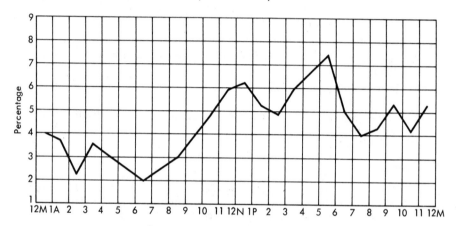

14

Tactical deployment of field forces

The allocation of field personnel according to the normal needs for their services by time of day, day of week, and area involves the simple matter of arithmetical computations and judgments based on experience. Such usual deployment criteria must be abandoned at times to meet the tactical needs of the moment under unusual conditions associated with such occurrences as major disasters, barricaded criminals, bomb threats, civil disorders, labor disturbances, or searches for lost persons.

GENERAL SUPERVISORY RESPONSIBILITIES IN UNUSUAL OCCURRENCES

Patrol units almost invariably are the first to respond to the scene of an unusual occurrence. They are responsible for taking whatever police action may be indicated. In almost all such cases, they must look to the field supervisor for guidance during those first few critical minutes when it is his responsibility to initiate control operations. He may not delay action in the expectation that he will soon be relieved of responsibility by higher authority. Rather, his actions should be predicated upon the assumption that he will not be relieved and that it will be incumbent on him alone to make decisions.

Any miscalculations he makes may cause irreparable harm. For example, failure to evacuate residents from an area endangered by a potential disaster resulting from a major fire, a rupture in a dam, escaping chemicals or dangerous gas from a broken container or line might result in untold loss of life with consequent civil liability. The accuracy of his evaluations of the field intelligence conveyed to him by field units, the correctness of his appraisal of the occurrence, and the effectiveness of his initial actions in deploying and directing the efforts of control personnel will largely determine the success of the police mission in containing the effects of the incident.

In incidents such as civil disorders where force is reasonably necessary, its sufficiency and decisive application are largely a supervisory responsibility. A delay in applying appropriate control measures may cause a relatively minor incident to escalate into one of major proportions.

BASIC PROCEDURES FOR UNUSUAL OCCURRENCES

Every supervisor should become familiar with the basic procedures applicable to the procurement and use of personnel, equipment, and facilities common to the policing of most unusual occurrences. Although practices may vary somewhat from place to place because of differences in reciprocity or mutual aid agreements or policy considerations, usually these will not substantially affect the immediate action the supervisor must take to initiate control measures. The application of the usual standard operating procedures will ordinarily require some deviations from normal operations to the extent that personnel, equipment, and facilities must be redistributed to meet the unusual conditions. The principal objective should be to deploy available personnel and equipment rapidly in the initial stages to prevent escalation of the incident or aggravation of the circumstances.

In implementing control activities initially at the scene of an unusual occurrence, the supervisor may perform or cause to be performed several very important tasks almost simultaneously. The sequence he will follow and the extent of his activities will depend largely on how well he organizes, systematizes, and delegates, how complex a police operation is required to control the incident and its effects, how many personnel he has immediately available, how proficient they are, and what equipment, supplies, facilities, and other support are available to him.

Although some of the following basic operating procedures may not apply to all situations, many of them will be found useful in most unusual incidents. They are recommended as guidelines to keep the supervisor from overlooking in a stressful situation some important procedures which may help him avoid later criticism.

Communicating field intelligence

One of the supervisor's first tasks at the scene of an unusual incident should be to quickly evaluate the occurrence, then communicate to his headquarters the field intelligence available. Wherever applicable, the following information should be transmitted as it becomes available:

1. The nature of the incident: fire, flood, civil disorder, barricaded suspect, or other.
2. The type and size of the incident: Data about the matter should include the extent of disturbance and the size of any crowd in a civil disorder, whether military or civil aircraft is involved in a plane crash, or other similar relevant characteristics.
3. The location of the incident and the type of area and property involved: residential area, brushy hillside, business district, bank building, school, manufacturing firm.
4. The potential effect of the incident on persons or property: danger from noxious substances or fire, disruption of specified utilities, water damage, looting or destruction of specified property by hostile and destructive persons, as well as direction of movement, direction of wind, and other applicable predictors.
5. Unusual circumstances present: crowd, barricaded streets, sniper armed with sidearm or rifle, explosives, broken water lines, and so on.
6. Need for evacuation: broken dam would endanger specified area, fire approaching specified residential area, poisonous or explosive gas blowing toward school, persons endangered by rifle fire, or other justification.
7. Antilooting measures required: based on need for evacuation.
8. Need for outside or traffic perimeter: area and sites where an outside perimeter should be established to control pedestrian and vehicular traffic into or out of area and locations which should be manned or barricaded.
9. Need for inside perimeter: at immediate scene.
10. Personnel needs: to patrol the inner and outer perimeters, for control duties, search, evacuation, or rescue. Special weapons teams, negotiators, or other specialists should be requested as needed.

11. Command-post location and location of staging area for personnel and emergency support.

12. Emergency equipment and personnel needed and routes available for their use into and out of the area.

13. Equipment, supplies, and facilities needed: portable communications, walkie-talkies, bullhorns, loudspeakers, flares, armor, gas equipment, gas masks, rope, barricades, flood lights, lanterns, rifle equipped marksmen, helicopters, etc.

14. Number of persons injured or dead.

15. Ambulances or hospital facilities needed.

16. Other: dogs for search; helicopters or aircraft for surveillance; ammunition; food and drink for control personnel; blankets; maps; special investigative equipment, such as a photographic booth so that pictures of arrested persons and the arresting officers can be taken as needed for future identification in court; other special equipment, such as bomb disposal gear, tow trucks, or torches.

The more field intelligence that is made available to headquarters personnel, the better they will be able to plan for the operational needs of personnel at the scene. In fact, without adequate field intelligence, support operations will probably be greatly impaired.

Establishment of command post

When a command post is needed, the supervisor should carefully select a suitable site. It should be easily identifiable on maps available to operational personnel. The location should permit radio communication without dead spots. It should be near the affected area but not exposed to attack or gunfire, fire, floodwaters, noxious gases, or other hazards. It should be located up-wind from the affected area, if practicable, in those situations in which the use of tear gas might be necessary. If possible, it should be positioned near a telephone and a power supply if electricity is needed to operate floodlights and mobile command-post equipment. To prevent clogging radio frequencies with the long messages often required and to provide the continuous communications with headquarters, land lines should be used and kept available.

The command-post location should also provide a staging area for personnel and their equipment as they arrive. The supervisor should also consider the accessibility of routes to and from the scene for emergency equipment such as fire trucks and ambulances. Routes should be selected which are not unnecessarily exposed to man-made or natural dangers and which can be protected from persons who might attempt to ambush control or support personnel as they approach or leave the scene.

The command post might be a radio car, a station wagon driven by the supervisor, another mobile radio unit, an office or building, the police station, or any other place that provides an immediate base of operations with communications equipment and other facilities. An officer or helicopter should be directed to scout the area for another site if the location initially selected proves to be unsatisfactory.

A formal command post may be necessary later should the incident require a major police effort. Care should be exercised, however, to avoid unnecessarily moving the command post as this may cause confusion and disruption of operations. The first choice is not necessarily the best. If another location is substantially better suited for the operation, the change in location should be undertaken. Command posts established for scheduled events will ordinarily pose no problems to the field supervisor because they are staffed and operated according to established plans.

Reconnaissance

As they become available, one or more radio units should be assigned to reconnoiter the affected area and its perimeter as might be necessary for the purpose of securing current field intelligence. When new information is obtained, it should be promptly relayed to headquarters.

Logistics aide and press relations officer

When the supervisor assumes responsibility for directing police action to control an unusual occurrence, one of his first acts should be to appoint an aide to assist him in performing the many tasks he cannot perform personally and to free him to concentrate upon directing the operation. Many of these tasks must be accomplished simultaneously at the beginning of the operation. Communications must be established and maintained with headquarters, the command post must be activated, supporting facilities must be set up, and security measures must be taken. The aide should be responsible for keeping a chronological log of control measures taken in all but the simplest of incidents. Such log should include the details of the operation from its inception. Names, unit numbers, and assignments of personnel should be recorded as they arrive at the staging area, and a list made of the department equipment they bring. They should then be assigned to units with designated leaders. Available equipment should be reassigned as needed.

Officers should be briefed, by the supervisor if practicable, given an assignment and dispatched to the scene of operations. They should be instructed to remain at their posts until relieved.

Supplies must be requested and distributed as needed. The area affected by the incident and the positions of control personnel and equipment should be plotted on a map to provide a ready overview of the entire operation. Such map should be part of each supervisor's field kit. It should be of small scale, ideally not larger than one inch per mile. A plastic overlay sheet and colored grease pencils should be available for plotting data. Such maps can be easily improvised by the individual supervisor and mounted on hinged plywood such as a checkerboard is mounted on its backing, if they are not provided by his department. They can be stored in the trunk of his vehicle or in a special map kit.

A well-selected public relations officer can be of great value in maintaining good media relations by collecting information and coordinating current news releases. He is also in an excellent position to secure media assistance in deterring onlookers from entering the area. Because of his position, he can also do much to prevent unrestrained media coverage that sometimes disrupts police negotiations and alerts terrorists to the tactics being used by the police.

OPERATIONAL GUIDELINES

Broad operational guidelines were included in the foregoing discussion for the supervisor responsible for directing the police activities required to control an unscheduled unusual incident for which a specific operating plan has not been established. Obviously, the nature of the occurrence will dictate which procedures are applicable in a given situation.

Some tactics that have been tried and found effective in handling specific types of unusual occurrences are discussed in the following pages. Basic procedures will be referred to briefly as a reminder to the supervisor of the essential parts of the operational procedures he must set into motion. He should become thoroughly familiar with local policies and procedures that may require him to perform certain tasks in addition to those described.

Usually, organizational rules will designate whether the uniformed field supervisor or a supervisor of investigators, who may be present, is in charge of the operation. Sometimes, both may believe they have responsibility for the direction of operations. If a barricaded suspect is involved they will reason that organizational rules give both uniformed personnel and detectives the responsibility for apprehending criminals. In such cases, it is imperative that they decide at the outset which should assume charge to prevent the confusion and conflicts that invariably result when there is no unity of command.

BARRICADED PERSONS

A potentially dangerous person may take refuge in a building or other structure to escape arrest, or he may be discovered in a building while committing a crime and barricade himself with the hope of a later escape. A direct assault upon him usually should be avoided, especially when he can be neutralized and apprehended by the use of special weapons without creating an unnecessary danger to police personnel or other innocent persons in the area.

Hostages

The suspect may capture a hostage, hoping to increase his bargaining power with the police. The presence of an innocent victim in the barricaded premises complicates the matter because his safety must be considered, but the basic problem of taking the suspect into custody remains substantially the same.

When the criminal has seized a hostage, he will usually demand that officers withdraw or provide him a means of escaping without interference. Time operates to the advantage of the police in such cases. Any delaying tactics will enable them to prepare more effective plans for dealing with the suspect. Delay may provide them an opportunity to seize the individual in an unguarded moment or give the victim an opportunity to escape.

Although there are no hard-and-fast rules applicable to such cases, the supervisor in charge at the scene must decide whether to accede to these demands or refuse to do so. Ordinarily, a general practice followed by the police in such instances is that no "deals" will be made. It has been shown all over the world that such arrangements encourage others to make the same demands.

The supervisor must judge each case on its own merits. He must weigh the danger to the hostage's life against the possibility that the suspect is bluffing. The supervisor should recognize that if he allows the hostage to be taken from the presence of the police, the police will no longer be able to provide any protection. Their mere presence may deter the criminal from harming the hostage. If they refuse to bargain with the criminal, he will be forced to continue to hold the hostage, to release him, to bargain for an opportunity to escape by himself, or to harm the hostage and risk capture or death.

If the suspect is not permitted to take the hostage from the scene, the hostage is probably in no greater danger. Assurances that the hostage will not be harmed if he is taken away by the suspect cannot be relied upon. If, however, because of unusual circumstances, the supervisor permits the suspect to remove the hostage, the route of escape should be surveilled by ground and air units. Should an attractive opportunity present itself to gain the initiative, these units should take advantage of it quickly and decisively.

Direction of operations

An attempt to rush a suspect who holds a hostage without careful planning and preparation might result in at least two deaths—the officer's and the hostage's. Any such attempt should be resorted to only after all other reasonable means to rescue the hostage or secure his release and the surrender of the suspect have been exhausted. The supervisor should make it clear to all personnel that he reserves the right to decide how and when organized force is to be used to achieve this objective.

If he enforces such directions, unity of command will be maintained. Personnel will be forced to act in harmony with each other rather than as independent agents. To permit each officer involved to decide such matters individually would only create unnecessary danger to others and considerable confusion. Generally, direct assault tactics have been proved to be the least effective course of action, especially when modern armor and gas equipment are available.

OPERATING PROCEDURES IN HOSTAGE AND BARRICADED SUSPECT CASES

As soon as a determination is made that a suspect has taken a hostage and barricaded himself in a structure, the supervisor should set into operation a tactical plan to neutralize and arrest him and to rescue or secure the release of the hostage.

Preliminary operations

The supervisor should perform the following tasks or delegate an aide to perform them. The sequence in which these tasks are carried out may vary, according to the circumstances:

1. Secure premises: When it is first learned that a suspect has barricaded himself in a structure, officers should be posted at the front and rear of the premises and in other locations as needed to prevent his escape. Nothing is more embarrassing to the supervisor than putting a major police operation into effect only to discover that the suspect has been allowed to escape because the premises have not been properly secured.

2. Command post: Locate in a safe, strategic area.

3. Injured persons: Give aid, interview, and remove.

4. Communications: Notify headquarters of situation as previously discussed.

5. Personnel support: Acquire necessary personnel for cordoning off area and for operations at the scene. Only personnel reasonably needed at the scene of operations should be requested. Too many may cause danger to each other by their crossfire. Special teams and trained negotiators should be summoned if available.

6. Special equipment: Request gas grenades and cartridges, masks, body armor, high-powered rifles and marksmen, portable communications equipment, loudspeakers for communicating with the suspect, portable lights and generators at night, helicopter patrol, materials suitable for cordoning off area to keep out curiosity seekers and uninvolved persons, ambulance, and fire equipment as needed.

7. Staging area: Locate staging area where officers and equipment are to report.

8. Identify officers as they report: Assign them to positions where they can secure escape routes without exposing themselves to each other's crossfire; assign other personnel as needed to cordon off area around perimeter.

9. Evacuation: Persons in area who may be endangered by sidearm, rifle, or shotgun fire should be removed to a safe location. Provisions should be made to protect their property if it is left exposed to theft or damage during their absence.

10. Field intelligence: Collate intelligence from police and civilians who can provide information regarding the suspect, his victim, and his precise location. Information should be obtained concerning the type of crimes he has committed, his purpose in barricading himself or seizing a hostage, his mental and physical condition, his attitudes concerning police and society, and complete physical description. Such a description should be disseminated to control personnel so that they may avoid shooting or unnecessarily taking other action against a person who is unidentified. The detailed description of the hostage should be given to control personnel so that they will not mistake him for the suspect.

11. Communications with the barricaded person: Establish communications with the suspect by telephone if one is available. The number can be obtained from the telephone company from the address. If a telephone is not accessible, communications might be established by a loudspeaker. A portable, battery-operated bullhorn is ideal for this purpose.

General considerations in hostage cases

Several alternatives are available to the supervisor at a scene where hostages are involved. Each situation is different; therefore, each alternative must be carefully evaluated in terms of its potential for a successful resolution of the problem with a minimum of danger to the hostage, the police, and the public.

The preferred procedure—*negotiation*—will buy time which operates to the advantage of the police. It gives them an opportunity to develop alternative plans of action should negotiations fail, it permits greater opportunity for the suspect to make a mistake that can be exploited by the police, and it often increases the suspect's affinity for the hostage. This reduces the likelihood that the suspect will take the hostage's life. Finally, time may give the hostage an opportunity for escape.

Skillful use of negotiation procedures has much potential for success. These activities should be supervised by a person especially trained for such purpose; but if one is not available, the supervisor should talk with the suspect, preferably by telephone. This type of communication generally tends to calm him and is more effective than natural voice dialogue or communications by amplifier or bullhorn.

The supervisor should be extremely cautious in allowing unskilled persons to communicate with such persons because of the ever-present danger that the dialogue might unintentionally aggravate the suspect's hostility and unnecessarily endanger the hostage.

Conversations with the suspect should always be carried out in positive terms, as discussed for rational or emotionally troubled suspects in later paragraphs. Patience and a calm demeanor are essential. These attitudes tend to have a calming effect upon the suspect. A negative, hostile, or antagonistic manner might only aggravate the delicate balance that exists between the hostage holder and the police and should be avoided.

The negotiator should proceed upon the premise that every issue is negotiable except that he must not agree to provide the suspect with offensive weapons or instruments, as these will only increase his capacity for violence.

The negotiator should adopt the position that he does not have authority to make final agreements with the suspect but must clear these with higher authority. Such techniques will buy further time. Every effort should be made to maintain constant communications with the suspect to focus his attention on negotiations and to divert his attention from the hostage.

Suitably equipped *snipers* should be strategically posted as soon as a hostage situation develops. If negotiations break down, it may become necessary to use them to neutralize the suspect should he become careless. This tactic may pose a danger to the hostage or other innocent persons and must be used with caution and restraint in controlling the activities of the suspect. *Assault* combined with the use of chemical agents as discussed later should usually be reserved as a last resort if other means fail to produce results.[1]

Rational suspect

If the evidence indicates the suspect is rational, an attempt should be made to point out the futility of his actions. A logical appeal in which he is informed that he is surrounded and cannot escape and that he will not be hurt if he gives himself up might be effective in inducing him to surrender. Such an appeal may have greater influence if it is made by a member of his family, a relative, a close friend, or his minister if the situation is such that any of these persons is available. Ordinarily, any of them should be allowed to converse with the individual, but they should not be permitted to enter the barricaded premises because they too might be taken hostage.

Emotionally troubled suspect

If the reason for his resistance is not obviously to escape arrest for a crime but appears to be based upon a real or imagined grievance of an emotionally troubled person, an attempt should be made to determine the cause of the grievance. It may be trivial, but to him it may be sufficient to cause him to destroy himself and his hostage. He should be given assurance that everything possible will be done to help him.

A calm, patient attitude should be reflected in all conversations with him. These should be directed toward convincing him that he should give himself up and, at the same time, stalling for time. He should be encouraged to talk. Time often has a settling influence upon such persons and may provide the police an opportunity to gain the initiative or give the hostage an opportunity to escape.

Whether the barricaded person is a rational suspect wanted for a crime or an emotionally troubled, irrational individual with a grievance sufficient to cause him to kill, every effort should be made to persuade him to surrender voluntarily. If he refuses, force may become necessary to take him into custody.

[1] Nathan F. Iannone, *Principles of Police Patrol* (New York: McGraw-Hill Book Company, 1975), pp. 253–56.

Assault tactics

In those cases where the acts and threats of the suspect indicate that he realizes he cannot escape and that his intent may be to harm a hostage, positive, direct action may be required. The use of tear gas and smoke to cover a direct assault upon his barricaded position by personnel in body armor, shields, and masks should be considered. To wait longer might unnecessarily endanger the hostage. The decision the supervisor must make should be based upon his evaluation of whether the hostage would be jeopardized more by the force necessary to rescue him than he is at the hands of the suspect.

When a decision is made to force entry into the suspect's position, plans previously formulated should be put into operation. Depending upon the type of structure to be entered, an entry team consisting of three to five officers should be dressed in protective armor and masks. They should be equipped with a pry bar, sledgehammer or battering ram, gas-gun, gas cartridges and grenades, and smoke grenades.

A cover team of at least two officers should be selected and equipped with gas masks and other protective clothing. They and the officers of the entry team should be thoroughly briefed by the supervisor in the tactics to be used in the operation. Precision in executing the established plan is vital to success.

The personnel of both teams should agree upon the safest route to approach the premises. Other officers, including expert marksmen equipped with rifles and scopes and their observers, should be strategically positioned to cover the advance of the approach team and to prevent the suspect leaving with the hostage.

A chalkboard is useful in illustrating the plan of attack, which officers involved must thoroughly understand. It may be used to depict the arrangement of rooms, hallways, and other interior features of the premises to be entered.

Diversionary tactics such as talking over the speaker system or bullhorn and loud noises on the side of the premises opposite the approach route or calling the suspect and occupying his attention may sufficiently divert his attention to allow the approach team to take their positions without being observed. Smoke might also be used to cover this operation if adequate concealment is not otherwise available.

When the approach team is in position to cover windows, doors, and other apertures through which the suspect might fire upon the officers, members of the entry team should make their advance to a position where entry is to be effected.

Upon a prearranged signal, the suspect's attention should be diverted away from the point at which gas is to be thrown or fired into the premises. This will permit detonation of the gas cartridge before it can be covered, kicked, or thrown away, or otherwise neutralized by the suspect. In one instance, a suspect was able to scoop several gas projectiles into a kitchen exhaust system, which effectively drew the gas out of the room in which he was barricaded. It was only after electricity to the exhaust system was shut off that the suspect was overcome by gas fired into the room and forced to surrender.

The gas should ordinarily be fired or thrown directly into the room where the suspect is believed to be. This will force him to take action to protect himself from it and will tend to divert his attention from the hostage. Such technique will also prevent him from shutting a door and sealing off the room he occupies.

Grenades and projectiles that dispel dust are preferred to those that dispel gas by combustion. These cause considerable heat and often ignite curtains, upholstery, and other inflammable materials with which they come in contact.

Simultaneously with the gas attack, the entry team officers should force entry into the premises. One officer should quickly assume a prone position in front of the place of entry, covering it with his shotgun at the ready position as the other members enter. The first should make a sudden entry, proceed to the right or left as previously agreed upon, flatten himself against the wall, and give protection to the others as they enter on signal and assume the positions agreed upon.

As each room is secured, officers should proceed to other rooms until the suspect is located, neutralized, and captured. Other officers should be assigned by the supervisor as they are needed to secure an area after it has been searched to prevent the suspect from moving back into it after the search. The success of the mission will depend largely upon the swiftness and precision with which the operation is carried out.

Search for other suspects

Even though one suspect is apprehended, the officers should not assume that there are no others in the premises. Rather, the same care should be used in searching the remainder of the building for others who may be present.

Arrest of suspect

At times, the suspect will voluntarily leave his position to surrender after gas has been employed against him. Should this happen, he should be directed to drop his weapons, hold his hands high above his head with fingers spread, and move beyond the immediate scene toward the officers. The supervisor should admonish the officers not to leave their cover positions to approach the suspect but to require him to approach them. From their positions, they can cover him while he is being secured and searched.

CIVIL DISORDER

Civil disorders may take several forms. They may involve mass civil unrest characterized by riotous mob action or may take the form of small assemblies bent on disrupting the public peace by demonstrating or by committing acts of vandalism or violence against persons or property.

Relatively small disturbances by a limited number of persons usually can be dealt with effectively by a small force of well-trained officers under the competent leadership of a field supervisor. A large riotous mob may require a major police effort involving hundreds of peace officers. In either event, the role of the supervisor is rather well defined by the basic admonition that a leader should not commit his forces until they are of sufficient strength to perform their mission with a reasonable expectation of success.

Minor unlawful assemblies

When a supervisor responds to a disturbance scene where a small group of persons has spontaneously assembled for an apparently unlawful purpose, he should evaluate the occurrence from a strategic location to determine what force may be needed to control the incident. He should establish communications with headquarters to notify his superiors of the nature of the incident, the number of persons involved, and their probable intent. Sufficient personnel to handle the matter should be requested, along with any special teams available to report to a specified staging location near the scene. Equipment that might be needed should be requested. Supporting reserve personnel should be alerted to stand by in reserve in the event that they are needed.

As personnel respond to the staging area, they should be directed to park their vehicles in a position least exposed to harm from the crowd and to lock shotguns in their racks and special equipment in the car trunks. Officer personnel should be assigned to guard this equipment. When sufficient officers have arrived to handle the crowd, the supervisor should form them into the appropriate squad formation with himself as squad leader. If more than one squad is to be employed, he should designate a leader for the second squad. These formations should then take action to disperse the persons unlawfully assembled.

The supervisor should direct the squads which are to be committed to advance in a close formation upon an assemblage that is fighting or engaging in other unlawful acts. Squad members should be commanded to carry their batons in a port arms position. Often such a display of force will cause a dispersal without the necessity of making arrests.

When the laws of the jurisdiction require the police to give a dispersal order to the persons unlawfully assembled, the supervisor should give such order from a position near the group. It should be given loudly and clearly to refute any later claim that the announcement could not be heard by those assembled. To avert such claims, an officer should be stationed at the furthermost border of the crowd to signal that the dispersal order was audible. After a reasonable time has elapsed, the supervisor should move his personnel forward to disperse the group into a predetermined escape route which has been left open to them.

Should arrests be indicated, the supervisor should concentrate the force of his squad formations upon the leaders of the group. When these have been arrested and moved quickly to the rear, the probability that further disturbance will occur is greatly reduced. When a group loses its leader, the members will often lose their desire to resist further and disperse on their own volition. At times, however, arrest of the real agitator who is not the group leader has more effect than arrest of the leader. The objective of an agitator is often to gain crowd support, cause a confrontation between the group and the police, then leave before he can be arrested. Often such an agitator can be followed and arrested away from the crowd to avoid precipitating further mob violence.

Once dispersal has been effected, officers should be directed to prevent small residual groups from forming. When they do, they should be dispersed promptly.

If persons have been arrested, they should be processed by officers best able to testify against them. Photographs of arresting officers and their prisoners, fingerprints, and the like are valuable evidence that may help in making proper identification of defendants later in court. Other officers not involved in arrests should be instructed to return to their former assignments.

When the incident is under control, the supervisor should communicate this fact to his headquarters. He may find it desirable to supervise the booking of prisoners and the preparation of routine reports.

A summary report of the incident should be made for future reference. Such reports are not only useful in court but for training in critique sessions that should follow.

MAJOR DISTURBANCES

A major police effort that is likely to be required in the control of an extensive civil disturbance will usually be directed by high-ranking police officials after the initial occurrence; however, during the critical initial period when units assigned to routine field duties first respond to the scene of the disturbance, the field supervisor bears the brunt of the responsibility for directing their activities.

What might start as an ordinary occurrence may turn swiftly into a widespread riot if improperly handled. Even a so-called "routine" incident may abruptly erupt into one of major proportions. The 1965 Watts riot in Los Angeles is a classical example of how a minor arrest expanded into a widespread riot marked by violence and destruction that lasted for six days.[2]

Analysis of many civil disorders has shown that the availability of good field intelligence, the accuracy of the evaluation of the initial incident, the effectiveness of the operational plan selected to deal with it, the speed with which personnel responded, and the decisiveness of their actions determined whether the incident remained a relatively minor one or developed into one of major proportions.[3] Upon the field supervisor rests much of the responsibility for collating and assessing facts and implementing the first course of action, which may well determine how much more serious the matter may become.

Basic tactical and operational procedures similar to those applicable to minor unlawful assemblies generally can be employed with good effect in major disorders. The very nature of major disturbances, however, will usually require more sophisticated planning and far more personnel in carrying out control operations. The following factors should be considered by the supervisor in such occurrences:

Communications should be established with headquarters to transmit information regarding the nature and extent of the incident and the mood of the rioters. Details should be given describing the area involved, what acts such as looting or rock throwing are being committed, the type of weapons being used, and the existence of snipers or other special conditions revealed by initial observations, reconnaissance units or observation posts. *Logistical support* should be requested as previously described. A *command post* should be established and an aide assigned to start an operational log and assist with coordinating the personnel, equip-

---

[2] State of California, "Violence in the City—An End or a Beginning," *A Report by the Governor's Commission on the Los Angeles Riots* (Sacramento, Calif.: California State Printing Office, December 2, 1965), pp. 1–9.

[3] Arnold Sagalyn, *The Riot Commission: Recommendations for Law and Order in Confrontation—Violence and the Police,* eds. C. R. Hormachea and Marion Hormachea (Boston: Holbrook Press, Inc., 1971), p. 160.

ment, and supplies as they arrive if it appears that the operation may last for an extended period. Its location and that of the *staging area* should be indicated so that officers responding may wait there in reserve or otherwise be assigned as they arrive. *Access routes* to this area should be specified if the situation requires. Sometimes, special efforts must be made to keep these routes open for emergency services.

Field tactics and standard operating procedures that have been adopted or are normally utilized in civil disorder control may have to be modified to some extent to meet the needs of a particular situation. Supervisory personnel should be thoroughly indoctrinated in these practices and should, as an integral part of their training function, acquaint their subordinates with the techniques and procedures that have been found to be most effective in such incidents.

If the supervisor decides that his force is not sufficient to commit immediately, he should wait until he has adequate personnel to overwhelm the riotous elements. This strategy of striking swiftly with adequate force to insure success should be the basic concept of civil disorder control.[4] He should, however, avoid any appearance of weakness because it might have an adverse effect on the morale of his subordinates.

If sufficient personnel have responded, however, he may conclude from his appraisal of field intelligence and his assessment of the problem, the area, and his logistical support that quick, decisive action should be taken immediately before the gathering becomes a riotous mob beyond what available personnel can handle.

The supervisor must make the decision concerning such matters. A limited number of well-trained officers acting in unison can ordinarily handle adequately a much larger group of hostile rioters; but it would be foolhardy to commit a grossly outnumbered force of officers to confront such a group.

Personnel available for the striking force should be assigned to squads or other duty as needed and thoroughly briefed regarding their mission, the type of crowd, its direction of movement, weapons being used, what specific tactics are to be used, the direction of dispersal, and other such matters of concern to control personnel. Squad members should be told that they must confine themselves to their primary mission of dispersing the crowd or making arrests of its leaders, as the case may be, rather than to become involved in secondary skirmishes which may jeopardize the entire mission.

If a dispersal order is required, it should be given as previously described. A standard squad formation might then be employed effectively in dispersing the group.

---

[4] Los Angeles Police Department, *Special Weapons and Tactics: The Specialist and the Field Officer, Command Strategy,* 1971, p. 1.

No particular formation is suitable for all situations. The supervisor should select the one which may be most effective depending upon his specific mission, the nature and structure of the riotous group, and the type of area involved.

Every effort should be made to avoid provoking the crowd into attacking control personnel. The supervisor should direct his squad in such a manner that the crowd may escape rather than be forced into a position where it must attack the police because no escape route is available. The supervisor should plan his operation so that the members of the hostile group will be forced to disperse into an open area where they can do little damage or into one where the crowd can be broken into small segments and dealt with separately as necessary. Sparsely settled areas or districts with few buildings and many escape routes can be used effectively for this purpose. However, the supervisor should alert his subordinates to be cautious that hostile elements do not disperse into buildings only to reform and attack the control force from the rear.

Care should be used that members of the crowd are dispersed away from residential or business districts foreign to them. Rather, they should be forced to move toward the area in which they live whenever practicable. They are unlikely to attack neighbors, destroy property, and loot the immediate area of their residence.

If sufficient control personnel are present, the supervisor may employ the tactic of dividing his force into two or more squads and attacking the crowd from two directions simultaneously. This may not be practicable if chemical agents can be used more effectively in bringing about a dispersal, but the method has been applied successfully in other cases when it was desirable to control the direction in which the dispersal was to take place. A pincer movement wherein the crowd is attacked from the front and both flanks may force it to escape to the rear. A flanking maneuver in which the crowd is attacked from the front and from one flank will usually force the group to disperse to the opposite flank. An attack from the rear and front of the crowd may force dispersal to the flanks but may permit hostile units to reform and attack the police from the rear, or the bottling effect may force the crowd to fight because there is no other acceptable option left to them.

Use of force in major disturbances

Only that amount of force should be exerted in dispersing the group or making arrests that will enable the control personnel to achieve their objectives. The use of excessive force beyond that which is reasonably necessary must not be condoned. It will only inflame a crowd and might result in violent reactions. In addition, the use of excessive force is illegal and may subject the individual officer involved and his entire organization to unnecessary criticism or civil liability.

Arrests in major disorders

When arrests become necessary, they should be made quickly with whatever force is reasonably necessary, equated, as far as possible, with the resistance involved.

Arrests of persons refusing to disperse or committing other serious violations should be made quickly when that course of action appears necessary. Police action in making arrests is usually most productive when it is directed toward leaders of the group. Persons arrested should be removed immediately from the scene for identification and processing.

Use of chemical agents

Chemical devices and other special weapons should be employed in dispersing hostile groups when such use is indicated. Local policies and procedures will ordinarily dictate how and when such measures should be put into effect. In making a decision whether chemical agents should be used, the supervisor should evaluate the wind conditions, the direction in which the crowd should be moved, the type of area the members of the group might disperse into, how the dispersal will expose innocent residents and businesses to vandalism, destruction, and danger, and what effects the chemicals might have on merchandise, supplies, materials, and property of innocent persons in the affected area.

Sniper fire

Protection against sniper fire, rock throwers, and other dangers to the control force may be provided by one or more officers assigned to observation posts in a high position above the affected area. These should be equipped with walkie-talkies so that they can communicate with the field supervisor concerning the number, identities, and positions of such individuals, who invariably operate from concealment behind buildings or at the rear of the crowd where they cannot be seen by control personnel. The observers can also provide the supervisor with valuable information regarding the most appropriate approach or strategy he can use to counter the tactics of the rioters, what overall strategy the crowd is following, what weapons are in evidence, the locations of snipers, and other hazards.

Limited withdrawal

The supervisor should withdraw his forces when the odds are overwhelmingly against the police and the danger of encirclement or flank attack by the mob make his position untenable. When a new defensible position has been reached, he should hold it until sufficient reserves arrive to permit the police to carry out their mission with reasonable assurances of success.

Withdrawal under the theory that the mere presence of the police at such occurrences is inflammatory and tends to generate hostility and violence should be avoided. There has been ample experience to controvert this theory subscribed to by some.

The strategy of establishing a control around the perimeter of the affected area and withdrawing police from the interior has been tested and generally has failed. When the police fail to carry out their responsibility for maintaining the peace and good order, chaos and not control is the likely result.[5] Law enforcement designed to control such occurrences should be extended to any place where it is required. There should be no sanctuary for lawbreakers.

Follow-up action

Follow-up action ordinarily will be necessary to prevent re-formation of small groups which break off from the main crowd. When dispersal has been accomplished, sufficient control personnel should be directed to remain in the affected area to prevent new outbreaks and looting, which often accompany rioting. Such control should be maintained long enough to allow a general cooling of the situation.

Mobile follow-up units can be used as an effective deterrent for this purpose. Units manned by four officers can usually disperse small isolated groups that re-form to harass the police, to loot, or to damage property. Teams of officers on foot may perform the same task in highly urbanized areas. Specially trained tactical teams can render valuable assistance if they are available.

LABOR DISPUTES

Disorders that arise from minor labor disputes ordinarily can be controlled by minimal police action. When a major strike is called that directly or indirectly affects a large segment of persons in an industry, however, considerable violence often results. Life and property are jeopardized and violent breaches of the peace might occur. Although it is not

[5] Los Angeles Police Department, *Special Weapons and Tactics,* Sec. 3, n.d., p. 2.

a police responsibility to settle economic disputes between labor and management, it is an obligation of law enforcement to take action when the public peace and good order are threatened.

Large-scale labor conflicts, unlike the usual civil disorders, do not occur spontaneously. Usually, the police have sufficient forewarning to make whatever plans are necessary to cope with the problem. Normally, the field supervisor must assume a major role in implementing such plans.

The brand of law enforcement at the scene of a strike has considerable impact upon both the labor and management segments involved. If the police act in unison, with confidence in their ability to cope with any problem that might arise, those involved might give second thoughts to conduct that might result in their arrest.

Strikes are a legitimate exercise of the right to protest, which must be protected as long as this right does not degenerate into license. When it does, and unlawful acts occur, the police must act; but their action must be impartial. When it is partial to one side or the other, they will be accused either of strikebreaking or siding with the strikers. In either case, their conduct might provoke violence. Their mission is to protect the rights of both parties and the public.

Maintaining impersonal attitude

The supervisor should admonish his subordinates assigned to strike duty that they must not allow themselves to become personally involved in the labor dispute. They must avoid overreacting when they are subjected to taunts, insults, and derision. If they become emotionally involved, their reactions may be exploited against them.

Avoid fraternizing

Fraternization with either the strikers or management, the acceptance of gratuities from either, or any other act that might be interpreted as partiality must be avoided. The supervisor should even caution his subordinates to avoid using management parking lots, telephones, and rest rooms for the same reason.

Display of weapons

Officer personnel at the scene should be cautioned against displaying their weapons unnecessarily. Special weapons should never be displayed in a threatening manner. To do so might unnecessarily provoke violent reactions.

Meeting with labor and management representatives

One of the supervisor's first acts at the scene of a labor dispute should be to arrange a meeting with the picket captain and a representative of management to discuss ground rules that both parties should be expected to follow. He should emphasize that his is a neutral position but that he must insist the strike be conducted lawfully. He should make it clear that damaging property, blocking sidewalks, streets, entrances and exits, interfering with lawful business and the rights of uninvolved employees and the public, or provoking incidents by either side cannot and will not be tolerated. Usually, such meetings will be welcomed by both sides. They can be extremely productive as a means of maintaining the peace.

Control tactics for labor disputes

The tactics used to control disorders arising from a strike should generally follow the same patterns as those used in the control of other civil disturbances. Slight modifications may be required to handle situations in which the acts of pickets become illegal.

Pickets may urge prospective patrons of a business establishment not to patronize it, but they may not use force or coercion to do so. When coercion is used for this purpose, violence is likely to follow.

Picket lines deployed to unlawfully block entrances and exits to businesses being struck must be broken by coordinated action by the police. The pickets should be clearly warned against such illegal action. They should be requested to allow patrons or vehicles of employees or persons delivering merchandise to the concern to pass. If they fail or refuse to do so, the supervisor should direct his subordinates to effect an opening in the line. Pickets should be permitted to resume their line of march on the picket line once this has been accomplished. To avoid giving the impression that they are encouraging or forcing persons in vehicles to enter the premises through picket lines, officers should not use the customary hand signals in directing vehicular traffic at picket lines.

Officers should be instructed to face the pickets when the line must be broken to allow persons or vehicles to pass through it. They may thus prevent their sidearms and batons from being taken and are in a more favorable position to observe the actions of the pickets.

The force used to breach picket lines should be firm but temperate. Acts which can be construed as harsh or officious will only incite resistance, which is contagious.

Strike scene arrests

Force sufficient to accomplish indicated arrests should be reasonable at all times. The police should not hesitate when violations justifying arrest occur. Vacillation may be construed as weakness and may encourage those involved to commit other acts that will eventually weaken police authority at the scene. The blocking of exits to keep persons inside buildings against their will may constitute false imprisonment or involve a breach of fire ordinances. Appropriate action to open such passageways should be taken in such instances or arrest of the offenders might be justified as a means of removing them. Should they passively resist by lying on the ground and going limp, such acts might constitute resistance to arrest and would justify their removal on stretchers.

The supervisor should direct his personnel to disregard minor acts that might best be handled by the picket captain. Drinking or littering are technical offenses, but the making of arrests for such minor violations would distract the police from their primary mission. The supervisor should maintain such a relationship with the picket captain that he will cooperate in dealing with incipient troublemakers. Should an officer be assaulted, however, other officers should quickly give him assistance in making an arrest. Evidence of the crime should be seized and the assailant should be quietly and promptly removed from the scene to a place where he can be identified, photographed, and processed.

Arrests for destruction of property should be made as in other cases. For example, if can openers, bolts, screwdrivers, ice picks, or other objects are concealed in the hands of pickets and used to maliciously damage vehicles as they pass, officers observing the act should seize the evidence and arrest the offender. If such acts are overlooked, others will feel they can break the law with impunity. This will only increase the police problem.

DISASTER CONTROL

The field supervisor is occasionally confronted with an occurrence of disaster proportions. It may cause directly or indirectly great destruction of property, loss of lives, and injuries. Such incidents may result from acts of nature or man. Floods, fires, earthquakes, explosions, aircraft crashes, broken chemical lines or containers, and the like can threaten the welfare and safety of vast numbers of persons. Although the police can do little to prevent these incidents, once they do occur, law enforcement forces must assume a major role in controlling and reducing the after-effects of the disaster. Sometimes, these after-effects are as destructive as the initial occurrence.

The field supervisor's effectiveness in directing control efforts during the period immediately following the disaster will have a vital bearing upon the success of the entire police operation. An error in selecting an evacuation route from an endangered area might result in utter confusion and chaos. Persons fleeing from an approaching fire might be trapped on roads cluttered with sightseers because perimeter control measures were neglected. Emergency rescue equipment might be deprived of access to the scene of an incident such as a train wreck or aircraft crash because access and exit routes were improperly selected and controlled.

Basic operational procedures

Field intelligence must be collected and transmitted to headquarters. A command post must be established, perimeter control must be initiated, reconnaissance units should be deployed, available support personnel should be assigned, and a disaster control plan should be put into operation. Other basic control procedures should be implemented as quickly as possible. Routine notifications and logistical matters should be assigned to an aide so that the supervisor may be relieved from the responsibility of handling details. This will enable him to concentrate on establishing control plans, making decisions, and directing the activities of control personnel.

Evacuation

Ordinarily, the decision to evacuate an area threatened by a fire, flood, poisonous gas, or some other major occurrence should be the responsibility of a superior officer of the highest position available because of the liability which might result from an ill-conceived act. Should the police fail to take action that might reasonably be expected to insure the safety of the public, considerable criticism and possibly civil liability may result. Likewise, they would undoubtedly suffer criticism if residents incurred injuries or if their property were damaged or stolen because they abandoned it when they were warned or forced to do so by the police acting beyond their authority. Any decision concerning evacuation must therefore be made judiciously. As the field supervisor may have to assume this tremendous responsibility, his decision must be based on the field intelligence he has received, an accurate assessment of this information, and an appraisal of the alternative courses of action available. He must give consideration to the consequences of each decision based on the presence or absence of imminent peril to the public.

If he decides that evacuation warnings should be given, persons affected cannot justly complain if they refuse to heed the warnings.

Rescue

Police units should be directed by the supervisor to confine their activities to their assigned missions. The responsibility for normal rescue operations can best be carried out by other elements of the control force specially equipped and trained to perform such functions. Emergency rescue and aid in exceptional cases must, however, be treated according to the needs of each situation.

AIRCRAFT CRASHES

When an aircraft crashes in a densely populated area or under circumstances that may jeopardize the public safety, responsibility for initiating control operations will fall upon the field supervisor. It is he who is most immediately available to coordinate the activities of field units that respond. His primary duty will involve directing their efforts in rendering aid to seriously injured persons, making appropriate notifications to headquarters, requesting necessary support, minimizing the danger to bystanders or victims, and protecting persons and property against looting. Where immediate rescue efforts are needed, these should be given prompt attention. Establishing traffic control at the immediate scene and at the perimeter and providing assistance to rescue or fire control units are secondary responsibilities.

Precautions in rendering aid

The supervisor should caution his subordinates that great care should be exercised in moving injured persons. If they cannot walk and are in danger of further injury by fire, explosion, or chemicals, immediate steps should be taken for their removal to a safe location. Ambulance or medical personnel at the scene should perform this task whenever possible. Injuries worse than those initially suffered might result if victims are improperly moved.

Security of military aircraft

The supervisor should post personnel in strategic positions where they can safely keep unauthorized persons from approaching military aircraft. Most of these are equipped with explosive charges which eject canopies and seats. Serious injuries may result if mechanical firing pins or gas charges are touched or improperly operated.[6]

Spectators should be discouraged from taking pictures[7] of such craft unless authorized military personnel request their services. Those taking pictures should be identified and their names transmitted to military representatives. News media cameramen should not be prevented from taking pictures, as control of their release is the responsibility of the military.

BOMB THREATS

When a supervisor responds to a call in which a bomb threat has been made, he should immediately notify his headquarters by telephone of the circumstances and request personnel and bomb specialists to help handle the matter. The radio should not be used as radio waves might detonate the bomb. If fire equipment is summoned, he should request that it be driven quietly to the scene without the use of sirens. Experience has shown that the more commotion bomb threat calls cause, the greater is the likelihood that the call will be repeated. Many of these calls are false, and it is likely that most are made by persons who derive some satisfaction from the noise, the commotion, and the concern they cause.

If a threat is made against a business establishment, a public building such as a school, an office complex or warehouse, or private property such as a commercial aircraft, that a hidden bomb is to be exploded, the person in charge of the premises is responsible for making the decision whether occupants should be evacuated. He will invariably look to the supervisor for advice. When this occurs, the supervisor should discuss the matter in private with him to avoid starting a rumor or alarming others unnecessarily.

A conservative approach should be followed if it becomes obvious that advice should be given. It is far better to advise evacuating persons who might be endangered, even though later evidence proves such action was unnecessary, than to advise against evacuation when that course of action *should* have been taken. The safety of innocent persons should be the supervisor's first concern.

The decision will ordinarily be based on the facts surrounding each incident. The supervisor should carefully evaluate the possible motives for destroying property—evidence of recent labor troubles involving the firm, the type of operations involved, and previous trouble

---

[6] Los Angeles Police Department, *Training Manual of the Accident Investigation Division*, 1971, pp. 18, 60, 87.

[7] *U.S. Code,* Title 18, Sec. 791.

with disgruntled employees—before he should consider giving advice. Schools often experience many such threats from students desiring a recess or holiday. Most schools give credence to all such calls until a search proves them groundless. Students are then required to make up the time involved in the search. Such action has proved to be an effective deterrent to other false calls.

Evacuation procedures for bomb calls

The supervisor should assign personnel to aid in the orderly evacuation of the premises once that course of action is decided upon. The distance occupants should be moved will depend upon the circumstances surrounding each case, the type of premises, and the existence and type of structures which may give protection in the immediate area against a bomb explosion.

Standard fire drill procedures in which lights are shut off and doors and windows closed should be avoided. Shutting off lights may trigger an explosion. Shutting windows and doors may cause unnecessary property damage from the blast effect, should an explosion take place.

The supervisor should dispatch officers to notify persons in surrounding buildings of the potential danger. Doors and windows should be opened there for the reasons previously discussed. Occupants should be instructed to remain in the building but go to a position furthest from the side where the explosion might affect them. They should be advised to stay away from windows and places where they might be injured by flying glass or debris.

The supervisor should advise the person in charge of the premises to be evacuated about the danger of theft so that guards may be posted to keep unauthorized persons out while the building is being searched. Persons making the search should be directed to leave the premises enough in advance of the time the bomb is to be exploded, if such information is known, to ensure their safety. They should not be permitted to reenter until it is reasonably safe to do so after the indicated time of detonation.

Traffic outside the building should be diverted if it might be exposed to an explosion. Gas and other utilities such as propane should be turned off if they might aggravate the effects of the explosion.

Searching premises

Whenever these exists a reasonable likelihood that a bomb or other device will be detonated in a structure, the supervisor should direct that a search be made. A warrant is not required. The usual limitations upon the scope of searches of this type do not apply because of the urgency of the matter.

An explosive device can be concealed in a building so that it is almost impossible to locate without a most careful search. The supervisor should recognize the extreme danger a hidden and triggered explosive poses to searching personnel. He should summon bomb specialists to the scene if they are available for the search or consultation. Officers should then be directed to conduct the search as quickly and thoroughly as circumstances permit. A minimum of search personnel should be used, depending upon the time available and the type of premises to be searched.

Mirrors and screwdriver sets should be obtained if possible and distributed to those making the search to aid them in looking on the undersides of furniture and equipment and behind wall plates and receptacle covers.

The supervisor should request some responsible person to assign employees most familiar with the premises to assist search personnel by pointing out to them objects foreign to the building. All persons engaged in the search should be cautioned against touching or moving anything that might trigger an explosion. They should be instructed to look in every conceivable place that might conceal a bomb. They should be especially alert for foreign packages or objects or those which appear to have been left behind by someone. Objects that are out of their usual places should also be suspect. Any of these may conceal an explosive device.

If no bomb or explosive is found, the supervisor should so inform the person in charge of the building, but he should avoid suggesting that the building is safe for occupancy. To do so might unnecessarily involve considerable liability for his department in the event persons reoccupy the building in reliance on his statement and are injured or killed from the explosion of a bomb which was not found.

Precautions when bomb found

When a bomb is located, the supervisor should summon experienced bomb disposal personnel to remove or neutralize it. He should not attempt to move such a device, nor should he permit inexperienced personnel to do so. If it clearly poses no danger, he should try to remove the device, if that is necessary, remotely, by using cords or protective shields. If its removal is not urgent, it should be sandbagged until it can be removed by experts. When it is essential to neutralize the bomb where it is found, it should be sandbagged to deflect the blast and reduce the danger from fragmentation and should then be detonated in place. Such action should be taken only with the full approval of a person authorized to permit such action. Preferably, his permission should be obtained in writing to protect the supervisor from liability for damage from the blast.

MAJOR FIRES

The police frequently are in a position to initiate control measures at the scene of a fire before fire personnel arrive. One of the first acts of the supervisor when he arrives should be to assure that appropriate notifications have been made to the fire department. Information transmitted should include the type and size of the fire, the type of property and area involved, wind direction, endangered structures and facilities, public utilities exposed to the blaze, and emergency routes to the scene.

Available personnel should be assigned to the immediate vicinity and to perimeter posts to control vehicular and pedestrian traffic that might interfere with fire-fighting efforts. This is the primary responsibility of the police. Other police units should be assigned as needed when they arrive.

The supervisor should consult with the commander of the fire-fighting units, who generally has overall command at the scene, to determine how the police might assist fire personnel. Should extensive police control measures be required, the supervisor should establish his command post near that of the fire department to facilitate maximum coordination. The police staging area should be located nearby so that personnel can be briefed and assigned to specific posts as they arrive. Usually, the assignments of personnel to traffic perimeter posts some distance from the scene can best be made by radio, not only to save time in setting up traffic controls but to reduce the confusion and traffic at the scene.

Evacuating fire area

Should it become necessary to evacuate an area endangered by the fire, especially when it occurs in a bushy area and threatens a residential or recreational area, residents and others affected must be notified of the peril. Radio units should be assigned to specific areas for this purpose, as the police usually must assume responsibility for such warnings. As each assignment is made, it should be logged and plotted on a map overlay, to reduce the possibility that some persons might be overlooked.

Officers should be directed to use sirens, horns, loudspeakers, and all other means available in making these notifications. They should be instructed to make personal contacts in those areas where residents live some distance off main roads and might not hear warnings from the street.

Sufficient personnel should be assigned to this very important task to permit them to give timely warnings to all persons who might be affected. The supervisor should keep in mind that only a limited number of notifications can be given in sparsely settled areas where residents live a considerable distance off the highways. This seems to be an obvious consideration, but, at times when a person is under stress, he tends to overlook the obvious. Units should be cautioned to be alert for radio broadcasts describing the progress of the fire so that they can clear the area safely.

The police fulfill their obligation to protect lives when they inform persons endangered by an approaching fire of the perils they face and help them leave the area. Should they refuse, it would be ill-advised to force them to do so. However, in unusual cases, where persons are mentally incompetent and incapable of providing for their own safety, another course of action may be required. Aged, young, crippled, or sick persons may require special help in escaping the fire.

Antilooting patrols

In the aftermath of widespread fires, many sightseers and thieves are attracted to the burned zone. Sightseers can ordinarly be turned back at the traffic perimeter. Thieves, however, are a special problem because they can often penetrate the inner exposed areas for the specific purpose of looting property that has been left unprotected.

Antilooting patrols should be assigned to specific beats in the burned-out zone to protect such property. Personnel in these units should be instructed to check persons who have no legitimate reason for being in the area. These should be directed to leave if legal authority prohibits their presence in the emergency zone. They should be checked for possession of property apparently stolen and handled accordingly. All contacts with persons encountered should be recorded for future reference. Information and evidence is often obtained from these contacts that is of value to investigators in determining how the fire started or who was responsible for it.

AREA SEARCHES

When a widespread area search is called for to locate a missing or wanted person and numerous officers are required, its effectiveness will be directly dependent upon how systematically it is conducted and how well it is coordinated. Operations of this type are somewhat unique in that specific plans cannot ordinarily be made beforehand. The supervisor must therefore develop them according to the needs of each situation; but even the best plans will not produce the desired results if they are not carried out under adequate direction and control.

LOST CHILDREN

In many law enforcement agencies, situations involving lost children are considered so important that supervisors are specifically made responsible for directing searches for them. The extent of the effort devoted to such incidents ordinarily is dependent upon the age of the child and the circumstances. The younger the child, the greater the need for locating him promptly. If a crime appears to be involved in the disappearance, its nature and the evidence available will usually dictate whether a localized or a broad search of the area is necessary.

In deciding how extensive an operation should be put into effect, the supervisor should consider several factors such as the age and sex of the child, the type of area involved and the attractive hazards in it, the circumstances surrounding the disappearance, the child's previous history of running away, the places he normally plays, his mental and physical condition, his fear of punishment, whether he has recently been scolded or punished, the circumstances under which he was last seen, and any other facts that might provide clues as to what happened to him or where he might be found.

Persons who might shed light on the child's whereabouts should be interviewed. Playmates usually provide the best information. Parents should be asked to notify the police immediately if the child returns home.

Should the evidence indicate that the disappearance involves a criminal act, the appropriate investigators should be notified immediately so that an investigation may be initiated. If a kidnapping is suspected, the parents should be requested to consult the police before they take any action if they are contacted by the kidnapper.

Broadcasting procedures

As in all cases of lost children, a full description of the child and the general circumstances of the case should be broadcast to all units in the area. Information concerning the child's interests, play habits, and circumstances surrounding his disappearance should be included to alert other police elements of the matter.

Initial search

Frequently, the child will be found in the immediate area from which he disappeared despite assurances of the parents that they have made a complete search. They are prone to look in only the most obvious places and often fail to search carefully.

Even though they insist that they have already made a search, a careful inspection of the inside and outside of the premises should be made. Children have been found asleep in unmade beds overlooked by their parents, in large chairs surrounded by their toys and dolls, behind furniture, and in other places where a careful search might have revealed their presence.

Every place that might offer concealment should be inspected. Containers, tanks, chests, and the like should be carefully examined inside and outside the house. Even though hasps are closed on large containers, they should be searched. Occasionally, a child will lock a playmate inside a container, then panic and fail to tell of the incident because he fears punishment.

Operating procedures for search

Should the initial search fail to reveal the child's whereabouts, a widespread operation may be suggested. Basic procedures should then be carried out. The supervisor should establish his command post near the center of operations. Usually his vehicle will suffice for this purpose. He should request sufficient personnel to conduct the search, depending upon the time of day, the weather, and other circumstances. As they arrive, they should be briefed and assigned specific tasks with instructions to return to the command post and report their findings when they complete their assignments. Data should be logged and search areas plotted on an overlay map to provide a ready reference of what is being done and to eliminate duplication of search efforts.

Units should be assigned to check playgrounds, recreational areas, and hazards that attract children. Other personnel should be directed to follow up leads that may be provided by playmates and other persons.

Search teams

When persons other than officers volunteer their help in the search, they should be assigned to teams under the direction of an officer. Each team should be given a specific area to search. Ordinarily, teams should consist of four officers or a combination of officers and volunteers.

Residential search patterns

Teams should be instructed to start their search of a residential area from the end of the block nearest the scene and work outward. Two persons should search the area on one side of the street while the other two should check the opposite side. They should inspect side and back yards, vacant lots, alleys, sheds and outbuildings, containers, garages, abandoned iceboxes and those in use outdoors, large boxes, chests, and every other conceivable place of concealment or hazard.

The more attractive hazards such as swimming pools, excavations, ditches, wells, cisterns, creeks, storm drains, lumber piles, or unsealed boxcars should receive first attention. Children have been found in these places after they have fallen in or entered and been unable to get out.

Residents of houses in the search area, especially children, should be questioned for information when they are first contacted regarding the search.

When the assigned area has been carefully checked, members of the team should meet at the end of the block to compare notes on their findings. If they have been equipped with walkie-talkies, they should transmit their findings to the command post. They should then move on to search the next block.

The supervisor will ordinarily be responsible for determining how extensive the search should be. Usually it will be continued until the child has been found.

Searches in open areas

When a child disappears in a sparsely settled, bushy, woody, or open area, the supervisor might utilize helicopters, aircraft, or mounted teams to good advantage if they are available. Sometimes dogs may be used effectively even though considerable time has elapsed since the disappearance. The sooner they are put into service, however, the more effective they will be. They may, however, follow false leads if the area has been contaminated by many persons walking through it.

Officers and volunteers available for the search should be organized into search lines in rough terrain. They should be instructed to walk from three to ten yards apart depending upon the nature of the ground to be covered. Lines should be kept relatively straight to avoid the loss of contact between persons. The line should be halted periodically to permit all searchers to proceed at about the same speed. This will permit a more thorough search.

Areas completely searched should be plotted on the supervisor's map to show what terrain has been checked. The search party should then be moved to another area to continue the operation. As with other searches, the supervisor is responsible for deciding when the search is to be terminated or providing the information that will permit his superiors to make that decision.

WANTED PERSONS

When a wanted person flees from the police into a residential or business district, sufficient units should be deployed to seal off his escape as quickly as possible and pin him down while a systematic area search is made. Disorganized police efforts may result in gaps in search patterns, and the suspect will almost certainly exploit them to make good his escape.

On-scene procedures

Upon his arrival at the scene, the supervisor should assume command of available personnel, organize them into search teams, and direct their activities to cover the widest possible area in a methodical manner. He should ascertain that a complete description of the suspect and the specific area into which he fled has been broadcast to units in the vicinity.

Other units should be assigned strategic fixed and mobile posts around the perimeter to prevent the suspect's escape should he elude the police in the interior search. These assignments may be made by radio to assure the most immediate coverage and prevent confusion at the scene. Units needed for the search should be instructed to report to a specific location for their assignments. The number required depends upon the type of area to be searched, the time the suspect has had to leave the initial contact spot, and the means he may have used.

Search strategies

Once the area has been tightly sealed off and the suspect immobilized, two strategies are available to guide the search. The choice depends upon the characteristics of the neighborhood, the number of personnel available for the search, its extent, the type of crime involved, and the time that has elapsed since it was committed.

One strategy is an inward search from the perimeter of the area. In a small, compact residential area, appropriately armed personnel should be directed to search inward from the perimeter in teams of three or more officers. Each team should be assigned a specific quadrant to search. If blocks of residences are to be searched, two teams should be assigned. They should be numbered so that search patterns may be complete.

Two members of one (odd-numbered) team should search all conceivable hiding places in and around the houses on one side of the street. The third member of that team should observe the street that faces the houses being searched. Simultaneously, a second (even-numbered) team should search the houses on the other side of the street. The third member of the second team should search the alley between two rows of residences as illustrated in Figure 14–1.

Teams should maintain contact with each other by portable radios,

FIGURE 14-1. Residential block search pattern

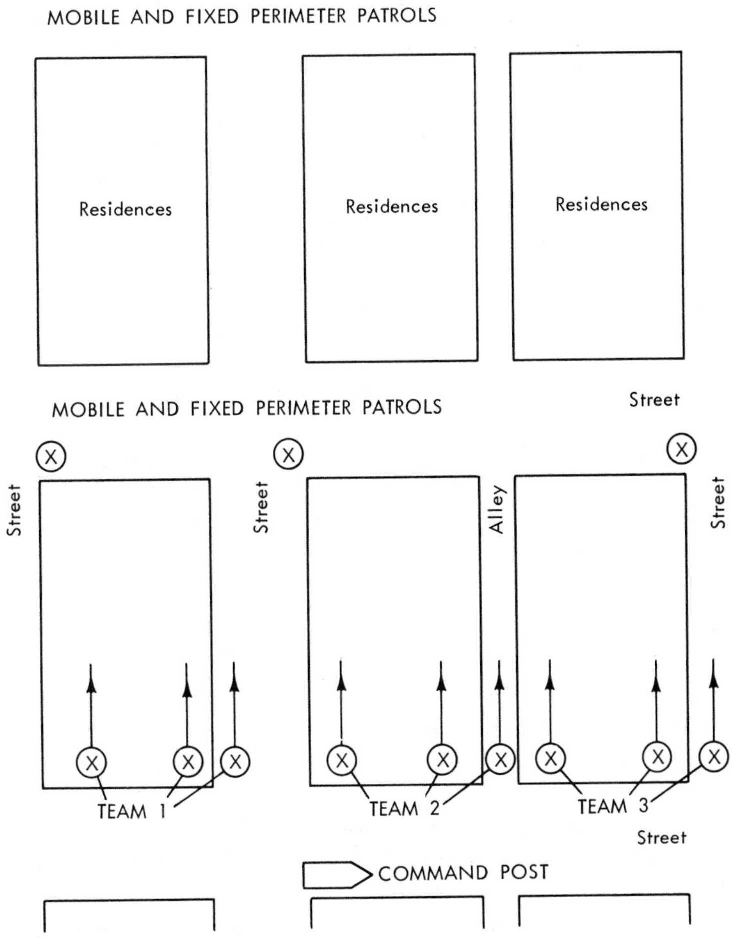

MOBILE AND FIXED PERIMETER PATROLS

if possible. Otherwise, they may communicate by voice and signals. They should proceed at about the same speed in their search to reduce the likelihood that the suspect can double back and conceal himself in an area already searched.

Officers should be cautioned to cover each other and to avoid crossfire between themselves and members of other teams in the vicinity.

Fixed observation posts should be established at the perimeter of the search area. These should be supplemented by mobile patrol units, helicopters, and foot patrols.

Officers should inform residents of the search and request permission to inspect yards, outbuildings, or the houses when it is essential. Searching personnel should be alert for evidence that the suspect is concealed in the premises and the householder is forced to mislead them about his presence.

The strategy of searching inward from the perimeter has the disadvantage of cornering the suspect, forcing him to resist if he refuses to surrender. The danger of crossfire, always present, may be greater when personnel converge at the center of the search area and are forced into a gunfight with a suspect.

The second strategy available is to search outward from the center of operations toward a guarded perimeter. If the suspect is moving ahead of the searchers, he will be forced into the hands of personnel guarding the perimeter.

Searches in business districts

In assigning teams to search a business district, the supervisor should consider the possibility that the suspect might try to take a taxi, bus, or streetcar from the scene. Motorized patrols should be alerted to this possibility. Other teams should be assigned to inspect nearby bars, rest rooms, restaurants, lobbies, markets, stores, and other places where he might remain inconspicuous.

Building searches

In many cases, criminals are discovered in a building during their commission of a crime. The procedures applicable to those types of searches described previously for barricaded suspects would generally be useful: Escape routes should be sealed off, and the suspect should be encouraged to surrender. If he refuses, forced entry into the premises may be necessary if the use of chemical or smoke agents is not desirable.

In many cases, the criminal will remain quiet and refuse to respond to police demands that he give himself up. The only means of determining if he has remained in the building then is to search it. The use of chemical and smoke agents is ordinarily not indicated for this type of case, but the need for great caution is always present.

Should reasonable cause exist to believe that a felony suspect or one considered to be a high risk is in the building, the supervisor should select two teams of officers, a search team and a cover team. These teams should be appropriately armed and protected, then briefed on plans and objectives to act in complete unison. Tactics similar to those employed by the United States Army in conducting a search should be adapted to the needs of the particular case.[8] The search team should enter the building under protection of the cover team in a manner similar to that previously described for barricaded persons cases but adapted to the needs of the moment. The number of persons permitted to make entry should be carefully controlled by the supervisor. As few personnel as necessary should conduct the search, depending upon the size of the premises to be searched and the characteristics of the interior.

All avenues of escape from the building should be secured by the cover team. The cover team should render whatever assistance necessary to the search team, such as the guarding of areas already searched.

All possible places of concealment must be searched systematically by the search team until the entire building has been inspected. In multistory structures, whenever practicable, the search should begin at the top of the building and proceed downward systematically. The suspect must either remain hidden where he can be located and arrested or be forced downward where he may be apprehended by the cover team. If he is forced upward by a search that starts in the basement of a structure, he may become more dangerous when he is cornered at the top of the building with no place to go or he may escape over the roofs of other adjoining buildings.

As each portion of the building is searched, personnel should be assigned to secure that area or keep it under observation to prevent the suspect's moving into it. The search team should then proceed to check the next room or portion of the building until it is completely searched.

SUMMARY

During the first few critical minutes at the scene of an unusual occurrence such as a disaster, a major disturbance, a barricaded criminal,

---

[8] U.S. Department of the Army, *FM 19-15, Civil Disturbances* (Washington, D.C.: Headquarters, Department of the Army, October, 1975), pp. 5/15–19; see also Jude T. Walsh, "Search of Buildings," *Law and Order*, 20, No. 4 (April, 1971), 20–24.

or some other important incident where a number of police personnel are engaged in carrying out control measures, the field supervisor is responsible for directing and coordinating their efforts. He may not delay action in the expectation that he will be relieved of his responsibility by higher authority. Rather, he must plan and set into motion an operation designed to minimize the effects of the incident.

Ordinarily, normal police practices, modified to meet the needs of the moment, will be adequate to cope with most unusual incidents. The supervisor's main responsibility is to distribute his forces in the initial period to prevent escalation of the occurrence and control its effects.

Many standard operating procedures are common to most such unusual incidents. Field intelligence must be collated and communicated to headquarters so that necessary logistical support may be provided. A command post and a staging area should be established in a strategic location near the center of operations. Directions for the operation will emanate from this post. A staging area nearby should be provided to accommodate personnel, their equipment, and the supplies needed to carry out the police mission.

Reconnaissance units may be required to provide current information that will enable the supervisor to meet changing conditions. Added intelligence might be provided by personnel assigned to observation posts.

Many of the initial tasks required by the initiation of a major police operation must be performed simultaneously. The supervisor should assign an aide to execute some of these, to relieve him of many details and permit him to devote his attention to planning and directing the operation.

At times, a criminal will barricade himself in a building, hoping to evade arrest, or he may take and hold a hostage in hopes of bargaining for his freedom. He may be rational or irrational.

Once the police seal off any escape route, the supervisor must decide what other action is justified under the circumstances. Usually, the police posture is that no "deals" will be made with criminals; yet, each incident must be decided on its own merit.

In these types of cases, time usually operates to the advantage of the police. Any tactics that will delay a showdown should be used. Talk is a most effective means of gaining time. Often the suspect can be persuaded that he has nothing to gain by resisting further. He may then release the hostage unharmed and give himself up.

Occasionally, he will refuse to surrender. When circumstances indicate that the hostage's life is in imminent danger and the decision is made to use force to rescue him and arrest the suspect, a cover team and an entry team should carry out a predetermined plan to force entry

REVIEW

Questions

1. What is normally the principal objective in deploying personnel during the initial stages of an unusual occurrence?
2. What factors will affect the supervisor's ability to perform or cause to be performed the many tasks needed during the initial stages of an unusual occurrence?
3. What factors should be considered in the establishment of a field command post?
4. What approach should be used with a rational barricaded suspect holding a hostage? an emotionally troubled one?
5. If chemical agents are to be used against a barricaded high-risk suspect in a business establishment, how should the gas be introduced into the building?
6. Why is a powdered chemical agent preferred over gas agents?
7. Why should a suspect be required to approach officers when he leaves his barricaded position to surrender?
8. What follow-up action should be taken after a mob has been dispersed?
9. What is the basic strategy of civil disorder control?
10. What are the primary police responsibilities in a major disaster?
11. What are the biggest dangers at the scene of a military aircraft crash?
12. Why should the radio not be used at the scene of a bomb threat?
13. What equipment should personnel use in making a search for a bomb in a building?
14. What types of objects should search personnel look for in making a bomb search in a building?
15. If a bomb is not found in a building after a careful search, what should the supervisor tell the person in charge?
16. What are the primary police duties at the scene of a major fire?
17. Why should a multistory building search be conducted from the top down?

Exercises

1. Give an example of how a supervisor's miscalculations during the first few minutes of an unusual occurrence might cause irreparable harm.
2. Enumerate and discuss the basic operating procedures that the supervisor should follow in most unusual occurrences.
3. Explain how the passage of time usually operates to the advantage of the police when a barricaded suspect is holding a hostage.
4. Explain the procedures which should be followed by the supervisor and the tactics which should be used if a barricaded suspect is holding a hostage in a large market.

5. Explain the procedures that should be followed in dispersing a small disorderly crowd.

6. Describe the factors the supervisor should consider in deciding whether gas should be used against a riotous mob.

7. Explain what the supervisor should do when he first assumes command at a major strike scene.

8. Describe the instructions a supervisor should give his personnel regarding their conduct at the scene of a strike.

9. Enumerate and describe the most common offenses committed by pickets at a strike scene; by the management sector.

10. Explain the procedures that should be followed in evacuating an office building because of a bomb threat.

11. Explain the precautionary measures that should be taken if a bomb is located in an office building after it has been evacuated.

12. Explain the procedures that should be followed if a bomb must be moved; if it must be blown in place.

13. Explain what factors should be considered in deciding whether a widespread search should be made for a missing child.

14. Describe how a search for a small child lost in a brushy area should be organized and conducted. How should one be conducted in a residential area?

15. Discuss how a search should be organized and conducted for a high-risk suspect in a dense residential district; in a business area. Discuss the two strategies that might be employed and their advantages and disadvantages.

16. Discuss how a single-story commercial building should be searched; a multistory department store. Assume that the suspect is dangerous.

15

The training function: problems and approaches

One of the principal duties of the supervisor and perhaps one of his most important responsibilities is the training of his subordinates. Of necessity, this activity occurs in all types of settings, ranging from the informal meeting with those who are performing their duties in the field to the formal lecture in the classroom. He must adapt his approach in each instance to the varied environments in which the need for training reveals itself. The supervisor must recognize that although various training techniques are available to him, all the methods of teaching have as common objectives not only to impart knowledge or change attitudes but to motivate the student to further his own learning by changing his behavior to more productive avenues than he has followed in the past.

The supervisor-teacher must constantly strive to establish an appropriate "climate" for learning. If he is to do this effectively, he must be familiar with the learning process, the obstacles to efficient learning, and the factors that influence it.

Theoretically, the existence of job-connected problems indicates that management has failed to provide adequate training.[1] It has been

[1] John M. Pfiffner, *Public Administration* (New York: The Ronald Press Company, 1946), p. 333.

stated that the incidence of personal misconduct and of performance failures is related to the quality and extent of the employee's training. This contention cannot be easily refuted since, if training were perfect— if it were to accomplish its objectives totally—every person subjected to it would react flawlessly to every stimulus. There would be no police scandals arising from misconduct and police effectiveness would be nearly absolute. Unfortunately, methods of accomplishing this state of perfection have not yet been developed. The supervisor can, however, make the greatest use of the time he has available for training by the skillful application of basic but proven techniques of teaching.

Regardless of the quality of material made available to the supervisor-instructor to pass on to his subordinates, the amount of learning which takes place will depend in a large part upon his ability to teach the information effectively. [2] No two teachers will utilize the same methods with equal success. Each must adapt his approach to his audience and to his own capabilities.

THE IMPORTANCE OF TRAINING

The training of the new employee to perform his basic duties with skill and dispatch is of utmost concern to the employer. It is a function vitally related to the introduction of operational rules and regulations, policies, specifications, and procedures of the organization. Its importance in indoctrinating personnel in changing laws, techniques, and police practices as a means of upgrading the service cannot be denied. Pfiffner [3] observed, "The skills, competence, and insight which are the products of effective training become the foes of waste, unproductive inertia, and bungling."

Causes and effects of training failures

Training failures are usually the result of administrative neglect to give supervisors an understanding of their responsibilities for this function and some instruction on how to proceed. It has been demonstrated that these failures can be prevented by systematic efforts to qualify supervisors to instruct. [4] Hall[5] contended, "The qualifying of supervisors to carry out their responsibilities for employee training probably is in

[2] *Ibid.,* pp. 342–43.
[3] *Ibid.,* p. 336.
[4] Milton Hall et al., *Employee Training in the Public Service* (Chicago: Civil Service Assembly of the United States and Canada, 1947), pp. 37–38.
[5] *Ibid.,* p. 37.

most agencies the one most fruitful training activity that can be carried on."

When the training function is performed poorly or not at all, low morale, waste, and preventable errors inevitably follow. All these are tremendously costly to the organization because they squander human endeavor. Inefficiency and loss of material things go hand in hand. These might be prevented if police effectiveness is developed to a greater degree by training.

Remedy for failure

Every organization must program its approach to the training problem or risk loss. Administrators and supervisors should endeavor to make maximum use of the time and wherewithal they have available for training. Personnel merely exposed to it may learn inefficiently and sometimes hazardously through the slow and wasteful process of trial and error or the "sink or swim" method, or they can be taught systematically by efficient supervisors who have been trained in the proven techniques of teaching and have been made aware of the great need to take advantage of whatever opportunities present themselves to train their subordinates, whether it is at shift briefing, in the field, or in the classroom. In each situation, the supervisor may be concerned with technical content or with some of the less tangible problems involving working relationships.

The instructor's approach to teaching

Customs, practices, or traditions might affect the form the supervisor's instruction will take. If, for example, the techniques of teaching personnel how to shoot have traditionally been adapted for single action target shooting, considerable resistance might be encountered if he attempts to shift emphasis to combat shooting. He will often be forced to improvise so that his methods will meet the needs of the moment.

The basic techniques of teaching apply to all forms of training, whether it is the teaching of an officer to photograph a crime scene, investigate a traffic accident, or prepare a crime report. If a police stakeout is involved, the instructor may be required to demonstrate how a shotgun may best be carried to the scene. He may be concerned with such simple procedures as loading, unloading, engaging, or disengaging the safety, or checking ammunition. He can never be certain that his subordinates are familiar with these critical procedures, and he can ill afford to assume that they will all remember such routine procedures or even that they have ever been exposed to them. At the scene of a crime, the supervisor may be called upon to refresh the new officer in the basic techniques of dusting a surface for latent fingerprints, photographing, lifting, and preserving them. He may be required to impart detailed tactical, technical, or procedural information in a more formal classroom setting relative to the control of public disorders or to instruct his subordinates in field deployment plans to be used in their response to robbery or burglary calls. He may be assigned the task of passing on specific information regarding a new procedure and its background, or he may be called upon to discuss the specific elements of crimes or selective enforcement procedures.

In each of these situations, his effectiveness as an instructor will be directly related to the degree to which he has acquired a knowledge of his subject, has gained an understanding of the learning process, and has displayed a willingness to work at the job of instructing. He will find that learning the rudiments of teaching is a relatively simple task. More difficulty will be encountered in applying them to practical situations. With reference to teaching, Brown and Thornton [6] stated succinctly, "Effectiveness . . . is not achieved through magical formula. It results, rather, from a happy combination of common sense, knowledge of subject, teaching skill, enthusiasm and force of personality, artful judgment and plain hard work."

INSTRUCTING AS A SUPERVISORY RESPONSIBILITY

The supervisory officer has a responsibility to train his subordinates by the most efficient and effective methods available to him. This vital function is an integral part of his job which he cannot afford to omit or perform carelessly. It is his responsibility to study the techniques of instruction so that he may do the best possible job of acquainting his men with the means of accomplishing their many tasks effectively and with the fewest possible errors. As Barlow [7] stated, "Good teaching does not just happen—it is not accidental. It is a result of careful preparation. Success or failure in any instruction program is seldom due to the efforts of the learner alone. The major portion of the responsibility rests upon the individual instructor. . . ."

CONSTANT NEED FOR TRAINING

There is no end to the need for training. Concept, theories, philosophies, practices, and procedures are constantly changing to meet current social needs. These changes are especially prominent in law enforcement. It has

[6] James W. Brown and James W. Thornton, Jr., *College Teaching: Perspectives and Guidelines* (New York: McGraw-Hill Book Company, 1963), p. 105.

[7] Los Angeles Police Department, *Instructor's Guide for Roll Call Training*, 1951, p. iii (quoting Melvin Barlow).

become a truism that the need for training police officers in our complex society is as great as the need for their services. The day when a new officer could be given a gun and a badge and sent into the field to perform police work has passed. Today's public demands more.

Many police administrators believe that they must deploy their personnel for training just as they do for vacations, days off, or sickness. To them, training is a function that requires the expenditure of vast sums of money and time; it must be recognized as a necessary component of public service, which must be paid for by the public that profits from a well-trained police force.

The benefits to be derived from an effective training program are not immediate nor are they easily measured. Rather, long-term results do occur, but these are subtle. A reasonably accurate assessment of the benefits of training can be made from the collective observations of those concerned with its effects and those responsible for its administration.[8] Precise measurements of results in activities such as law enforcement are difficult because of the many abstract reactions brought about by training. Results may be reflected in a multitude of factors such as higher morale, greater esprit de corps, a lessened need for punitive discipline, greater effectiveness in crime suppression, increased public support and confidence, fewer errors, better decisions by the police, and a feeling of security by members of the community. The benefits which accrue to the police agency will, in the long run, be directly proportionate to the efforts expended by supervisory and administrative personnel in establishing and carrying out a progressive training policy.

PRINCIPLES OF LEARNING

The supervisor will perform his training mission with greater effectiveness if he is armed with an understanding of the several principles of learning and teaching which have emerged from studies by psychologists and educators.[9] Their findings have indicated that people learn according to some well-established rules of which the following have special significance to police trainers.

Principle of readiness

When conditions in the learner's environment are such that they establish in him an attitude favorable to learning, he is said to be in a

[8] William E. Mosher, J. Donald Kingsley, and O. Glenn Stahl, *Public Personnel Administration* (New York: Harper & Row, Publishers, 1950), p. 428.

[9] See B. R. Bugelski, *The Psychology of Learning Applied to Teaching* (Indianapolis, Ind.: The Bobbs-Merrill Company, Inc., 1964), pp. 35–64 for a discussion of Thorndyke's theories of learning. See also E. L. Thorndyke, *The Fundamentals of Learning* (New York: Teacher's College, Columbia University, 1932), pp. 53–194.

state of readiness to learn. The teacher's efforts in establishing such favorable conditions is of vital importance to the learning process. If the job is pleasant, the learner's mind is receptive to learning. If the job or environment is unpleasant, an emotional block is likely to occur and learning will be retarded. The instructor must therefore direct much of his effort toward stimulating the learner so that he will want to learn and will make an effort to do so. An application of some of the basic techniques of teaching will contribute to this.

Effective learning will rarely take place, and if it does the process will be slow and inefficient, if the learner is not ready to absorb what is presented to him. Therefore, the instructor must show him why he needs the things to be learned and how he can use them either to improve his proficiency or his personal welfare. The learner must be given the opportunity for early success in some phase of the learning process so that he will achieve some sense of satisfaction from his accomplishment. The instructor will help this to come about if he displays a sincere attitude of interest in the learner as an individual and avoids annoying distractions and pressures which act as obstacles to learning. The student subjected to ill-prepared, disorganized, overly difficult material will soon lose his desire to learn because of utter confusion and frustration. The absence of the satisfaction of accomplishing something, or of making progress, will often cause him to, "shut his mind" to learning. Motivating him to a receptive state wherein he is ready to learn once again may be exceedingly difficult.

Principle of effect

When the learner is in a state of readiness in a favorable environment, efficient learning is possible. The effect of his success in learning is a pleasurable sense of satisfaction. The student strives to continue that which provides a pleasant effect so he continues to learn. Lack of success or a failure to learn causes unpleasant feelings of frustration which may make the student want to quit that environment or avoid that condition and to do something else that may give him a pleasant and satisfying experience instead of an unpleasant, frustrating or annoying one. In unusual cases, it may be necessary to set up annoyances to overcome bad habits and encourage the learner to perform correctly. The boxer attempting to deliver a blow to his opponent by leading with a right cross soon finds to his annoyance that he is sitting on the mat looking up. He will soon discontinue that procedure.

Usually, the instructor should give the learner an opportunity to learn each small unit in an operation in its proper sequence before moving on to the next so that by completing something he may derive a pleasant feeling of achievement. In addition, the completion of these small units in the operation will enable the learner to perform in a logical, orderly manner and learn sequentially. If commendation for successful achievement is given sincerely by the instructor, it will tend to provide a pleasant and satisfying effect which will prompt a desire for more success and further effort.

Principle of repetition

When experiences are pleasing or satisfying, there is usually an accompanying desire to repeat the experience. Repetition builds habits which, if correct, lead to success, satisfaction, and a desire to repeat what produces pleasure. Thus the repeated use of what is learned strengthens the learner's performance. Failure to use what is learned weakens performance. Hilgard and Bower [10] refer to this concept as the law of use and disuse.

The instructor can improve the learner's ability to perform an operation by having him repeat it correctly until he is adept at it or, when necessary, by having him repeat it to refresh his memory if the operation is not performed frequently. Merely having the learner repeat what he learns for the sake of keeping him busy is wasteful. Busy work does not necessarily result in productive learning. Repetition, if required, should be purposeful. The amount will depend upon the ability of the learner and the adequacy of the instruction he receives.

The better a person learns by using a procedure, the longer he retains that which is learned. The teacher should remember, however, that every learner forgets in varying degrees with the passing of time. Therefore, he must be again exposed to the training from time to time to keep him proficient. Special weapons procedures, self-defense techniques, and the like are not ordinarily used with such frequency in the everyday work routine that the individual can maintain a satisfactory level of skill. The supervisor-teacher should thus provide the needed refresher training periodically to maintain such skills at an acceptable, safe level.

THE LEARNING PROCESS

Some of the factors that psychologists, trainers, and educators have found to affect the learning process vitally are of concern to the supervisor in

[10] Ernest R. Hilgard and Gordon H. Bower, *Theories of Learning* (New York: Appleton-Century-Crofts, 1966), p. 19.

his training function. The effectiveness of his teaching and the learning efficiency of the student are dependent upon how these factors are applied.

Learning rate

It is commonly recognized that students learn at varying rates depending upon the presence or absence of several conditions:

The student's *apperceptive base,* his past training and experience, and his ability to integrate these with his new learning and experiences will materially affect his learning rate. Therefore, the teacher should adapt his approach to the types of students in the group, their past experiences, and their previous exposure to learning in subjects similar to those being presented. He should attempt to link the new knowledge to the old so that the student may interpret it by associating it with his past experiences.

The *personality of the instructor* may vitally affect the rate at which learning takes place. The overly demanding instructor may or may not motivate his students to speedier learning. He must therefore continually test his approach to determine its effectiveness. If it does not work, he should experiment with other approaches that may produce better results.[11]

Individual differences in the personality and in physical or mental characteristics of students will cause them to learn at varying rates of speed and efficiency. The shy, diffident, insecure student may learn slowly until he is sparked by the instructor who inspires self-assurance. The student's rate of learning may then climb precipitously.

There are many individual differences among people. Some of these are inherited and little can be done by the teacher to change them. Size, physical debilities, or mental capacity may have a profound effect upon learning. Even in law enforcement agencies which screen personnel, some hereditary characteristics that detract from a person's learning capacity will be found. The instructor must be aware that these exist, try to recognize them when they are present, and alter his training approach as circumstances may dictate. Patience and understanding are essential if he is to accomplish the objectives which he sets out for himself. Many factors, such as class size, time available for training, or physical facilities, will have a bearing upon the individual attention that can be given the student by the instructor. Those with the most pronounced problems will require the greatest personal attention if they are to be brought to the level of the rest.

Numerous individual differences result from the influences of the

[11] Brown and Thornton, *College Teaching: Perspectives and Guidelines,* p. 105.

student's environment. The classroom environment itself may contribute adversely to learning. If the student is easily distracted or annoyed by conditions such as noise, poor ventilation or light, excessive heat or cold, or other discomforting conditions, he may concentrate more upon the effects these have upon him than upon the instruction. His home conditions, past experiences, economic insecurity, lack of friends or acquaintances, poor grades, or frustrations from any one or a combination of these factors may affect his learning capabilities. Personal characteristics such as the inability to concentrate, lack of interest because of preoccupation, poor general health, faulty vision, or inferior hearing might likewise affect drastically his learning rate. The teacher must appreciate the potential effect of these deleterious conditions and endeavor to compensate for them in his teaching and in his personal relationships with the students.

Motivation and its effects upon the learning rate

The degree of motivation by the teacher has a direct bearing upon the student's learning rate and performance. Special effort by the instructor to individualize his teaching and encourage students with special abilities will contribute to accelerated learning and improved performance. Brown and Thornton [12] have concluded:

Learning proceeds best when the student is motivated to learn—when he *wants* to learn and when he puts forth *effort* to learn. Achievement of these conditions is aided when the learner considers course goals and learning tasks as having intrinsic worth and value for immediate or eventual use, or both.

One of the greatest spurs to motivation is the recognition of the student that his personal or professional growth will be directly dependent upon the effort he expends to improve himself, to gain greater insight into the problems affecting his position, and to increase his proficiency. The recognition of these factors combined with a sense of accomplishment and a feeling of satisfaction gained from his learning efforts will contribute greatly to his motivation. Here, the teacher can play a prime part.

Interest and learning effectiveness

The interest the instructor generates in his students plays an essential role in the rate at which they learn. He must hold the student's

[12] *Ibid.,* p. 115.

attention since attention precedes effective learning. The degree of a learner's interest, in turn, depends upon the internal motivation he gains from a sense of achievement and the external motivation inspired by the teacher though the use of incentives such as the spirit of competition, grades, and the like. The positive use of stimulation is superior to the use of fear to increase motivation and interest. Yet undoubtedly the fear of competition, of poor grades, or the fear of being dismissed because of them, is a powerful, although negative, influence upon performance.

LEARNING PATTERNS

There seems to be a definite pattern in the learning process. At first the learner gains accuracy, speed, and self-confidence slowly. As motivation occurs and self-assurance increases, speed and accuracy increase more rapidly. The learner's state of mind is directly involved in this process. If he is receptive to training—if he recognizes the value and need for it—if he gains satisfaction and acquires a feeling of success from the process, the speed with which he learns will accelerate greatly. Self-confidence and a feeling of security will increase in direct proportion to how well the worker learns to perform his tasks.

Sequential teaching

Ordinarily, from a strictly learning standpoint, it has been found most desirable to teach an operation as a whole in the same sequence that will be followed in practice. If this sequence is logical, it will be most meaningful to the student because he will be able to apply logic and common sense to aid him in remembering what he needs to know. Of course, there are many exceptions to this procedure. In the case of complicated, lengthy operations, sequential learning may not be practicable because the student will not be able to remember all the critical steps upon which later ones are based.

SUMMARY

A principal duty of the supervisor is the training of his subordinates since the level of their proficiency is directly related to the amount of the training they receive. Personnel constitute the most important and costly of all items in the police budget. The supervisor-teacher must therefore make the greatest possible use of the time he has available for training. He must take advantage of every opportunity which presents itself to improve the performance of his subordinates through the most efficient training methods available to him. Inefficient, careless teaching methods must give way to effective artful instruction. Without it, low morale, waste, and costly errors inevitably infiltrate the police operation.

Training failures which allow personnel to sink or swim by the slow process of trial-and-error learning will eventually take a toll upon resources of a force in the form of lowered public confidence brought on by ineffectual law enforcement, costly lawsuits arising from performance derelictions by police personnel, and a general withering of the morale and esprit de corps of the organization.

The effectiveness of the supervisor in his training function is dependent upon his knowledge of the various components of the job, his understanding of the learning process, and his common sense, imagination, and willingness to work at his training task. The techniques he uses will depend upon the setting in which training takes place. Much of this will occur on the job. Some will be of a more formal type in the classroom; but wherever it takes place, the basic principles of teaching will be applicable with perhaps only a change of emphasis in the specific methods used.

REVIEW

Questions

1. What are some of the effects of training deficiencies?
2. How might traditions, customs, and habit affect the teacher's approach to training? Give examples.
3. How can the administrator or supervisor determine the effects of training?
4. Define the principles of readiness, effect, and repetition and give an example of how each may be applied to the learning process.
5. How are these three principles interdependent?
6. What are some of the factors that affect the learning rate of students?
7. What is meant by motivation? How can the teacher bring this condition about?

Exercises

1. List as many individual differences as you can and indicate how each might affect learning.
2. List at least ten environmental factors that might affect learning and indicate which of them might be controlled by the teacher. Explain how this might be accomplished.

16

The instructional process

Once the teacher selects or is assigned a subject for presentation, the general and specific objectives to be accomplished should be determined. Information must be gathered, analyzed, and arranged so that it may be adapted to the four-step method of teaching involving the introduction, presentation, application, and test, as discussed later in this chapter.

GENERAL AND SPECIFIC OBJECTIVES

The instructional objectives which are to be accomplished by a single presentation or a series of lessons must be carefully developed to ascertain what *general* goals are to be achieved in changing the behavior of the learner in terms of his ultimate job performance. Such goals are called *general objectives*.

Specific objectives are those specific goals which are to be achieved in the various segments of the lesson or lessons. These require similar care in developing. They must be related to the specific desired changes in behavior, attitudes, or performance that the instructor intends to bring about through his teaching. As Mager [1] stated, the instructor, "must then select procedures, content, and methods which are relevant to the objectives [and] cause the student to interact with appropriate subject matter in accordance with principles of learning."

JOB ANALYSIS

The instructor must evaluate the particular job and the operations necessary to complete it. The operations should then be listed in some logical sequence. Key points that should be emphasized should be noted. This job analysis will comprise the presentation step of the lesson plan.

Instructional material is then collected from the most authoritative sources available. It must be carefully analyzed so that it may be organized into a lesson plan which will aid in a thorough, logical, and systematic presentation. The amount of material taught can be adjusted to the time available and the needs of the particular group to which it will be presented.

In analyzing the needs of the group, the instructor should take into consideration the trainees' experience, the methods they have used in performing their jobs, their past training in the particular subject area, and the type of presentation likely to work best with the group. Nonessential detail and material extraneous to the subject should be excluded. Ordinarily in police training, the amount of time available is minimal. Consequently, the instructor cannot afford the luxury of developing in minute detail each point he must present. Unfortunately, training sometimes suffers because of this time limitation. Therefore, he should ask himself what portion of the material the trainee must know to perform his job adequately and what part would only be nice to know. He will then be able to eliminate whatever is least necessary, emphasize what is necessary, and make maximum use of the time available to him.

The bulk of the material retained for the lesson will be used in the presentation step; however, the instructor should be alert for items which can be adapted to meet the needs of the introduction, application, or test. Each of these steps, but especially the introduction, can be strengthened by an artful, imaginative approach.

THE LESSON PLAN

When the instructor has completed the preliminary procedures of developing general and specific objectives, obtaining lesson materials, and

---

[1] Robert F. Mager, *Preparing Objectives for Programmed Instruction* (San Francisco: Fearon Publishers, 1962), p. 1.

analyzing them, he is ready to prepare his written teaching plans. If these are carefully prepared, they will guide him toward his objectives and help him avoid some of the common teaching failures. Most will agree that blueprints are necessary for the fabrication of material objects but sometimes it becomes difficult to convince teachers of the need for a planned approach to teaching. Even those with considerable experience can seldom teach effectively without some plan to guide them in presenting their material in an organized, systematic manner.

The instructional plan involves a simple listing in proper sequence of the several steps to be followed in completing a particular job, or it may involve a logical arrangement of material if the lesson is to consist of a discussion of a procedure, law, technique, or philosophical concept. The first consideration is that the points to be covered should be arranged in a logical teaching sequence. The instructor should add the knacks, techniques, "tricks of the trade," and the basic facts that go with each point. These are the "interest getters" that give meaning to the various points covered. A liberal scattering of pertinent, practical examples that have been well thought out in advance will do much to clarify abstract principles and assist students in applying them to their work. Illustrations, questions, and special procedures should be carefully prepared and included in the teaching plan if the instructor plans to use them during his presentation.

Form of lesson plan

While the lesson plan is a personal matter with each instructor, it should be more than a scribbled note or two. It should be geared to the four-step plan of teaching that will be explained later in this chapter and should follow a definite format to meet his particular needs as exemplified in Figure 16–1. This will require that he make definite decisions regarding what he intends to accomplish and how he expects to reach his objectives in each of the four steps.

The plan should cover every stage of the instructional process from the beginning to the accomplishment of the objectives.[2] The plan serves mainly as a guide to systematic teaching. It should consist of a series of notes that will enable the instructor to recall in an organized manner the information he plans to use, to use the teaching aids he has developed to best advantage and at the most appropriate time, and to test the students to determine the extent of their learning. The plan may follow a topic outline form, a detailed sentence outline, a narrative with appro-

[2] F. Dean McCluskey, *Audio-Visual Teaching Techniques* (Los Angeles: University of California Press, 1949), p. 1.

```
                          LESSON PLAN

                                Name_____

                                Date_____

          NAME OF COURSE OR SCHOOL IN WHICH TO BE USED


     COURSE:          (Title of Course or the Subject of which
                      this Lesson Plan is a part.)
     LESSON:          (Title of Lesson.  Should be short, com-
                      plete, and descriptive of the content.
                      Should be stated in terms of "HOW TO...",
                      i.e., HOW TO SEARCH FOR LATENT FINGERPRINTS
                      etc.)
     OBJECTIVES:      (List of specific knowledge, skills, and
                      abilities students will gain from lesson.)
     MATERIALS        (List of handout materials, supplies,
     NEEDED:          equipment and teaching aids needed in
                      presenting this lesson.)
     ASSIGNMENT:      (Specific assignment for next session.
                      If outside project is expected, Assign-
                      ment Sheet should be handed out.)
     REFERENCES:      (List of materials used in developing
                      this lesson.)
 I.  INTRODUCTION:    (List what has been planned to prepare
                      the student for the information he is to
                      be given.  List what will be done to gain
                      Attention, arouse Curiosity, stimulate
                      Interest and create Desire to learn.
                      (ACID Test of Introduction).  Specify
                      what student will be told to stress im-
                      portance of lesson material.)

 II. PRESENTATION:    (List of teaching points in step by step
                      sequence, in outline form.  Key points,
                      examples, and illustrations should be
                      included to make points clear.  In this
                      step, the instructor tells how, demon-
                      strates how, presents new information,
                      and summarizes.)

III. APPLICATION:     (Cite hypothetical problem that will re-
                      quire students to apply the principles
                      given him in the Presentation to the
                      solution of the problem or require the
                      student to perform under instructor's
                      supervision the task taught.)
 IV. TEST:            (Have student perform the job taught
                      without aid from instructor or ask how
                      or what questions to test depth of his
                      understanding of the information presented.
                      Specify exactly what the student is to do
                      in the Test step.  Include copy of written

                      test questions in lesson plan.  Oral how
                      or what questions best for short presenta-
                      tion.  These will test understanding,
                      recall, and will reduce guessing.  Periodic
                      paper-pencil tests constructed from
                      written test questions.)
```

FIGURE 16-1. Form of lesson plan (adapted from material used in the
California Peace Officers training program, *Teacher Training,*
California Community Colleges, Division of Vocational Education, Sacramento.)

priate markings of key teaching points and subordinate items, or marginal references keyed to the main teaching points. Some teachers make effective use of a single word (or phrase) outline to refresh their memories and help them organize their presentation.

Determining teaching sequence

The instructor should consider the point of view of the learner when the lesson material is analyzed and the teaching plan is being prepared so that his presentation may be arranged in the most logical order and will best meet current needs. Any one or a combination of several basic criteria may be used in determining the most appropriate sequence to be followed in each presentation. For example, the instructor may wish to progress from the *simple to the complex* if he were giving instruction in the field use of the primary fingerprint classifications. He may wish to proceed from the *safe to hazardous* if he were discussing such subjects as defensive driving or the use of firearms. The *easy to difficult* approach may be utilized with good effect in teaching subjects such as the disassembling of weapons or physical defense tactics. By giving his presentation so that it proceeds from the *known to the unknown,* the instructor might best acquaint the students with such subjects as laboratory procedures or accident investigation techniques. He can also utilize this sequence to establish a basis for clear understanding of even the most difficult material relating to law enforcement; but if his presentation involves merely a "rehashing" of what is already known, little will be accomplished in terms of bringing a greater understanding to the student despite his knowledge, background, status, or personality. These factors have a bearing upon the instructional approach, but they will not substitute for good planning.

The *time element* involved in performing a job such as writing a traffic citation, the *need for accuracy* in such operations as indexing and filing, *chronological sequence* as in report writing, *cause-and-effect* relationship, *pleasant to unpleasant, comparison to contrast, least to greatest, general to particular, enumeration of items,* or some other logical approach that might be involved in a lecture on report writing or interrogation would form a basis for the systematic organization of instructional material. When logical, systematic plans are employed, "material ceases to be mere hodge podge; it takes on sequence of some sort, progress has meaning. Beginning sounds like the start of something; the middle part develops substance and significance for the topic; the conclusion sounds like the end." [3]

---

[3] Cecil B. Williams and Allan H. Stevenson, *A Research Manual for College Studies and Papers* (New York: Harper & Row, Publishers, 1951), p. 14.

Regardless of what criteria for logical presentation are used, the objective is to give the student the knowledge or ability that will enable him to perform his duties properly. When the arrangement of the teaching plan is completed, the instructor should review it to make sure it is workable and that critical points have not been omitted.

LEARNING BY ASSOCIATION

Things to be learned should be presented so they can be associated with other familiar things. The process of remembering by association is described by William James in his classical statement, "In mental terms, the more other facts a fact is associated with in the mind, the better possession of it our memory retains." [4]

The instructor who has planned well will have constructed his lesson material so that the learner can relate it to his own background and experiences. This process of learning by association is of special importance when the material deals with jobs, operations, techniques, or principles foreign to the learner. The philosophy behind the law, for example, or the psychological principles involved in the interrogation of suspects may be difficult to convey to the student if he cannot associate the material in some way to his past experiences.

When facts and ideas are presented only in isolated bits and fragments, considerable difficulty will be encountered in communicating them to others. They can be transferred profitably when they have been given meaningful associations. [5] The development of pertinent examples will tax the imagination of the teacher but the returns for his efforts will amply repay him.

THE FOUR STEPS OF TEACHING

In every teaching situation there must be an orderly procedure for imparting information to the learner if best results are to be realized from the training effort. First, the learner's attention must be focused on the subject and his interest titillated. This is how teaching begins. Then the information must be conveyed to him. This is the substance of which teaching is made. Then he must be given an opportunity to apply what he has learned under the supervision of the instructor. Last, the teacher must appraise his own effectiveness in terms of the learner's understanding.

[4] William James, *Principles of Psychology* (New York: Holt Publishing Company, 1908), p. 294.
[5] *Ibid.*, p. 14.

Introduction

The introductory step in the instructional process will perhaps tax the imagination of the teacher more than the remaining three steps of instruction. The introductory remarks should focus the attention of the student on the subject, gain his interest, and place him in a state of readiness to learn. If these conditions are not present, the value of the remaining steps of the process will largely be lost.

The introduction should result in an arrangement of ideas and experiences already present in the learner's mind in such an order that he will be receptive to new ideas and experiences to be taught. This step does not involve the imparting of new knowledge, but it provides the instructor an opportunity to develop a basis upon which instruction can rest. When properly used, this step gives the learner motive and enthusiasm for learning and will establish a relationship between the subject and his past experience.

There are a multitude of ways of securing the attention of the learner, stimulating his interest, and creating in him a desire to learn. This can usually be accomplished by:

asking leading questions

directing rhetorical questions to the students

making use of suggestions, illustrations, or demonstrations

relating personal or other practical examples

placing emphasis on present or future needs which the learner may satisfy by the information

citing group or individual experiences

discussing why it is imperative to learn how to perform the job correctly

indicating how increased proficiency may benefit the learner personally or economically

In the introductory step of the instruction, the instructor often finds the individual approach has several advantages over the group approach. It is a more personal and informal approach to training and can be given at any time or place. No special physical facilities are required since contacts are usually short and impromptu and occur on the job. Psychologically, the learner is receptive to the training since he can apply it immediately to the job and ordinarily needs no other motivation. The instructor can alter his approach to allow for individual differences among trainees.

When the training is given in a group setting, considerable planning is needed for the introduction since the entire group must be motivated to learn. The introductory remarks must be adequate for this purpose; however, the introduction seldom achieves this objective if it is devised primarily to appeal to the average learner in the group. The result is that often it fails to provide motivation to learners outside the middle group. Difficulty is sometimes encountered in altering the teaching approach to compensate for individual differences unless the group is quite small.

Presentation

The objective of the presentation step is to impart new knowledge or skills to the student or to refresh his memory of what he has once learned. To be most meaningful, the material must be related to ideas and experiences already known to him. This is the process of association previously discussed.

The material should be presented in an orderly, systematic manner by showing, telling, explaining, or demonstrating so that the learner understands the proper procedures and methods of performing a task. Preplanned demonstrations might well supplement the lecture. Imaginative teaching aids will assist the instructor in vividly describing concepts to the student. Discussions and relevant examples will give the learners an opportunity to clarify misconceptions.

The advantage to be gained by the teacher in presenting information on an individual basis is that he can make allowances for individual differences by speeding or slowing his presentation. When it is given in a group setting, he must gauge his speed to meet the needs of the average learner. He sometimes loses the interest of the speedier or the slower ones thereby. The amount of emphasis of key points and the pace of instruction must be continously adjusted to accommodate varying group abilities; however, the information can be presented to more persons in groups than individually. This advantage of the group method cannot be overlooked.

Application

In the application step, the learner is provided an opportunity to try out or use the information he has learned. This step should disclose how much of the new material he has grasped and how ready he is to progress into a new area of learning. The instructor should carefully supervise and assist the learner when necessary during the application step to insure that what has been taught is applied correctly and that bad habits are not formed. The instructor should check key points as they are being performed and require the learner to repeat the operation if repetition is necessary to increase his proficiency to an acceptable level. There is wisdom to the adage, practice makes perfect.

Problem solving or role playing are excellent teaching devices to determine if the students are able to solve practical problems by applying the principles given them in the presentation.

The instructor can more closely supervise the individual in this step than he can a group. He can also answer questions more readily as the need arises and can detect and correct errors more quickly. In the group setting, equipment needed by students to apply what they have learned is often unavailable and participation thereby suffers. In addition, errors may occur without prompt detection, bad habits develop more readily, and retraining is needed more frequently.

Test

The fourth step, the test or follow-up, is the last in the instructional process and consists of an evaluation of the learner's progress. Like the application step, the test enables the instructor to determine the present ability of the learner and his readiness to proceed to a new phase of instruction. The learner must know the extent of his successes and failures and their nature to encourage him to further effort and to enable him to correct his weaknesses. Regardless of the type of tests given, whether they are oral, written, or manipulative, they must be constructed so that they will measure the effectiveness of the teacher through an evaluation of the learner's progress or lack of it. This step is closely related to the application step in which the learner demonstrates the extent of his learning and his ability to apply what he has learned. On occasion, the test step can be appropriately combined with the application step.

"How" or "what" questions are best when asked orally in testing the student's understanding of the principles presented.

Thorndike and Hagen [6] contend, "Testing procedures control the learning process to a greater degree, perhaps, than any other teaching device." As diagnostic instruments to show gaps in learning and as a medium for applying principles to practice, the value of tests is unquestioned. They should never be relegated to a place of unimportance in the teaching process. Test questions should be based not on trivia but on objectives. Although tests are not easy to construct, they deserve a great deal of attention because they will, if properly formulated, give the teacher some clues to whether he is achieving his general and specific objectives.

[6] Robert L. Thorndike and Elizabeth Hagen, *Measurement and Evaluation in Psychology and Education*, 2nd ed. (New York: John Wiley & Sons, Inc., 1961), p. 28.

GENERAL PROBLEMS AFFECTING TEACHING METHOD

The real problems encountered by the instructor in applying the four-step method of teaching are not failures of the method but are failures of the instructor to make proper use of the steps and to alter his approach to teaching as necessary when confronted with specific training problems. The method has been widely used with great success, as the training of massive numbers of troops during World War II by similar methods will attest. The theory and method are sound. They can be adapted to any teaching situaton. The emphasis placed on each step of the method depends upon the particular training need which has to be met.

On occasion the instructor can eliminate the introduction because the learner is self-motivated. He may reveal this by asking a question or requesting instruction. The instructor may then proceed immediately to the second step. The third step may not be required because the fourth may serve two purposes. All four steps in the process are important at times but the appropriate emphasis for each changes. The instructor must make his own value judgments regarding his method of approaching a particular training situation in the classroom or in the field. No method suitable for one instructor is necessarily suitable for others. Uniform training material can be provided to him, but the effectiveness of the specific methods he employs to impart knowledge to his subordinates depends upon his individual teaching repertoire and his ability to avoid the pitfalls that contribute to teaching failures. He can be told what methods have been found effective, he can be acquainted with the many and varied techniques of teaching, but unless he diligently and imaginatively applies himself to his teaching responsibilities, he will achieve little more than mediocrity in this activity.

COMMON CAUSES OF TEACHING INEFFECTIVENESS

Perhaps one of the most common faults in presenting instructional material arises from *oversimplification*. The inexperienced teacher is often prone to include too much detail in his lesson because he fails to allow for the basic intelligence of the learner. When he includes too much material for the time available, he will have a tendency to "cover the ground at any cost." Either too much is attempted, in which case the learner retains few of the key points because time limitations make it necessary to gloss over them, the teacher uses the allotted time without completing his objectives, he fails to complete the steps of instruction, or he improvises at the last moment and proceeds without an organized plan. In any event, the student suffers by having been exposed to too much and having learned little. Another common weakness contributing to teaching ineffectiveness is *aimlessness*. Klapper [7] observes most appropriately, "Aimlessness is the most important single cause of ineffectiveness in teaching and of frustration of educational effort." This condition usually results from a failure to plan and organize teaching material properly. Deficiencies in teaching often result from the inclusion of *unnecessary* or *irrelevant material* in the teaching plan. The cause usually can be traced to the failure of the teacher to discriminate between necessary material and trivia which is only nice to know. Once a mass of information has been accumulated, the teacher often finds it extremely difficult to discard any of it; but he must strip his material to the essentials or risk failure.

Too frequently the teacher assumes that the learner knows more about the job than he actually does. This ill-founded assumption often causes the instructor to leave out key points which are essential, to gloss over them without sufficient emphasis, or to fail to define unusual terms. The learner thereby fails to grasp the necessary facts; he misunderstands or fails to understand. The result is performance failures and costly errors.

Often a *lack of competency* or a failure on the part of the supervisor to prepare himself for his training role is the cause of his teaching ineffectiveness. It is highly desirable that he be occupationally competent to perform the task he expects his subordinates to learn about; but having technical proficiency does not insure that he can impart it to others. It would be erroneous to assume that just because an individual is an excellent burglary investigator, he can effectively teach others how to catch burglars. Rather, the technically competent supervisor who is also a good teacher will achieve a high degree of success in the training function because one ability will complement the other.

TEACHING TECHNIQUES

There are numerous approaches to teaching, each with its own characteristic advantages and disadvantages. The instructor must recognize that there is no "ideal" approach for all situations and that no single method can be used to the exclusion of the others. Some of the most common techniques of implementing the four-step method of instruction are included here as reminders to the supervisor-teacher of the need for an imaginative approach to teaching.

---

[7] Paul Klapper, "The Professional Preparation of the College Teacher," *Journal of General Education*, 3 (1959), 229.

Lecture

The pure lecture method of instruction is greatly overworked because many instructors find it the easiest way to present instructional material. Good demonstrations, use of teaching aids, questions and discussions, and the development of the more sophisticated supplements to teaching require time and energy that many instructors do not feel are worth the results. The contribution of these various approaches to learning will, however, more than offset the time required to prepare them.

The lecture method of teaching is quite often the least effective method since it assumes that all members of the class progress at the same rate. It can be used advantageously if the lesson is presented in extremely short sessions, however. Even under this condition, the presentation should be supplemented by some teaching aids if nothing more than the chalkboard, which is readily available and easy to use. Some humor, showmanship, and even a little histrionics at times will help to improve the learning environment.

When explanations are made of procedures, techniques, or manipulative tasks, they must be simple, clear, and concise to be most effective. They should be given in language suitable to the backgrounds of those being taught. Recruit officers will be less familiar with police jargon than will seasoned officers. An unfamiliar term used without definition or explanation may hinder the learner's understanding of the entire lesson. Unusual jargon, vernacular, or technical terms should be defined or avoided in favor of language with which the learner is familiar.

Often the teacher makes an erroneous assumption that his material is understood because questions are not raised. In reality, questions may not be asked because the learner desires to remain inconspicuous in the group or may be self-conscious about not understanding what he is afraid is common terminology.

Questions from students should be handled carefully since they may indicate that understanding has not taken place or that review is needed. They should be treated patiently by the instructor. He should be guided by the nature of the question in determining the extent of the answer required, but answer it he must to clarify any misunderstanding. As Bugelski [8] has indicated, "Misunderstanding and understanding can occur with exactly the same feeling of assurance." The student may believe he has understood the instructor perfectly when he has not done so at all. The only clue to the instructor that this has occurred might be a simple

[8] B. R. Bugelski, *The Psychology of Learning Applied to Teaching* (Indianapolis, Ind.: The Bobbs-Merrill Company, Inc., 1964), p. 202.

question. The absence of questions cannot, however, be relied upon as a reliable indicator that understanding has taken place.

Demonstration

Instructors and students find relief from the boredom of the pure lecture method when preplanned demonstrations with actual equipment or implements are used to supplement other teaching techniques. While demonstrations are a useful device in almost any training situation, they are of particular value when manipulative skills are the subject of instruction. The student can be shown one step of the procedure at a time, he can be allowed to apply what he has learned under the watchful eye of the teacher, and then he can be advanced to the next step until he has received instruction in and been able to perform satisfactorily the entire job.

The object of the demonstration should be made clear to students. They should be told the important points to be looked for and their overall relationship to the completed task. The student is thus prepared for the instruction by being familiarized with the ways he can utilize the information to help him to do the job.

Ideally, the teacher should place himself in a position where students can observe him performing the demonstration from the same relative position as they would assume when actually performing the operation. An explanation of why the operation is performed in a certain way will give the student a greater understanding of the procedure and will tend to fix the steps in his mind. The task should be repeated as many times as necessary to assure student proficiency at about the level where he could effectively and safely execute the task on the job. The need for too much repetition should cause the instructor to reassess the effectiveness of his teaching techniques. Changes in his approach might be indicated. As the demonstration is conducted, the instructor should test students by asking them how to perform the next step and why it is done to ascertain the degree of learning that has taken place and the effectiveness of his methods of presentation.

Group discussion

A change of pace may be of great value in reviving lagging interest, fostering partcipation, and refocusing attention on the subject. The instructor may often accomplish this by stimulating discussion among the students. Problem solving by students with the accompanying benefits derived from their participation provides them an opportunity to contribute pertinent information, evaluate it, and draw conclusions. This procedure is extremely useful for synthesizing much information from a variety of sources. It is also a useful device for determining the extent of learning which has taken place since it involves the application of stated principles to practical problems. The discussion technique used in conjunction with the lecture or demonstration, or a combination of these, provides balance to the presentation, gives it vitality, and adds color and interest.

When the instructional technique involves a presentation by specialists with audience participation permitted, it is called a *forum*. When the discussion is between a group of specialists without audience participation, the technique is referred to as a *panel discussion*. A modification of this procedure is to permit the audience to ask questions of the panel. It is an excellent problem solving medium and is very useful in clarifying many knotty issues which cause much insecurity and misunderstanding among personnel. Such a training technique has the disadvantage of limiting the content to the information imparted by the panel, however.

USE OF QUESTIONS

Questions requiring thinking and reasoning by the student can be used to reveal the extent to which he has absorbed the material he needs to perform a task or has gained an understanding of the more abstract types of instruction. Additionally, they can be used to spot check the student's progress or reveal the need for review. These may be of several types. *Overhead questions* are those directed to the entire group with the instructor then choosing one student to answer. This type of question is the one most commonly used. Sufficient time should be allowed for the named student to formulate an answer. Every effort should be made by the instructor to aid him, without actually answering the question, to give the learner a feeling of success and achievement. *Relay questions,* those asked by one student and relayed by the instructor to another member of the group for an answer, can also be a useful tool of instruction. The instructor should avoid using the relay question as a means of evading a response to a question which he is unable to answer. The *reverse question* is one that the instructor "throws back" to the person who asked it. It can be used to advantage to cause the student to solve his own problems with perhaps some prompting by the teacher or others if necessary.

Questions should never be used as a club to embarrass, chastise, or reveal the ignorance of a student. To do so would tend to close his mind and set up barriers to effective learning.

TEACHING AIDS

The aids available to the teacher to help him carry out his teaching function are practically unlimited. Too often he relies only upon the spoken word to put his material across; yet, investigation has revealed that the largest portion of man's knowledge has been gained not through the auditory sense alone but through the use of this sense combined with the others, principally sight. The teacher who performs his instructional function most effectively is the one who utilizes every possible means of assistance in carrying his message to the student in a manner calculated to enhance learning efficiency.

USE OF INSTRUCTIONAL AIDS

Instructional aids help the teacher to avoid too much telling and too much reliance on words to carry ideas. They will help him and the student to develop meanings in common and, when used properly, will help prevent misunderstandings arising out of merely verbal presentations.[9] They do not supplant good instruction but supplement and improve teaching. Dale[10] observes, "Teaching aids can make the learning experience far more concrete and memorable." Student interest and participation are enhanced by the addition of color and variety to the instruction and the presentation of live problems and situations. Monotony can be avoided by the use of these teaching supplements when they are imaginatively employed to vary the presentation. Many avenues of learning are opened when senses other than hearing are brought into play and combined with it.

Knowledge is acquired through the senses and stored in a system of symbols. Teaching is concerned with the art of stimulating a desire to learn and developing the ability to perceive symbols accurately and clearly. When this is done, increased learning is possible. It will be enhanced by any communication media that aid perception and understanding.[11] Ideally, as many senses as possible should be appealed to when the teacher presents ideas, principles, facts, and problems. Although he should use as many aids as are available to him, no one type should be used to the exclusion of all others. Each type has its own value and should be used to serve a particular purpose. This is particularly important in the introduction and presentation steps.

[9] McClusky, *Audo-Visual Teaching Techniques*, p. 1.
[10] Edgar Dale, *Audio-Visual Methods in Teaching* (New York: Holt, Rinehart and Winston, Inc., 1946), p. 6.
[11] G. Umstaatd, *College Teaching* (Washington, D.C.: University Press of Washington, D.C. 1964), p. 204.

Audiovisual instruction need not be confined to manipulative skills. The Armed Forces have used these methods to good effect in changing attitudes, in motivating personnel, and in developing morale.[12]

TYPES OF TEACHING AIDS

Elaborate aids are not essential. Simple, inexpensive ones can be used to fill a real need. Sometimes the aid made with a felt pencil or a wax crayon on butcher paper is more effective than a sophisticated, expensive mock-up.

Display aids

The simple chalkboard, bulletin board, or specially prepared chart can be effectively used for display purposes to supplement oral instruction. These are especially useful when material is being taught in a small area where the entire class can see them. Pictures, diagrams, charts, or other matters depicted must be large enough to show details clearly if the teacher expects them to be effective. Color adds variety and value to posters and should be used whenever possible to stimulate student interest. Discretion and good taste are always in order. If charts, tables, or diagrams are prepared beforehand and are complex, parts should be used separately to reduce the span of the student's attention. When the chalkboard is employed, the material placed on it should be well arranged, simple, and clear. If the teacher desires to draw diagrams while lecturing, he should plan carefully what he wishes to depict so that the drawing will not detract from his presentation. A series of tiny dots previously arranged on the board will guide his drawing if it is a complex one.

Duplicated aids

Duplicated aids can be prepared by a multitude of mechanical and chemical processes now available to the teacher. They may consist of instruction sheets, information sheets, diagrams, charts, illustrations, outlines of the fill-in type, conventional outlines, or other types of data useful to the student. The material should be punched so that it may be included in the student's notebook.

[12] United States Office of Education, Committee on Military Training Aids and Instructional Materials, *Use of Training Aids in the Armed Services,* Bulletin No. 9, (Washington, D.C.: Federal Security Agency, 1945), pp. 10–12.

These handout materials should not be made available to the student as a substitute for study. Rather, the information should represent matter rather difficult to obtain but valuable to his progress.

Projected aids

The teaching aids available for projection on a screen are almost unlimited. Some are easily and cheaply prepared and make a splendid contribution to teaching. The equipment necessary to project these materials, however, is often expensive and not easily available. Videocasts and tapes, stereographs, overhead projection equipment, motion picture projectors with or without sound, opaque projectors, slides with narrated tapes, and a multitude of other devices will add greatly to the teacher's instructional efforts if they are properly used. He must not rely upon them as a crutch. They are only a complement to his own efforts. Neither should this type of aid be looked upon as a form of recreation for the student.

When films are used, it is essential that they be ordered sufficiently far in advance so that they may be delivered and the necessary equipment set up for their use prior to the time of the class meeting. They are part of a planned lesson and must be used carefully and with discrimination to be most effective. A few selected slides, for example, studied carefully by the student might provide more learning than the use of many, which may only cause confusion. Students should be prepared in advance to observe important points. Careful introduction paves the way for learning. Note taking during the presentation generally should not be required since it tends to distract attention from the film. Ideally, students should note and discuss key points after the film has been observed, discuss major concepts depicted, and answer pertinent questions to demonstrate the amount of learning which has taken place.

Three-dimensional aids

Equipment parts, cutaways, mockups, simulated scenes common to police work, sandboards, table models, and many other such devices overcome the difficulty of depicting items on a flat surface. The flannel and magnetic boards (Figure 16–2) are very useful in giving the student an overall perspective of a problem although these ordinarily have flat surfaces. They do, however, have the advantage of simplicity of preparation, economy, and portability. Sandboards or mockups do not have these advantages. In addition, the flannel or magnetic boards give the

FIGURE 16-2. Magnetic board. Field tactical problems can be simulated by figures representing persons, equipment, buildings, streets, or objects glued to magnetic strips and placed on the board. Students can deploy personnel and equipment as the various exercises indicate.

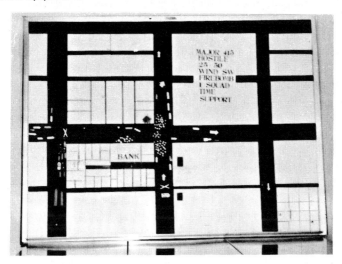

student some of the same advantages obtainable from the sandboard, namely, the opportunity to deal with movable objects. This type of aid is unmatched in some presentations having to do with police tactics and field operations since it places the learner in a position that simulates those encountered in practice. He is also afforded an opportunity to exercise his judgment or apply principles in a hypothetical setting. Sandboards, for example, may be used to make clear the small details of a scene through the application of large-scale models. Problems involving such police incidents as civil disorders, major disasters, barricaded criminals, or other unusual occurrences can be simulated to give the student experience in the classroom.

Field trips

Trips carefully planned to accomplish a specific objective are a useful type of teaching aid which will allow the students to learn at first hand through observation of an actual operation. They should be oriented in advance to the objectives of the trip and pertinent points to look for so that the trip might be most meaningful. Trips should be carefully controlled to prevent them from becoming purely recreational.

SUMMARY

When the subject matter has been selected for training, the instructor must first decide upon the general and specific objectives he wishes to accomplish. Objectives should be thought of as goals to be accomplished by the instructional process. The teacher should look upon them in terms of the desired changes in attitudes or behavior that he wishes to bring about by training.

Material should be collected from the most reliable and authoritative sources available after the instructor establishes his objectives. It must then be analyzed to determine what operations are most necessary to complete the job and how much of the material can be presented in the time available. That which is of secondary importance should be discarded. Only that which is pertinent and can be presented in the allotted time should be retained.

The instructor should then prepare a written plan to teach. It should be devised to guide him in presenting the subject matter to his students in a logical, systematic manner. It should be adapted to the four-step method of teaching and should include notations regarding when and how the teaching materials and aids are to be used in each step. Proper, careful planning is essential to proper application of this four-step method.

The introductory step is useful to motivate the student to learn, to secure his interest, and to focus his attention on the subject. The objective of the presentation step is to develop understanding, impart knowledge, and prepare the learner better to accomplish a task. In the application step, he is given an opportunity to apply what he has learned. The test step enables the teacher to evaluate his effectiveness in teaching and the learner's comprehension of the subject matter.

The teacher must be cognizant of the advantages and disadvantages of the various approaches to teaching in order to minimize failures. He should recognize that the four-step method is basically sound. Failures are the result of the instructor's shortcomings in applying the proven principles of teaching. He fails to accomplish his objective when he tries to teach too much in the time available, when he fails to discriminate between necessary and trivial material, or when he oversimplifies or overcomplicates his presentation. His teaching effectiveness is also reduced when he fails to appeal to the learner's several senses and supplement his verbal presentation through the proper use of teaching aids of all kinds.

If the teacher does not relate the material he presents to his students to things they already know or if he fails to convince them of the importance of the information either in terms of what it can do to make the job easier or more effective or how it can personally benefit them, they likely will not retain it. If the information is not presented so that the student can see clearly what he is supposed to learn, confusion will result. The student who is unable or unwilling to make use of what he has learned will not remember it long. He will probably have wasted his time and that of the instructor.

REVIEW

Questions

1. What are teaching objectives?
2. What two types of teaching objectives should the teacher prepare in readying himself to teach? Distinguish between the two.
3. What factors should the instructor take into consideration in analyzing his teaching material before presenting it?
4. What is a lesson plan? How may it be used?
5. What should the lesson plan contain?
6. What form should the plan follow?
7. Why is learning by association important to the student?
8. List the four steps of teaching discussed in this chapter and explain what each step should accomplish.
9. What are some of the ways of stimulating attention and securing interest of the learner?
10. What are the advantages of the individual approach to teaching over the group approach in each of the four steps of instructions?
11. What are the advantages of the group approach over the individual approach in each of the steps?
12. What step controls the learning process most? Explain why this is so.
13. List the most common causes of teaching ineffectivenesss. Discuss briefly what can be done to avoid it.
14. Discuss the advantages and disadvantages of at least three of the most common methods of teaching.
15. Name three types of questions and explain how they can be used in a teaching situation.
16. Name four general categories of teaching aids, give a specific example of each, and explain how each might be used in a training session.

Exercises

1. List at least ten bases upon which the teacher can establish a logical sequence in his teaching and give a concrete example of how each might be used in a practical teaching situation.

2. Prepare a lesson plan from information you have collected for a thirty-minute lesson on one of the subjects listed below. Be prepared to give your lesson from this plan to the class.

How to make a primary fingerprint classification
How to use a primary fingerprint classification in the field
How to plan for handling a special event
How to make a station inspection
How to make a personnel inspection
How to make a vehicle inspection
How to deploy personnel to handle a barricaded suspect incident
How to conduct a search for a lost child
How to handle an explosion incident
How to handle a plane wreck in a business district
How to deploy personnel to handle a major fire
How to deploy personnel at a flood
How to develop command presence among supervisors
Defensive driving
Range safety
Acceptance of gratuities
How to recognize symptoms of low morale
How to recognize symptoms of civil unrest
How to handle a major disorder
How to combat a special robbery problem
How to handle an unusual burglary problem
How to combat a rapist-burglar problem
How to establish good public relations in traffic law enforcement
How to establish good community relations among minorities
Supervisory liability for acts of subordinates
How to motivate the lazy worker
How to operate a driver safety program
How to implement a firearms safety program

3. Prepare and use at least two teaching aids other than the chalkboard in your teaching exercise.

17

Conference
leading

A conference is an interchange of views between persons with common problems and related interests. It is a mutual consultation involving the pooling of ideas and experiences by selected individuals for the purpose of analyzing problems and seeking solutions to them. Solutions to problems which affect an organization can often be found by means of a conference when other means cannot be used effectively. By this technique, persons who are well qualified in a particular field can pool their knowledge in a search for a solution.

COMPOSITION OF CONFERENCE MEMBERSHIP

Ideally, members of a conference should be somewhat equal in position or rank if they are drawn from the same organization to avoid stifling of individual participation. These are called horizontal conferences. They tend to be more productive than vertical conferences, which consist of persons with widely differing backgrounds, ranks, or positions. A patrol officer would ordinarily be somewhat reluctant to differ with his commanding officer in the same conference. Members should have had some common experiences with the type of problem selected for discussion. The problem might thus be soluble through group participation.

VALUE OF CONFERENCES

One of the main benefits of the conference procedure is that it is a useful tool in solving difficult organizational problems. Another benefit is that those who are performing the actual operation can be given an opportunity to participate in making decisions that affect them. They will usually respond more favorably when given this opportunity. Consultation between management and the members of an organization wherein employees share in the decision-making process will enhance morale and give employees a special feeling of status. The conference is particularly valuable when used by supervisors as a means of sharing information and experiences with subordinates and learning of their needs and desires.

Even when all members agree to disagree, at least management learns that the subject matter is likely to be highly controversial. As Hunter [1] observes, "A conference which results in a disagreement which all clearly understand may be just as fruitful educationally as a conference in which all agree." This flexible device can be useful as a training medium to secure better understanding of organizational objectives and to solve problems affecting operations. Ideas can be drawn out, evaluated, and integrated into concrete recommendations. Effective plans of action can often be developed from the systematic discussion that a well-conducted conference can produce. Good planning and the application of proven techniques of conference leading will be of material assistance to the leader in deriving maximum benefits from the experiences of the group. Although the conference procedure takes more time to develop a subject or solve a problem systematically than do other methods, the arbitrariness of other methods may be avoided. Parliamentary procedures are seldom followed, and there are no rules of order to stifle discussion. Almost full freedom of action is thus possible.

CONFERENCE LIMITATIONS

Since conferences deal primarily with a discussion of ideas and problems, they are not the most economical and effective medium for imparting

---

[1] H. Jack Hunter, *Conference Leadership for Use in Supervisory Training Program* (Washington, D.C.: Office of Industrial Resources, International Cooperation Administration, 1958), pp. 6–7.

new knowledge and developing skills. Other training techniques are usually more suitable for this purpose and consume less time.

Members of a conference are not always familiar with the procedures to be followed, but they gain skill in working together. For this reason, usually a single, short meeting of a group which has not previously conferred is not very practical.

Another limitation on the conference technique is that skillful leaders are not always available to conduct the discussions. It is better that a conference not be held if the result will be a distressing waste of time for everyone participating. A well-planned and well-handled conference, on the other hand, will achieve results impossible for even the most articulate orator.

CONSIDERATIONS AFFECTING THE CALLING OF A CONFERENCE

The mere fact that a problem is present and in need of a solution does not, in itself, justify the calling of a conference. It can sometimes be solved by other, more economical means. Before a decision is made to attempt to find a solution by calling a conference, certain practical questions should be considered. The Department of the Army [2] lists eleven of these:

What are the objectives of the conference?

Can the objectives be attained as well or better by other means?

Is attainment of the minimum objectives of the conference likely at this time?

Are references currently available containing the facts essential to the success of the conference?

Is time so vital that correspondence or visits would delay too long the agreements needed?

How much time can be gained by the conference?

Are suitable participants available?

Can an appropriate place with suitable facilities be provided?

Are the proposed scope, duration, and agenda appropriate?

Are the issues clearly defined?

Can adequate preparation for the conference be made in the time allowed?

WHY CONFERENCES FAIL

While there are numerous causes for conferences failing to achieve established objectives, most of them can be eliminated by practice, which is

[2] Department of the Army, *Staff Officers' Field Manual—Staff Organization and Procedure, FM 101-5* (Appendix VIII) (Washington, D.C.: Headquarters, Department of the Army, 1960), p. 499.

the key to successful conference leading. Cooper [3] contends that, "Most poor conferences suffer from the leader's having overlooked a minor point or so in technique, rather than from his being entirely wrong in procedure." The leader should therefore strive to make his techniques more effective. The improper selection of subject matter and failure to prepare thoroughly are also major causes of conference failures. Other failures result from the inability of the leader to inspire the confidence of members in the purpose of the conference. This will usually dampen their interest and enthusiasm in really trying to find a solution of the problem. The leader must make every effort to avoid saying or doing anything from which the participants will infer that they are being "humored" by the administration by being allowed to participate in problem solving or decision making or that the conclusion they drew was one which *had* to be drawn. If they gain the impression that the problem has already been decided upon and a conclusion has already been reached by superiors, the conference is doomed to fail.

Failure on the part of the leader to summarize contributions and crystallize opinions will also detract from conference effectiveness and result in failures to accomplish objectives. Likewise, overstructuring of the proceedings by too much emphasis on formality will stifle results. The expert leader will conduct the conference in an informal, impersonal manner. Taylor and Mears [4] contend, "In the early stages, the fewer the rules the better, as friendliness, tolerance and a keen desire to exchange ideas flourish best in a free atmosphere."

The experienced and effective leader will avoid expertising each point as it is made. If he does, the members will soon tire of his attempts "to impose his views upon them." As Cooper [5] points out, "There is no better way to wreck any conference than for the leader to participate too frequently or for too long a period at a time." He will lose the participation of members one by one as they will soon conclude that their contributions are not needed since he has all the answers to all the problems. He will do his job best only when he realizes that the group knowledge of the subject is superior to his own. His job is to lead the group, not monopolize the conversation. There will be times, however, when he will be required to exert some rigid control on the group in the interests of harmony. He should then act positively and without hesitation to minimize disruptive influences which often crop up.

Most of the novice conference leader's mistakes will be made

[3] Alfred M. Cooper, *How to Conduct Conferences*, 2nd ed. (New York: McGraw-Hill Book Company, 1946), p. 20.
[4] H. M. Taylor and A. G. Mears, *The Right Way to Conduct Meetings, Conferences, and Discussions*, 6th ed. (London: Morrison and Gibb Ltd., 1964), p. 117.
[5] Cooper, *How to Conduct Conferences*, p. 11.

because of his fear of losing control of the group.[6] He will either fail to assume control when it is needed or will exert it when it is not needed.

On occasion, conferences will not achieve desired results simply because of improper or careless selection of conferees. If they have no background to qualify them for participation in the area to be discussed, they are not likely to arrive at satisfactory conclusions and should not have been selected to participate in the first place.

Conferences also fail because the problem to be discussed has already been solved or is not soluble and such facts are known to the conferees. Perhaps an erroneous impression to this effect is gained from an inadequate introduction of the problem by the leader at the outset. This can be avoided by careful planning of the introduction and statement of the conference problem.

CONFERENCE PLANNING

The degree of success of the conference will be closely related to the type of planning done by the leader in preparing for it. Unfortunately, it is often the inexperienced leader who needs good preparation most who makes the least. Leading a conference might appear easy to those who have had no experience. This is an appearance purposely created by the experienced leader to give an impression that will deemphasize his own role.

Good conference plans will help make possible the maximum accomplishment during the time allotted to the discussion. Hunter[7] concludes that, "The most basic and most important element in preparation for conference leadership is the discussion plan." This is often called the conference "hot sheet."

Although it is not necessary that the leader be an expert in the matter to be discussed, he should become familiar with the subject so that he can properly introduce it and can stimulate discussion which is necessary to solution of the problem. This will require that he review the material available so that he will be informed of past developments, present trends, and future possibilities. Analysis of the material will also aid him in determining if the problem is soluble.

Any good conference plan should indicate the alternate channels available as a guide to the leader in leading the group toward this end. It should suggest the objectives to be accomplished and should include a statement of the problem with alternate statements the leader might find

TABLE 17-1. Sample conference-leading plan

Subject: SERGEANT'S LOG

Introductory Statement (4 minutes)
Need for information from supervisor's log
Benefits to be derived from this information
Requirements of the organization
Possible uses of such information
Etc.

Statement of Problem
What information should the Sergeant's Log contain?
or
Why is it desirable to have a record of the Sergeant's work?

Problem Analysis Chart Heading
      INFORMATION
        or

INFORMATION NEEDED	USES OF INFORMATION
1. Calls answered	1. Budget data
2. Observations of personnel	2. Manner of performance
	Quality of work
	Need for training
3. Unusual incidents	3. Discipline or other corrective action
	Training
	Keeping superiors informed
4. Etc.	4. Etc.

Possible Conclusions
List major conclusions likely to be reached

Possible Recommendations
List possible courses of action

---

necessary to use if group reactions to the first statement of the problem are negative, as shown in Table 17–1.

Introductory materials such as charts, statistics, concrete examples, or illustrations should be developed by the leader to aid him in introducing the problem to the group and impressing upon members the need for its solution. Chart headings for problem analysis should be worked out together with alternate headings to be used if necessary. Preliminary discussion in the group might indicate that an approach different from the one originally planned would be more productive. The *probable* major contributions or key points the leader could expect the group to make should be listed to give him guidelines to follow in leading the discussion to a logical conclusion. Probable questions from the conferees should be anticipated so that a plan to secure answers from the group can be developed. The possible conclusions with suitable alternatives should be listed. These should reflect the major objectives of the conference. Possible recommendations which might be forth-coming from the group should be listed so that the leader will have thought through what course of action the group might recommend. This forecasting process will enable the leader to avert some of the pitfalls of conference leading by recognizing potential problems in time to circumvent them.

Conference checklist

The wise leader will develop a checklist for use before the conference to insure against a failure to do those things which have to be done in preparing for it. The list should include in orderly sequence the steps that he should have taken in his planning activities (such as determining and reviewing the conference objectives), making ready the necessary aids for his introduction (such as charting materials, background data, and check sheets for evaluation purposes), preparing to make demonstrations or use other aids, preparing a concise statement of the problem with suitable alternative statements, preparing an appropriate introduction, developing and studying carefully the conference outline, preparing pertinent questions, arranging for proper notifications to participants of the meeting place, time, and agenda, and determining that arrangements for all physical facilities have been made.

Formulating the conference problem

The conference problem should be clearly stated so that it will not be misunderstood by conferees. It should be framed in a manner that will enable them to direct their thinking toward the same objectives. This will prevent loss of time resulting from the need to redefine the problem, delimit its scope, and restate it.

The leader should ask himself several questions when he analyzes the problem: Is it a real problem? Will the group feel that it is? Has it been solved already? Is the conference the right method for solving it? Can the problem be stated fully and clearly and, if so, how? Is the group selected capable of solving it? Are their backgrounds and experiences adequate for this purpose? Is the problem sufficiently concrete so that it can be discussed fully and probably solved in a reasonable time? The conference leader should make necessary revisions in his planning on the basis of his responses to the aforementioned questions so that the problem will meet the tests of solubility, concreteness, and clarity.

Even the poor conference leader can do an adequate job of leading a conference and can attain satisfactory results if the subject matter is appropriate. If it isn't, he will do poorly regardless of how skilled he is.

Once it has been determined what the conference problem is, that it is soluble by this method, and that it has not already been solved, the leader should formulate it in a positive manner rather than in a negative one. Ordinarily it should be framed as a question in clear terms which delimit its scope.[8] For example, the following is a positive statement of the problem: What can be done to improve the coordination between patrol officers and detectives? This is preferred to the following negative statement of the same problem: What can be done to avoid impairing the coordination between patrol officers and detectives?

CONFERENCE PROCEDURES

Overview

Once the conference problem has been specified and the subject introduced by the leader, discussion should be started to gather the facts, impressions, and opinions needed for a solution. As contributions are made by conferees, the leader must analyze them, pick out pertinent materials, and crystallize them into summary statements for entry on the chart. As the discussion progresses, other summary statements will be recorded. From these an overall summary along with the decisions reached by the group and its conclusions will be developed. These will provide a basis for the preparation of a plan of action or a means of carrying out the group recommendations.

General considerations

The first meeting of a conference to be held in a series is perhaps the most important because the success achieved and the impressions gained by participants will largely influence their acceptance of the procedure. Therefore, the new leader should make a special effort to provide the members a feeling of accomplishment from their first efforts.

Ordinarily, if the leader is not acquainted with the conference members, he should have someone from the organization involved introduce him to them. If they are acquainted with each other, he should prepare a seating chart to enable him to identify them. Name cards sufficiently large so that they are readable from any position should be

[8]Russell H. Wagner and Caroll C. Arnold, *Handbook of Group Discussion* (Boston: Houghton Mifflin Company, 1950), pp. 46–47.

provided if some of the participants are not known to each other. These cards can be made simply and effectively with broad-tipped marking pencils and five- by eight-inch cards folded in the middle.

The leader should ask members to pronounce unusual names. He will often relieve tensions if he asks each member of a strange group to identify himself and give a brief account of his job and background. This procedure will also tend to encourage members to participate.

When members are not experienced in conference procedures, these should be described briefly and the general steps to be followed explained. The leader should acquaint participants with his duties and should familiarize them with their individual responsibilities to the conference.

If several sessions are to be held, the group should discuss the sequence of topics to be discussed so that scheduling of future meetings will be facilitated. Details of the next meeting should be announced as soon as possible after the subject sequence has been decided to enable members to arrange their work schedules accordingly. All conferences should be started and concluded promptly as scheduled.

CONFERENCE LEADER DUTIES AND RESPONSIBILITIES

The qualities of leadership and the responsibilities of the leader were appropriately summarized by Loney [9] when he stated, "To accomplish the goals of a conference, the leader must be a monitor, not a mentor. He must act as a friendly, impartial, alert, interested referee. To achieve these goals, he should be personable, sincere, patient, fair-minded, a good listener, and endowed with a sense of humor."

Introduction of subject

Once the leader has dispensed with the general mechanics of acquainting the participants with conference procedures, he should introduce the problem in accordance with his plan. A proper statement and introduction of the problem will contribute materially to conference success since it is at this stage the conferees are either convinced of the existence of a real problem and the need for its timely solution or they will reject the objectives and doom the conference to failure.

Opening remarks should be brief and concise. Perhaps five minutes at the most should be taken for this purpose. Two or three minutes

[9] Glenn M. Loney, *Briefing and Conference Techniques* (New York: McGraw-Hill Book Company, 1959), p. 161.

would usually be even more appropriate. The longer the introduction, the more the group will tend to become passive and the more difficult it will be to arouse members into a state of active participation.[10]

Stating the problem

The problem to be solved should be stated as planned when introductory remarks have been concluded. If it has been well thought out in advance, the leader will be able to avoid the necessity for restating it later, which would weaken his position.

Leading the discussion

Once the problem has been properly stated and recorded on the chart or board in the form of an appropriate question, the wise leader will avoid any appearance of "badgering" the conferees into an immediate response. Rather, he will allow them to mull over the matter. Ordinarily, the pause will be followed by some responses from the group.

An appropriate use of good follow-up questions to the initial responses will tend to elicit further responses. A good conference leader can be distinguished from a poor one usually by the quality of his follow-up questions and the timing with which they are employed.[11]

The leader need not be an expert in the subject area, although some familiarity with it is helpful to him in leading the group to a logical conclusion. His principal job is to lead and guide others along the lines they must follow to solve the problem at hand. There is little that can happen during the conference that is beyond the power of the adept leader to control. He is the key person in the discussion group and it is his responsibility to keep the conference progressing. But, as Wagner and Arnold [12] point out, "Progress in discussion is not necessarily insured by careful preparation of the subject, by free participation, or by conscientious leadership. There must also be thoughtful, diligent, and conscious use of correct procedures. These procedures are necessarily determined by the laws of group thinking as modified by the general conditions of discussion and the special limitations of time, place, and persons." The application of proper techniques and procedures will help the group in a systematic attempt to solve the conference problem.

[10] Cooper, *How to Conduct Conferences,* p. 25.
[11] *Ibid.,* p. 29.
[12] Wagner and Arnold, *Handbook of Group Discussion,* p. 84.

Encouraging participation

The leader should promote the discussion by encouraging all conferees to participate. He should retain an open and receptive mind to contributions even though the expressions may at times be hostile or negative. Whether they are directed toward the management, other supervisors, or himself, he must accept them with composure. These often have value as a catharsis in releasing tensions which might be present.

Maintaining permissive attitude

A permissive attitude will lend informality to the proceedings and will foster active participation, which is the key to conference effectiveness. Participation involves a process of active learning quite different from the passive type, which is usually less productive. Since the very success of any conference is dependent upon the quality and nature of each member's opinions and conclusions, the leader must constantly be alert for any conditions which may depress their participation. He should avoid evaluating their opinions. He should give no clue by attitude or remark that he agrees or disagrees with their contributions. This should be left to the others in the group. Once they sense the permissive climate, they will respond freely and will often quickly agree or disagree with each other's contributions. Thus they will usually police themselves and make it possible for the leader to remain in a neutral position.

It is of especial importance that reticent members of the group be encouraged to make an occasional contribution. Since a feeling of status and self-confidence is usually the forerunner to their active participation, the leader should sincerely acknowledge the value of their expressions whenever he can so that ego inflation will occur. When other members of the group accept the contribution as worthwhile, the backward member will often be inspired to participate more actively. If he does not, the leader should ask him questions.

Reflection

Competition between conferees will usually have a very beneficial effect upon them. The leader can foster such competition by the skillful application of the techniques of reflection. This psychological principle can be applied in one of three levels. *Reflection of content* involves a rewording of what the member says, without trying to interpret or change its meaning. For example, if the conferee states, "I think we do a poor job in orienting the new employee," the conference leader reflects the content of the statement back to the group by saying, "You feel that our present methods are inadequate?" Further discussion might then be in order.

Reflection of feeling involves the process of clarifying or drawing out the feeling behind the statement or inflection. It is a means of showing that there is an understanding of what the person is experiencing inwardly or how he feels. For example, if the member says, "Supervisors here are not really a part of management," the leader reflects the feeling behind the statement by responding, "You feel that management doesn't have confidence in your opinions?" Thus an opportunity is provided for the leader to clarify and draw out the true feeling implied by the member.

Reflection of core is a summary made to insure or gain an understanding of what has been said.

The benefits to the conference gained from this process of forcing complete, accurate contributions from members are inestimable since reliable conclusions cannot be easily drawn from abstract, vague statements without the danger of distortion. Further, this process of reflection is a form of therapy in which the individual is encouraged to examine his statements in their true perspective. This provides him an emotional release and promotes further discussion.

Giving credit

The leader should give credit to the whole group for results achieved as they are group results and not those of any one individual. Likewise, the wise leader will assume the responsibility for failures and not attempt to shift the blame to others since he, and he alone, was in control of the proceedings and was responsible for results.

Respecting confidence

During the course of conference discussions there will be occasions in which overly frank or plainly indiscreet statements will be made by members in the heat generated by the discussion. These should be received by the leader with equanimity and, except under the most extraordinary circumstances, should not be carried outside the conference room in such a way that a particular individual will be held accountable. To do so would destroy the confidence of the group in the leader and in the conference procedure. Without doubt, it would seriously jeopardize his future relationships with conferees.

Summarizing contributions

As the discussion progresses, the leader should frequently summarize contributions, crystallize the thoughts of the individuals, and record such summary statements on the conference charts for later reference when the conference report is prepared as discussed later.

A good leader will avoid summarizing the obvious or nonessential contributions. Too much repetition of statements in the form of summaries will detract from the discussion. When made, they should be timely to show that there has been general agreement in a segment of the discussion and to prepare the group for the next part of the discussion. Summary statements can also be valuable devices for restructuring a wandering discussion and to eliminate repetition.[13]

USE OF QUESTIONS IN CONFERENCE

Well-formulated questions are among the most useful devices the leader can use to stimulate and direct a conference or to avoid taking sides or participating excessively in the discussion.[14] Although he cannot always avoid giving an opinion, he may use a question to obtain a response from a member of the group at times and thus avoid responding himself.

To promote thinking, questions should be framed so that the person to whom they are directed must respond with more than a "yes" or "no" answer. If they are begun with *why, how,* or *which* rather than *what,* they will provoke thoughtful answers. *What* questions usually require factual responses and may be used with good effect if that kind of information is wanted.[15] The specific objectives to be achieved by a question will determine the type which should be used. With practice the leader will gain skill in selecting the right type of question or combination for each occasion. An admonishment the leader must always keep in mind is that those questions that might have a tendency to embarrass, antagonize, humiliate, or depress the group or any member should be religiously avoided.

Overhead questions

The general query, directed to the entire group is phrased so as to be answerable by any member. Usually it is answered by voluntary

---

13 J. V. Garland, *Discussion Methods* (New York: H. W. Wilson Co., 1951), p. 37.
14 See Chapters 6 and 11 for a further discussion of the use of questions.
15 Sidney S. Sutherland, *When You Preside,* 4th ed. (Danville, Ill.: Interstate Printers and Publishers, 1969), pp. 130–33.

response. It is useful to start or stimulate discussion on a contribution requiring emphasis or elaboration. It may be *rhetorical,* that is, the answer is implied in the question, or *factual,* that is, the question calls for a specific answer.

Directed questions

This form of question receives its name from the fact that it is directed to a specific participant for response. It is useful to force the reticent member to participate or to take advantage of the views of one who is especially knowledgeable. It may be used effectively to dampen the zeal of the overtalkative person if it is framed in such a manner that it is difficult or impossible to answer. It can be used with good results in reframing a response from one member and redirecting it to another when further discussion is desirable.

Reverse questions

The leader should discourage conferees from looking to him for opinions or answers to their questions or to "expertise" the conference. They may try to have him support one point of view or they may be looking for advice only. In order to avoid overparticipation, he can remain in a neutral position by reversing or "bouncing back" a question to the member who asked it. This procedure forces the member to reflect upon an answer to his own question. With slight reframing, the original question can be directed back for a response based upon the experience and background of the asker. A simple question such as, "What has been your personal experience in this area?" may elicit the desired response. In some cases, several questions may be necessary to obtain an answer to the original one.

Relay questions

The leader can also avoid answering questions directed to him by relaying them on to other members of the conference. This enables several persons to participate and often provides a well-balanced answer. Use of the relay question will enable the leader to increase his structuring of the conference and keep it within the boundaries he desires.

Follow-up questions

Follow-up questions are a useful means of gaining further information or clarification of a contribution, increasing participation, emphasizing points, stimulating discourse, and "shaping" the conference. They should be pertinent to the discussion and brief to avoid any stifling effect. Their high quality is the badge of an effective leader.

Ambiguous questions with double meanings should be avoided as they only cause confusion and loss of time. They invariably require restatement.

Leading questions suggest the answers desired and, as such, give the impression of too much structuring. These should be avoided for that reason. Controversial questions may or may not be provocative. For example, the question, "Don't you think modern supervisors are too prone to overact their human relations role rather than maintain a firm discipline?" has the characteristics of an ambiguous, leading, controversial, and provocative question and is likely to give rise to animosity, controversy involving the leader, and downright ill feelings.

USE OF CONFERENCE CHARTS

Just as any other teaching aid is of value in a teaching situation, the conference chart is useful to supplement the discussion in a conference. It also provides a record of group contributions. Organization of the chart entries assists the conferees in logically and systematically approaching the problem under discussion.

Charting materials

Newspaper pads or chart pads made from butcher paper approximately 2½ by 3 ft. are perfectly adequate for charting purposes. Black grease pencils are useful for recording chart entries.

Chart headings

The general pattern of the problem analysis chart and main headings that may be considered as pathways leading toward the objectives of the conference should be formulated by the conference leader. The specific items making up the analysis of the problem should be left for the members of the conference to formulate. [16]

Clearly worded chart headings properly presented to the conferees will assist them in directing their thinking toward solution of the problem, will stimulate their interest, and promote their participation. Some examples of chart headings which have been used effectively are:

Arguments for		Arguments against
Incident (example)	Cause	Remedy
Advantages		Disadvantages
Favorable points		Unfavorable points
Difficulties		Causes
Causes	Effects	Remedies
Problems		Solutions
Direct		Indirect
Acts		Reactions

These possible headings may be refined to meet the needs of a particular situation. They are limited only by the imagination of the leader.

Charting procedures

Proper use of the chart will prevent needless repetition of contributions. The mere fact that it is used for recording contributions will force the leader to make frequent summations.

Numbers should be run ahead when recordings are made on the chart. Psychologically, this causes members to become curious and to think ahead for other items to include in the discussion.[17] As evidence increases that progress is being made toward solving the problem at hand, the group members will gain a sense of satisfaction from their accomplishments. This will often accelerate their interest and will lead to even greater effort.

As each chart is filled with contributions, it should be removed from the mount and tacked or attached with tape or otherwise hung where it can be readily viewed by the group. This will tend to prevent duplication of effort and repetition of contributions.

Since the conference chart will serve as a record of the proceedings,

[16] California State Department of Education, *Conference Leader Training: A Manual for Training Conference Leaders for War Production Industries* (Sacramento, Calif.: California State Department of Education, 1943), p. 11.

[17] Sutherland, *When You Preside,* p. 54.

it should be prepared in such a manner that future references can be made to it with assurance that it properly reflects group contributions. At times, a vote should be taken to reflect the attitudes of members upon a particular issue. The leader may desire to poll the group with respect to final conclusions and recommendations so that he can report the consensus when the final report is prepared. This procedure might be especially desirable if the subject is highly controversial. The chart recordings will be relied upon heavily by the leader as a basis for his report of conference results several days or even several weeks later. Contributions should therefore be recorded legibly, accurately, neatly, and systematically. Items placed on the charts may be perfectly understood at the time of the discussion. Several weeks later, their meaning may become dim and vague if entries are not carefully made. They may be made in longhand or printed depending upon the leader's writing proficiency. Correct spelling, especially of common names, will not only improve his image but will aid him in preparing his report. Standardized abbreviations will shorten and speed chart entries, but they should be avoided if they might later cause confusion when their meaning is no longer fresh in the leader's mind. For example, the abbreviation "Sup. Ct." might mean either Supreme Court or Superior Court.

Each recorded contribution might contribute significantly in the final plan of action; but the leader must bear in mind that the group, not the chart, is most important during the conference. It is not until long afterward that the chart becomes important. This suggests that the chart be used in such a manner as not to sterilize the discussion.

Other devices

Although contributions should be recorded upon the chart for future reference, the conference leader will find a need for the blackboard, overhead projector, or other aids to clarify concepts, make needed computations or illustrations, and otherwise visualize contributions as the group progresses from point to point. Use of the conference chart for this purpose will only result in garbling or confusing it.

PITFALLS FOR CONFERENCE LEADERS

The conference leader should appraise the conferees as soon as possible after their selection so that he will be aware of their backgrounds, experience, reputation, and capabilities before meeting with them. He might thus gain some insight into potential problems which may arise and prepare himself to avert them. Although this cannot always be done, it is one step in preparing for the conference and might provide some clues that would be helpful in selecting techniques likely to be most effective in dealing with participants. Some of the most troublesome problems confronting conference leaders are discussed in the following pages.

Overtalkative members

Every conference leader will sooner or later encounter the garrulous individual or the overly talkative one and will be hard put to control his attempts to monopolize the conference. This type of individual might be extremely knowledgeable or he might have little to offer the group except talk. In either case, it is necessary that he be controlled. If he is not, the orderly progress of the entire proceedings may be jeopardized. His contributions may be extremely logical, in which case he might best be called upon to summarize major conclusions. As a summarizer, he may be of considerable help to the leader. Some control can usually be exercised over his volubility by giving credit to someone else for his contributions, by using his comments to initiate the conference or, as a last resort, calling his attention to the rule—no speeches!

Hostility

The hostile individual occasionally disturbs the meeting by arguing or criticizing others. He must be controlled before he becomes a disruptive influence to all participants. He will tax the ability of the leader, who must refrain from losing control of his emotions. If he does, he may lose control of the meeting. Often the members of the conference will exert sufficient pressures to restrain such persons. This will leave the leader in the desired neutral position, neither defensive nor offensive; for if he assumes the offensive posture, he risks the danger of turning the others against him. If he becomes angered or defensive, he risks losing control of the conference. The premise of Taylor and Mears [18] with reference to audiences also pertains to conference groups; that is, they "take their tone from the presiding officer and irritability and loss of temper by the chairman will react adversely on the meeting." Instead, the leader might ask the person to allow others to give their points of view or direct a thought-provoking question to him to consume some of his energy and divert his mind from hostility toward constructive thought. At other times, he might be asked to record entries on the chart

[18] Taylor and Mears, *The Right Way to Conduct Meetings, Conferences, and Discussions*, p. 117.

or to act as scribe for the group. On occasion it may be necessary to call the "no speech" rule to his attention or talk to him privately at a recess to ask for his cooperation.

The retiring member

The friendly but retiring member often participating in such group discussions should be given help whenever possible to build his confidence and to integrate him into the group as rapidly as possible. He, like the hostile person, will tax the ability of the leader. He should be encouraged to participate so that he will gain a feeling of belonging to the group. His comments should never be ignored. Questions which suggest an answer may be used with good effect in developing his self-assurance, especially if they are directed to him in such a way as to give him the impression that he is talking with the leader rather than to the group. His confidence may be built through an interpretation of his statements in such a way that others will appreciate his opinion. This will also tend to slow the discussion if the pace is too fast. If others of the group are encouraged to recognize his contributions, the process of building his confidence will be hastened. A sincere compliment for his first contribution may aid in accomplishing this.

The leader should be especially alert to rescue such an individual if he appears to "bog down" in his response, although he should be given a fair opportunity to express his views without being proffered help too hastily. If he is not given assistance when he needs it, he may believe his contribution was unproductive. This will only contribute to his feeling of insecurity. The leader can often help most by stating, "Let me repeat what you have said," rather than by asking, "What you meant was this?" The latter approach may be resented because of its patronizing flavor.

Handling the obstructionist

Usually, the uncooperative obstructionist with the "I am against" attitude can be controllen if his remarks are completely ignored, if he receives no credit for his statements, or if the group takes it upon itself to "police" him. The leader may find it necessary at times to interrupt him with a follow-up question to the group based on someone else's previous comment. Sometimes, he "gets the message" when he is challenged by another participant.

There are times when the "anti" member can add materially to the conference, however. If he is handled properly by the leader, his contributions may force the group to explore the issues more fully than might otherwise be the case. The majority might strive harder to justify its decision once it is opposed.

Handling the dogmatic or prejudiced member

The conferee who has a predisposition toward the matter under discussion, won't change his opinion, or will not accept the point of view of others probably should never have been selected as a conference member in the first place, but sometimes one does become a participant. The adverse influence his presence makes upon the group cannot be overlooked in the hope he will disappear. Rather, he can often be an asset to the discussion if handled properly. The leader might find out his interests and ask him pertinent questions regarding them or encourage others to do so. If he becomes argumentative or controverts every response, he should be asked to accept the group viewpoint for the time being, or the leader might tell him that they can discuss the matter between them later rather than use the time of the whole group in unproductive argument. Often, it is possible to control this type of individual by giving credit for a contribution made by him to another member of the group. If he becomes too dominating, the leader might direct a technical question to him in such a manner that he will likely be unable to answer it.

Lack of group interest

There are many reasons for lack of interest in the conference discussion. Predominantly, however, it is caused by poor selection of the subject matter, a poorly introduced subject which fails to state a real problem or to convince the group that it is real and soluble, or the fact that the discussion of the problem has been exhausted. Occasionally, improper selection of participants without appropriate backgrounds in the subject will contribute to shallow conclusions and a general lack of interest.

The remedy often lies with the leader. He may take complete responsibility for an improper or weak statement of the problem, attempt to rephrase it, and continue, or he may provide a break in the proceedings by an anecdote or by a recess. If taken, recesses should be short because of the difficulty in starting the discussion again. As a last resort, when the leader detects a total lack of interest and is unable to rekindle it, he should terminate the proceedings as graciously as possible.

Disturbances

Members may be distracted from giving their full attention to the discussion by annoying disturbances caused by other conferees from time to time. These may arise from matters under discussion or from personal conversations; but, whatever the cause, they should be controlled without humiliating or embarrassing those involved. This might be accomplished by directing an easy question to one of them or by asking him to speak so that all may hear what he has to contribute. The leader might on other occasions ask the individual's opinion of a contribution made by another person. If necessary, it should be repeated to avoid causing embarrassment. Distractions might otherwise be curtailed by the leader if he discreetly moves to a position where he can stand close behind the persons involved.

Handling delicate controversial problems

Many controversial problems will spring from conferences because of the very nature of the procedures involved. These controversies must be handled with the utmost tact and discretion lest they stifle participation. This is especially necessary if the members clash and divide into factions. The leader must be quick to sense and prevent abusive treatment of one member by others. He should direct abuse away from a member and absorb it himself if necessary to preserve decorum. The leader must be alert for such happenings and act quickly to prevent a breach in the proceedings if they occur. If this is not done, the harm caused often cannot be repaired. If the occurrence cannot be avoided, the leader might contain it and prevent it from expanding by asking members to avoid allowing personalities to become involved and pointing out the conference objectives. He should remain neutral if possible; but if he cannot, he should face the problem forthrightly and attempt to resolve it with equanimity. If the matter involves an obvious conflict with established rules or policy, it may become necessary for him to stop the debate by telling the members of the conflict.

Avoid making promises

On occasion, the leader is asked by the members to represent their interests to management. If he finds it necessary to act in such a capacity, he should avoid making any promises he might not be able to fulfill.

CONFERENCE MEMBERS' DUTIES

Each member of a conference group has a responsibility to participate in achieving the objectives for which the meeting was called. All should cooperate in solving problems of mutual interest by devoting their full attention to the discussion. Success will be in direct proportion to the degree to which each individual carries out his obligation to the group. Participants should give the group the benefit of their experiences. In doing so, they should avoid speech making and arguments although discussions should be continued as long as they are productive. Each member should recognize the points of view of others. None can be deprived of prejudices but all should control them.

Contributions should be frank and honest. Each member has the right to expect that such frankness will be treated with confidence and that, except under very aggravated circumstances, he will not later be made to suffer because of a breach of confidence by the leader or by another member.

CONFERENCE EVALUATION

Every supervisor having occasion to utilize the conference method of problem solving should develop his techniques so that he will be able to use most effectively the most valuable resources available to him— expert personnel. His conference-leading ability will be enhanced if he will analyze each problem to be presented, if he makes complete plans for leading the group, and if he evaluates results to detect weaknesses in his techniques.

While there are no precise approaches to the evaluation of conferences, every leader should attempt to appraise his performance to determine his weaknesses, which should be guarded against, and his strengths, which might be helpful in the future. He should refine his techniques, especially in practice sessions, by analyzing his own performance and having other participants do likewise on a Conference Leader Rating Chart such as that depicted in Figure 17–1.

FACILITIES AND MATERIALS

Proper physical facilities are extremely important in conferences as in other types of training situations. Inadequate facilities may constitute an insurmountable handicap to the proper fulfillment of conference objectives. Whenever possible, conferences should be conducted in well-

Leader _____ Date _____

Subject _____

	Rating			
	Excellent	Very Good	Average	Poor
1. How clearly and concisely was the problem stated?				
2. How effectively did the introduction give members confidence that a real problem existed?				
3. How well were supplementary illustrations used?				
4. How well were questions used?				
5. How well was the discussion controlled and held to the main topic?				
6. How successfully was the discussion distributed?				
7. How well was a helpful, permissive and friendly manner maintained?				
8. How frequent and concise were recorded summaries?				
9. How well were accepted and proven conference techniques utilized?				
10. How well were distractions, arguments and controversies handled?				
11. How well was the chart organized?				
12. How well did the chart provide a record of the proceedings?				
13. How well was the conference time used?				
14. How well prepared was the leader?				

FIGURE 17-1. Conference leader rating chart

lighted, ventilated, and distraction-free surroundings. A conference table should be suitably arranged. Figure 17–2 illustrates several seating arrangements found to be effective for conferences.[19] If a table is not available, chairs should best be arranged in a U-shape to permit the informal interchange between members in a face-to-face relationship. Ashtrays, nameplates, pencils, and paper should be provided at each seat.

FIGURE 17-2. Conference seating arrangements

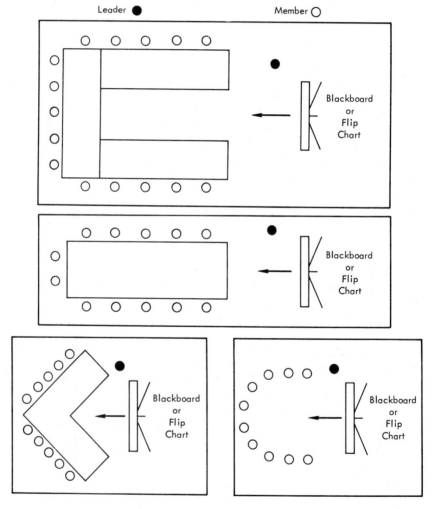

[19] Adapted from California State Department of Education, *Conference Leader Training*, p. 32.

A flip chart mounted on a stand, frame, or piece of plywood and wax marking pencils of various colors should be placed at the open end of the seating arrangement so that all members can view the chart. Precut paper for charts may be used although inexpensive butcher paper cut into suitable sizes is a very adequate substitute. Chalk, blackboard, thumb tacks, masking tape, and other materials should be available for use by members or the leader as needed.

STAFF MEETINGS

Well-conducted meetings with subordinate personnel provide the supervisor an excellent opportunity for training. These meetings, usually called staff meetings, may be scheduled periodically at specified intervals or only as needed. In a newly established unit or in one with newly assigned superior officers, staff meetings probably should be held frequently at first; but once the operational personnel become acquainted with any changes in policy or procedure, such meetings will be necessary less frequently.

They are useful in passing on new information and in solving problems within the organization. As a means of developing coordination and integrating efforts, they are without equal if properly handled. They are sometimes held as coffee or breakfast meetings which give them a desirable degree of informality.

Usually, staff meetings are called by superior officers, although every supervisor should take advantage of this medium for training. Those with common interests, even though assigned to another unit, should be invited to participate. The patrol supervisor would miss a splendid opportunity to achieve greater coordination between uniformed personnel in his unit and investigators in another unit if he failed to invite the detective supervisor to such meetngs.

Planning

The most "mileage" can be gained from staff meetings if the supervisor responsible for their conduct prepares a plan of action. Problems which require discussion should be noted as they occur so that they can be included in the agenda. Facts necessary for complete resolution of the problems should be collected and organized, and an agenda should be prepared and transmitted to concerned personnel before the meeting so they will have time to think about the items to be discussed. If the meeting is to produce maximum results, a portion of it should be devoted to training. A specialist, one of the members of the unit, or a representative of another allied unit might be asked to prepare a short training presentation for the group on some pertinent topic.

Follow-up

Minutes of the proceedings should be prepared so that policy determinations, solutions to operational or other problems, and group decisions will become a matter of record. Follow-up observations or action necessary as the result of the decisions arrived at by the group should be made by the supervisor or his delegate.

Use and misuse of staff meeting procedures

Staff meetings are usually conducted in one or a combination of three ways: as a democratically led conference, as an autocratically controlled assembly, or as a training session. When they are conducted democratically by use of the conference method, employees are encouraged to participate in the decision-making process by expressing their opinions and making recommendations. By being encouraged to become involved in the solution of problems that affect them, they will likely accept the decisions made as their own.

If the supervisor looks upon staff meetings as a place in which he can give orders and monopolize the time by doing all the talking and none of the listening, the meetings will eventually turn into "silent sessions" with little or no response from those assembled. They will soon consider such meetings as ordeals with themselves as a captive audience. Many supervisors recognize that the problems which arise within a unit are their responsibility. They are therefore inclined to tell their subordinates what to do about the problems rather than solicit their ideas for solving them. They become one of several types, as Sutherland [20] classifies them: The absolute dictator falls into the habit of telling. He rarely listens effectively. The benevolent dictator discusses. His subordinates listen. The responsibility dodger does not dictate, but he does not lead either. The democratic leader shares problems with his subordinates. He also shares his decision-making power by encouraging suggestions and initiative.

[20] Sutherland, *When You Preside,* p. 149.

SUMMARY

A conference is an interchange of ideas and a pooling of views and opinions of persons selected because of their backgrounds and experience to analyze and solve problems. It is a valuable medium for securing better understanding of the objectives of an organization by operating personnel who have been asked to participate in the making of decisions which affect them.

The conference method of training is an inefficient means when new skills or knowledge must be imparted to participants but is one of the best for problem solving. The absence of skilled leaders limits the widespread use of conferences; yet leaders can be trained. Opportunities must be made available to them to gain experience, however, by actual practice.

The individual selected to lead a conference should plan his approach by analyzing the subject to be discussed; preparing a clear statement of the problem with appropriate alternate statements which he might find necessary to use; developing broad contributions, recommendations and course of action statements that the conferees are likely to propose; and developing charting procedures he expects to use. In this way, he will be able to obtain maximum results from the proceedings by systematically leading participants to the fulfillment of conference objectives.

The leader will come to the conference with appropriate introduction, describe the procedures to be followed when necessary, state the problem in positive terms in the form of a question, motivate the group by convincing members that the problem is real and can and must be solved, and start the discussion. He will attempt to obtain the participation of all conferees. He should maintain a permissive, informal atmosphere so that participants may be induced to respond to the discussion in an easy, impersonal manner.

The leader should avoid evaluating contributions but should summarize and crystallize them frequently and record such summaries on the chart. In this way, he can reduce excessive overlapping of ideas and give conferees a sense of satisfaction from the progress shown. He will encourage reflection by participants to obtain the true meaning behind their statements and feelings. Indications of hostility should be received with equanimity. These may contribute materially to the objectives of the conference although remarks should not be allowed to reach the abusive state against another person.

The effective leader will apply all the techniques available to him to guide the discussion toward a productive conclusion. He will use questions to start the discussion, to provide positive guidance when needed, to obtain participation from all persons, to stimulate and promote thinking, to bring out overlooked points, to determine the degree of interest present from time to time, to slow or speed the discussion, or to reshape it to arrive at a conclusion.

An overall conclusion will be drawn from the discussion. It will be the basis of recommendations and proposals of a course of action that should be agreed upon before termination of the conference proceedings.

The wise leader will evaluate the manner in which the conference was conducted for the purpose of detecting weaknesses in his techniques that might be avoided in the future. He will also attempt to appraise those procedures he found to be effective so that they might be repeated as part of his conference-leading repertoire. This self-appraisal will involve a critical view of his performance for the purpose of self-improvement.

The conference technique combined with other appropriate training methods will provide an excellent medium for the conduct of staff meetings. If they are operated on a democratic basis, the supervisor will be able to convey new information to his subordinates, confer with them on problems, resolve problems by developing workable solutions, and make acceptable decisions as needed.

REVIEW

Questions

1. Define a conference and discuss the benefits obtainable from it. What are its limitations?
2. What are the factors to be considered before a conference is called?
3. Discuss the reasons for conference failures and how they may be prevented.
4. Enumerate the steps the conference leader should take in planning to conduct a conference.
5. Describe briefly the steps the leader takes from the time he first appears before the group until the discussion is well under way.
6. What is meant by reflection? What are the three types of reflection?
7. Discuss some of the general principles concerning the use of questions.
8. Why should frequent summaries of contributions be made?
9. Describe briefly how conference charts should be used.
10. Discuss how the conference leader might best handle the problems

occasioned by the following: group or individual hostility; overtalkative members; lack of individual participation; the retiring member; the obstructionist; the prejudiced person; loss of group interest; disturbances; delicate, controversial issues; situations involving promises.

11. Describe briefly the duties and responsibilities of a conference member.

12. What are the most needed materials for the conference leader and members?

13. Constructively critique a staff meeting you have attended, describing what was done that could have been done better, and how; what was done that should have been avoided, and why. Discuss the favorable aspects of the meeting. Do not identify the meeting unless you feel that its identity adds to your description.

Exercises

1. Choose a subject from the topics listed below, prepare a conference-leading plan, and be prepared to lead a thirty-minute practice conference. Other members will evaluate the exercise orally and on the rating chart form provided.

Topics

1. Rewards for good work
2. Incentive systems
3. How to make commendation systems work
4. What to do with the overly talkative worker
5. What to do when personal problems affect the employee
6. How to handle the chronically tardy subordinate
7. How should the department handle reprimands?
8. How can morale be kept at a high level?
9. How can morale be assessed?
10. How to manage a suggestion system
11. Procedures to follow at roll call
12. How to handle prejudices among employees
13. Improving relations between uniformed and investigative personnel
14. Improving cooperation between units
15. Exchange of information between divisions or units
16. How to give orders
17. Department charity programs
18. Employee participation in controversial political issues
19. Discipline procedures in the department
20. Eliminating damage to vehicles
21. Reducing personnel injuries
22. Shooting policy in field operations
23. Overtime pay

24. Improving work conditions
25. Supervisory follow-up methods
26. How to orient the new officer
27. How to justify additional personnel for your unit
28. How to justify additional equipment
29. How to develop command presence
30. Fleet safety award system
31. Procedures for booking perishable property
32. Organization of a laboratory
33. Recruitment methods
34. Use of tear gas
35. Carrying weapon off duty

2. Choose five subjects from the list in Exercise 1 and prepare chart headings which could be used in a conference on those topics.

3. List the *specific* points you would look for under *each* of the fourteen items in the Conference Leader Rating Chart in this chapter.

4. Sketch as many workable seating arrangements as you can think of in addition to those included in this chapter for use in a conference. Include single table designs that might be justified in a budget request for conference facilities.

Selected references

ADAMS, THOMAS F., GERALD BUCK, and DON HALLSTROM, *Criminal Justice: Organization and Management.* Pacific Palisades, Calif.: Goodyear Publishing Company, 1974.

AL-ANON FAMILY GROUP HEADQUARTERS, *The Dilemma of the Alcoholic Marriage,* New York: Al-Anon Family Headquarters, Inc., 1971.

ANDERSON, E. H., and G. T. SCHWENNING, *The Science of Production Organization.* New York: John Wiley & Sons, Inc., 1947.

ARGYRIS, CHRIS, *Executive Leadership: An Appraisal of a Manager in Action.* Hamden, Conn.: The Shoe String Press, Inc., 1967.

BARRETT, RICHARD S., *Performance Rating.* Chicago: Science Research Associates, Inc., 1966.

————, E. K. TAYLOR, J. W. PARKER, and L. MARTENS, "Rating Scale Content I: Scale Information and Supervisory Ratings," *Personnel Psychology,* 12 (1959), 157–73.

BASS, BERNARD M., *Conformity, Deviation, and a General Theory of Interpersonal Behavior in Conformity and Deviation.* New York: Harper & Row, Publishers, 1961.

————, *Leadership Psychology and Organizational Behavior.* New York: Harper & Row, Publishers, 1960.

BATTEN, J. D., *Tough Minded Management*. New York: American Management Association, 1963.

BAVELAS, ALEX, "Communication Patterns in Task-Oriented Groups," *Journal of the Acoustical Society of America*, 22 (1950), 725–30.

BAYROFF, A. G., and J. H. BURKE, "The Rater's Guide," *Personnel Psychology*, 3 (1950), 461–65.

BECK, AARON T., "What to Do When You're Under Stress," *U.S. News and World Report*, 13 (September 24, 1973).

BERRIEN, F. K., and W. H. BASH, *Human Relations: Comments and Cases*. New York: Harper & Row, Publishers, 1957.

BINGHAM, W. V., and BRUCE VICTOR MOORE, *How to Interview*. New York: Harper & Row, Publishers, 1959.

BISHOP, MAXINE H., *Dynamic Supervision: Problems and Opportunities*. New York: American Management Association, 1969.

BLOCK, MARVIN A., *Alcohol and Alcoholism: Drinking and Dependence*. Belmont, Calif.: Wadsworth Publishing Co., Inc., 1975.

———, *Alcoholism—Its Facets and Phases*. New York: The John Day Company, 1965.

BOGARDUS, E. S., *Leaders and Leadership*. New York: Appleton-Century-Crofts, 1934.

BOPP, WILLIAM J., *Police Personnel Administration*. Boston: Holbrook Press, Inc., 1974.

BROWN, JAMES W., and JAMES W. THORNTON, JR., *College Teaching: A Systematic Approach*, 2nd ed. New York: McGraw-Hill Book Company, 1963.

BUGELSKI, B. R., *The Psychology of Learning Applied to Teaching*. Indianapolis, Ind.: The Bobbs-Merrill Company, Inc., 1964.

BUTLER, JOEL R., FELICIA A. PRIOR, and HARRY E. ADAMS, "Psychoanalytically Oriented Therapy," in *An Introduction to Clinical Psychology*, ed. Irwin A. Berg and L. A. Pennington. New York: The Ronald Press Company, 1966.

CALHOON, RICHARD P., *Personnel Management and Supervision*. Englewood Cliffs, N.J.: Prentice-Hall, Inc., 1967.

CALIFORNIA PERSONNEL BOARD, *Supervisor's Handbook, 3: A Guide to Employee Discipline*. Sacramento, Calif.: California State Personnel Board, 1965.

CALIFORNIA STATE DEPARTMENT OF EDUCATION, *Conference Leader Training: A Manual for Training Conference Leaders for War Production Industries*. Sacramento, Calif.: California State Department of Education, 1943.

CARROLL, CHARLES R., *Alcohol—Use, Nonuse and Abuse,* 2nd ed. Dubuque, Iowa: William C. Brown Company, Publishers, 1975.

CHRUDEN, HERBERT J., and ARTHUR W. SHERMAN, JR., *Readings in Personnel Management,* 4th ed. Cincinnati, Ohio: South-Western Publishing Company, 1976.

COLEMAN, JAMES C., and CONSTANCE L. HAMMEN, *Contemporary Psychology and Effective Behavior.* Chicago: Scott, Foresman and Company, 1974.

DALE, EDGAR, *Audio-Visual Methods in Teaching.* New York: Holt, Rinehart and Winston, Inc., 1954.

DAVIS, KEITH, *Human Behavior: Human Relations and Organizational Behavior,* 5th ed. New York: McGraw-Hill Book Company, 1977.

DEPARTMENT OF THE CALIFORNIA HIGHWAY PATROL, *Field Operation Management Series—Supervision and Leadership.* Sacramento, Calif.: Department of the California Highway Patrol, 1960.

———, *Supervisor's Handbook: No. 1: Personal Development; Programs and Forms.* Sacramento, Calif.: Department of the California Highway Patrol, 1968.

DOLLARD, JOHN, NEAL E. MILLER, LEONARD W. DOOB, O. H. MOWRER, and ROBERT R. SEARS, in collaboration with Clellan S. Ford, Carl Iver Hovland, and Richard T. Sollenberger, *Frustration and Aggression.* New Haven, Conn.: Yale University Press, 1943.

DRUCKER, PETER F., *The Practice of Management.* New York: Harper & Row., Publishers, 1954.

DUDYCHA, GEORGE J., *Applied Psychology.* New York: The Ronald Press Company, 1963.

———, *Psychology for Law Enforcement Officers,* Springfield, Ill.: Charles C Thomas, Publisher, 1976.

EISENSON, JON, J. JEFFERY AUER, and JOHN V. IRWIN, *The Psychology of Communication.* New York: Appleton-Century-Crofts, 1963.

FAVREAU, DONALD F., and JOSEPH E. GILLESPIE, *Modern Police Administration.* Englewood Cliffs, N.J.: Prentice-Hall, Inc., 1978.

FAYOL, HENRI, *Industrial and General Administration,* trans. J. A. Conbrough. Geneva: International Management Association, 1930.

FEDERAL AVIATION AGENCY, *Management for Supervisors.* Washington, D.C.: U.S. Government Printing Office, 1961.

FIDLER, GAIL S., and JAY W. FIDLER, *Occupational Therapy.* New York: Macmillan Publishing Co., Inc., 1965.

FLESCH, RUDOLPH, *The ABC of Style: A Guide to Plain English.* New York: Harper & Row, Publishers, 1964.

FLESCH, RUDOLPH, *The Art of Plain Talk.* New York: Harper & Row, Publishers, 1962.

———, *Art of Readable Writing.* New York: Harper & Row, Publishers, 1974.

FORD, GUY B., *Building a Winning Employee Team.* New York: American Management Association, 1964.

FRYER, DOUGLAS H., "Motivation and Self Direction," in *Handbook of Applied Psychology,* ed. Douglas H. Fryer and Edwin R. Henry. New York: Johnson Reprint Corp., 1969.

FULLMER, DANIEL W., and HAROLD W. BERNARD, *Counseling: Content and Process.* Chicago: Science Research Associates, Inc., 1964.

FULMER, ROBERT M., *Supervision: Principles of Professional Management.* Beverly Hills, Calif.: Glencoe Press, 1976.

GAINES, LARRY K., and TRUITT A. RICKS, *Managing the Police Organization: Selected Readings.* New York: West Publishing Company, 1978.

GARDNER, BURLEIGH B., and DAVID G. MOORE, *Human Relations in Industry: Organizational and Administrative Behavior,* 4th ed. Homewood, Ill.: Richard D. Irwin, Inc., 1964.

GARLAND, J. V., *Discussion Methods.* New York: H. W. Wilson Co., 1951.

GILKINSON, H., S. F. PAULSON, and D. E. SIKKINK, "Effects of Order and Authority in an Argumentative Speech," *Quarterly Journal of Speech,* 40 (1954), 183–192.

GOETZ, RACHEL, *Visual Aids for the Public Service.* Chicago: Public Administration Service, 1954.

GRAICUNAS, V. A., "Relationship in Organization," in *Papers on the Science of Administration,* ed. Luther Gulick and L. Urwick. New York: Institute of Public Administration, 1937.

GULICK, LUTHER, "Notes on the Theory of Organization," in *Papers on the Science of Administration,* ed. Luther Gulick and L. Urwick. New York: Institute of Public Administration, 1937.

HAIRE, MASON, *Psychology in Management.* New York: McGraw-Hill Book Company, 1964.

HANER, CHARLES F., and PATRICIA ANN BROWN, "Clarification of the Instigation to Action Concept in the Frustration Aggression Hypothesis," *Journal of Abnormal and Social Psychology,* 51 (1955), 204–6.

HAYAKAWA, S. I., *Language in Thought and Action,* 3rd ed. New York: Harcourt Brace Jovanovich, 1972.

HECKMANN, I. L., JR., and S. G. HUNERYAGER, *Human Relations in Man-*

agement, 2nd ed. Cincinnati, Ohio: South-Western Publishing Co., 1967.

HERZBERG, FREDERICK, BERNARD MAUSNER, and BARBARA B. SNYDERMAN, *The Motivation to Work,* 2nd ed. New York: John Wiley & Sons, Inc., 1959.

HILGARD, ERNEST R., and GORDON H. BOWER, *Theories of Learning,* 4th ed. Englewood Cliffs, N.J.: Prentice-Hall, Inc., 1975.

HUNTER, H. JACK, *Conference Leadership for Use in Supervisory Training Program.* Washington, D.C.: Office of Industrial Resources, International City Management Association, 1971.

IANNONE, MARVIN D., "A Descriptive Study of the Internal Disciplinary Program of the Los Angeles Police Department," Unpublished Master's thesis. California State University at Los Angeles, 1967.

IANNONE, NATHAN F., *Principles of Police Patrol.* New York: McGraw-Hill Book Company, 1970.

INTERNATIONAL ASSOCIATION OF CHIEFS OF POLICE, *Managing for Effective Police Discipline.* Washington, D.C.: International Association of Chiefs of Police, 1976.

INTERNATIONAL CITY MANAGEMENT ASSOCIATION, *Local Government Personnel Administration.* Washington, D.C.: International City Management Association, 1976.

———, *Local Government Police Management.* Washington, D.C.: International City Management Association, 1977.

———, *Municipal Police Administration,* 7th ed. Washington, D.C.: International City Management Association, 1971.

JELLINEK, E. M., "Phases of Alcohol Addiction," *Quarterly Journal of Studies on Alcohol,* 13, 1952.

JUCIUS, MICHAEL J., *Personnel Management,* 8th ed. Homewood, Ill.: Richard D. Irwin, Inc., 1975.

KASSOFF, NORMAN C., *Organizational Concepts.* Washington, D.C.: International Association of Chiefs of Police, 1967.

KELLER, LEONARD A., *The Management Function: A Positive Approach to Labor Relations.* Washington, D.C.: BNA Incorporated, 1963.

KING, ALBION ROY, *Basic Information on Alcohol,* rev. ed. Mt. Vernon, Iowa: Cornell College Press, 1960.

KIRCHNER, W. E., and D. J. REISBERG, "Differences Between Better and Less Effective Supervisors in Appraisal of Subordinates," *Personal Psychology,* 15 (Autumn, 1962), 295-302.

KLAPPER, PAUL, "The Professional Preparation of the College Teacher," *Journal of General Education,* 3 (1959), 229-30.

KOONTZ, HAROLD, and CYRIL O'DONNELL, *Principles of Management*, 5th ed. New York: McGraw-Hill Book Company, 1972.

KRECH, DAVID, and RICHARD S. CRUTCHFIELD, *Psychology: A basic course*. New York: Alfred A. Knopf, Inc., 1976.

LATEINER, ALFRED, *Modern Techniques of Supervision*, 13th ed. New York: Lateiner Publishing Company, 1975.

LEAVITT, HAROLD J., *Managerial Psychology*, 3rd ed. Chicago: University of Chicago Press, 1972.

LEE, IRVING J., *How to Talk With People*. New York: Harper & Row, Publishers, 1952.

LEONARD, V. A., *Police Enterprise: Its Organization and Management*, 3rd ed. Brooklyn, N.Y.: The Foundation Press, 1969.

LEVINSON, HARRY, *Emotional Health in the World of Work*. New York: Harper & Row, Publishers, 1964.

LIKERT, RENSIS, "Motivation: The Core of Management," In *Human Elements of Administration*, ed. Harry R. Knudsen, Jr. New York: Holt, Rinehart and Winston, Inc., 1963, pp. 72–75.

————, and STANLEY E. SEASHORE, "Motivation and Morale in the Public Service," *Public Personnel Review*, October, 1956, pp. 271–76.

LONEY, GLENN M., *Briefing and Conference Technique*. New York: McGraw-Hill Book Company, 1959.

LONG, CHARLES H., "Clear Thinking and Its Relationship to Clear Writing," in *Proceedings of the 1962 Institute in Technical and Industrial Communications*, ed. Herman M. Wiesman. Fort Collins, Colo.: Colorado State University, 1962.

LOS ANGELES CITY CIVIL SERVICE COMMISSION, *Resolution on Discipline Policy*, December 9, 1966.

LOS ANGELES POLICE DEPARTMENT, *Daily Training Bulletins: Volume I*. Springfield, Ill.: Charles C Thomas, Publisher, 1954.

————, *The Department Manual*, 1977.

————, *Instructor's Guide for Roll Call Training*, 1951.

————, *Special Weapons and Tactics: The Specialist and the Field Officer, Command Strategy*, 1971.

————, *Tactical Manual*, 1976.

LYNCH, RONALD G., *The Police Manager*. Boston: Holbrook Press, Inc., 1975.

McCLUSKY, F. DEAN, *Audio-Visual Teaching Techniques*. Los Angeles: University of California Press, 1949.

McCORMICH, ERNEST J., and JOSEPH TIFFIN, *Industrial Psychology*, 6th ed. Englewood Cliffs, N.J.: Prentice-Hall, Inc., 1974.

McFARLAND, DALTON E., *Management Principles and Practices,* 2nd ed. New York: Macmillan Publishing Co., Inc., 1964.

MAGER, ROBERT F., *Preparing Instructional Objectives,* 2nd ed. San Francisco: Fearon Publishers, 1975.

MAIER, NORMAN R. F., *Frustration: The Study of Behavior Without a Goal.* Ann Arbor, Mich.: The University of Michigan Press, 1961.

MARROW, ALFRED J., *Making Management Human.* New York: McGraw-Hill Book Company, 1957.

MASSIE, JOSEPH L., *Essentials of Management,* 2nd ed. Englewood Cliffs, N.J.: Prentice-Hall, Inc., 1970.

MEGGINSON, LEON C., *Personnel: A Behavioral Approach to Administration.* Homewood, Ill.: Richard D. Irwin, Inc., 1967.

MEIER, NORMAN C., "The Psychology of Human Relations," in *Psychology for Law Enforcement Officers,* ed. George F. Dudycha. Springfield, Ill.: Charles C Thomas, Publisher, 1966.

MEYER, PAUL J., "Fear—Money—Inspiration; Which Motivates Best?" *The National Sheriff,* January–February, 1968.

MOSHER, WILLIAM E., J. DONALD KINGSLEY, and O. GLENN STAHL, *Public Personnel Administration.* New York: Harper & Row, Publishers, 1950.

MUNN, NORMAN L., *The Growth of Human Behavior,* 3rd ed. Boston: Houghton Mifflin Company, 1974.

NATIONAL CENTER FOR PREVENTION AND CONTROL OF ALCOHOLISM, NATIONAL INSTITUTE OF MENTAL HEALTH, *Alcohol and Alcoholism.* Washington, D.C.: U.S. Government Printing Office, 1967.

NEWMAN, WILLIAM H., *Administrative Action,* 2nd ed. Englewood Cliffs, N.J.: Prentice-Hall, Inc., 1963.

NIGRO, FELIX A., *The New Public Personnel Administration.* Itasca, Ill.: F. E. Peacock Publishers, Inc., 1976.

———, and LLOYD G. NIGRO, *Modern Public Administration,* 4th ed. New York: Harper & Row, Publishers, 1977.

ORR, DOUGLAS W., *Professional Counseling on Human Behavior: Its Principles and Practices.* New York: Franklin Watts, Inc., 1965.

PARKER, WILLARD E., and ROBERT W. KLEEMEIER, *Human Relations in Supervision: Leadership in Management.* New York: McGraw-Hill Book Company, 1951.

PARRY, JOHN, *The Psychology of Communications.* London: University of London Press Ltd., 1967.

PEREZ, JOSEPH FRANCIS, *Counseling: Theory and Practice.* Reading, Mass.: Addison Wesley Publishing Co., Inc., 1965.

PFIFFNER, JOHN M., *The Supervision of Personnel.* Englewood Cliffs, N.J.: Prentice-Hall, Inc., 1951.

———, and MARSHALL FELS, *The Supervision of Personnel: Human Relations in the Management of Men,* 3rd ed. Englewood Cliffs, N.J.: Prentice-Hall, Inc., 1964.

——— and ROBERT PRESTHUS, *Public Administration,* 2nd ed. New York: The Ronald Press Company, 1967.

———, and FRANK P. SHERWOOD, *Administrative Organization.* Englewood Cliffs, N.J.: Prentice-Hall, Inc., 1960.

PIGORS, PAUL, and CHARLES A. MYERS, *Personnel Administration: A Point of View and a Method,* 8th ed. New York: McGraw-Hill Book Company, 1977.

QUICK, THOMAN L., *Person to Person Managing: An Executive's Guide to Working Effectively with People.* New York: St. Martin's Press, 1977.

ROETHLISBERGER, FRITZ J., "The Foreman: Master and Victim of Doubletalk," *Harvard Business Review,* Spring, 1945, pp. 283–98.

ROGERS, C. R., *Counseling and Psychotherapy.* Boston: Houghton Mifflin Company, 1942.

———, "Psychotherapy Today or Where Do We Go from Here?" in *Readings in Abnormal Psychology; Human Values and Abnormal Behavior,* ed. Walter D. Nunokawa. Chicago: Scott, Foresman and Company, 1965.

———, and F. J. ROETHLISBERGER, "Barriers and Gateways to Communication," *Harvard Business Review,* July–August, 1952, 46–52.

ROSENBERG, SAUL, "Frustration as an Experimental Problem. VI: General Outline of Frustration," *Character and Personality,* 7 (1938), 151–60.

SAGALYN, ARNOLD, *The Riot Commission: Recommendations for Law and Order in Confrontation—Violence and the Police,* ed. C. R. Hormachea and Marion Hormachea, Boston: Holbrook Press, Inc., 1971.

SASLOW, GEORGE, and JOSEPH D. MATARAZZO, "Psychosomatic Phenomena," in *An Introduction to Clinical Psychology,* ed. Irwin A. Berg and L. A. Pennington. New York: The Ronald Press Company, 1966.

SAYLES, LEONARD, "On-the-Job Communications," *Supervisory Management,* August, 1967.

———, and GEORGE STRAUSS, *Managing Human Resources.* Englewood Cliffs, N.J.: Prentice-Hall, Inc., 1977.

SCOTT, WALTER DILL, ROBERT C. CLOTHIER, and WILLIAM R. SPRIEGEL, *Personnel Management,* 6th ed. New York: McGraw-Hill Book Company, 1961.

SELZNICK, PHILIP, *Leadership in Administration: A Sociological Interpretation.* New York: Harper & Row, Publishers, 1957.

SHERTZER, BRUCE, and SHELLEY C. STONE, *Fundamentals of Counseling,* 2nd ed. Boston: Houghton Mifflin Company, 1974.

SHOUT, HOWARD F., *Start Supervising.* Washington, D.C.: The Bureau of National Affairs, 1972.

SIMON, HERBERT A., DONALD W. SMITHBURG, and VICTOR A. THOMPSON, *Public Administration.* New York: Alfred A. Knopf, Inc., 1961.

SMITH, BRUCE, *Police Systems in the United States,* 2nd ed. revised by Bruce Smith, Jr. New York: Harper & Row, Publishers, 1949.

SOURYAL, SAM S., *Police Administration and Management.* St. Paul, Minn.: West Publishing Co., 1977.

SPRIEGEL, WILLIAM R., EDWARD SCHULZ, and WILLIAM B. SPRIEGEL, *Elements of Supervision,* 3rd ed. New York: John Wiley & Sons, Inc., 1964.

STAHL, GLENN O., *Public Personnel Administration,* 7th ed. New York: Harper & Row, Publishers, 1976.

————, and RICHARD STAUFENBERGER, *Police Personnel Administration,* 7th ed. North Scituate, Mass.: Duxbury Press, 1976.

STATE OF CALIFORNIA, "Violence in the City—an End or a Beginning," *A Report by the Governor's Commission on the Los Angeles Riots.* Sacramento, Calif.: State Printing Office, December 5, 1965.

STOCKFORD, LEE, and H. W. BISSELL, "Factors in Establishing a Merit Rating Scale," *Personnel,* September, 1949.

SUTHERLAND, SYDNEY S., *When You Preside,* 4th ed. Danville, Ill.: Interstate Printers and Publishers, 1969.

SYMONDS, P. M., *Dynamic Psychology.* New York: Appleton-Century-Crofts, 1949.

TAYLOR, H. M., and A. G. MEARS, *The Right Way to Conduct Meetings, Conferences, and Discussions,* 6th ed. London: Morrison and Gibb · Ltd., 1964.

TEAD, ORDWAY, *Administration: Its Purposes and Performance.* New York: Archon Books, 1968.

THOMAS, W. I., *The Unadjusted Girl.* Boston: Little, Brown and Company, 1931.

THORNDYKE, E. L., "A Constant Error in Psychological Ratings," *Journal of Applied Psychology,* 4 (1920), 25–29.

THORNDYKE, E. L., *The Fundamentals of Learning.* New York: Teachers' College, Columbia University, 1932.

THORNDYKE, ROBERT L., and ELIZABETH HAGEN, *Measurements and Evaluation in Psychology and Education,* 2nd ed. New York: John Wiley & Sons, Inc., 1961.

TRICE, HARRISON M., *Alcoholism in America.* Huntington, N.Y.: Robert E. Krieger Publishing Co., Inc., 1977.

UMSTATTD, J. S., *College Teaching.* Washington, D.C.: University Press of Washington, D.C., 1964.

UNITED STATES ARMY LOGISTICS MANAGEMENT CENTER, *Principles of Management: Special Text 38–1.* Washington, D.C.: U.S. Government Printing Office, n.d.

UNITED STATES DEPARTMENT OF THE ARMY, *Civil Disturbances, FM 19–15.* Washington, D.C.: Headquarters, Department of the Army, October, 1975.

———, *Military Leadership, FM 10–100.* Washington, D.C.: U.S. Government Printing Office, 1961.

———, *Staff Officers' Field Manual—Staff Organization and Procedure, FM 101–5.* Washington, D.C.: Headquarters, Department of the Army, 1960.

UNITED STATES DEPARTMENT OF DEFENSE, *The Armed Forces Officer.* Washington, D.C.: U.S. Government Printing Office, 1950.

UNITED STATES OFFICE OF EDUCATION, COMMITTEE ON MILITARY TRAINING AIDS AND INSTRUCTIONAL MATERIALS, *Use of Training Aids in the Armed Forces,* Bulletin No. 9. Washington, D.C.: Federal Security Agency, (1945).

URIS, AUREN, *How to Be a Successful Leader.* New York: McGraw-Hill Book Company, 1953.

———, *Techniques of Leadership.* New York: McGraw-Hill Book Company, 1964.

URWICK, L., *The Elements of Administration.* New York: Harper & Row, Publishers, 1943.

VAN DERSAL, WILLIAM R., *The Successful Supervisor in Government and Business.* New York: Harper & Row, Publishers, 1975.

VARDAMAN, GEORGE T., *Communications in Modern Organizations.* New York: John Wiley & Sons, Inc., 1973.

———, "Language and Semantics," in *Proceedings of the 1962 Institute in Technical and Industrial Communications,* ed. Herman W. Wiesman. Fort Collins, Colo.: Institute for Technical and Industrial Communications, 1962.

WALSH, JUDE T., "Search of Buildings," *Law and Order,* 20, No. 4 (April, 1972).

WALTON, FRANK E., "Selective Distribution of the Police Patrol Force," *The Journal of Criminal Law, Criminology and Police Science,* November–December, 1958.

WHYTE, WILLIAM FOOTE, *Men at Work.* Westport, Conn.: Greenwood Press, Inc., 1974.

WIESMAN, WALTER, "Effecting Better Management Communications in Technical Organizations," in *Proceedings of the 1965 Institute on Technical and Industrial Communications.* Fort Collins, Colo.: Colorado State University, 1966.

WILLIAM, CECIL B., and ALLAN H. STEVENSON, *A Research Manual for College Studies and Papers.* New York: Harper & Row, Publishers, 1951.

WILSON, O. W., *Police Planning,* 3rd ed. Springfield, Ill.: Charles C Thomas, Publisher, 1977.

———, ed., *Parker on Police.* Springfield, Ill.: Charles C Thomas, Publisher, 1956.

———, and ROY CLINTON MCLAREN, *Police Administration,* 4th ed. New York: McGraw-Hill Book Company, 1977.

WOLFE, MALCOLM E., et al., *Naval Leadership,* 2nd ed. Annapolis, Md.: United States Naval Institute, 1960.

WOLFE, MALCOLM E., and E. J. MULHOLLAND, eds., *Selected Readings in Leadership,* 3rd ed. Annapolis, Md.: United States Naval Institute, 1965.

YODER, DALE, *Personnel Management and Industrial Relations,* 6th ed. Englewood Cliffs, N.J.: Prentice-Hall, Inc., 1970.

———, *Personnel Principles and Policies: Modern Manpower Management,* 2nd ed. Englewood Cliffs, N.J.: Prentice-Hall, Inc., 1959.

ZALEZNIK, ABRAHAM, *Human Dilemmas of Leadership.* New York: Harper & Row, Publishers, 1966.

Index